Pulitzer Prize and
National Book Award winner
TRACY KIDDER
unravels the myth of Everytown, USA,
in the national bestseller
HOME TOWN

"A remarkably detailed, accomplished, and empathic portrait. . . . Kidder's acutely observed, crisply written, and utterly absorbing documentary proves that there is nothing on this spinning earth more amazing and full of grace than everyday life."

—*Booklist* (starred review)

"Kidder's protagonist . . . is Northampton itself. And there's no better way to see it than with a Kidder's-eye view."

—*The Boston Globe*

"*HOME TOWN* is a masterwork."

—*Grand Rapids Press* (MI)

"Tracy Kidder brings Northampton so vividly to life that it's a temptation to call Amtrak for tickets."

—New York *Daily News*

"Tracy Kidder has a gift. He can make complex subjects readable and intensely personal as well."

—*The Denver Post*

"He takes something superficially glittering and reveals its dense, lumpy, and endearingly eccentric ordinariness."

—*Entertainment Weekly*

"Harkens back to a nostalgic and perhaps mythical moment in American history when small towns across the country seemed bucolic."

—*St. Louis Post-Dispatch*

"[Northampton] is a place, as Kidder demonstrates, where all things are possible, uplifting and otherwise."

—New York Newsday

"Like the best nonfiction, *HOME TOWN* reads like a novel, full of riveting action, a vivid sense of place and larger-than-life characters, caught at stress points in their lives. Kidder reminds us of the complexity of people's experiences and the nobility of their struggles."

—The Des Moines Sunday Register

"There is a touch of paradise in Kidder's portrayal of this small town near the Berkshires."

—The Christian Science Monitor

"Kidder has rendered a real place into a narrative as dramatic and archetypal and life-affirming as those towns found on stage, film, or fiction."

—Denver Rocky Mountain News

"The journey does not merely teach us about Northampton, but ultimately about the human pull toward a hometown, this one or our own."

—St. Petersburg Times (FL)

"It is a well-told, human story of a place with a pulse we all know. Even when the perfect grid of streets is kept clean, people are complex."

—The Plain Dealer (Cleveland)

"Kidder's vision combines the realistic detail of a documentary with the broad sweep and imagination of a nineteenth-century novel of the streets."

—Publishers Weekly (starred review)

Also by Tracy Kidder

THE SOUL OF A NEW MACHINE

HOUSE

AMONG SCHOOLCHILDREN

OLD FRIENDS

Tracy Kidder

Home Town

WASHINGTON SQUARE PRESS
PUBLISHED BY POCKET BOOKS

New York   London   Toronto   Sydney   Singapore

Grateful acknowledgment is made to Harcourt Brace & Company and Faber and Faber Limited for permission to reprint four lines from "Little Gidding" in *Four Quartets* by T. S. Eliot. Copyright © 1942 by T. S. Eliot and copyright renewed 1970 by Esme Valerie Eliot. Rights outside the United States are controlled by Faber and Faber Limited. Reprinted by permission of Harcourt Brace & Company and Faber and Faber Limited.

<u>Libby Roderick</u>: Excerpts from "How Could Anyone," words and music by Libby Roderick. © Libby Roderick Music 1988. From the recording *If You See a Dream,* Turtle Island Records, P.O. Box 203294, Anchorage, Alaska 99520. (907) 278-6817, libbyr@alaska.net, www.alaska.net/~libbyr/. Reprinted by permission.

A Washington Square Press Publication of
POCKET BOOKS, a division of Simon & Schuster Inc.
1230 Avenue of the Americas, New York, NY 10020

ISBN: 0-671-78521-4

First Washington Square Press trade paperback printing May 2000

10 9 8 7 6 5 4 3 2 1

WASHINGTON SQUARE PRESS and colophon are
registered trademarks of Simon & Schuster Inc.

Cover design by Brigid Pearson
Front cover photo by David Ryan/Index Stock Imagery

Printed in the U.S.A.

For

Nat and

Alice

This is a work of nonfiction. Most of the spoken words that appear in this book were uttered in my presence, some recounted to me. I have attributed thoughts to some of the characters, and all of these were plausibly described to me. All names are real, except as noted here. The following are pseudonyms: "Carmen," "Francisco/Frankie Sandoval" (and "Samson/Sammy Rodriguez"), "Hearth 'n Home Construction," "Jackie," "Rick Janacek," "Willie," and "Tyrone."

I describe a criminal proceeding and cite various documents relating to it. Some of those documents were part of official court proceedings, and the others were supplied to me by the defendant. I also refer to various criminal records, which I obtained in accordance with Massachusetts law.

CONTENTS

PART IV

PART V

FOREWORD

In the days of rutted roads and horse-drawn transportation, tourists by the thousands trekked to western Massachusetts and ascended to the summit of Mount Holyoke. Charles Dickens and Henry James made the climb. Thomas Cole and other, lesser nineteenth-century romantic painters set up their easels near the precipice. The scene they gazed at was, for a time, the most famous landscape in America. Now an interstate highway and a marina intrude on the view. Otherwise, it hasn't changed much. You look out on the valley of the Connecticut River, an expanse of cultivated fields and of forest sweeping away across the horizon, and, at the center, the old town of Northampton.

It nests within natural boundaries. To the east the wide river bends its arm around Northampton's Meadows, planted mostly in corn. To the north and west the foothills of the Berkshires rise up in the blue distance, higher than the town's steeples. When Cole painted his famous picture *View from Mount Holyoke, Northampton, Massachusetts, After a Thunderstorm*—it now hangs in New York's Metropolitan Museum of Art—the town was already more than 180 years old. It was nearly 200 when an entrepreneur, hoping to cash in on the view, erected the Mount Holyoke Prospect House. A cable car used to carry up the tourists. It vanished years ago. The hurricane of 1938 battered the hotel and closed it down for good. Only the shell remains. Standing on the old front porch on a windy summer day, at the edge of an eight-hundred-foot drop, you feel grateful for the railing. Down below, the river glistens in the August light. A small airplane wobbles like a gull as it descends toward Northampton's tiny airport in the Meadows. Sylvia Plath visited this promontory and in a poem described the sweet illusions of the view. "All's

peace and discipline down there," she wrote. Surrounded by
what she called "the high hush," the only sound the wind in
your ears, you gaze northwest at the town.

It seems as natural as the hills around it. Among the myriad
trees, you can make out some of the roads and white houses
and steeples and the back side of Main Street—a line of buildings, tiny from here, a patchwork of red and brown behind the
greenery. Only thirty thousand people live in Northampton,
roughly the same number as forty years ago, not many more
than at the turn of the century. And it still preserves the old
pattern of the New England township, a place with a full set of
parts. It has rich farmland by the river, an industrial park, a
hospital, a courthouse and registry (Northampton is a county
seat), and a college (Smith, the famous school for women). A
shopping strip follows the line of the railroad tracks and the
Interstate, north toward Vermont, for a mile or so. Tree-lined
streets of clapboarded houses from the last century surround
the old downtown. In recent years, ranch-style houses have
sprung up along outlying roads. Their backyards merge into
forest where coyotes howl at night.

From the summit, the cornfields are a dream of perfect
order, and the town seems entirely coherent, self-contained, a
place where a person might live a whole life and consider it
complete, a tiny civilization all its own. Forget the messiness of
years and days—every work of human artifice has a proper
viewing distance. The town below fits in the palm of your
hand. Shake it and it snows.

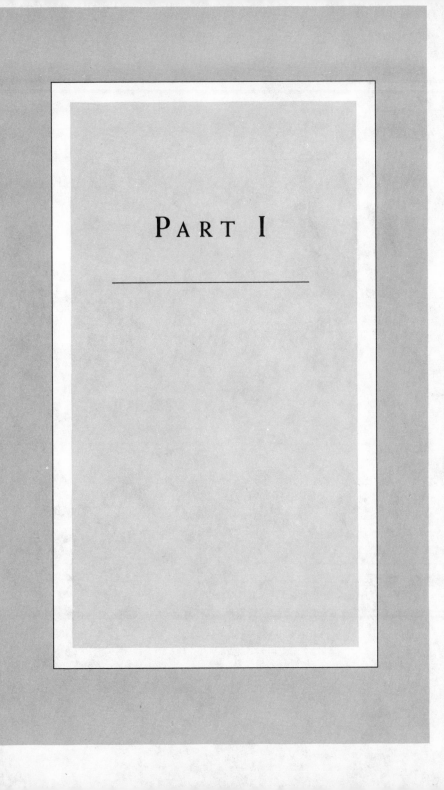

PART I

CHAPTER 1

Townie

He grew up here. He was the youngest of Jane and Bill O'Connor's seven children. His oldest sister called him Todder when he was an infant. His high school friends shortened up his surname and rechristened him Oakie. To teachers and other adults he was usually Tommy. His wife would call him Tom. All his nicknames and the diminutive accompanied him to adulthood. If you do all your growing up in the same small place, you don't shed identities. You accumulate them.

One day when he was ten years old, Tommy O'Connor's Little League baseball coach made him the starting pitcher. A signal honor, but then Tommy couldn't get anyone out. He walked the first batter, and from their lawn chairs on the sidelines the parents called, "Make him be a hitter, Tommy." So he threw an easy one right over the plate, and the batter nailed it. His teammates in the field behind him did as they'd been taught: they talked it up, they chattered, squeaky voices calling, "Hum chuck, Tommy. No batter, no batter. Hum it in there, Tommy baby." He threw harder and walked the next two batters. He eased up and the next kid hit it over *everything*. Many games of Little League reach this kind of impasse. Five runs in, the bases loaded once again, and still nobody out, the fielders grumbling, the parents looking on in silence, all except for one, someone else's father, who cares more about a good ball game than his neighbor's son, and shouts, "Get him outa there, for Christ's sake!" Tommy stood on the mound, staring at his shoes.

The coach called time and went out to talk to him. If sports build character, they can also test it prematurely. What if the kid can't take it? What if he begins to cry? "You all right?" the coach asked.

Tommy lifted his eyes toward the sky. It was a fine summer afternoon at Arcanum Field. Not a cloud in sight. Tommy looked back over his shoulder, as if just making sure. Then he looked at the coach, and he smiled. "Think it might rain?" he asked.

The coach told the story to Tommy's father, Bill, the treasurer of Hampshire County and the region's preeminent master of ceremonies and after-dinner speaker. Bill put that story about Tommy in the vast repertoire he employed at the Elks, the Legion, the Ancient Order of Hibernians, the John Boyle O'Reilly Club, the family's kitchen table. There it grew as smooth as the bits of glass that Tommy found on the beach during the family's summer camping trips to Cape Cod. Tommy's mother kept scrapbooks about him, even when he was an adult. He was her last child, the youngest of the six who survived. He had brown curly hair, and a little cockeyed grin that made girls and women smile back.

Tommy spent his childhood and adolescence on Forbes Avenue, just off Elm Street and a few blocks from Smith College, in a quiet neighborhood of both grand and ordinary homes. He was raised in a wood-framed house that a family of modest means could afford back then. The house was full to bursting with exuberant youth, and the neighborhood was so full of children that Tommy never felt a need to go beyond it, except for the sake of adventure. Early on summer mornings he would stand on the sidewalk in front of his family's house and hear a cry or lift it first himself—"*E-awkee!*"—and then the same call, from voices that hadn't changed yet, would sound up and down the streets, and soon barefoot children would appear from all directions, apparitions out of the gray dawn. Tommy's friend Rick emerged from just three doors up Forbes Avenue, and from their homes came Ethan and Lisa and Bobby and half a dozen more. They'd converge on the sidewalk and make plans, naming destinations—"Meet ya at the Hill," "Meet ya at White Rock," "Meet ya at the dirt mounds."

The fastest, easiest route to Hawley Junior High—named for a local Revolutionary War patriot—would have been by sidewalk, but Tommy and his friends rarely went that way. From September until June they traveled with their bookbags through the backyards of the Elm Street neighborhood, sliding through hedges, ducking under fences, wading through snow. They paused to gather chestnuts at Slawson's chestnut tree, for the after-school chestnut wars with the Washington Street kids. They crossed the Smith College campus, past stately buildings and views of Paradise Pond, though years would pass before Tommy noticed the postcard beauties of the place. It was just their playground then. They stopped outside the college art museum and climbed on the Rodin, a statue called *The Walking Man*. They detoured through the backstairs spots that made perfect hiding places during games of Kill. They hunted frogs in the pond beside the college greenhouse, until someone came out and chased them away—class consciousness began to bloom in Tommy at that pond, the day he saw a group of kids and a teacher from the private Smith day school catching frogs without interference. The campus was so rich in diversions—the Foucault pendulum inside the science building, which they set swinging wildly; the elderly college security guards, Creepy Kreps and Mooney, whom they could usually get to chase them—that by the time they'd passed under the Romanesque shadows of the town's public library, they were nearly always late for school.

Tommy's world widened bit by bit, to take in other neighborhoods and villages within the town such as Bay State, Leeds, and Florence, and every widening seemed dramatic to him, a journey into a vast territory, called Northampton. But the old neighborhood remained its center, and the friends from it his most enduring. The oldest friend of all was Rick Janacek. Tommy knew him before he knew Northampton. Rick was left to play at the O'Connor house when Tommy still slept in a crib. He was two years older, and became something like a leader for Tommy and many of his gang. "Let's go see what Rick's doing," he'd often say, on the mornings when Rick didn't join them on the sidewalk outside Tommy's house.

The O'Connor family had lost a child some years before, but the Janaceks' misfortunes were astonishing. Two children had died in infancy from blood disorders. One had cerebral palsy. In the most lurid of the family's catastrophes, the second son accidentally shot and killed the eldest. Not long afterward, that second son lost half his arm in the meat cutter at the family store. And a year after that, the family store burned down. The city took up a collection. Tommy's father had organized the fund-raiser.

All of this had happened before Rick and Tommy were born, but Tommy heard the stories, of course—"the old Irish," as his father called them, whispering that the one Janacek boy was maimed in fateful retribution for killing the other. Between Rick and Tommy, those troubles remained for years a thing known and not discussed. Rick didn't bring up the subject, and Tommy didn't want to meddle. Family was a sacred subject even then for him.

The hallway outside Rick's bedroom always seemed to be half filled with boxes. You got past by walking sideways. Rick's house always seemed dark, heavy-curtained, a bit eerie, but that didn't bother Tommy much, partly because of Rick's mother, who was forever feeding Tommy snacks and loading him up with boxes of damaged crackers to take home.

Sometimes when he came looking for Rick and Rick wasn't there, she invited him to sit with her on her porch, and talked about relatives and people she knew who were doing good works, while feeding him another snack. She brightened the house considerably for him.

In the background of a group of old snapshots, a corner of Rick's bedroom appears—a crowded bureau, a clutter of coats and shirts hanging on a wall, and a desk completely covered with model paints, the pieces of a model in progress sitting on some newspaper. A heavy curtain blocks the window. Tommy, who is just eleven, stands in the foreground, pink-cheeked and chubby with a Dutch-boy haircut, striking various poses: joyfully giving Rick the finger, spraying deodorant at Rick, and, wearing a maniacal grin, holding the deodorant can as if to spray an armpit with it. Rick took the pictures from his sickbed. He was laid up for six months with a badly broken leg, and for six months Tommy visited him after school, almost every single day. They spent the countless hours of Rick's convalescence playing an early electronic game called Talking Football and building models. Rick's creations had a craftsman's perfection; Tommy's had gobs of glue hanging from their joints.

A friend two years older is a prized possession when accomplishment is still marked by years acquired and inches grown. Tommy pestered Rick for information about the adult world. Rick had *Playboy* magazines. He could answer some of Tommy's insistent queries and clear up his wild misconceptions about the facts of life. Tommy got drunk for the first time with Rick: he threw up on the couch in Rick's living room; Rick walked him home, put him to bed, and cleaned up the mess. One day when Tommy was fifteen, Rick said, "I got a joint." Rick held up a bedraggled-looking thing vaguely like a cigarette.

"What are you gonna do with it?"

"Want to try it? Nobody'll know."

So it was that for the first and last time in his life Tommy tried to taste an illegal drug. In his memory, it only made him cough. He still thought they'd tried to smoke oregano.

Tommy was a tender child, utterly dependent on his parents' affection for each other—bawling, he vividly recalled, when they got into mock arguments. He shared a room for years, and the same bed for several, with his older brother Jack, who was big, handsome, and wild. He adored Jack, and was, like many little brothers, oppressed by him. Tommy came to adulthood with a proclivity to worry, which seemed allied with the anger that he felt when someone tried to "get over" on him, and maybe that was part of the residue of growing up with Jack. But they were great friends now, and Tommy had decided to feel grateful to Jack when he returned to his memories of childhood. In that fine, assembled place, Jack had toughened him up—cured Tommy of his fear of the dark, for instance: when their parents went out, Jack used to lock Tommy in the basement and turn off the lights.

On one day out of many like it at the O'Connor house, Jack slapped Tommy and Tommy started crying and Rick said, "You're disgusting." Jack said, "Yeah. Mama's boy." Afterward Rick started saying to Tommy, "Why don't you stand up to him?" And one day he did. Tommy actually wrestled Jack to the ground, and looked up at Rick with startled eyes, as if to say, "Wow, it actually worked." Then Jack recovered and pummeled Tommy once again. But this was the beginning of Tommy's years of fighting back, a period that ended in a donnybrook conducted all over the O'Connor house. It concluded in the cellar in a draw, when he and Jack realized that one of them was going to kill the other.

By then Rick no longer guided Tommy. In many ways their positions had changed. By the time they got out of high school, Rick would say to mutual friends, "I taught O'Connor all about life. And he came back and told me what it was like."

Tommy was the kind of student about whom teachers say,

"If only he'd apply himself." He was also the kind that teachers remember with special fondness and amusement out of the legions they've taught. One of his report cards read, "He's doing better. But he's still talking." Through every stage of school, he was surrounded by the warmth of popularity. Though he was hardly the best student or athlete, his high school classmates chose him to deliver their commencement address. "No jokes," the faculty adviser said, and Tommy obeyed. His classmates tittered anyway.

Rick grew taller and handsomer, but Tommy had the charm, and the first girlfriend. For a while Rick and another pal, Mark, tagged along when Tommy went out on dates. Then came their Smith College days. Some doctors and professors lived in their neighborhood but Tommy and Rick belonged to the quotidian part of Northampton, the part that ran the stores and local government and policed and plowed the streets and went to public school and attended high school football games on Friday nights and listened to the local AM radio station. To date a Smithie was, as Rick would put it, "every townie's dream." Tommy accomplished that first. His parents couldn't afford to send him away to a private college. Tommy lived at home and worked his way through two state schools in the region. The initials on his sweatshirt, "HCC," stood for Holyoke Community College. Now and then he told a Smithie they stood for "Harvard College Crew." He brought Rick along to parties at Hopkins dormitory, where they became something like mascots, interim boyfriends for the young women whose real ones weren't around. For Tommy too, these were mere flirtations with another life. He always felt a slight relief in June, like the feeling of returning home, when the Smithies left and he went back to older, native friends.

A lot of friends eventually moved away. Tommy stayed in town, and he became a local cop. In his neighborhood this wasn't an unusual thing for a boy to do when he grew up. Several had become cops—Tommy's brother Jack in Richmond, Virginia; Tommy's friend Mark on Martha's Vineyard; and also Rick, who joined the Northampton force a couple of years after Tommy. But Tommy's case was special. For as long as anyone could remember, he'd dreamed of becoming a policeman. At five years old he stood in the middle of Forbes Avenue dressed in a round postman's hat and pretended to direct the scanty traffic. In fourth grade he founded the O'Connor Detective Agency. He borrowed his father's old sewer commissioner's badge. His family's garage was the station house. Most of his friends were deputized. They made up flyers and distributed them around the neighborhood: "If you have any mysteries or anything missing call the O'Connor Detective Agency." Soon bikes expanded their territory, and took them into the old downtown.

Back then, in the early seventies, Northampton's Main Street looked like a lot of others in New England towns—the upper stories of many commercial buildings abandoned, some of their windows covered in plywood; moneylending and furniture stores occupying what once had been prime commercial space. Pleasant Street off Main was essentially a skid row, lined with buildings sheathed in tar paper and with what the local cops called fighting bars, where brawling men rolled around on sawdust-covered floors. The lovely old train station was crumbling, its roof half caved in. Downtown had its attractions, though: Charlie's, where Tommy and his pals bought penny candy, and old drugstores with creaking wooden floors and soda fountains that produced ice cream sodas, cherry Cokes. On their bikes he and his deputies followed suspicious-looking cars down Pleasant Street. In Tommy's memory, he got so good at mimicking a siren that now and then a driver actually pulled over, and he rode by looking innocent.

In junior high, he joined the Police Explorer Scouts and

stayed with them through high school, and in due course he went from being a ward of the town to one of its wardens, dressed in blue polyester. In all his dreams, Tommy spent the rest of his life in Northampton. He made a plan. He would remain a cop and rise to sergeant—and no higher for a long time, because higher office meant mostly desks and paperwork. He would marry and have a bunch of kids who would reenact his own Northampton childhood—why not, when his had been so nearly perfect? And then after he retired, he would run for mayor.

By the end of high school he'd already met the woman he wanted to marry, Jean Kellogg, a Yankee girl from a small neighboring hill town. She wasn't so sure about him. He courted her assiduously, and eventually won her over. They made an old-fashioned couple, for the 1980s. He and Jean bought a house. Tommy was supposed to move into it, alone: Jean didn't want to live with him before their wedding. That was fine with him—he knew his parents wouldn't approve. But when the day arrived for him to pack up and leave his childhood home, he felt overcome by the prospect. He said he couldn't do it that day, he had to deal with an emergency at work. So Jean and his mother did the packing for him, and Jean fixed up the new place. Tommy was twenty-three, with his own bachelor pad, and he knew he should feel emancipated. But when he climbed into bed that night, all he could think about was home. This was the first time in his life he'd gone to bed without saying good night to his mother. He called her up.

"You did it to me," he said. "Your youngest is gone."

She didn't take the bait. "Yes. Yes," she said wearily. "Good night."

After a few years of marriage he and Jean began trying to conceive a child. None appeared, but they assumed it was just a matter of time. Meanwhile, Tommy's professional career proceeded much as planned. As the years went by, he rose through the ranks on the Northampton force, from patrol officer to detective, and finally, after ten years, to the sergeant in charge of patrol on the evening shift. He now commanded half a dozen young officers—a well-trained, grown-up version of the O'Connor Detective Agency.

Superficially, Tommy had changed. He had been a chubby little boy, and trim and handsome in his twenties. Now he was about six feet tall and burly, not fat but with a layer of flesh concealing muscle, and his curly hair was gone. If he was going to be bald, he'd decided, he'd be bald emphatically. Sergeant O'Connor shaved his head into a great expanse of skin and shined it up with aftershave before he went on duty. "Helmet Head," one of the other sergeants called him. Without hair above, Tommy's large nose looked larger. At times on duty, his face looked hard, which was the effect he aimed for. The skinhead look was meant to be part of his policeman's uniform, but it didn't entirely conceal the softness of his hazel eyes.

In crayon on the wall inside his bedroom closet on Forbes Avenue Tommy had written:

Tom O'Connor September 29, 1972
I want to be a policeman
I am in sixth grade.

Twenty-three years later, the inscription remained in the closet. Tommy went up to his old room and looked at it once in a while. It was like opening a scrapbook.

Sometimes Tommy O'Connor would be out on patrol at the summer evening hour when streetlights began competing with the sky, a thick forearm resting on the windowsill of the supervisor's cruiser, and he would find himself driving down Elm Street on the hill above downtown. As he approached the Smith College gate, Northampton's quintessential landscape filled his windshield—a green wedge of the Holyoke Range above the Victorian rooftops of Main Street. For a moment he'd imagine he was driving, not toward the center of Northampton, but into a western place at sunset, into a cowboy, frontier town, framed against real mountains.

The Mount Tom and Holyoke Ranges arise just beyond the southern border of the town. The Connecticut cuts a gap between them. They aren't really mountains, just a line of steep green hills. But in Tommy's windshield, they always looked more distant and much taller than they are. They looked grand and not quite real. They looked like Northampton's painted backdrop, and they gave him both a faraway and a comforting feeling. They made Northampton seem like places that he'd never seen, and yet defined the cozy scale of a place he knew by heart—miniature mountains for the miniature city that lay before him down Main Street.

A real Main Street, U.S.A., in general outline much the same as the dying downtown he'd known as a boy, but utterly transformed. Trees along the sidewalks decorated rows of refurbished nineteenth-century commercial buildings, three and four stories tall. Most were made of brick, with fancy Victorian cornices at their rooflines, all slightly different and all of a piece, like faces in a human crowd. Most of the public buildings stood apart, some behind tall trees and little lawns—the old stone courthouse, the old First Church, the Unitarian Universalist Society, city hall (the Castle, as some called it, because it looked just like one, with crenellated turrets on the corners of its roof). Downtown had a little park, Pulaski Park, wedged between Memorial Hall and the Academy of Music, America's first municipally owned theater, where Jenny Lind sang in the middle of the nineteenth century. Tommy couldn't drive down Main Street—no one could—without feeling the presence of history. Layers and layers of past were sedimented under the broad, curving avenue, the bottommost layer dating back to 1654, to a settlement made of wood on the first dry land above the ancient riverside cornfields of the Indians. Downtown's principal streets still followed the Puritan settlers' paths. Main Street still climbed their Meeting House Hill.

In the downtown now before him, the old crumbling train station was entirely restored. It had become a busy, fancy restaurant. So had a lot of other once moribund storefronts. Downtown encompassed only half a dozen city blocks. It was just a patch of city. But it now contained about forty restaurants serving a variety of national cuisines, eleven jewelry and twenty-two clothing shops, a dozen bookstores, seven crafts and art galleries, several nightclubs, two movie theaters. The plywood had come off all the upper-story windows of the commercial blocks. Lawyers and psychologists and hair salons now occupied the second floors. Tommy vividly remembered the era when, after graduation day at Smith, a stillness settled over Main Street and lingered for the summer. Now it was as if he'd blinked and looked again and the place was packed.

From one summer evening to another, the scene through the cruiser's windows looked much the same. The yellow streetlights and gaily colored lighted signs above storefronts illumined crowded sidewalks, down which flowed a mainstream of the middle-aged—mostly white, but with some black, brown, and Asian faces. They made up the human background of downtown, normal-looking and casually dressed, in slacks and jeans and khakis, in sandals on these summer nights. Men and women, women and women, strolled arm in arm past the street musicians. Now and then Tommy would see a cellist seated on a chair outside a coffee shop, or a troupe of Bolivian panpipers on the sidewalk by the Unitarian church. Most evenings the more ordinary sounds of a steel drum, a guitar, an accordion, a saxophone, came in the cruiser's open windows as he drove slowly by. Lines spilled out the doors of restaurants. People with that drifty academic look headed for the readings at the bookstores, and people of the avant-garde, in collarless shirts, the occasional beret, headed for the old bank building that had been recycled into an art gallery. Tommy would glance, and glance again, at the little knots of costumed youth loitering in Pulaski Park and by the Information Booth—skateboarders with their baseball caps turned backward, homeboys with baggy pants and gold chains, Goths in torn black clothes, adorned with spiky jewelry. Often, out in front of the Haymarket coffee shop, a group of Gothically attired youths sat in a circle on the sidewalk—some of Northampton's vegetarian anarchists, talking revolution and for now impeding only foot traffic.

The new downtown was lively and various. And, remarkably to Tommy, it was very peaceful. In the crowds, he spotted the familiar faces of city officials, local entrepreneurs, lawyers and judges he knew from court, doctors and professors from his old neighborhood—people who rarely got in the kind of trouble that he dealt with, though some of their children did. He would watch through his cruiser's windows as, unbeknownst to them, those respectable citizens walked down the sidewalks right beside drug dealers, local felons, a paroled murderer or two. Many of the people on the summer streets came from out of town, looking for a good time. From years of checking license plates, Tommy knew that on any given summer evening some visitors, sometimes more than a few, had long and violent criminal records. Yet there hadn't been a murder on the streets of Northampton for two years or, for several, anything more than minor disturbances on Main Street. Tommy thought his department deserved some of the credit. "I think some local officers have made it hard to be a criminal here," he said. But he felt that something more mysterious than good policing had to be at work. He gazed out the cruiser's windows at busy, peaceful

Main Street, and he shook his head. "I don't know what it is about this place. We get some serious criminals here, but they always seem to do their bad deeds someplace else." He put on a homeboy's accent. "Up here they're chillin', chillin'. "

Tommy had a gift for mimicking accents. His own had the plain sound of what linguists call standard American English, a sound typical of Northampton and the region. One heard many nonnative accents around town these days—Brooklyn, Asian, East Indian, Latino. But once an accent is established in a place, it tends to stick, surviving immigrations. Probably because Northampton was settled by people from Connecticut, the local accent lacked the broad "a" of Boston. Tommy's was as plain as New England accents get.

Northampton was an old Yankee town twice altered fundamentally, first by nineteenth-century immigrations from Ireland, Canada, and Poland, and much more recently by an influx of generally well-heeled members of the well-educated class, the people largely responsible for restoring downtown, and for redefining it. Current local theory divided Northampton in two opposing camps: a trendy, liberal-minded part made up of newcomers and nicknamed Noho, and a mostly native part called Hamp. According to this theory, natives were supposed to take politically conservative stands on every issue and to resent the changes newcomers had wrought, especially the revision of downtown.

The distinction was too neat, but not entirely inaccurate. Most of the natives Tommy knew did their shopping on King Street, the town's shopping strip, a slice of chain department stores, auto dealerships, fast-food restaurants. They didn't shop downtown much because its stores were expensive and didn't sell many necessities—in all of downtown now, you couldn't buy a wrench or a tenpenny nail.

Tommy never shopped here anymore. "What would I buy?" he said, glancing at the boutiques. "Maybe a pair of sandals to write my *Ph.D. thesis* in." He wasn't fond of his hometown's new, prevailing politics, a kind of Democratic liberalism that described itself as progressive. In recent years it had displaced the old ethnic Democrats like Tommy's father, and, it seemed clear to Tommy, now wanted to exclude them altogether—conservative "old Democrats," in the parlance of the new ones now in control of city government. For years Tommy's father had presided at every Democratic mayor's inauguration, but not, rather pointedly, at the most recent of those. His father's jokes, it seemed, were thought to be unsuitable for current sensibilities.

One evening Tommy spotted a man dealing drugs right out in the open, in front of a Main Street coffee shop. A small scene ensued: On a crowded sidewalk, a bald-headed, burly cop running his hands up and down the pants legs of a young black man, who stood with his hands behind his head, protesting loudly, "Man, why you hasslin' me?" And, about ten feet away, a white woman with a silk scarf around her neck, watching the proceedings like an angry sentinel, hands on hips, glaring at the cop.

No doubt this woman was a well-intentioned citizen, summoned to moral outrage. It was reasonable enough to see what she saw—one of society's vulnerable members suffering from the prejudice of an agent of the law. She couldn't have known that the man Tommy was frisking often worked for him as a drug informant and also dealt drugs himself, or that he had a long criminal record and a history of psychosis. But to Tommy, the angry-looking woman was the prejudiced one. He imagined that he knew exactly what was going through her mind. "Obviously I'm hassling a black man, and the next thing I'm gonna do is call him the n-word," he'd thought as he'd glanced at her. Her silent reproach got to him. "It almost makes you feel like you're doing something wrong," he told a fellow cop afterward, back at the police station. Then he repaid the woman in kind. He put on a falsetto, a parody of the voice he imagined for her: " 'How can that bald-headed cop indiscriminately pick on that nice man just because he's black. *I* know a black man. I don't know his name, but I've actually sat down at a table and spoken to him.' " Angrily, Tommy had concluded, "Yeah, well, she wouldn't like it if T.C. was selling drugs to *her* kid."

Some natives, particularly those of Tommy's father's generation, actively avoided Main Street and its spectacles—the people in outlandish costumes and the women with butch haircuts holding hands and kissing. The people of Hamp were supposed to feel deeply aggrieved that their town had acquired a national reputation as an enclave of lesbians. Unquestionably, some natives did feel that way.

Tommy couldn't claim that some of his best friends were homosexuals, but three of his favorite colleagues on the force were openly gay. So were two of his favorite crime victims, a lesbian couple whose house had been robbed—he'd solved the crime and they were grateful, and so was he, for their gratitude. Imagining homosexual sex made him uneasy, and he couldn't keep from imagining it. But lesbians here didn't commit any crimes to speak of, and they'd shown themselves to be some of Northampton's most conscientious parents. "Lesbians are great!" he once exclaimed, catching sight of several female couples as he cruised down Main Street. "Gimme more! Why? They don't cause any trouble."

One thing that had certainly improved in Northampton was the police force. In the late 1970s, a local cop was indicted for attempted murder, and two others went to jail for burglarizing stores. Other malfeasance was dealt with quietly, and the force had essentially been rebuilt around the time Tommy joined. A young cop once said to Tommy that he couldn't imagine cops beating up prisoners in Northampton. "It used to happen," Tommy replied. "And that's one reason why it doesn't now." On this subject his tone was as righteous and reflexive as the one he imagined around him on Main Street. "There's an extreme brotherhood among police," he liked to say. "But I wouldn't stick up for a dirty cop. No way, shape, or form."

Tommy expressed most of his views as declarations, and his views of Main Street were declaratively mixed. He stopped the cruiser at pedestrian crosswalks before people had even left the curb. He did this partly to set a good example for the other drivers, but it wasn't really necessary. Once they hit downtown, most drivers seemed to become pacified, to rediscover manners, to remember driver's education. People could amble across Main Street with alarming carelessness. Some cast lofty glances at the cars. Especially at cop cars, Tommy thought. "Gets my ass out," he muttered, remembering a young woman who had walked, slowly and haughtily, in front of his cruiser the other night, even though he had his blue lights on.

He watched the pedestrians pass before his windshield. On any given summer night, they might include, mixed among the average-looking, a couple of young women with garlands in their hair, an earnest-looking young man with a slinky ferret on a leash, a woman in a pair of platform shoes so tall they nearly qualified as stilts. "How can she do anything serious in those shoes?" said Tommy. A man in a black cape, carrying a wand. "There goes Mr. Magico. Why doesn't he make himself disappear?" A former mental patient, a special ward of Tommy's and of some other cops, striding across the street, lifting his knees high, his fingers splayed rigidly apart. He wore a furry hat with a feather in it. "I believe he'd call that a plume," said Tommy. A group of boys and girls with burgundy hair, orange hair, India-ink hair, hair that stood up in spikes like a rooster's comb. He'd asked one of those kids for the secret: heavy applications of Ivory soap. He liked these motley promenades. They enlarged his town. He hadn't had to leave Northampton to sample the sights of urban America. The world had come to him. "In downtown Northampton, every day is Halloween," he said. "And every night is New Year's Eve."

On a summer evening, stopped at the central traffic light on the corner of Main and Pleasant Streets—no right turn on red allowed—Tommy peered at the bumper sticker on the car in front of him. QUESTION AUTHORITY, it read. Sergeant O'Connor's jaw stiffened. He started talking softly to himself, as if talking to the driver, saying, "Free Tibet. Save the whales. Hey, dude, go for it all. I hope you make a right turn now." But then, a moment later, a beautiful young woman appeared on the sidewalk. Her hair was dyed green, yellow, and white. She had a ring in each nostril and, hanging from her septum, a beaded chain that looked just like the pull chain on a lamp. Tommy's eyebrows rose. His eyes widened. His tongue came forward, almost between his teeth, almost ahead of his words. He looked ten years younger, or maybe ten years old, like the boy who used to go to special classes because he stuttered when he got excited. "This is the greatest community to live in!" he exclaimed. "All the lunacy, that's half the beauty of it. This is a great town to work in. What other town this size has this much going on at night?"

In a decade of police work, Tommy had seen a seamy side of Northampton, and through it a spectrum of dispiriting human qualities, including, in one appalling murder case, the very incarnation of what his parish priest had meant by the word "evil." A lot of people never saw that side of the town. Tommy suspected that a lot of residents didn't think that it existed. He felt impatient with their naïveté and he felt protective of it— rather like the parents who want their children to know the world has many dangers, which they don't want them to encounter. "We deal with the same people over and over again, so that the rest of the people don't have to deal with them. We're like trash collectors," Tommy said once, in a tone that carried more pride than complaint.

Working here as a cop, he often said, had cost him his innocence. But the loss hadn't simply come with the job. It had also been a project. As a young cop, he'd gone with older ones to houses and apartments that had corpses in them—some of which no mortician's art could make presentable. Tommy often cracked jokes at the scenes. Once, while watching the medical examiner peel the scalp off a body, he was reminded of the reflection of his own shaved head in the mirror, and he said, "See, everyone's bald in the end." And everyone in the autopsy room had laughed. A joke made him feel alive in the presence of death, like carousing at an old-fashioned Irish wake, and when he was a younger man, a joke had also made him look worldly-wise in the presence of older cops at the scene.

Maybe he had managed to lose his innocence, but he hadn't lost his capacity for repossessing youth. One time he was rooting around in a trunk at home and found a wig and fake mustache that he'd worn in his years as Northampton's drug detective. He held them in his hands, smiling at them. Utter boyhood reclaimed his face. "I'm saving these," he said. "If we ever have a kid, he'll love to play with them." He added, "I know *I* do."

The town and childhood were inextricably connected for him, and in spite of all the newcomers and the alterations on Main Street, a great deal of Northampton still felt the same. When he drove away from festive Main Street near the end of the evening shift, he found himself almost at once in dim and quiet places. He might have left a party around a bonfire on a beach and, one sand dune away, found himself enveloped by the immensity of night. A mile from downtown, out past the college and the hospital and the fields of the Smith Vocational High School Farm, Northampton's village of Florence would look as calm and quiet as a churchyard. Florence used to be Tommy's beat. He'd patrolled it on the midnight shift for years as a young cop, through its almost always peaceful slumber. He passed through Florence often in the evenings nowadays, but he'd gone for years without seeing it in its early-morning hours.

One night he agreed to work a tour as the substitute

sergeant on the midnight shift. Florence still went to bed early. The morning of his brief return to Midnights, Tommy discovered that the village still woke up early, too. At four A.M. the lights went on inside the Miss Florence Diner—Miss Flo's, the village's old central landmark, quaint-looking enough to have made it into several coffee-table books. For old times' sake, and feeling hungry, Tommy pulled up beside Miss Flo's right at four, for the first time in half a decade. He opened the door, and he thought he must be dreaming. There behind the counter, scrambling eggs as always, stood the bent and twisted figure of Battlin' Bob, the short-order cook, as ever undeterred by his disabilities. Tommy stood in front of the counter in his sergeant's uniform, looking around, his eyes growing huge. The same small group of men, less one, sat in the diner's booths. And not just any booth, but each in the same one he had occupied five years ago. In a moment, the paper man came in with a stack of the Springfield *Union-News.* Tommy looked at his watch. It was the same paper man, and he was right on time, five-years-ago time.

Tommy turned to one of the men who sat drinking coffee in a booth. "Joe, you're still here! How many years since I used to come in here?"

Joe couldn't remember. He filled Tommy in on what had happened since he'd been away. There wasn't much to tell. The missing regular had died. Joe himself had retired from construction work but still got up and came to Miss Flo's before dawn every morning.

"You're still here!" Tommy said again.

"I'm in the same pew, too," said Joe. "Nothin' ever changes, huh?"

One thing Tommy liked about his job was that every evening brought something unexpected, but he'd never liked unexpected changes in his own life—maybe because, on the whole, his own life had always seemed so well arranged.

A few years ago he and Jean had moved. It was because of his job. Tommy found a message spray-painted on the North-ampton bike path: FUCK O'CONNOR'S WIFE BECAUSE SHE LIKES IT. Then someone he arrested said he knew where Tommy lived and at what hour his wife walked their dog. So he and Jean bought a house in a neighboring town. The night they moved into it—he hated the whole experience—Jean pointed out to him that, so long as they lived here, he wouldn't be able to run for mayor of Northampton.

"I never thought of that!" Tommy had yelled. He'd felt sincerely upset.

Their new town was rural, Republican, and Protestant, but only a few miles from downtown Northampton and from Mike Bouley's garage, where Tommy still got his car serviced, and Ed's Electric, where he got appliances fixed, and the Dunkin' Donuts on King Street, where he went for his coffee while on duty and the woman at the cash register always called him "honey," and the Look Restaurant, where he usually ate when he ate out and where, without his asking, the waitresses placed his order for him, saying, "I know. A tuna melt and a chocolate milk." And he was just a short drive from Forbes Avenue and his childhood home, where his father still lived.

Tommy's mother had died suddenly, in 1994. He was on duty and made it to the emergency room just in time to say good-bye. He couldn't go back inside that place for months. Jean said he had to put a stop to this, and face the ghost in the ER. He finally forced himself. Walking into that brightly lit place, he felt sweat trickling down his back beneath his protective vest.

Now, more than ever, his father's house pulled him toward it. In the winter, after snowfall, he'd steal ten minutes from his sergeant's duties and shovel out his father's drive-way. One morning he arrived at the front door and asked his niece, who was staying there for a few months, "How's Himself today?"

"I don't know," said the niece. "He hasn't gotten up yet."

Tommy brushed past her, ran through the kitchen, and bounded up the stairs. He came back a few minutes later, his face flushed. "Sleeping like a baby. Phew."

Almost every evening around six, Tommy turned his cruiser back toward Forbes Avenue, heading for supper with his father. A meal eaten on duty was, in police parlance, a "forty." He was allowed about half an hour for his. Sometimes Jean joined them, and did the cooking.

As Tommy drove down Forbes Avenue, he noticed small changes in the old neighborhood. That house he remembered as run-down was newly painted. That old barn they'd used as a fort during those chestnut wars had been made into an artist's studio. And there weren't nearly as many children around. But oaks and maples taller than the houses still lined the narrow street, their roots wrinkling the sidewalks, and the O'Connor homestead was essentially unaltered. Tommy entered through the kitchen door, and on most evenings his father, Bill, turned from the stove and right away seemed to stand behind an imaginary podium. "Well, Tom, I was walking around this morning, and I was singing, and I thought of a great song for Northampton. 'I Saw Daddy Kissing Santa Claus.' Now whaddaya think of that? It's a hit, isn't it?" Then his father made his laugh—it was famous in old-time Northampton, one grand exhalation, mouth opened wide.

Tommy smiled, thinking, "Jesus, Mary, and Joseph, I hope he doesn't use that one at the St. Patrick's Day breakfast."

Bill O'Connor was seventy-nine, and spry. He had long ago retired from his day job as treasurer of Hampshire County; before that, he'd run an insurance business, so small that when he sold it and entered politics, the entire operation fit in a shoebox. His work now was entirely as an Irish storyteller, a *seanachie*. He always presided at Northampton's St. Patrick's Day breakfast, and the phone still rang with requests that he serve as master of ceremonies at functions in the city and region. Bill rarely refused.

Physically, Tommy didn't take after his father. For one thing, Bill still had his hair, and his nose made a fascinating sharp left turn. Bill used to tell Tommy and Tommy's older brother Jack that his nose was wounded on the beaches of Normandy. Bill really had been there, in the navy. But his nose was congenital.

Years ago, when Tommy and Jack were making noise at bedtime upstairs in this house, their mother would come to the door and say, "If I hear another peep out of you two, your father's coming up." "Peep, peep," he and Jack would say in unison, and then, as threatened, Bill would arrive, sit down on their bed, and start telling stories. They had counted on this. A forty at Bill's house was nearly as predictable. On the nights when Jean wasn't there, Tommy and his father both pitched in at the stove. Then they sat down at the long kitchen table, the one Tommy had always known, Bill at the head and Tommy to his right, and in a moment, without preamble, Bill started telling a story.

He had hundreds of stories. Many were tales of the good old days in Northampton politics, when the town still had more than a smattering of Republicans. There was the one about the bibulous city councillor—"He was a Democrat, usually," Bill said—who went to a meeting to cast his vote on the Yankee Republican side of an important issue, but disappeared on the way to city hall. The mayor, a Yankee Republican, declared that the councillor had been kidnapped. Actually, two old Democrats, one Tunker Hogan and one Wally Puchalski, had intercepted the councillor and offered him the sort of bribe he found irresistible. The three men spent the evening drinking in the Polish Club bar across the river, where they watched the TV news story about the councillor's kidnapping.

Tommy gazed at the old man, and scraped his right

thumbnail, deformed from high school football, against a front tooth. Jean liked to study him at these moments. Listening to his father's stories over supper, dressed in his sergeant's uniform and fearsomely equipped, his gun on the table, Tommy looked, Jean thought, just like an eager child.

Bill took a bite of supper, and resumed. "Now it's after midnight. As I found out later, they decided to bring him home."

"And you were nowhere around at that point," said Tommy.

"No. I was home with my wife," said Bill.

The councillor lived at the top of a steep grassy hill, and he was now asleep. His kidnappers, Hogan and Puchalski, had to carry him up the slope. They made an awkward pair of bearers, one too big, the other too small. "Hogan's a big man, oh, Hogan's over three hundred. I can see him now. He had a little pin head," said Bill. He added, "Puchalski's frail. Frail all over." Puchalski once defeated Bill in a mayoral election and used to run the city from his candy store. The two kidnappers weren't entirely sober themselves, and they managed to carry the councillor only halfway home before they slipped and fell in a heap on the grass. Then Tunker Hogan, who liked a bit of mischief, reached over and took the still-sleeping councillor's pulse. "Son of a bitch, he's dead!" Hogan said to Puchalski. "You killed him!"

"Puchalski believed it," said Bill. "I think he was thinking of resigning from politics, and isn't it funny, he went on to be mayor four terms. And Hogan says, 'I'm not gonna get caught in this thing. I'm goin' to my car. If you want to come, all right.' So. They both ran away."

"They left him lying on the grass?" said Tommy.

"They left him lying on the grass," said Bill sadly.

"One of them thinking he was dead!" said Tommy.

"And the Recreation Department picked him up later in the morning," said Bill.

The next night he might tell about the time when he was a

boy and his mother sent him to pay a long-overdue doctor's bill: he hands over the dollar bill his mother has given him, and the doctor says to his nurse, "My God! This boy is paying for his own delivery." And maybe the night after that, the one about Puchalski and his cronies stealing the U.N. flag from city hall and pleading patriotism when they got caught, Bill saying, "I never laughed so much. That was politics. It made no sense at all." Sometimes he told a story that Tommy hadn't heard before, but the routine was always about the same. After supper Tommy helped clean up, then strapped on his laden gunbelt. As Tommy headed for the door, Bill said, "Hey, thanks. Thanks for visiting an old man."

Tommy looked back quickly, in time to see his father winking.

Like one loved long ago, Northampton has saved many keepsakes, among them old journals and diaries, and stored them in Forbes Library instead of in bureau drawers. The most important come from a nineteenth-century newspaper editor and antiquarian named Sylvester Judd. He gathered up a huge assortment of documents and memorabilia about the town in its colonial youth. He recorded this story from the time of the seventeenth-century Indian wars: Samuel Strong and his son left town one morning to fetch some grain and were ambushed by Indians. Other townsfolk heard the shots and came running. The boy was dead, Strong only wounded. But he imagined he was dying as he was carried back toward town. "He used to say that when they reached a hill where Northampton could be seen, he took, as he supposed, one last look at his beloved home and town, with feelings that cannot be described."

As for his own feelings about Northampton, Judd was usually reserved. In his journals, he mainly recorded small details of the place, the locations of its houses, the clothes its people wore, its daily temperature. But there is feeling here. Surveying Judd's old documents, so intensely local and precise, you sense that he was working in an already retrospective frame of mind, trying to construct the entire place without him in it. Once in a while he got carried away and made what, for him, amount to exclamations. He might have been writing to an old flame to tell her how she once appeared. Of a Northampton winter scene in the 1840s, he wrote, "The night was very still; no wind, and the trees this morning are if possible more resplendent and glittering in the morning sun than yesterday. It seems an enchanted scene from the Arabian Nights. The trees seemed filled and covered with transparent silver like foliage." After you have spent some time with him in his journals, you can feel the disappointment with which he wrote this entry, recording the town's nighttime and early-morning sounds during the summer of 1842: "I have heard no whippoorwills this season." Judd must have been overwhelmed with pleasure when, three summers later, he sedately wrote: "A whippoorwill was heard at Broughtons Meadow April 28th and it has been heard there every day since—early in the morning and evening."

People who spend their lives in one small town don't necessarily grow blind to it. Some natives of a comely place take its beauties in so deeply that the place becomes almost identical with the senses that perceive it. Since marrying Jean, who was geographically adventurous, Tommy had traveled some, on vacation trips. But his journeys were few. He'd never seen the West Coast. He'd never seen New York City, though it was only a three-hour drive away. When he did travel, he carried Northampton with him. If he saw a pretty hillside belonging to another place, or smelled another place's river, he knew those things by contrast and comparison with the hills around Northampton and the great river that made its eastern boundary. These were, for him, reality. And if he woke up somewhere else, on a vacation trip or in the neighboring

town where he now lived, and heard a whippoorwill outside—three syllables, the first and last accented "*Whip*-poor-
weel, Whip-poor-*weel*"—he would be transported back to his
bedroom on Forbes Avenue. Opening his eyes to the gray
daylight in the window and listening to that ancient song,
he'd remember himself remembering, "Oh yeah, oh boy, it's
summer." In his mind's eye, his frayed shorts lay on the floor,
right where he had left them. He'd pull them on, hurry
through breakfast, then run out to meet Rick and his other
friends on the street.

In his first years as a cop, when he worked the midnight
shift, and it was very early in the morning and almost everyone else was still asleep, Tommy would drive west toward the
forested part of Northampton. Out Ryan Road to West
Farms Road, then up a dirt track toward the top of a hill that
he thought of as Turkey Hill. There, deep woods behind and
an open vista before him, he'd get out of his patrol car, his
coffee cup in hand, and, gazing toward Mount Tom, watch
the sun rise over a corner of Northampton. He could see
some of the town laid out below and imagine the rest, and he
felt lordly, watching Northampton emerge from the dark,
almost as if he were watching its creation, almost as if it all
belonged to him.

Years ago, on foot patrol downtown, he'd walk into an alley
off Main Street and imagine that a great metropolis lay at the
other end. But he knew he was scarcely a big-city cop, and, he
often told himself, he was better off for that. A lot of those
cops spent half their careers doing nothing but traffic work,
whereas he dealt with all sorts of crimes and problems. Real
trouble arose less frequently here than in many places that
called themselves cities, but he figured he could work in
Northampton for forty years and, on the day he retired, his
successor would still have plenty to do. In the meantime, he'd
be working in a place where, he often told himself, a cop could
make a difference.

It would be hard to prove that police work matters more where it's needed less, but sometimes he could have an effect inconceivable in a large and violent city. One day back in 1993, a former member of the Latin Kings gang hailed Tommy and told him that a carload of Kings had just tried to abduct him. And they would have succeeded, this young man said, if Tommy hadn't happened to drive by and scare them off. "The Kings got a termination out on me," the former member said. Tommy took off after the car. He stopped it at downtown's busiest intersection, right in front of the courthouse. Although he knew he was on shaky legal ground, Tommy ordered the young men out of the car and searched it—the kind of decision that had made him most unpopular among several local defense attorneys.

A crowd of citizens had gathered on the corner. Aware of many eyes on him, Tommy thought he might as well state his case publicly. He'd found necklaces of gang beads in the car. He held them up for all the crowd to see, and he bellowed at the young men, "Gang activity in Northampton will not be tolerated! You will not come to Northampton wearing your colors and displaying gang signs!"

The young men denied that they were Latin Kings.

Really? Tommy asked. Then how come they were wearing T-shirts that read ALMIGHTY LATIN KING NATION?

"Yo, man, you can have my shirt," one of them said, disrobing on the spot.

About a year after that incident, Tommy was talking to a former gang member named Felix, a young man he'd known as a baby. Tommy asked him if many gangsters came to Northampton, and Felix said, "No, not too many, man. They don't want to come here. They get hassled by cops. Yeah, they say *you*, O'Connor! They say you go up there and the bald-headed cop takes your shirts!"

It isn't given to many to know a town as well as Tommy knew Northampton. A state detective friend who had never worked a long time in one place occasionally called Tommy to ask for information about Northampton residents. A certain person had come to his attention. Did Tommy know him? The detective would start laughing as Tommy answered, without a moment's hesitation, "Yup, he's going out with Daisy. Hangs at the Information Booth. Drives a blue Mustang. You want the license number?" This really was the right-sized town for him. Working here, he could arrest the person who was selling cocaine to his friend's kid. He could make a gang think twice about colonizing the place, just by taking a youngster's T-shirt.

He was thirty-three years old, and it seemed like an enviable way to spend the next thirty years, working in a town he could see entirely and feel he understood, all in one view from the top of Turkey Hill. Tempting from up there to think that he could protect it all, and keep it just as orderly and safe as it had seemed when he was a boy.

On his way home to Jean after the evening shift ended, Tommy almost always took a last drive down Forbes Avenue, through his old neighborhood. This was called performing a check on "the well-being."

One summer evening, Tommy had been sitting with his father on the screened porch facing the street, and he'd seen a couple of young men he knew very well playing hacky-sack in the front yard of the house next door. A heroin addict and thief, and a drug dealer supposedly connected to an Asian gang from Lowell—both had moved in next door to his father. Tommy was sitting there, astonished, when a car pulled up and another familiar young man got out and walked up the path to that neighboring house, carrying a huge, potted, robust-looking marijuana plant.

Tommy went inside and called Peter Fappiano, the current drug detective, and told him to come in the back door of his father's house. Together they wrote up an affidavit for a search warrant. They found the pot, but not the *pot,* as Tommy put it.

They couldn't arrest his father's new neighbors. So Tommy called the owner of that house and told him about his tenants. Tommy also told the landlord the government might confiscate his house—which was most unlikely. Tommy laid it on thick. By the end of the conversation the man was apologizing. Two days later those renters were gone. "It's not the neighborhood for them," Tommy said afterward. "Even if they hadn't been doing anything wrong."

All had been peaceful ever since, and was peaceful still on these summer nights, as he made his last night watchman's checks on Forbes Avenue, his car windows down, the cicadas and tree frogs filling up the air with insistent, inland sea sounds, summoning memories. The morning cry of "*E-awkee!*" The delicious feeling of grass and pavement on bare feet—you went barefoot and toughened up your feet, because that was what Indians did. Driving slowly down Forbes Avenue, the place full of living ghosts, he could imagine the promise of snow in the warm moist August air. It wouldn't be very long before he and his pals had headed out for fresh territory, dragging toboggans toward Hospital Hill.

Tommy would pause in his car for a moment in front of his father's house. Thinking of his mother, he looked for the flickering light in the living room windows that signaled Bill was watching TV. Then he drove away toward bed, the world of home and neighborhood and town still intact behind him.

CHAPTER 2

The Morning Polka

NORTHAMPTON'S DAY, IT might be said, officially begins around nine, when the mayor walks into the Castle, city hall, at the apex of Main Street's broad curve. On her way upstairs to her office, the mayor—Mary Ford, a heavy woman in her fifties—walks down a high-ceilinged corridor, past wooden doors darkened with age. Only the elevator, which she usually rides, looks modern. City hall speaks of ancestry and evolution. The old woodwork and the small signs that stick out beside doorways, representing just a handful of the city's twenty-five departments—"Board of Health," "Retirement," "City Auditor," "City Treasurer," "City Clerk"—make the place feel like a museum of complex, everyday necessity. Those who still dream of transporting American-style democracy to fledgling republics, all at once and in one piece, might well despair at the sight.

Local government has functioned here for 341 years. It has been continuous back far beyond memory, back beyond its occupation of this century-old building. The mayor isn't a native—she grew up in Pennsylvania—but she doesn't represent a newfangled breach of tradition. Calvin Coolidge was mayor of Northampton, and he didn't grow up here either.

Letters, computer printouts, forbiddingly thick bound documents cover the mayor's desk, a sturdy oak table. The room
makes you think of musty rugs and mothballs. She sits beside a
huge old double-hung window. She could look out over
rooftops toward the Holyoke Range, if there weren't an air conditioner plugged into the lower half of the window, and if the
blinds above weren't lowered. She works mainly under fluorescent light. Visitors sit in straight-backed chairs lined up in
front of her desk. Her aides, Mike and Corinne, sit in them
now. This day starts with a long-range strategy session. The
mayor stands at an easel. On a huge sheet of paper she's laid
out the big picture of what she hopes to accomplish during the
rest of this term and her next. She will run unopposed this
November, so she doesn't have to campaign. She has two years
and several months more in office, guaranteed. "It's a big luxury. I can put my stamp on things," she says.

On her easel she has written, "Jobs," "Schools," "Community Building," and placed long lists under each. These
include items like "Marketing Outreach" and "Efficiency,"
"Morale" and "Computer Progress," "Homeless" and "Old
Buildings," "Coke—When Is Peaking?" and "School Change?"
One notices the question marks. It looks as if the budget
might be balanced by next year, just one year later than she
first planned. Barring disaster, that is. She wonders whether
they'll have enough free cash to plow the streets if it snows a
lot this winter and whether they shouldn't take out snow
insurance. The new Coca-Cola factory is running, but not at
full capacity—all two hundred new jobs may not materialize if
Americans don't take to the drink Fruitopia. A crack has
appeared in the junior high's new swimming pool, still under
construction. She worked very hard, along with others, to persuade the town to improve the junior high. "And I'm proud of
it. Because it's a very positive thing for the community," she
says. Then she laughs, hard enough to shake all over. "But if
the swimming pool crumbles, that's it. That's my career, down

the tubes." Northampton's mayor still doesn't directly control
the various financial departments or the Department of
Public Works. ("You don't control the DPW?" the mayor of
Somerville once asked Mayor Ford. "Then what's the point of
being mayor?") And, of course, the mayor has little control
over what the state government does, and no real way of
redressing the fact that new state educational funding formu-
las unfairly penalize Northampton and threaten her dreams of
improving the schools.

Standing beside her easel, the mayor sums up the prospects,
in a high, cheery voice. "Hard as it is to change anything, it's
even harder because there are so many structures in place." She
chuckles. "And we may end up with very little change."

Her aides return to their desks. Mayor Ford sits down at
hers. She has just begun to sort through all the papers there,
when through the open door Corinne calls, "Mary, the chamber of commerce is here." After the chamber comes a woman
from the Feldenkrais Learning Center, who wants to sell the
city classes for its clerks, classes in how to avoid the injuries of
deskbound life. "All those new phrases in my head," the
mayor murmurs afterward. " 'Surviving in a culture of
chairs.' " All morning long the big picture on her easel atom-
izes. One who has mastered the Esperanto of the managerial
class might say that even on "proactive" days she is forced to
be "reactive." A parade of petitioners comes and goes—the
chair of the volunteer committee that is trying to arrange for
a new fire station, various department chiefs, her son in
search of lunch money. And the phone keeps ringing.
Corinne calls from the outer office, "Mary, someone who
can't make the Cable TV Committee meeting tonight wants
to speak to you about what she feels is the lack of public-
access programming."

Then Tom, her budget analyst, walks in. The mayor tells
him that the personnel director wants her to spend some
money on Feldenkrais training.

"That's going to be the least of your worries, after you hear all of this," says Tom. He hands her a draft of next year's budget.

The mayor gazes at the sheaf of papers, then cries out, "We'll only have a hundred and fifty thousand in free cash by January, before snow season?"

Tom narrows his eyes and stares at her.

"Okay, okay, okay," she says. The mayor takes out a package of antacids and gobbles one.

The old town clock on the stone steeple of the First Church is telling the wrong time over Main Street. It is nearly two o'clock, in fact. A code of studied informality seems to guide most of the people on the sidewalks. Women tend to wear pants and not skirts, clogs and not pumps. In every street scene, people assert something, through the ways that they dress and act. But what do they say here? No one seems in a great hurry, but many seem serious. No one dresses to say, "I'm rich." If anything, most say with their costumes, "I'm smart." Many could be blue-collar workers or perpetual graduate students, or both. Or financiers. Guessing professions on Main Street is tricky.

When you see people in suits, though, it's a good bet they work at the courthouse. Two such men stroll side by side past the First Church. Court recesses at one o'clock and resumes at two. They are heading back from lunch. The tall one is a middle-aged lawyer, the other a rather small, trim man of about fifty, with wire-rimmed glasses, gray hair, and a full gray beard. He looks detached from time, like a historical figure. This would be Judge W. Michael Ryan, of the District Court. He is a native and a former district attorney. The first time he ran for D.A., he came in fifth in a field of five candidates. "I never could decide if it was because I wasn't well enough known, or too well-known," he likes to say. "Probably the latter."

Now from behind his beard comes a brightening look, in his eyes and around his mouth, a suggestion that he has tasted and enjoyed what he's about to say. "Between the two of us we probably know almost everyone in town," Judge Ryan tells his friend. "But we probably only know a few of the same people." He points across Main Street toward a chain drugstore. "You look over there and you see CVS. *I* see Woolworth's where I used to go as a kid." The judge pauses. "As we walk down this street, we see two completely different towns."

This piece of wisdom, the ascendancy of the subjective, dominates a lot of contemporary thought. Of course, the judge is right. Viewed through the eyes of individual inhabitants, all places are disparate, Northampton notably so.

It has achieved numerical stability through flux—about two-thirds of native children leave when they grow up, and newcomers replace them. Some of its thirty thousand residents work elsewhere and some people come from elsewhere to work here. A sizable proportion, about 16 percent, are students, and another 5 percent or so provide education at all levels, but Northampton is far from being a mere college town. About 13 percent of residents are children under eighteen, about 11 percent have retired, about 5 percent describe themselves as "homemakers" (all but a few female), only about 2 percent are unemployed, and about 10 percent make up what could be loosely called the working class. For a town its size, North-ampton has an unusually large number of lawyers, doctors, clergy, judges. An extraordinary number, about two hundred, work in the psychological trade—a few earn half their incomes analyzing fellow analysts. The yearly census leaves it up to citizens to define themselves however they choose. A number pursue fairly unusual professions. There is a stump grinder, a storyteller, a quilter, a missionary, a rugby coach, a rug restorer, a buttonmaker, a weapons technician, a kayaker, an opera singer, a ballet accompanist, a bridal consultant, a fish smoker, an aircraft mechanic, three brewers, and three millwrights. A fair number of academics eschew the simple title "professor" and call themselves economists, astronomers, historians, philosophers. Northampton also has an aesthetician and a nail technician, a comedian, a green thumb, a collector, a domestic engineer. It has two residents who describe themselves as poets and one who calls herself a factotum, also two copy consultants, one key associate, one feminist, and five activists.

All those eyes see many different towns. The Gay, Lesbian, and Transgender Pride March, once a rather grim and tense affair, has become a peaceful rite of spring and the March for Jesus follows, a few weeks later. The largest denomination in town is Roman Catholic. The largest single church is Christian evangelical, which stands for salvation through Christ, and the second largest is Unitarian Universalist, where God isn't usually mentioned and parishioners are encouraged to create their own systems of belief. In the one, the hymns are soft rock tunes, and in the other, classical—played on a Steinway and an organ, occasionally a flute. Meanwhile, New Age mysticism flourishes here. The town has American Legion baseball and contra dancing, a small Buddhist church and a very active Elks club, homes that cost $400,000 and many boardinghouses and halfway houses. Somehow it works. Northampton is the kind of place where a professor, potter, unemployed musician, former mental patient, a woman with a handsome alimony, can all be found on Sunday mornings sitting near one another at sidewalk tables outside the coffee shops. Somehow—is it the sum of unconcerted efforts?—a cohesive property seems to bind the place, as if it were a liquid held by surface tension.

Dave McDowell is a giant of a man. He came close to winning the national collegiate wrestling championship some years ago, and was invited to try out for the Dallas Cowboys. He couldn't imagine why he'd want to play football, though, when he had a chance to go to seminary. Dave never sweats or shouts when he preaches, in the old gym of the former Northampton School for

Girls, but he packs them in. The Episcopal priest sometimes sneaks over in mufti to listen. Dave's church, the evangelical College Church, was the first in town to provide emergency shelter for the homeless. It also runs a clinic for people without health insurance.

A homeless man with a murder in his past needs help in getting lodging. Dave gives him $25 to tide him over and calls the manager of a local rooming house on his behalf. Afterward Dave says, "There's a passage early in John. 'And Jesus did not entrust himself to any man.' The most important thing is not to get disillusioned. For every ten, one guy's gonna make it. You can't stop trying. Do you trust 'em? No. But you can't stop trying. I think Jesus loved people. Maybe he didn't trust 'em."

Main Street thrives, and some restaurants gross more than a million dollars a year. But success has boosted rents, and also brought in groups of kids. They pack downtown, clogging the sidewalks, impeding tourist shoppers, alarming some. The merchants have called for a meeting with the police chief. They sit together at a long table, in a city building a few blocks from the Castle.

"Every word I hear is 'fuck.' It's getting really trashy," says one shopkeeper.

"It's just not friendly anymore," says another.

The chief is, as ever, calm and reassuring. "Believe me," he declares. "I know how important downtown is. Police chiefs come here for dinner, because it's safe for their kids."

"Can we set up something in the park to make it uncool to go there?" one of the merchants asks. "Play Vivaldi all night long?"

"I wonder if there could be designated areas for street entertainers," a shopkeeper says. She adds, smiling, "This is where I really get to sounding like my mother."

• • •

Downtown used to have a large department store. Now it has Thorne's Marketplace, built inside the old store's shell, full of separate trendy shops, the air scented with incense, but with the wooden floors intact. Two of the owners, Brink Thorne and Mazie Cox, a handsome couple, middle-aged, sit in their living room, discussing Northampton.

She says, "In a community it's like a musical score and all of these people are playing their parts. I think Northampton represents community." She goes on, "In New York people used to say, 'Northampton? Is that part of Long Island?' Now they say, 'Northampton. Oh, you're so lucky. I have a boyfriend, a cousin who lives there.' Maybe it's the density of something we are craving in our society."

He says that in some ways Northampton resembles southern France. "Geography created dense, tight neighborhoods surrounded by natural features. How does that come to be and succeed? Through real relationships. Elasticity that can survive tragedies."

They remember coming upon Main Street, in 1972. "It was an incredible place," he says. It looked moribund, but most of the old buildings had survived. "It hadn't had any teeth knocked out." They were both architects, and young enough to imagine their professional ideals realistic. They also came with capital. They campaigned against the plans to bring urban renewal to downtown. They bought and renovated several buildings. They played a part in the revival. Those were wonderful years. "The SoHo image," he says. "Loft living. People like ourselves who were going to make things better. Living in spaces where no one had lived before, in lofts. You could make up, create your own life." He laughs. "And then we end up living in white clapboarded houses."

Loitering kids notwithstanding, downtown still looks wonderful to many ordinary citizens. Pat Coonerty strolls down Main Street with her string bag, heading for the open-air farmer's market. The sidewalks are crowded, all the sidewalk tables in front of the coffee shops filled. The place has what she thinks of as "a little European flavor." Pat buys *The New York Times* and fills up her string bag with fresh vegetables. This takes a while, because she keeps running into friends.

All her life she has worked for causes—for peace during the Vietnam War, for runaway children, for battered women here. She once taught a course in assertiveness at a small women's college. She teaches school now, in a nearby city. She and her husband came to town twenty-three years ago. They were just passing through. "It looked like, just a lovely town. I wanted a neighborhood," she remembers. They didn't have much money. They found a little house they could afford in the leafy South Street neighborhood. "A handyman's special," she says. "A handy*person's*." A little Victorian, all spruced up now, painted pink, but a pink so pale and tasteful it deserves to be called rose, with rhododendrons in the little lawn out front, and a Korean dogwood, and a saucer magnolia. "I love my house," Pat says. "I mean, other people, other people stop and take pictures. It's just really nice. I mean, I love my house."

Northampton turned out to be most of what she hoped for. "I could walk the streets with my toddler. Downtown is where she got her first undies, just like Mom's." She used to chat with other mothers on the way. The neighborhood was warm. She remembers block parties. "The kids learned to ride their bikes together," she recalls. "It has a lot of history and memories. Not to mention that my house is a hundred and eight years old." Her child is grown now, but Pat's journey downtown still has a lot of the old gregarious flavor.

She stops in half a dozen stores to schmooze with the shopkeepers. Then she walks into Thorne's Marketplace. Pat plans to do some shopping, but is suddenly waylaid by a disturbing sight—a young mother carrying a screaming baby in a sling and holding a screaming toddler by the hand, a lost and helpless-looking young mother. Pat thinks the young woman bears all the telltale signs of someone stoned on drugs. Crowds pass by, ignoring this mother in trouble. Pat marches up and asks if she needs help.

The woman says she wants Pat to leave her alone.

"No. You *need* help," Pat says. "Somebody *has* to help you."

The woman heads for the back stairs. Pat calls 911.

"I think children, like, *belong* to the community," Pat explains afterward. "One needs to sort of *take action*."

For most people, the workday is almost over when, at a few minutes after three, Sergeant O'Connor emerges from the side door of the police station, a block away from Main Street. The sun glints off his shiny head. He wears a blue polyester shirt with sergeant's stripes on the sleeves, dark polyester pants, black boots, and a clip-on necktie (because a real one could become a noose). All uniforms make the people in them seem easily understood. When Tommy emerges in uniform onto the streets of Northampton, leather creaking and hardware softly jangling, he rolls his shoulders and holds his arms bowed out a little from his sides, as if he fancies himself a weight lifter and gunfighter all in one. The impression he makes, of confidence and force, isn't altogether wrong, or unintended. But in fact, he rolls his shoulders to adjust the protective vest he wears beneath his shirt, and all the equipment on his belt forces his arms out from his sides.

About ten pounds of hardware hangs from his uniform—pistol, pepper spray (the safest means all around of subduing suspects and mental patients who have begun to fight), pouches full of ammo and rubber gloves, two pairs of handcuffs, a kielbasa-sized flashlight for the dark hours of his shift, a PR-24 baton (a modern version of the old nightstick). He's heading for the supervisor's cruiser when he spots a man in a wheelchair rolling by on Center Street.

An informant has told Tommy that this man is using heroin

again. Tommy walks over to him. The man's legs look like a rag doll's. Tommy hooks his thumbs over his belt buckle. He stands with his feet wide apart. He looks immense beside the man, but he is smiling. After a little small talk, Tommy says, "By the way, you ever hear of C-smack? Comes in a yellow package, says 'C-smack' on it?"

The man in the wheelchair shakes his head. He looks away, then up at Tommy. "I'm clean now, Tommy. You know that."

"Good man," says Tommy. "But just a heads-up, in case you fall. Stay away from that stuff. Last week? We took a guy out of an apartment in Florence who died from it."

Tommy watches the man roll off toward Main Street. "I haven't had the heart to bust him. I don't know. If I was in a wheelchair, I might take heroin too."

He walks over to his cruiser, a big Ford with head-snapping acceleration. He opens the trunk and inspects the gear inside— emergency medical equipment, extra pairs of rubber gloves for handling bloody situations, a life preserver ring for emergencies along Northampton's riverfront, antibacterial soap for washing his hands after various potentially infectious incidents. He climbs in and tests his radios—they connect him to all the police forces in western Massachusetts and to the dispatcher at the station and his patrol officers. Beside the driver's seat he places his binoculars, especially handy for observing drug deals from a distance. He tests the cruiser's gaudy strobe-light show and medley of piercing siren noises. He takes the 12-gauge shotgun out of its rack on the floor and makes sure it's loaded—not that he's likely to need it, but, he reasons, you never know. He rolls down the windows and turns the air conditioner on full blast. Then he puts the cruiser in gear. "I'm in a ridin' mood," he says.

Tommy hasn't driven far when he hears trouble unfolding over his radio. One of his young patrolmen is right now arresting a citizen for driving an improperly registered car—not an arrestable offense. Tommy flicks on his blue lights and siren and races to the scene. He arrives just as the patrolman has finished snapping handcuffs on the driver. Tommy jumps out and strides toward them. "Officer! Officer! Take those handcuffs off that man! This man is a *good* man!" The young cop obeys and steps aside. Tommy stands before the citizen, and lifting his right hand high, makes the sign of the cross over him. "You are unarrested! Go in peace." It works. The citizen sticks out his hand to shake with Tommy.

Tommy tells the young cop to meet him back at the station. There Tommy takes him to an office, closes the door, and says, "Go and arrest someone else, but make sure you have the right to do it. Remember, this is the largest power you have." The young cop apologizes. Tommy says, "Be thankful it was an ignorant civilian and not a lawyer. But it was an honest mistake, and it's not goin' past here." Tommy pauses. He smiles. "Unless the guy complains."

He spends a part of every shift following his officers to accidents and to calls from citizens in distress, and in between he does his own patrolling. Each of the junior officers is confined to a sector of town, but Tommy's jurisdiction encompasses all of Northampton, thirty-six square miles of land, crisscrossed by 170 miles of road. In the course of a week, he drives all of it, varying his rounds so as not to make himself predictable to Northampton's criminal class. He drives past ranch houses on the suburban roads and past the supermarkets, car dealerships, fast food restaurants on King Street, Northampton's Anywhere U.S.A. He drives through the small and usually quiet villages within the town and explores the wooded spots by the railroad tracks where homeless people sleep in cardboard shelters, under plastic construction wrap. He cruises slowly past the playgrounds and through the parks and parking lots and old residential neighborhoods, past the apartment complexes, rooming houses, and public housing projects.

On a housing project street, he rolls up beside two brown-skinned Hispanic boys, who stand outside one of the units. Even though the air is warm, they wear hooded sweatshirts, probably for the pockets: a cop can't look in pockets without probable cause.

"Whussup, O'Connah?"

"Whussup wit' you, my man?"

"Chillin'."

"Ricky, I been knowin' you since you were a baby and I've never seen you look this stoned before."

"That's where you're wrong, O'Connah. I ain't smoked a blunt today."

Tommy shakes his head at him. "Stay out of trouble."

He pulls up beside a boy carrying a metal pipe, fashioned into a club. Last evening Tommy heard rumors of an impending gang fight, kid talk that will probably come to nothing. But the pipe is real enough. "Hey!" says Tommy, pointing out the window at the pipe. "Give me that!"

The boy obeys. "These fuckin' guys with guns and shit."

"Where?"

"I don't know."

"So what you gonna be? Superman? Banging bullets with your pipe? You call me. I got a gun."

"You won't get here soon enough."

"I'm always here."

"All right, O'Connah, I'll call you. I will."

"Good man. Stay out of trouble."

He drives a little farther on and stops, and a group of small boys and girls crowd up beside his window. Some shyly stroke the cruiser's spotlight, and others ask if they can make announcements to the project on the PA system. Tommy hands them the microphone and plays the siren for them, just as he used to do for the young man with a wild-looking shock of hair, like a tassel on a cornstalk, just now walking past. "Suck my nuts, O'Connah."

"Hey! Come here, Rodolfo!"

The young man turns, grabs his wild-looking hair, and says, "You want some hair, O'Connah?" Then he puckers up his lips and makes a kiss, and saunters on.

The muscles flex in Tommy's jaw. "Oh, man, sometimes I wish I worked thirty years ago," he says. "So when Rodolfo blows a kiss at me, I could stop and split his head wide open." According to the stories, in days gone by, Northampton's cops didn't suffer insults from teenagers, but took them to the station and beat them up with phone books. In his time, Tommy has wrestled with a number of people he's come to arrest, but, rumors notwithstanding, he has never beaten up a prisoner.

He sometimes looks as though he might—when, for instance, he yanks open the back door to a patrolman's cruiser and glares at the teenage boy sitting in the backseat. The boy has repeatedly given the patrolman a false name. Tommy sticks his head in the door and gives the boy his stare.

For years Tommy studied and practiced street tactics. Nowadays, to supplement his pay, he teaches them at the police academy in a nearby, larger town. Some tactics he invented for himself—his stare, for instance, which he uses on tough guys and people who are clearly lying. Frozen in the stare, his jaw thrust forward, his bald head glistening, he looks implacable and cruel, and staring usually works. Tough and distraught people usually grow docile. The look did not come naturally. He had to spend a long time practicing in mirrors, lifting one eyebrow, lowering the other, and fixing his eyes on the glass as if to look right through it. He stares that way at the boy in the backseat now. "What's your name?" he growls.

The boy gives him the same false reply.

Tommy yells in his face. "You're lying! You have candles in your eyes!" He adds more softly, "As my mother used to say."

It takes some time, but the boy comes clean, and Tommy resumes his patrol.

Early in his career, he went to a local ophthalmologist, complaining of eyestrain. The doctor concluded he was scanning the landscape too intently, trying to look at too much all at once. Tommy's eyes are conditioned now, though. Vision is by far the strongest of his senses, and the main path to his memory. He rarely forgets a face. Once he's looked at a license plate, he can remember the numbers for half an hour. He has to see only the writing on one of his file folders, not what the words say but the way they look, to remember the whole case described inside, and he remembers cases as if they were movies playing in front of him.

Ten years have filled his patrols with memories. They wait in the landscape. He drives through the old industrial neighborhood called Bay State, past what used to be the Clean Bore factory, and in his mind's eye the summer evening turns snowy. He remembers following footprints in the snow from the factory's front door and along the bank of the Mill River. He was an almost brand-new cop. It was getting dark when he saw the burglar up ahead. Tommy started running, his flashlight in one hand, his pistol in the other, yelling for the thief to halt. And then the figure turned, and in the beam of his flashlight Tommy saw a boy with a harried, frightened face, holding a shotgun. The double barrel, the gun's two large empty pupils, pointed at Tommy's chest. Tommy raised his pistol, about to shoot. But he didn't. The police department brass had questioned Tommy rather harshly afterward. Why hadn't he shot the kid? How could he have been so sure the shotgun wasn't loaded? Tommy still couldn't name his reasons. There was just something about the scene, the look on the boy's face, the way the kid had held the weapon.

As far as Tommy knows, no one has pointed a gun at him since. Almost a decade has passed since a cop got shot at or shot at someone here. Northampton is a peaceful town. Tommy often tells himself that thinking so is dangerous. He takes target practice and cleans his guns regularly, rehearses situations in his mind at night in bed, and, as he drives by, makes himself remember that long-ago evening in the snow.

Dramatic incidents come rarely. He spends a large part of every evening shift making friendly greetings, beeping at old friends and the parents of old friends in passing cars, waving to an old classmate, now a reporter for the local paper (the *Daily Hampshire Gazette,* published continuously since 1786), calling, "Good evening, Your Honor," to the mayor as she walks out of city hall. He spots a lawyer, one he likes, on a sidewalk and calls to him through the cruiser's PA system, his amplified voice echoing off the buildings, "Charlie! It's good to see you wearing men's clothes again!" He turns down a side street and calls to a staggering drunk, "Hey, Campbell! You told me you weren't gonna do anything stupid. Go home and go to bed!" He rolls up beside a respectable-looking middle-aged man, a former coach of his. "Did you get your kid to say where he got it?" "It" is marijuana.

"No," says the man. "Not yet."

"Okay," says Tommy. "Let me know."

Over the radio the dispatcher's voice announces an elderly woman in trouble. Tommy finds her upstairs in a bedroom of her house. She lies groaning on the floor, an overturned chair beside her. A neighbor has already called for an ambulance. Tommy strips a blanket off the bed and arranges it over the old woman. She moans on, looking up at him with frightened eyes. Tommy sits down on the floor beside her. She says that she was watering a plant and fell off the chair. She has a thick French Canadian accent. She doesn't want to go to the hospital. That's where people go to die, she says. Tommy puts a hand on her shoulder. "No. No. I know the people there. They're very nice. They'll fix you up in no time." Then he changes the subject. They talk about her relatives, her years here in town, until the ambulance arrives. "I'll come and see ya," Tommy says as they carry her away.

On many evenings he makes arrests, sometimes one that he has looked forward to. Shortly after dark, hiding in the shadows at the rear of Pulaski Park, he catches a young man selling LSD—a young man with a small goatee, who dresses in black, occasionally with a cape, and who, Tommy believes, wields a malign influence over the younger teenagers always loitering in the park. Those kids, at any rate, refer to him as God. Tommy usually chats up people he's arresting, but God is one of those old adversaries who have taunted him. "So I guess this makes me Pontius Pilate, right?" says Tommy, snapping handcuffs onto God. Tommy makes a loud, braying laugh.

He catches a boy skateboarding up King Street, in violation of local ordinance. "Crime of the century," says Tommy, a former skateboarder himself. "But you're outside the city limits. I just moved them up. Have a good night."

On the sidewalk beside a quiet street in Florence, the cruiser's headlights brush across the figure of a boy, unsteady on his feet. Tommy gets out and walks him home to his mother's house. They stand together on the front porch, the boy protesting. "*Dude.* How can you say I'm drunk?"

"Because most people, when they try to crack their knuckles, don't punch themselves in the chin," says Tommy, pressing the doorbell.

He still likes all this—dealing with the undramatic, playing ombudsman to the lost, the needy, the unsteady in his hometown. Administering stern reprimands to the boys he catches throwing snowballs at cars, as he once did; wagging a finger at the drivers who don't think he saw them make illegal turns; saying to a carful of gray-haired women who ask if he knows the way to Alumnae House at Smith College, "Follow me, ladies." Many nights he stops at the emergency room in the Cooley Dickinson Hospital, to follow up on an accident, to interview a suspect, to help the staff with a dangerous patient. The charge nurse, Mary Lou Greene, used to baby-sit Tommy. "I can remember changing your diapers," she'll say. Sometimes, once he finishes his work there, he gets Mary Lou or one of the other nurses to take his blood pressure. Repeatedly, the measurements have told him that it rises, not dangerously but markedly, when he is in uniform. Ten years as a local cop in his small native place, and he still feels excited when he goes out patrolling his town and hears the desk officer's voice come over the radio, calling for him.

"Eighty-three," says the desk officer's voice. "We have a call for a dog locked inside a car."

The desk officer's voice sounds weary. Tommy's voice rises. "Why do people call the police because of a dog in a car?" he cries, as he heads toward the scene. "Why not? Who else they gonna call? This is a great job."

As Judge Ryan says, there are many different Northamptons. Tommy doesn't know them all. He doesn't get invited to the cocktail and dinner parties in the fine houses of Northampton's rich. Or to the after-hours card games or the golf tournaments of the town's hard-drinking, high-living crowd. One time he was told to post some traffic guards for a wedding at "St. John's." He looked puzzled. "Where?"

"St. John's. The Episcopal church."

"Oh, yeah," said Tommy. "The English church."

"Jesus Christ, O'Connor. You've lived in this town your whole life and you don't know the name St. John's?"

Tommy smiled. He put on a brogue. "And what would be the need to know?"

But in Tommy's own subjective view, the town is a single place and worth preserving, worth a lifetime's effort at stamping out the bad or keeping it at bay or cleaning up the messes that it leaves behind. He always had a compulsion to be busy, and ten years of compulsively busy police work have made a great deal of the town transparent to him. He knows the insides of most of the larger buildings and of thousands of houses and apartments, and he knows where flaming youth repairs to drink and experiment with drugs. He knows the escape routes that burglars and hit-and-run drivers are likeliest to take, and, not always but often, he has gone to just the right spots for intercepting them.

He doesn't know everyone in town, not by any means, but it seems as if he might know half and as if more than half know him. All evening long, voices call to him as he passes in his cruiser—friends, acquaintances, adversaries. All evening long, people he once arrested, young and middle-aged, white, black, and Hispanic, come up to his window. He knows their family histories, their special weaknesses. They tell him what exemplary lives they're leading now. "Hey, O'Connor! I'm working seven days a week. Nine dollars an hour under the table." "I'm working! Eighteen weeks!" "Oh, man, I got in trouble once, but I'm stayin' out of trouble, workin', man." "I got a job now, got a wife. I'm clean, too, man. Hey, O'Connor, I got a kid now." He pulls into a housing project and Willie, a notorious scammer and crack addict, walks over and says, "Have no fear, Willie's here. That's because I go to the hospitals and do all the laundry, you know what I'm sayin', O'Connor?"

Maybe people like Willie simply hope to get him off their backs, but it usually sounds as if they want something else besides, something like approval, or absolution. By the midpoint of a shift, Tommy often begins to feel like Northampton's father confessor. He plays the role. He half believes in it. To all of those anticonfessions, Tommy replies, "Good for you. Stay out of trouble." As he drives away, he muses, "I wonder if they think I actually believe them. They probably do. It makes them feel better."

Sometimes he seems neither priest nor cop, but more nearly social worker, a comparison he would resent. He stands inside a cramped living room, in a small rented Northampton house. A young woman sits before him, her face in her hands. Her wrists look thin as wishbones. The room contains what furniture dealers call a living room set, the kind that newlyweds buy. The plaid upholstery is stained.

The young woman glances up at Tommy. In his black boots and tidy uniform, he looks, as always, too large and martial for a domestic scene, like a soldier barging in. She says in a reedy voice, "I don't want to go to jail."

"We're not here to arrest you," Tommy tells her. His voice sounds very loud and brassy, the voice of social norms, feared and resented and, this time, strangely at odds with what he says. "We didn't advise you of your rights, which means that anything you talk to us about we're not gonna use against you. We're gonna leave here, you're gonna stay here, and that's gonna be the end of it. We're not here to charge you criminally. We don't *want* to charge you criminally. That's what we want to *avoid*. Okay? So if you have heroin here you want to get rid of, give it to the detective, and it's gonna be out of here and you'll never hear about it again."

But she puts her head back in her hands, weeping softly.

Tommy tells her, "Look at me." She hardly seems to dare. He counts on his fingers. "One, you're not going to be the mother that you are and can be for your kids. And two, you're gonna get a hot load some night, and that's gonna be the end of it. Then you got a bunch of pretty little kids with nothin'."

She clears her throat. "I'm so embarrassed."

"Well, don't be embarrassed. And we can hook you into the right things to try to get you some help. You're the only one that can help yourself, but at least we can get you in the direction that *maybe* you can do something for yourself, or for your kids."

She starts crying again. "I don't care about myself," she sobs.

"Well, you gotta learn to care about yourself. How bad a habit do you have now?"

"Basically, I just need some time." Her voice rises. "I don't want to get in trouble."

"Honestly! Hey lookit, you're *not going to get in trouble.*"

"I just . . ."

"How old are you now?"

She looks up at him again. "Twenty-five?"

"You got a lot of years ahead of you."

She puts her face back in her hands. "I'm so embarrassed."

"*Don't* be embarrassed." Silence descends on the room, except for her sniffles. "Will you take my suggestion, or at least hear it?"

"Sure." But she doesn't look at him.

"Take the advice of the detective here. Talk to your friend, who wants to sit down with you. A person concerned about you. Have that person help you. Don't let this guy you're living with influence you. Have someone who cares about you, who's really interested in you. Not *him*."

She seems to stiffen. She stares at the floor. "Tell ya honestly," says Tommy. "If you *don't* listen to us and you just continue on? I'll think it's sad, but it's not gonna make me not sleep at night. Because there's a lot more people out there with the same problem. You're getting an opportunity here to do something, and I would take it. How are your kids doing?"

"Oh, *they're* fine."

"How old are they?"

"Eight and five?"

"Well, the eight-year-old's old enough to start to figure things out."

She says she'll let her friend come and talk to her, but isn't ready to do more.

"All right. Good luck," says Tommy.

It is dark when he comes outside. He looks back at the lighted windows of the little house. "That could be enough to bottom her out. Maybe not. Would it surprise me if a week from now we go there for an overdose? Not in the least bit." He climbs in his cruiser and starts driving, back on his rounds, musing aloud. "I don't get discouraged over it anymore, because if I went in there thinking that the Royal Canadian Mounted Police and Dudley Do-Right just walked in and now the world's gonna be fine for her, and then I find out differently and I'm bothered by that—and I would be, she's a nice kid!—

then I'd be bothered all the time. Because the vast majority of people don't take up on your advice. Like domestics. You go back there and the woman's still with the freaking moron. There's more to it than what we see."

During the past few hours peace has settled over the emergency room at the Cooley Dickinson Hospital. But it's about eleven now, and Mary Lou Greene, the veteran charge nurse, figures peace will end soon. She's dealt for years with local injury and illness and hypochondria, and has discerned a pattern that seems timed to television. About 86 percent of households in Northampton, 9,577 at last count, have cable and almost a third contain two TV sets or more. (Only 137 customers haven't paid their bills.) Prime time on television is quiet time in the ER, but shortly afterward, at a little after eleven, a small epidemic hits—a young woman who thinks she has pneumonia and only has the flu, a drunk with no other place to go, a man with a compound fracture of the ankle, a restaurant worker with a bruise on his head from a falling can, and a dozen more. If a TV special has publicized a new disease, some are sure to think they have it.

At midnight supine people dressed in johnnies fill the beds behind the curtained enclosures while worried-looking relatives stand by, and Dr. Ira Helfand goes bustling among them, talking fast. He is the current president of the American chapter of Physicians for Social Responsibility, the international antinuclear group. But he works here in town. He stitches like a London tailor.

The beds empty slowly. A few people come in around three-thirty in the morning, and then the place grows quiet for a while. Dr. Helfand says, "This night for drunkenness is not bad at all."

"Shhh," says one of the nurses.

"It's four-thirty A.M. We're not going to get any now."

"They just haven't found them yet," the nurse replies.

Out in Northampton and the towns around it—the doctors and the nurses know this happens many nights—a couple of people, sometimes more, lie awake in the dark in their beds. In one house a woman with pain in her chest, in another a man with an aching left arm. They lie there telling themselves it's probably nothing, they can wait until their doctors' offices open. Around dawn they change their minds. They troop into the ER around six-thirty. At the local hour of the suspected heart attack, civilization isn't art and architecture. It's a nurse's hands and the smell of antiseptics, a short drive away.

Little indoor nighttime dramas fade. The town is waking up. Out on Main Street the lights shut down with an audible click. From several alleys comes the smell of baking bread, and in the distance beyond the rooftops, to the rising chatter of downtown's birds, the sun clears the top of the Holyoke Range. It etches silhouettes of buildings on the façades across the street. For a moment Main Street is empty.

Then down the hill from Elm Street, rattling, come the trucks of the Honor Court. If Northampton were a town in Paraguay or Haiti, you might think a coup had begun. The men, mostly dressed in army fatigues and all in orange vests, climb out and straggle into position, carrying brooms and shovels. A reformed drunk founded the Honor Court; his son is in the state legislature now. The inductees perform civic chores in return for room and board, and often in lieu of jail. Some local homeless advocates call the program authoritarian, but not many residents complain. The service is virtually free to the city and all but unwitnessed because of the hour. The Honor Court platoon sweeps up the sidewalks, empties the municipal trash barrels, then rattles off toward Florence.

In some households, a large minority, mostly ones with natives in them, radios are tuned to Northampton's own AM station—WHMP, 1400 on the dial. For nearly forty years, old-timers have awakened to a deep and slightly ominous voice, full of pregnant pauses, saying, "Goo-ood morning. I'm. Ron

Hall." Ron is part of the "1400 Team." He reads the news. "Employees and patrons of the pizza shop chased the man after the robbery. And beat him with a. Shovel!" Soon the cheery voice of Ron Hall's sidekick, Dennis Lee, takes over: "I had a strange dream last night that I forgot to play the morning polka. Here's the 'Tuba Polka,' on WHMP! With Ray Jay!" Everyone listening knows what this means: that it's right around six-forty. Some snap off their radios. Others, not all of Polish descent, leave theirs on, and climb out of bed to the cheery strains of a brassy orchestra, evoking women in babushkas, men in boots, clomping from side to side in a barn.

When the music ends, Dennis Lee returns. "Yes, the 'Tuba Polka.' Life's okay."

CHAPTER 3

A Restraining Order

Tommy O'Connor pulled into the parking lot beside the police station around nine o'clock on the night of August 17, 1995. He was ending his patrol much earlier than usual to catch up on reports. He had a reputation, which he didn't think he deserved, for forgetting administrative details. Once a week or so he hunted through the police station for his misplaced cruiser keys or patrol diary, muttering, "If you do twice as much as everyone else, you have twice as much to forget." But even though no one in the department believed it—in a small society, as in a marriage, reputations long outlive the traits they memorialize—Tommy really had become much more diligent about paperwork.

The station that squatted before him is tucked away downtown, on Center Street off Main, in the shadow of much taller, older, grander buildings. It was a shameful-looking thing, Tommy thought, an offense to its setting and his profession. Unpruned shrubbery clawed at its few windows. It had a low, flat roof and the general appearance of an abandoned blockhouse. Tommy let himself in the side door by the parking lot, into a hallway of scuffed linoleum tile, with partitions made of plasterboard covered in paper that was supposed to look like wood. Some of the walls had fist-sized holes in them, souvenirs of difficult arrests and of stressful moments in the lives of cops. He went into the Records Room, a cluttered chamber. Tacked to a wall above some filing cabinets was a print in the Rockwell manner—a traffic cop turning from his duties to smile down at a little girl who is offering him an apple. Tommy liked the picture, though he felt it ought to have a frame. He had just sat down at one of the computers when his old friend Rick Janacek walked in, dressed in civilian clothes.

Tommy was glad to see Rick but mildly surprised to see him in the station at this hour. Rick worked the day shift, and besides, Tommy had thought he was taking some vacation time. He looked up at Rick, and then he looked again. Something was wrong.

Rick was as handsome as many movie stars. He had a strong jaw and high cheekbones. He was six foot three, broad-shouldered, and athletically thin, and he carried himself with the erectness that makes a person look confident and proud, and in Rick's case, a little superior. At this moment, though, he might have been stoop-shouldered, raggedly dressed, unshaven. He was none of those things in fact, but all of them in the image Tommy saw, like a picture of an embodied soul. The effect came from Rick's face. His eyes looked blank, as if he was exhausted. And he was making little uncomfortable-looking movements with his mouth. Tommy knew exactly how his friend's mouth felt—dry, like the mouths of people being interrogated. In his years as a detective, Tommy had made himself a reader of faces. He'd had a life-time's practice reading Rick's.

"We gotta talk," said Rick.

Many old friends from the neighborhood now lived far away. Another kind of distance had opened up between Tommy and Rick. Years ago, when they'd both joined the Hamp police department, Tommy had imagined himself and Rick as two old buddies, side by side, moving on in life. But in their years on the force, they had rarely worked together, and the brass had made Tommy the favored one, the one who got the special training and promotions. Just a year ago Tommy was promoted to sergeant instead of Rick. An awkward moment for Tommy, standing beside Rick in one of the captain's offices and receiving the good news. Rick was still a patrolman, though the head of their union.

Like many old friends, they had drifted away partly because of their marriages. Jean didn't like Rick much, and neither she nor Tommy cared for Rick's wife. She was a Smithie. She came from money. She seemed stuck-up to them. At Rick's wedding, a string quartet had played Polish polkas—exactly right as a symbol for that marriage, Tommy and Jean had thought. The two couples went out together a few times, but uncomfortably. Anyway, Rick and his wife soon had small children, and then their lives had become fundamentally different.

But strong first friendships always leave something immutable behind. Rick would forever be Tommy's oldest friend. He belonged to a precious part of Tommy's life, a glorious remembered place. When he reminisced about growing up, Rick was almost always there, playing important roles, often in scenes that made Tommy smile. He cared about Rick, and about the idea of Rick.

About two weeks ago, Rick had asked Tommy out for coffee and told him his marriage was coming apart. Tommy had tried to counsel and console him. He was good at this—notoriously. "Father O'Connor," his patrol officers called him, partly because he preached to them about the importance of marital fidelity, and partly because so many people, both cops and civilians, seemed drawn to him when they were in trouble.

On the face of it, this seemed odd. He was famously irreverent. Once when he was a boy, Tommy coaxed a Jewish friend into attending Catholic confession. He himself had often knelt and confessed to venial sins he hadn't committed, so that, as he put it, the priest could have "his juice." That side of him endured.

As a rule, if he said something serious in public, he took it back right away with a joke or a quip. But in the privacy of his own confessional, Father O'Connor was entirely earnest. "I'd take some time off and work on this," he'd told Rick over coffee a couple of weeks ago. "Family's the most important thing."

Now on this night in August, Tommy's face fell into its priestly, whatever's-wrong-we-can-fix-it mode. He quit the computer at once. He took Rick into a little office off Records, and closed the door.

During the day a clerk occupied this room. At night it belonged to the sergeants. Tommy sat behind a metal desk, Rick on the edge of a chair. Tommy didn't think it showed, but he felt a slight discomfort as Rick began to talk. Here they were, two old friends alone again in a room, and yet the atmosphere felt stiff and formal and strained. Maybe because of the setting. He was the sergeant, Rick the patrolman. They weren't quite equals here.

In their conversation two weeks ago Rick had declared himself an alcoholic. Surprising news to Tommy. No one had ever seen Rick drunk on duty or smelled alcohol on him then. Many cops were harder drinkers. "It's not how much you drink, Tom. It's why," Rick had explained. Maybe that was true. At any rate, Rick had quit drinking, and had just endured two wretched weeks. His wife had said she wanted him out of the house, and he couldn't turn to the bottle, and maybe on top of everything else he was suffering symptoms of with-drawal. He couldn't sleep. Not even sedatives worked. He woke up after sleeping all of two hours, then went for a predawn run, then worked the day shift for eight hours, then spent half the night on a road job at the Coolidge Bridge. Then, on his day off a week ago, he took his four children to an amusement park, worked the job at the bridge, came home, went to bed, and shortly afterward woke up realizing that tomorrow was the birthday of one of his daughters and that he'd forgotten to decorate the house, as he always did. So he got up and strung crepe paper around the living room, and afterward, around two o'clock that morning, he and his wife had a conversation. The next day Rick went to a psychiatric ward in Holyoke Hospital. He stayed there for most of a week. He'd just gotten out today.

"I checked *myself* in, Tom."

"You were smart to do it, Rick," said Tommy. "If you felt you needed it."

"Yeah." Rick's voice was full of irony. The hospital wasn't all. While he was there, his wife had taken out a restraining order against him, barring him from having any contact with her or his children.

That would be a blow to anyone, especially a cop, Tommy thought. And to Rick an intolerable one. He was always talking about his children, about the cute things they said, about all he did with them. "Hey, Rick, that's no big deal," Tommy told him. Rick knew about restraining orders. He could go to court tomorrow and fight this one and get it changed, so at least he could see his kids.

"Well, there's more to it." Rick leaned farther forward in his chair and slid the official document, the restraining order, across the desk. "Read this."

Tommy picked up the sheaf of paper and read for a moment. Then he yelled, "What the hell is this!"

The affidavit accused Rick of sexually abusing one of his daughters. Tommy looked at Rick. He felt very angry. Some wives nowadays took out restraining orders full of trumped-up allegations in order to gain the advantage in divorces. The strategy was shabby. But this was evil. Tommy knew Rick. He wasn't what was known contemptuously around here as a "diddler." Tommy felt ready to explode. He still felt as if he knew Rick so well that he could read his thoughts. In a moment Rick was going to say that his wife, or someone, had made up this slander. And Tommy was going to tell him that whoever it was wouldn't get away with it, not if he could help it.

But the conversation didn't go that way.

Rick said that he knew from his rape investigation course that his daughter might actually have been abused by someone. "Tom, my daughter needs to get interviewed. Possibly the others." It was true that he'd been drinking a lot up until a couple of weeks ago. But he had no memory, none at all, of assaulting any of his kids. "The only way anything could have happened with me is if I was in a blackout," Rick said.

He was still talking. He was saying that the only time he'd had a blackout while his children were at home was on the night of October 22, 1994, the day Tommy had been promoted to sergeant instead of him. Tommy listened, but his thoughts were traveling. *The only way anything could have happened with me is if I was in a blackout.* The moment he'd heard Rick say those words he'd felt a tingling in his extremities and free fall in his chest. He'd felt those sensations as acutely only once before, when he'd heard his mother was lying on a gurney in the emergency room. But now, as the tingling subsided, he felt a more usual kind of alertness. He had composed his face, into what he thought of as his "game face." He had put it on so often in his years on the job that the act had become all but reflexive. He suddenly felt like a cop. He was thinking, "If I were investigating this, I'd want to know he said that." Tommy looked at Rick appraisingly for a moment. Rick looked haggard and distraught. He looked ripe for interrogation. Tommy thought, "I could work him now."

Tommy had questioned thousands of people on patrol and hundreds as a detective. Sometimes all it took to make a suspect crack was to stare at him and yell, "You're lying!" But most interrogations called for subtler techniques. The classic one, far from infallible, was to conjure up a ruthless sympathy, sympathy that seemed real enough to Tommy to seem real to the suspect, even if he loathed the person.

In one of his early cases, a girl out for a walk with a friend had been run over and killed by a car on the edge of a cornfield in Northampton's Meadows. A suspect was brought in. Tommy had sat alone with him for a long time, in an interrogation room at the state police barracks. Tommy felt certain that this was the hit-and-run driver. Tommy figured he was drunk and had chased the girl into the corn for fun. But he wouldn't even admit that he'd been at the scene, in spite of all the cornstalks they'd found stuck in his car's chassis, in spite of other evidence. Tommy started telling the man that he and his buddies used to drive through those cornfields—"field-beating," it was called. Actually, Tommy had never joined in the sport. "Jesus, that must have been scary when you saw her hit the windshield. Christ, I'd get the hell out of there, too. Hey, I understand. Things happen. That's why we call them accidents. I know you didn't mean to hit her." The man still wouldn't admit he'd even been in the Meadows. He seemed to be weakening, though. He seemed to be trying to hold himself back. The signs of this effort were classic—he uncrossed and recrossed his legs, he covered his mouth with a hand, he kept making little yawns. In a while, Tommy moved his chair closer to the man. Saying again, "I know you didn't mean to hit her," he touched him on the leg. He'd been taught that trick at interrogation school. And this time it actually worked.

"Yeah, all right, I was there."

"Gotcha!" Tommy had thought. He'd known that the rest of the confession would follow. He had felt exuberant in the stomach.

A veteran Northampton detective named Rusty Luce had helped to train Tommy. Luce often said, "Everybody lies." This was Tommy's first working assumption. The second was that guilt tends to reveal itself, signaling its presence in movements and gestures, in tones of voice, in the lies themselves. All honest detectives know that they sometimes misread the signals. Every so often Tommy brought a suspect right up to what seemed like the brink of a confession and the suspect didn't crack and Tommy tried another route to no avail, and then another, and then he went away for a while to think and something would tell him, "This guy *didn't* do it." But in his experience, when suspects conceded that they could have committed a crime— "Yeah, I was there, but you got the wrong guy," or "Yeah, I had sex with her, but like you said, it was consensual"—they were usually three-quarters of the way to confessing everything. *The only way anything could have happened with me is if I was in a blackout.* That certainly sounded like a first concession. He could build an interrogation on it, Tommy thought.

This line of speculation lasted only a moment. How could he have imagined interrogating Rick? He didn't want any part of this case. He thought about Rick's mother, an old woman now, probably sitting on her porch looking out at the night. This was all she needed.

"Rick." Tommy made his voice emphatic. "I don't want you to tell me anything more."

"Tom." Rick opened his hands. "I don't have anything to hide."

"I'll be there to help you as a friend," Tommy told him. "But I don't want you to tell me anything more about this. *Anything,* Rick." He took Rick through the likely scenario. The D.A.'s office must already have begun an investigation. Suppose Rick told him something, as a friend, that sounded incriminating. Then Tommy would end up in court testifying against him.

Tommy said all this sincerely. On his drive home after the end of the shift, he realized that he'd issued his warning too late.

Many of the people Tommy helped send to jail came from rooming-house and housing-project Hamp. Many never had much chance in life, he figured. And it often seemed as if the criminals and their victims were merely swapping roles, the one doing to the other what the other would do to him tomorrow. Recently, a case like that had come to court. Watching the defendant being sentenced to state prison, Tommy wondered if justice really was being served. A few days later, out on his rounds, he started thinking about that case again. He wondered aloud, "If you commit a crime in hell, is it still a crime?" But doubts like those came rarely. His moral code and the penal code were not identical, but they weren't often inconsistent.

Tommy once hunted a woman who had taken up with a young teenage boy, and he'd expressed no qualms about helping to send her to jail. "If it'd been a man, everybody would have wanted him fried. I thought what she did was just as wrong as if a man had done it."

Tommy said, "Pet peeves. I have a lot. You could call it a zoo." Fellow cops cheating on their spouses, for instance. "Most people don't take that vow very seriously. You stand up in front of your church and your family and make a promise, and then you break it. Why should I trust such a person one iota? If you'll destroy *that* institution, then who am I? You'd have no problem lying to me."

One time an old friend back in Hamp for a visit remarked that Tommy didn't recognize much of the "gray" in the world. He told Tommy, "You like things black and white." Tommy ruminated about this for a couple of weeks, and then, heading out on patrol one evening, declared, "That gray is just the thing that boggles you. It isn't worth anything."

The world was full of confusing situations. All the more reason to choose a clear path. Now and then cops from other jurisdictions would call to say they'd gotten parking tickets while eating out in Hamp, and to keep up good relations Tommy would tell them he'd fix the tickets. And he would—by paying the fines himself. Small detours were permissible, but you had to know where you were headed. "Do the right thing" and "Do your job": those were his categorical imperatives. He had another, though, which was infused with sentiment, with the feelings of the boy who had visited Rick in his sickbed nearly every day for six months.

Tommy had a favorite movie, *Stand by Me.* He'd first seen it years ago at the old Calvin Theatre downtown, a place of sticky floors, redolent with ancient popcorn fumes. He'd sat down in one of the old plush seats, and listened as the voice-over described a town in Oregon: "There were only twelve hundred and eighty-one people, but to me it was the whole world." Four boys on the brink of adolescence appeared. They had a club-house, too, and one of them had breathtaking news. There was a body by the river, a person killed in a car wreck, some miles away. Why the boys should hunger to be the first to find the body might not have been clear to everyone, but it was very clear to Tommy. By then all his attention was fastened on the screen, and he was worrying his right thumbnail. The gang of friends set off down the railroad tracks. They met adversity. They bickered and they teased one another, but they also talked heart to heart out in the woods by their campfire, and *when the chips were down,* they were *there* for one another.

Tommy wished the movie would never end. The figures on the screen dissolved, like childhood itself. At the close, the narrator wrote down these words: "I never had any friends later on like the ones I had when I was twelve. Jesus, does anyone?" Tommy left transported. He'd seen that movie half a dozen times since, feeling every time that he'd just seen the truth of his childhood retold.

"Stand by your friends" and "Do your job"—he'd never imagined that those commandments could be at odds. Now, as he drove home on this August night, he replayed the conversation with Rick in his mind. Rick hadn't confessed, but in essence he had said, "I could have done it." That kind of admission could be crucial in an investigation. Tommy had no use for people who betrayed friends, and little use for cops who withheld information in order to protect a colleague. Though he mocked himself for it, Tommy believed in omens, and in a Fate that designed his life. Right now it seemed as if a trap had been laid for him. He had only two options, and neither one seemed exactly right. But he knew what to do first. He'd talk to Jean.

Tommy had various terms of endearment for his wife, such as "my little shorty." She was small, though not tiny, and gracefully proportioned, with thick, sandy hair. Jean had grown up on a hill farm outside Northampton. She descended on both sides from some of the first English settlers of the Connecticut River Valley, and her face had an heirloom quality that kept it from being merely cute. She had a beautiful downturning nose and her eyes had what seemed like an ancestral steadiness. They looked grave, even when she smiled. Jean was a good shot with a pistol, and Tommy often thought it was a good thing they lived in a peaceful town, because he didn't want her to have to kill anyone. He thought she wouldn't hesitate to shoot an intruder in their house, if she was there alone, as she often was in the evenings. Jean managed their marriage. She had moved him, literally, out of his parents' house, and also out of town on trips. She picked out his clothes, which was why, in court, he didn't look like most other cops, like a kid at his first dress-up occasion. His court suits fit him, thanks to Jean. Tommy couldn't balance a checkbook. Jean was the head auditor at Florence Savings Bank, and she handled their household finances.

Eleven years ago, when he was a minor-league cop at Look Park, taking his job very seriously, Tommy caught some friends of his drinking and smoking dope. He was courting Jean then, and they went downtown for ice cream. He told her he was having second thoughts about becoming a Northampton cop, because he now realized it would mean arresting friends. She said, "Maybe they aren't very good friends, if they put you in that position." Tommy had held on to that thought ever since. Over the years, out of his high school class of about three hundred, he'd arrested about 10 percent. As a rule he acted kindly when locking people up and harsh when giving them a break.

Jean thought things through, listened carefully, and measured her words. Tommy counted on her for advice on ethical matters as well as all practical ones. Usually they agreed. They often talked about the cruel irony of child abuse, that some of the people with the luck to have kids should neglect and mistreat them. In the abstract, general case, Tommy had no sympathy for those kinds of criminals. In particular cases, he thought, "I'm sure something was done to them when they were kids, but that's no excuse for wrecking someone else's life." Child abusers deserved punishment, Jean believed. Tommy felt the same way.

She was still up when he got home. He told her about the charges against Rick, and her jaw dropped. "You're kidding!" She looked at him warily. "Tom, this isn't a joke, is it?" Then he told her what Rick had said to him. He told her he felt that he had to do the right thing, and the right thing was to report the conversation to the D.A.'s office. Jean agreed, which came as no surprise. In her own professional career, Jean had often chosen probity over self-interest. Maybe the charges were true. If so, she said, Tommy had to think of the interests of the innocent victim.

He didn't wait long to act. He and Jean had a dinner date with some close friends the next night. The husband, Steve Gawron, was a state trooper whom Tommy had worked with. Steve's wife, Jane Mulqueen, was a local prosecutor who specialized in rape cases. Tommy once said of her, "If she told me green was blue, I'd get my eyes checked." In the restaurant over dinner, Tommy asked Jane if Rick was being investigated. She nodded. Then Tommy recited the gist of his conversation with Rick. He asked her if she thought Rick's words seemed significant, and she said she did. Jane also said she would report what Tommy had told her, which was what he'd expected.

In effect, he had offered his testimony to the district attorney. He'd wrestled with the question of what to do, not for long but intently. He'd asked himself if his father would approve, and he felt sure his father would. He knew that Jean did. So hadn't he done the only thing he could do?

• • •

Soon after the night when Rick showed Tommy the restraining order, the chief called the department together and told them about the allegations, warning them not to let a hint of the news leave the station. That very day someone on the force leaked the story to a reporter. Tommy couldn't imagine why. Some people disliked Rick. They called him a know-it-all. But he had never injured a fellow cop. Tommy thought of him, banished from his home and family, temporarily suspended from his job, and now publicly accused of the most scandalous kind of crime. Wherever he went in town, he would feel eyes on him, imagine people whispering about him. Tommy remembered a story, famous around the department: serving papers some years ago on a man accused of molesting a child, Rick had taken a bullet from his pistol, placed it on the table in front of the man, and said, "Do the right thing." Instead, the man had thrown the bullet back at Rick. Would Rick now take his own advice?

Rick was staying at a fellow cop's house, a small ranch house on the outskirts of town. Tommy sat down facing him in the living room. Naturally, Rick wanted to talk about the case. Tommy wouldn't let him.

Rick said, "Tom, I want to find out what happened. I'll do the right thing."

"Honestly, Rick, I don't know what happened or if anything happened, and I don't want to know. But right now I want to get you where you don't do anything stupid." Tommy came right out and asked the question. "Are you thinking of killing yourself?"

Rick said the doctor at the hospital had called him suicidal.

"Well, you owe it to your kids not to do anything stupid."

"Tom, I owe it to my kids to provide a living for them, and how am I gonna do that if it's true?"

At one point Tommy told him, "If you do it, don't do it in Northampton." But Rick saw this as a joke and laughed, though in fact Tommy could imagine the scene, standing over Rick's corpse, pulling on rubber gloves. Anyway, Rick told him, "Don't worry. I'm not gonna do anything stupid."

Tommy visited Rick often over the next few weeks, sometimes not just as a friend but in uniform. One afternoon, the captain in charge of administration handed Tommy a document, an official notification of Rick's suspension from the city payroll and the police department. "Would you take this to Janacek, Tom?"

"Couldn't you find someone else?" Tommy blurted out.

"Well, Tom, I can, if it makes you uncomfortable."

"No, if it's an order, I'll do it," Tommy said, thinking maybe it was better that he be the courier. There were a few people on the force who might hand Rick the papers and say, "Here you go, diddler."

All his talks with Rick followed the same pattern. Rick would want to discuss details and Tommy would refuse to hear them; then he'd ask about Rick's family or start cracking jokes. Rick had bought a bunch of new police uniforms. Tommy smiled at him and asked what size uniform he wore. Rick got the joke. "Fuck you, Tom." But he laughed, which was the effect Tommy aimed at. Rick would know that Tommy still considered him a fellow cop if he was still subjecting him to cop humor. And then one day Tommy came into the little ranch house and found Rick red-eyed as if he had been crying, and smiling, as if he were elated.

The state police had finally interviewed his daughter, Rick told him. Rick had taken a course in rape investigation not very long before he'd been accused, and the same female state police detective who'd taught him had conducted the interview. "Tom, I was never so relieved in my life." He handed Tommy the document and insisted that he read it. Tommy felt he shouldn't, but he wanted to. He sat at the kitchen table reading silently, bending over the document.

It was five and a half pages of questions and answers—questions from the detective, answers from the six-year-old girl. Tommy had some training and experience in child sexual-abuse investigations, and to his eye the questions followed a proper pattern. They didn't suggest their own answers. On the face of it, this didn't seem like the kind of interview calculated to mold a child's thoughts and words into an accusation.

Nothing that the little girl had said would have sustained the lurid images that terms like *rape* and *sexual assault* inspire. She knew what her "private parts" were and clearly knew the difference between "inside" and "outside," and she told the detective she was sure that her father hadn't done anything to her on the "inside." But she also said that she had taken showers with Rick, that he had touched her "private parts," that she had often touched his penis and at least once had touched it with her mouth.

Tommy read, looking for anything that might clear Rick. This was, after all, the record of an interview of a little child. Naturally enough, a lot of what she was quoted as saying seemed ambiguous and contradictory, to adult ears. The document wasn't entirely clear, but it suggested enough to leave Tommy feeling slightly queasy. He looked up at Rick, and he tried to assemble a noncommittal face. This time he didn't feel it was convincing. Rick must have noticed; Rick tried to explain why the interview exonerated him. He said that this daughter was his mischievous child, and that there were perfectly innocent explanations for everything she'd said. Rick also told him that the D.A.'s office was offering a deal—probation and counseling and no jail time if he would plead guilty to a single count of indecent sexual assault. Otherwise they'd charge him with both that and rape of a child. Rick said something about that being the kind of deal they'd offer if they knew their case was weak. Rick wasn't going to take a plea. If they wanted a trial, so be it. Rick also said something dramatic. "The last few weeks the only thing that kept me from eating the business end of a revolver was not knowing. Now I know."

Over the following days, Tommy found himself trying to solve the case in his own mind. He knew all the people involved in the investigation, and trusted them. He was part of the prosecutorial system, as Rick had been. "I live by it. I believe in it," Tommy thought. They wouldn't be out to get Rick, not a cop with a good record. On the contrary. And they'd also want to spare the child from testifying against her father. You didn't have to look any further, Tommy figured, for the likeliest reasons that the D.A.'s office was offering him a lenient plea bargain.

He thought about the interview with Rick's daughter. Of course, small children made up and misinterpreted things. The interview was hardly conclusive. It was just a first interview and the detective hadn't probed very deeply, or explored an alternative line of questioning that might have exonerated Rick. But Tommy thought that if he were the investigator, what the girl had said would make him very suspicious. And there was also the fact that when Rick had first been accused, he'd checked himself into a psychiatric ward. Rick seemed to think that the interview with his daughter cleared him. But Tommy knew investigations. He knew this one was just beginning.

He stuck to his plan not to ask for information about the case, but every time he saw Jane, his friend from the D.A.'s office, he'd say, "I don't want to know any facts, but is it a strong case?" Again and again, Jane nodded—maybe a little more emphatically each time.

He tried to imagine innocent explanations. One night Rick's estranged wife called him at the station. She told him that she thought Rick might have violated the restraining order. She'd found her car's parking lights on, so she thought Rick must have been lurking around their house. She lived in a neighboring town. Tommy felt very relieved that he could tell her he had no jurisdiction and she should call the state police. Another time she'd called him with a question: Did Tom know anyone who might need size fourteen shoes and boots? Rick had size fourteen feet. She asked the question in such a cheer-

ful, offhand way, and there was so much malice in it that
Tommy had to wonder. He had never trusted the woman. Out
on patrol the next evening, he thought aloud, "Whether he's
guilty or not, she's a horrid bitch." He pursed his lips. "Or
maybe not. If he did it, and I was her, I'd fuck with him all I
could." He'd heard that she was telling perfect strangers about
the case. "It's weird," Tommy said. "But it's almost like trying to
make somebody laugh before they laugh at you. Your bringing
it up before others do makes it more palatable."

Anyway, Rick's wife couldn't have manufactured this case.
The allegations hadn't started with her, but with a neighbor,
the mother of a playmate of Rick's daughter. Apparently Rick's
daughter had said to her friend, "My daddy likes it when I put
his penis in my mouth." And the playmate had repeated the
conversation.

Tommy had heard that story around the police station. He
couldn't avoid hearing stories about the case. Supposedly,
when he got out of the hospital, Rick had said something to the
chief about having been sexually abused himself, by a sibling.
Tommy didn't want to believe that, and he wasn't going to ask
anyone about it.

Soon the D.A.'s office called. As he'd expected, they wanted
him to give a formal statement about his conversation with
Rick that night in the police station. Tommy wrote his statement as accurately as he could. He described himself as
"shocked" when Rick had told him he was being accused of
sexually abusing his daughter. And if a defense attorney should
later ask him what he meant by that, Tommy would say that
although they'd drifted apart the last few years, he'd known
Rick all his life and *never* come across any reason to think that
Rick could commit a crime like that. He'd say what was true:
that they talked a lot about sex as boys, back when Tommy
imagined that intercourse had something to do with urination,
and if Rick had ever mentioned carnal relations with a sibling
he'd never have forgotten it.

Tommy submitted his statement. The plodding ways of the criminal justice system guaranteed a long delay. He figured it would take months, maybe even a year, for Rick's case to reach trial. Maybe he wouldn't have to testify. If he did, he'd probably have company. The night Rick had left the hospital he'd gone all around the station telling other cops essentially what he'd told Tommy: *"The only way anything could have happened with me is if I was in a blackout."*

A CROWD OF about thirty, a large crowd by local standards, was gathering behind city hall, outside the Wallace E. Puchalski Building. It was Thursday, September 21, the first day of fall. The evening was balmy. Tommy and Jean and Bill O'Connor felt reluctant to leave it. They lingered outside. Thursday night was city council night, and a ceremony was scheduled as well. Tommy wore his gray court suit. Jean straightened his tie. She wore a dress. Bill, in shirtsleeves, gazed at the plaque outside the building. It bore the name of his old rival Wally Puchalski. Bill smiled, shaking his head. Recollection was obvious on his face.

One time back in the 1970s, the Northampton School Committee spent two hours arguing about the color of the shoelaces the high school football team should wear. In 1969, the local police ordered the high school to burn all its copies of *Manchild in the Promised Land*, because the book had obscene words in it. "Chitlins" was one of the bad words, the police brass had thought. Those days were gone. The good old days of kidnapped city councillors, when local politicos went by monikers like "Tunker" Hogan, "Black Jack" Kern, "Big Jim" Cahillane. The days of widespread patronage, when nearly all the public-school principals were related to one another. The days when a mayoral candidate could dust an opponent by revealing that he drove a foreign car—one of Wally Puchalski's successful campaign strategies. Gone were the councillor who had wanted to put a quota on the number of newcomers Northampton would admit, and the councillor who used to drop to the chamber floor and do push-ups during heated debates. Gone, too, were more recent spectacles, from Mayor Mary Ford's first term, which many used to watch with delight on cable TV—the mayor chasing after a councillor, scolding him for his intemperate remarks as he retreated toward the men's room, yelling bravely back at her.

Two years ago the voters had returned Mayor Ford to office by a wide margin, and had thrown out her bitterest opponents. Some citizens complained that city council meetings weren't worth watching anymore, they were just so dull. Nowadays when a city councillor aired strong feelings, the subject was apt to be the clear "gender bias" in the wording of ancient city ordinances. Mayor Ford would sit at the head of the rectangle of tables, gazing studiously over her reading glasses and smiling warmly at her colleagues in Northampton government, her hands folded before her, the city's matriarch, presiding over a peaceful feast of issues. What to do about the crumbling cafeteria wall at the high school? Could the city afford to buy the fire chief a new car? Should they take out snow insurance this year? And did the council agree with the mayor and wish to issue proclamations: that Northampton stood firm against the Nazi Holocaust, revered the memory of Dr. Martin Luther King, Jr., supported National Homeless Animals Week? Indeed, the council did.

Of course, in politics some things never change. A few years back the mayor got into a battle with the DPW and tried to force the chairman of its board to resign. The mayor often talked about openness in government, but when the chairman refused, she went behind the scenes and threatened privately not to reappoint one of his friends. The DPW got even. It snowed a fair amount that winter, and the mayor and her neighbors often found their street unplowed. About half the present council, and the mayor herself, had come to Northampton as adults, as sophisticated people, bringing new ideas to town, ideas formed out in the wider world. But they brought them to a stage that hadn't really changed. It was still very small.

Curious how Northampton drew some people in, like the people who settled here because the place seemed bohemian, and ten years later realized they'd become soccer moms and dads. Some people came here after years of living in great cities and decided to attend a city council meeting, out of curiosity and expecting to be amused. They usually were. Amused at the little council chamber in the Wallace E. Puchalski Building, with its all-over-brown decor; at the folding metal chairs for the audience; at the framed photographs of bygone mayors and councillors that seemed to be sinking into the walls. Amused, especially, at the tone of the proceedings, earnest out of all proportion to what was being discussed. But Northampton still had an adequate supply of citizens, both sophisticated settlers and natives, who had discovered the dignity of proceedings in here, and also the pleasures that came from having their voices heard, from dealing with matters both tangible and near.

Tonight uniformed cops and their families filled the chairs in the audience. Tommy, Jean, and Bill sat down among them. As the mayor discussed preliminary business, Tommy leaned forward over his knees. "We have to sit through this crap," he whispered, smiling at Jean.

"*And,*" said Mayor Ford. "The first but probably not the last transfer of free cash for this year. The new litter baskets for downtown." She looked around. "Any discussion?"

"Hallelujah!" cried one of the councillors. Then the councillor from Leeds declared that she wanted some trash barrels too, for her ward's swimming hole. The first councillor said that Leeds could have downtown's old litter barrels. The other councillor glared. "We don't want your leftovers." The two rival newspaper reporters from the *Gazette* and the Springfield

Union-News looked up from their notebooks and smiled, grateful for anything that resembled an argument.

"Next item," said Mayor Ford. "Chief Sienkiewicz."

Chief Russ Sienkiewicz, a tall man, came forward and stood at military attention before the council. He wore gold stars on his epaulets. He looked like a general. "I think it's important that the officers who have done these deeds be recognized in the appropriate fashion," he said. The chief called the name of a cop and the cop marched forward and stood at attention as the chief read out the citation. "While on patrol on January 27, 1995, you, Officer Dombroski, heard an explosion at the Smith Vocational High School. . . ." The officer had found a homemade bomb and done the right things. The ceremony went on, each uniformed officer coming stiffly forward to receive a citation, applause, and handshakes from the councillors and the mayor for his good deed—saving an infant who had stopped breathing; preventing a distraught man from jumping out his apartment window. Then the chief intoned, "And last but not least: Sergeant Thomas O'Connor, please come forward."

Tommy walked to the center of the room. He placed a hand on top of his shiny shaved head, and said, "Dim the lights." Which got a laugh, the councillors looking at each other and shaking their heads.

Mayor Ford aimed one of her motherly smiles at Tommy. She remembered, without warmth, another little joke of O'Connor's, made at a heated city council meeting in 1993, during a debate about special pay for local police who got college degrees. It had been a warm night like this one, and through the open windows had come the sound of someone beating a bongo drum on Main Street. The drum had ended up playing a small part in the defeat she'd suffered that night, at the hands of young O'Connor, a dreadful defeat, it had seemed at the time.

When Mayor Ford first took office, in 1991, the city had a

deficit of between two and three million dollars. The causes were complex, her first attempt at a solution simple. She'd asked the voters to agree to an increase in property taxes. They'd turned her down. So she and her budget director had devised a long-term plan to cut the city's expenditures, and they had stuck to it—ruthlessly, some felt. For her part, the mayor hadn't gone into politics to lay off public employees, or to promote what she believed were regressive forms of taxation—increasing the fees people paid for necessities such as water—or, God knows, to cut the budget for schools. But she'd felt compelled to do some of all of those. In the circumstances, granting pay raises to cops seemed absurd.

There had been a lot of parliamentary maneuvering. Her opponents outflanked her and prevented her experts from speaking. But Mayor Ford made a forceful argument against the special pay. She thought she still had a chance, until O'Connor got up, walked confidently to the microphone, and said, "I thought I'd be up here by seven-fifteen, and I only paid for the bongo player until eight o'clock."

It wasn't *that* funny a line, but she had to admit that the timing was perfect. All around her, the mayor saw smiles, even on the faces of her allies on the council. Then O'Connor made his serious pitch. He talked about morale and public safety. But in the mayor's view, he was really talking about a pay raise for some cops. "We shouldn't be doing this here," she thought. "This should be done in collective bargaining." O'Connor talked about the costs to the city. He underestimated them, by her calculations. He didn't even acknowledge the effect the incentive pay would have on retirement benefits. "He doesn't know this, in spite of the fact that his father *ran* the county retirement system," she thought. "His father only taught him how to get his way," she said angrily to herself.

The mayor stewed, and at the same time, in that part of her mind removed from the moment, the part that was purely professional, she studied the young cop's technique. He spoke briefly. He was straightforward. He threw in his jokes at just the right moments. She wasn't handy with jokes herself. She hadn't expected to be outdone in this way, not by a cop. She felt as if her jaw would drop if she let it. Then she thought, "It's in the genes."

In the end, the police got their raise, and for forty-eight hours she considered pulling out of her reelection campaign. Then she got over it. A year later, when the old police chief retired, she actually considered O'Connor for the job. It was out of the question, of course. He was much too young. Now on this first night of fall, 1995, Mary opened her eyes and smiled as the new chief, the one she'd selected—an excellent appointment, everyone agreed—declared, "Sergeant O'Connor has been selected as the new detective sergeant of the Detective Bureau."

The councillors all clapped. Mayor Ford clapped, too. Then the chief described O'Connor's largest drug bust, which had started in Northampton but taken him across state lines. Reading from the citation in his hands, the chief intoned: "In August of 1994, Sergeant O'Connor initiated a local investigation that led to the largest seizure of marijuana in New Hampshire to date. Therefore, in recognition of your valuable service to the Northampton Police Department and the city of Northampton, I hereby award you the exceptional service certificate."

The mayor went on smiling, watching as O'Connor moved around the room, leaning over the councillors' tables to shake each one's hand. She thought she might be watching one of her successors perform.

Not everyone grows up wanting to be president. For Tommy, the chief's announcement was more than just good news. It was the reward for ten years of striving. Detective sergeant. He had dreamed of becoming such a person since the days of the O'Connor Detective Agency. The chief had already told Tommy he wouldn't assume his new duties at once—the department had to solve some personnel problems first. Tommy could wait. Street sergeant was the next best job he could imagine.

Tommy left the Puchalski building feeling proud and happy, and it was a while before he realized again that he wasn't altogether comfortable in his mind. "Everything happens for a reason." That was Tommy's motto. He used it to console himself over disappointments. It meant things would eventually turn out for the best. But he found it hard to imagine a reason why Rick's troubles had arisen at this time, just when his own professional world had become nearly perfect.

Since that day about a month ago when Rick had declared his innocence, Tommy had stopped worrying that his friend might kill himself. He'd stopped visiting Rick, and called him only occasionally, not knowing what to say. But Rick was often on his mind.

On a gray autumn afternoon, Tommy sat in his cruiser, in a back lot on King Street, watching a couple of shabbily dressed men root through a Dumpster. "If he did do it, now he's all cleaned up and to realize he did it must be awful," he said. "It'd be awful, too, if he didn't do it and everyone in town thinks he did. But I'm out of it. *If* he did it, I have no knowledge. *If* he was molested as a child, I have no knowledge."

Tommy paused. One of the men was climbing out of the Dumpster, as if up through the hatch of a submarine. "Poor bastards," he murmured. "They go through the Dumpsters and find broken VCRs and try to fix them."

He drove out of the parking lot, back on his rounds, saying, "He could be innocent. He's pleading innocent, the way a really good guy would."

These days he and Jean didn't have abundant opportunities to talk. Jean worked regular hours. She had to get up early and was often asleep when he got home near midnight. Some conversations were brief—the night Tommy came home after dealing with a suicide, for instance. He usually left his clothes outside after dealing with a corpse, but this body hadn't been dead very long. He felt too tired to shower. Eyes closed, still asleep, Jean wrinkled up her nose. "What smells in here?"

"Me. You want me to take a shower?"

She stirred and rolled over. "No, I'll just hold my breath."

Sometimes they chatted for a long time, Jean answering him from out of her dreams and almost making sense. Tommy tape-recorded a few of those chats for her. Those were some of their longest conversations for days at a time.

Jean had always listened patiently to troubles he'd brought home from work. But now, when they did have an evening together, she seemed unable to let him talk about Rick. If he brought him up, she'd say, "Oh, he's such a jerk. I'm so mad at him." Rick wasn't her friend. She'd never felt warm toward him. The charges against him offended her, and she didn't find it very hard to believe them. Tommy understood. But when Jean responded that way, referring to Rick as "Richard" in an icy voice, he didn't feel like continuing the conversation. He didn't want to talk to anyone else about Rick's case. So, for the most part, he was left alone with his thoughts.

Many nights, he came home, found Jean asleep, got into bed, and read until the page began to blur. He turned off the light, and woke right up in the sudden dark. An old familiar feeling washed over him. He remembered times when he'd gotten in some trouble as a boy and had awakened the next morning imagining all was right with the world, and suddenly realized he was still in trouble—"Oh, shit!" He stared at the ceiling. His thoughts came braided. "I hope he's innocent. What if he is? If you had good times with a kid long, long ago in another world, what's the whole concept of a friend? Someone who's there for you when you're in trouble. What if he didn't do it? Then I'm a schmuck."

On the perimeter of sleep, Tommy had often imagined making the wrong snap decision out on a Northampton street or in a Northampton rooming house. Shooting someone by mistake seemed the likeliest of the possible irreversible errors he could make. He imagined being hauled into court before one of the local liberal judges, who would fry him. This old *argumentum ad horrendum* usually ended with him in jail. He couldn't imagine being accused of sexually abusing a child. He wouldn't let himself imagine that. But if he were accused of a wrongful shooting, he'd expect his best friends to defend him loudly and in public. Not refuse to discuss the facts with him. Not offer evidence against him. You never ratted out a friend to his parents.

His old friend Mark, who was Rick's friend, too, got in a lot of little trouble when they were teenagers. Mark didn't do anything they didn't do. He just got caught. One time Mark's father called Tommy and said, "I'd like to discuss Mark with you." Tommy had thought fast. He'd said, "But, sir, I'm only seventeen." The memory made him smile. Then it reproached him. Shouldn't he be protecting Rick? What kind of friend hears his old buddy say, "I didn't do it," and goes off thinking, "I *hope* he didn't."

What if Rick was guilty and the motive had been planted a long time back, right under his nose, inside the house three doors down Forbes Avenue, and had lain there dormant until a year or two ago? If he'd stayed closer to Rick the last few years, he might have seen what was happening and intervened and gotten Rick into treatment, without charges being filed, without a public scandal to humiliate Rick's mother, without a trial.

Tommy stared at his bedroom ceiling. "It'd be better if he robbed a bank. I'd much rather he shot someone in a bar."

Tommy wished all those thoughts away. And little by little, first for a week, then for two, then for whole months at a time, he nearly succeeded.

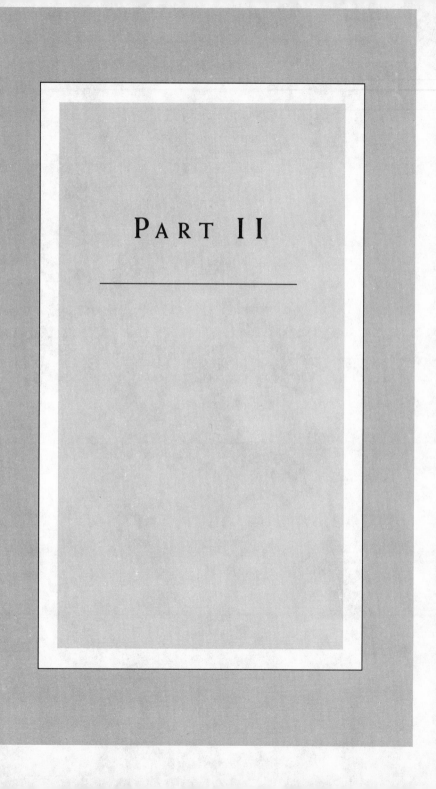

PART II

CHAPTER 4

A Moral Place

IN THE DAYS before it had a town clock, Northampton paid a citizen to sound a trumpet, calling all to Sunday Meeting. Attendance was required. Proper Sabbath behavior was enforced by tithing-men, each one of whom was also charged with checking on the morals of a dozen families. They carried black canes tipped with brass as symbols of their office. In Northampton nowadays, local ordinances policed a great deal of what went on outdoors, such as skateboarding and street music, and the tobacco control coordinator prowled around with a camera, looking for violations of the ban against smoking in restaurants. Even downtown, for all its flamboyance, had a serious air. Off and on, little groups stood in front of Memorial Hall, protesting international arms dealing and whatever war was current. Battles against homelessness, racism, domestic abuse, the burning of black churches in the South, were carried on from pamphlet-laden tables in Pulaski Park, and in lectures and discussion groups inside the Unitarian Society and the First Church. In spite of the nightly masquerades and all the luxuries for sale, Northampton was a moral place.

On a billboard out by the Interstate, an ad for a Main Street shop read, STUFF YOU WANT; below that someone had written, in artfully drippy red paint, WHILE OUR GHETTOS BLEED. That message had lingered for months. The fading graffito on the back wall of Thorne's Marketplace—GENTRIFICATION IS WAR, FIGHT BACK—had remained undisturbed for years. On Main Street, inside the shop that caters to recreational runners, a middle-aged customer tells the clerk that he must be fitted to only one brand of sneaker. "It's the only kind that isn't made by sweatshop labor in China," he explains. In a dress and accessories shop a block away, a woman gazes longingly at a pair of shoes—black with a gold-colored adornment like a snaffle bit on top. Then she turns away. Of course, she could afford the shoes, she tells her husband that night. But she doesn't actually *need* them, and there are so many problems in the world—starving children, threatened species, political prisoners—that she can't help but think the money would be better spent elsewhere. Besides, she says, smiling sheepishly, she's afraid she'd feel pretentious wearing fancy shoes in Northampton. People who dyed their hair green were more comfortable here, it seemed, than people who bought leather pumps.

Downtown had a tone, and the tone had a history. It probably stretched back to the Puritans' sumptuary laws, which were intended to keep average citizens from aping the rich. There were exceptions, of course, but anecdotes from the town's annals suggest that by the time of the Revolution the rich of Northampton were endeavoring not to look too different from everyone else. In the early 1800s a resident recorded in his diary a story he'd heard, an object lesson on this theme: In 1775 or thereabouts, a young tradesman came to seek his fortune in Northampton. He carried letters of introduction to the town's leading men. First he visited the famous soldier Seth Pomeroy, hero of the French and Indian Wars, soon to fight, at the age of sixty-five, at the battle of Bunker Hill. "But to his surprise found Col. Pomeroy clothed with a leather apron and arms naked, busy at the Anvil . . ." Then he called on a Major

Hawley. He found him living in an old, plain house, sitting in a ratty old armchair.

> The young man had doubts whether this man could be the famous Major Hawley and received the affirmative reply that his name was Hawley—the young man presented his letter of introduction and soon found the Great Man and that Greatness did not consist in splendid buildings or courtly dress and was taught the useful lesson of not Judging a man by his outward dress.

Timothy Dwight, the president of Yale, visited Northampton in the early 1800s and noticed a peculiarity about the town's three hundred homes. "A considerable number of the houses are ordinary, many are good, and not a small proportion are handsome," he wrote. But the handsome ones weren't situated together. The rich hadn't settled down in exclusive neighborhoods, the way Dwight seemed to think they should. The handsome houses were "so scattered on the different streets as to make much less impression on the eye than even inferior buildings in many other places."

During the 1980s Northampton had indulged in a spree, extravagant by local standards, with money and real estate. But the boom had ended now. Many of the bon vivants of the eighties had moved away, been indicted, or simply calmed down. And the wealthy had generally become retiring again. Gossip had punished ostentation in the past. It still did today. The rich were especially vulnerable, because they were greatly outnumbered. For years the town's median income had stood below the Massachusetts average, and as of the 1990 federal census, only seventy-nine households, fewer than one percent, considerably less than the national average, had incomes of $150,000 or more. Wealthy people here tended to live on remote hilltops, far away from inquiring eyes, or else discreetly, in houses with plain exteriors but interiors that contained kitchens good enough for restaurants, and private libraries, and art collections of great worth. The wealthy of Northampton drove good cars but not the very best. They didn't have live-in servants, though some maintained the equivalents of staffs, in caterers, cleaners, gardeners. One tier below, there was a much larger prosperous class, the upper middle by local standards—academics, business owners, various professionals. Many people had given up a little something to live here, forsaking their chances to maximize profits.

As long as they avoided ostentation, people could be wealthy in Northampton and still be called "progressive." In fact, the combination was likely. One way to achieve it was to open one's house to fund-raisers for a worthy cause. Mayor Ford once remarked, "It does seem to me that the rich here are quite benign." Of course, she was a beneficiary of fund-raisers, but she had a point. In Northampton inequality was more muted than in many American places.

Not that unanimity prevailed. A while ago the progressive forces had gone too far for some, and now the town was fighting over a proposed local statute, called the Domestic Partnership Ordinance, a gay rights initiative of sorts.

In other places, this kind of argument usually came mixed with practical questions about municipal finance and economic fairness, about discrimination in the workplace and freedom from harassment. Not in Northampton. The ordinance would allow an unmarried couple, whether heterosexual or homosexual, to license themselves as domestic partners at city hall for a ten-dollar fee. In return, one partner would have the right to view the school records of the other partner's child, with the partner's written permission. But anyone could do that already. One domestic partner would also have the right to visit the other in any city-owned jail or hospital. But Northampton didn't own a hospital, and the only jail under its control was the lockup at the police station, which didn't allow visitors of any sort. So the ordinance would grant rights that either didn't exist or that everyone already possessed. It wouldn't cost the town a penny. Maybe in other places the DPO wouldn't have seemed worth arguing about. But it had any number of symbolic meanings here. It set the town up for an election of great purity, an election about principle alone.

"This has always been a tolerant community," some natives liked to say. But not all that long ago, in the 1950s, the police had arrested a Smith College professor named Newton Arvin, winner of the National Book Award for a biography of Melville. His crime was possessing pictures of scantily clad young men. Exposed as a homosexual, and too weak to resist pressure from police, Arvin snitched on some of his best gay friends, was retired from Smith, and checked himself into the state mental hospital.

Gay-bashing in Northampton seems to have grown, along with the numbers of openly gay residents, until the early 1980s, when Judge Ryan, then the district attorney, prosecuted a man for making harassing phone calls to a local lesbian. Ordinarily the culprit would have gotten a stern warning, but the people who spoke for gay residents had been demanding action. Ryan pressed to have the man be given jail time. The judge remembered that case with mixed feelings. "He was just some poor slob and we made an example of him. But it seemed to work."

A place often gets known for one of its parts. In tabloids as far away as England, Northampton was now described as over-run by lesbians, teeming with weird and florid sexuality. The city census didn't ask the citizens what kind of sex they preferred, but a careful, between-the-lines analysis by the city planner suggested that lesbians constituted only one of many sizable minorities in town. Perhaps they only seemed more numerous than retired persons, because here they felt safe enough to come out of hiding. Several churches now performed gay marriages and the *Gazette* carried the announcements alongside traditional ones. Lesbians had become some of the city's sturdiest burghers. They ran thriving businesses.

They served on civic boards. Three of the city's cops were openly gay, after all, and so were two city councillors. The first cop to come out had found FAGGOT written on his locker, but that was years ago, and if some people on the force still didn't like the idea of gay colleagues, they knew better than to say so. The First Church, scion of the Puritan church, had, after a little struggle, officially declared itself to be "open and affirming"—that is, to people of all sexual persuasions.

Nowadays so many people in Northampton, both gay and straight, referred to their significant others as "my partner" that you might have thought it was almost entirely a town of lawyers. So when the council proposed the Domestic Partnership Ordinance, it hadn't seemed likely to arouse much opposition. But an organization called Northampton for Traditional Values hastily assembled, and in no time at all they collected three thousand signatures, forcing the ordinance onto the ballot.

Tommy O'Connor watched from a little distance. He thought the DPO gave gay people here a way of sort of getting married, a state that he approved of. "It'd be kind of nice for them," he said. What he didn't like about the ordinance was its licensing of unmarried heterosexuals—another assault, he felt, on the sanctity of marriage. And what he disliked much more was that this seemed like an attempt to rub new lifestyles in old-timers' faces. This wasn't a simple argument between newcomers and natives, between Noho and Hamp, but elections make an issue two-sided. He felt that newcomers were trying to declare that they'd taken over. He lived across the border now. He didn't have a vote. If he had, he'd have voted against the ordinance.

The opposition, Northampton for Traditional Values, declined a grand public debate. In lieu of real public discourse, lawn signs sprouted up all over town and the papers printed hundreds of letters to the editor. The backers of the DPO said, among many other things, that the DPO would represent a start, one small stand against the scorn and persecution that gay people had forever suffered. They said their cause was civil rights. Nonsense, said the opposition. The ordinance didn't ask for tolerance, which gay people here already had, but for official recognition, corporate approval, of gay and out-of-wedlock cohabitation. It asked the town to vote for lifestyles that many people here could tolerate but not in good conscience affirm. That seemed to be the essence of the argument at its most decorous. Both sides, of course, uttered meaner thoughts behind closed doors.

The camps held strategy sessions. They conducted phone-banking. The proponents even did some sophisticated polling. They raised far more money than the opposition, and no wonder. They had better fund-raisers: name tags, cocktails, and elevating surroundings. At one pro-DPO fund-raiser, cocktails ended with the bright sound of a bell, and the host, standing on a rug that looked like a work of art, said to the crowd, "This Tibetan bell can be heard for miles, and sometimes even in the kitchen." Short, inspiring speeches followed.

On election day, people who listened to National Public Radio the rest of the year tuned into the 1400 Team. You could hear Ron Hall's voice coming out of car windows and through doorways all morning. It rained that afternoon. Campaigners stood their ground, lining streets outside the polling places, holding up their competing signs: VOTE NO ON 1 and VALUE ALL FAMILIES. Many actually looked cheerful.

"This is democracy," said one sign-holder, as waterfalls of rain spilled off his hat.

"As good as it gets," said another.

For the first time in Northampton's history, the votes were counted electronically, so the results came in much earlier than ever before. Against most expectations, Northampton for Traditional Values had prevailed—but by a margin so narrow that the contest looked like a dead heat.

Two religious services followed the vote. The winners held

theirs on election night in the World War II Club, a smoky bar on Conz Street. When the returns were announced, someone cried, "It's a miracle. Hallelujah!" A group of about thirty gathered in a circle, holding hands, bowing their heads, while Father Honan of St. Mary's said a prayer. "We had a cause worth fighting for," he said afterward. Then the father raised up a glass, thanking the electorate and, presumably, God.

The losers put on a more elaborate service. They called it "A Healing Ceremony." It was held two weeks after the election, in the grand hall of the Unitarian church—by far the loveliest in a town full of churches. It has a vaulted ceiling, as tall as the Sistine Chapel's. It looks like a religious place without religion's somber side. The place is warm and bright and airy. The pews are comfortable, the architecture neoclassical, with authentic Tiffany windows fifteen feet tall and Corinthian columns. The place seems designed less for worship than for thought.

A photographic exhibit of gay and lesbian families hung on the walls, and the crowd—the majority female—filled up every pew. Victoria Safford, the Unitarian's pastor, the local rabbi, three different Christian ministers—Congregational, Episcopal, Methodist—and several lay speakers mounted the high pulpit in turn and offered consolation. As they spoke, sounds of sniffling, now and then of weeping, came from the congregation. The hall was full of handkerchiefs. But one lesbian couple was giggling softly, and whispering loud enough to attract the attention of someone nearby.

"Shhh. You shouldn't laugh in church."

"She's a recovering Catholic."

They giggled a little more and then composed their faces. They at least seemed to have emerged from grief. Perhaps the music helped. First the assembly sang a Unitarian hymn, one that doesn't mention God, called "We Sing Now Together":

> We sing of community in the making
> In every far continent, region and land

Then Andrea Ayvazian, for many years a lecturer on racism, now a seminary student, and the owner of one of the town's finest voices, stood near the Steinway and sang a more modern sort of song. Her lovely, deep voice filled the hall. She gestured with her arms, pulling the congregation with her, sing-along style. She could have worked a crowd in Las Vegas, but the song belonged in new Northampton. It was entitled "How Could Anyone." It began, "How could anyone ever tell you you were anything less than beautiful?" Andrea wore an enormous smile. "Sing with me," she called, and after another verse or two, she asked, "Is it too low for you?"

It was not. The congregation had the hang of it by then, but Andrea's voice could still be heard, shining among the rest. "How could anyone fail to notice that your loving is a miracle?" she sang. "Now get angry!" She showed them how. "*Don't* let *anyone ever* tell you you are *anything* less than beautiful. *Don't* let *anyone ever* tell you you are less than whole." She called for "one more *don't*" and then let her voice begin to fall. Still filling up the nave, it fell toward the vocal embodiment of great calm after a storm: "How could anyone ever tell you you were anything less than beautiful . . ."

Of course, in a democracy, if one group of people asks the electorate questions such as "Do you agree with us?" and "Do you like us?" they ought to be prepared to hear them answer, "No." But it would be a while before some women in Northampton stopped bursting into tears and a while before many others could look at fellow citizens without wondering, "Which way did you vote?"

Liberalism had seemed to be in season here. It had seemed like the political philosophy against which all others had to struggle, or else shut up. But now it looked as if Northampton's current residents stood almost equally divided in their strong opinions about their town, about how people ought to conduct their private lives inside it, about the way Northampton defined tolerance, about who owned the place. Was the town destined to remain forever split in two camps, forever scowling at each other? Only if less than half of a town can be said to define it. As usual, a majority of the adult population hadn't even bothered to vote.

Thirty thousand souls. Plato's ideal city-state was about that size, Northampton's size. To relieve the squalor and congestion of Renaissance Milan, Leonardo da Vinci devised a scheme for building ten new cities. Like Northampton, each was to have a population of thirty thousand. And thirty thousand was roughly the size of the famous "garden cities" dreamed up by Ebenezer Howard at the end of the nineteenth century. Howard intended his ideal towns to serve as antidotes to the overcrowding of great cities such as London, and to the growing impoverishment of the English countryside. And his utopias were most unusual in that a few approximations actually got built.

Howard's perfect garden city was neither quite a city nor a country town. It combined the best of both. It wasn't an American-style suburb, but a truly self-sufficient place, with farms and rural scenery, urban entertainment and variety. Northampton had become a place rather like that, where many people went for weeks without leaving because they found some of everything they needed and wanted here. But Howard's garden city depended on a collectivist vision. The garden city itself would be the only landlord. And, Howard figured, his new towns wouldn't need more than a few cops, because, like Northampton, they would contain only thirty thousand people, "who, for the most part, will be of the law-abiding class." Utopias by definition ignore some stubborn realities. If a place is big enough to provide all the variety that the law-abiding want, it's likely to be big enough to harbor most varieties of human nature unrestrained.

Most of Northampton was asleep. Only the occasional, distant sound of a lonesome trailer truck on the interstate broke the silence outside the rooming house at 129 Pleasant Street, Northampton Lodging. The building looks like a motel, shaped like a big shoe box. You could drive by a hundred times and not notice it. Five detectives sat inside, on the floor of the second-story hallway, a long, narrow shaft lined with bedroom doors. On one end of the hall, a door led out to an exterior staircase. At the other end, a small window opened east onto Pleasant Street. The hallway looked like a tunnel now, maybe because of the hour, the bleary hour when the world feels all used up. This building once contained the classrooms of the Northampton Commercial College. Hopeful, earnest youth once horsed around in here. The place was different now. A mingled smell of tobacco and night sweats was suspended in the air. A rust-colored stain in the hallway carpet, Caribbean blue, was what remained of a former tenant named Freddie. The stain lay in front of one of the bedroom doors. It marked the site of what seemed to be Northampton's first murder in several years.

The victim, Freddie, had been a drifter. The detectives had pieced together a detailed account of his last days. He'd spent them in Northampton with a local homeless man, who was living on the streets because his wife had thrown him out. This man didn't know Freddie's last name. Rooming-house Hamp had its rules of etiquette too, and one was not to ask people their last names. In their three days together, the new friends drank at least two thirty-packs of beer and a quart or two of vodka. They had "a few" in local bars. They also took a great deal of heroin. On the afternoon of the third day of the binge, Freddie was found lying in this hallway with a grave-looking wound over one eye. He had died yesterday, and the detectives hadn't stopped working since. Right now they figured that someone beat up Freddie to get his heroin. They had come to the rooming house to search Freddie's room, mainly to see if there was any heroin still inside it. But proper procedure required that an evidence expert examine the scene first. They sat in the hallway waiting for the expert to arrive.

The chief had taken Tommy O'Connor off patrol to help with the investigation. Tommy would go back to uniform once this case was solved. His eyes were bloodshot now, but he seemed in high spirits. He looked up and down the empty hall. "This would be hell if you suddenly fell and woke up living here," he said cheerfully.

Birdsong came in the window at the east end of the hallway. It arrived like the tinkling of a bell. The detectives turned toward the sound. "The sun's coming up," said Kenny Patenaude, Northampton's lieutenant of detectives. Abruptly, the window turned orange. Then the sound of a door opening came from the other end of the hall. They turned their eyes that way. "Oh, God," said one of them.

A very thin man emerged, barefoot and shirtless. His chest looked concave. With an odd, tiptoeing gait, he walked to another door, knocked, waited, got no answer, then went outside and leaned on the railing on the landing of the exterior staircase.

The detectives looked at one another. "He was hoping for a solid blue-veiner from the guy in there," said Tommy. He stood up and pushed open the door to Freddie's tiny room. A box of breakfast food stood on the small refrigerator.

"Cereal killer."

Lieutenant Patenaude made as if to hit Tommy.

Then another door opened. Out came another bare-chested man, with a flabby build and long black hair that reached his waist. In a moment other doorways opened. All up and down the hall men emerged—obese and skeletal bodies, weathered faces, tattooed arms. They passed by as if sleepwalking, as if they didn't notice the cops.

"This could be a documentary," said Tommy softly. "You know how they take a picture of a flower opening up? Good morning, thirty-nine." He added, as if speaking to himself, "The fucking rock has been lifted, and we're under it."

A man in a porkpie hat with a pipe in his mouth came out, down at the end of the hall.

"Go talk to him, Tommy."

The man's name was Bob. He told Tommy that he'd almost been a witness to the murder. He said he'd heard a thump outside and opened up his door. Looking down the hall, he'd seen a body lying on the carpet. Then Bob had looked across the hall and seen the man who lived in the room directly opposite standing in his doorway, too. Bob had looked at him, he'd looked at Bob, and then both men had closed their doors, so as to see no more.

Finally, the evidence man showed up and did his work. Then, donning rubber gloves, Tommy and another detective went into Freddie's room and began to search his bureau drawers. They didn't find any heroin. "But here's an appointment slip for a substance abuse program," said Tommy. The slip of paper lay amid several hypodermic needles.

"He's the number one student."

"All druggies have pornography. Videos, magazines, pictures of girlfriends, and, if the girlfriend lives there, dildos," said Lieutenant Patenaude.

"Bingo," said Tommy. He held up some snapshots of a naked woman. "Here you go, dude. Airbrush. Live it."

"Live the legend."

A few lone figures were walking on Main Street when they drove back to the station in the dawn. They stopped at the central traffic light and Tommy and the other detectives started laughing. A colorfully dressed man walked briskly past the unmarked cruiser, talking angrily to himself. "Orange shorts, red knee-length socks, tan shoes, a lovely coat, and to top it all off, a leather chapeau," said Tommy. "Just shoot me." Northampton had never seemed so strange. But maybe that was because of the hour and the view through sleepless eyes.

Back at the station, two other detectives were interviewing the prime suspect, and all the detectives' theories were beginning to fall apart.

In some big cities, cops jaded by mayhem called this kind of case "a misdemeanor homicide." But not in Northampton, regionally renowned for its peacefulness and safety. There was no such thing as routine mayhem here. And when a nasty little mess occurred, plenty of people arrived at once to clean it up. Most of the city's detectives and four from the state police, two of them lieutenants, worked for about forty-eight hours straight investigating Freddie's death. The D.A.'s office sent over a lawyer to help with writing affidavits for search warrants. Tommy loved a team. This one was good. All its members were well trained and willing. The lieutenants didn't have to tell the subalterns what to do. There was no grumbling, only voices saying, "I'll take care of that." But in the end, they realized that they'd never know for sure if there had even been a murder. "I think it may be a case of Fred dead from a fall in the hall," one of the detectives said.

All their good intentions, backed up by diligence and competence, all amounting to a strong assertion about the sanctity of life—all came to nothing. A brutal drive-by murder on Main Street would have been worse, of course—a shocking event, unheard-of in this town. This death had its own small horror: the invitation to despair that comes from not knowing what has really happened and what, if anything, it means.

While investigating Freddie's death, the detectives interviewed every resident in the rooming house, knocking on the doors, looking for potential witnesses. They came across, among others: an old classmate of Tommy's who had fallen on hard times; Woody the blind poet who had put his own eyes out during a bad LSD trip many years ago; a father and son who were both notorious child molesters; an adolescent boy who had also been convicted of molesting children; a man who had shot himself in the stomach once, probably in an attempt to collect insurance, though that had never been proven. One of the state police lieutenants knocked on one of the rooming-house doors and when it opened he saw before him a man he hadn't seen in years, not since he'd looked up at a motel balcony in another town and seen this very person aiming a rifle at him. This man had destroyed a state trooper's house and car with a pipe bomb, he had done his time, and now he had settled in Northampton.

In the police station late at night, the detectives sit chatting, as if around a campfire. Tommy muses about the rooming-house residents they've interviewed. "I really enjoy dealing with these people. I don't know why," he says. "Maybe because I can figure them out." He opens his filing cabinet. "All these files, all these names, all these confidential *un*reliable informants, drug addicts, thieves, volunteer firemen. Here's the guy who was arrested for rape last week. He went home to his wife, raped and sodomized her, used *twigs.* And this guy, over twenty arrests, a frigging teacher at a college . . ."

Northampton was the region's social services capital. Scattered through the town were an organization for wayward youth, dozens of big-hearted churches, a shelter for battered women, myriad counseling services. The rooming house where Freddie and his new friend had spent three days filling up on alcohol and heroin stood only half a block from the headquarters of a worthy substance abuse program. One block in the other direction was a methadone clinic, itself only a few blocks from the busy needle exchange, a concession that in many cases methadone and counseling don't work. "The downside of the rehabilitation movement," the assistant D.A. said during the investigation. "People come here for help, and when they fall off the wagon, they stay in town."

This was part of the fabric of the place: rooming houses full of misery and excess and anonymity right across the street from fancy restaurants and bookstores, and just a short walk away from a famous college and from houses where cocktail parties for charity were regularly held, bartenders wrapping crystal glasses in napkins, waitresses carrying canapés on silver trays.

• • •

It has long been fashionable to speak of the importance of public spaces, but all over town doors were mercifully closed on affairs too frail to withstand public view. In their separate offices, the town's army of psychologists listened as patients tried to specify their fear. Behind the closed door of his office, the evangelical pastor Dave McDowell sat beside a troubled parishioner, who said, "I'm emphasizing the material part of my life. I'm not open to God. I want to be."

"I'm only a man," said Dave. "Why don't you just tell Him?" Dave knelt on the rug. "Let's pray together, man."

Behind a door at the rear of the Unitarian church, the minister, Victoria Safford, sat at her old oak desk, helping a couple plan their wedding. Victoria was thin. She had a boyish haircut and couldn't have looked more feminine. The couple sitting before her were young and wearing sneakers. The young woman said, "We've got a bed now."

Victoria smiled. "Well, that's a good start," she said, and then turned gently solemn. "What I presume is that a couple is ready to be married, and unless you prove otherwise, I presume that it's true. But I will put to you a few questions, because I feel that as your accompanist, I can't not ask them. Because for half of the people who do this, it doesn't work out."

A great deal lay hidden and half-hidden in this small, peaceful town. Well before you understood all of it, you would feel you understood too much. Northampton wasn't New York or Calcutta. It wasn't even as large as the little cities to its south. As places go, it seemed so orderly. But what an appalling abundance it contained. If all of the town were transparent, if the roofs came off all the buildings and the houses and the cars, and you were forced to look down and see in one broad sweep everything that had happened here and was happening, inside the offices, the businesses, the college dormitories, the apartments, the hospitals, the police station, and also on the playing fields and the sidewalks, in the meadows and the parks and the parking lots and graveyards and the boats out on the river, you'd be overcome before you turned away. And not just by malignancy and suffering, but by all the tenderness and joy, all the little acts of courage and kindness and simple competence and diligence operating all the time. To apprehend it all at once—who could stand it? No wonder so much remains invisible in towns.

CHAPTER 5

Hands

ON PLEASANT STREET, just around the corner from Main, stands a little brick building, wedged between two bigger ones. They have fancy cornices, like tiaras in a wealthy matron's hair. This building's façade is plain, and some of its windows lean slightly toward each other, like rhombuses. Some colonial English diarists and poets imagined human form in buildings. This building was not unstable—it had settled to its present shape more than a hundred years ago. But it looked a little drunk, standing there with its slightly lopsided windows.

Tommy drove up Pleasant Street. As he approached the odd little building, a figure emerged through the narrow doorway beside the ground-floor wool shop. Tommy noticed a lot—a drug deal in progress that to other eyes would look like just a handshake; the silhouette of a wanted man hastily turning down a side street; the glances that other drivers gave him and, usually more significant, the ones they didn't give. All were like figures in a carpet that only trained and eager eyes could see. But it would have been hard for anyone to overlook the person coming out of the doorway.

He was a man of slightly less than medium height, with a bushy mustache meant to hide his damaged teeth. He wore shorts and running shoes and calf-length socks. And he came out onto the sidewalk at a fast, dangerously athletic-looking pace, a gait like an Olympic race walker's, wearing a hunted look on his face, and holding his forearms locked together and pressed against his chest, his hands encased in plastic bags. Sometimes he wore rubber gloves.

"That's Alan Scheinman. Another local nut," said Tommy. "Actually, he's not a bad guy."

Tommy had met him once. A few years ago Scheinman came up to him on the corner of Main and Pleasant while Tommy was dressing down a kid for public drinking. Scheinman told him he'd seen the kid put a half-full, uncapped liquor bottle in the corner mailbox. Another boy standing there said, "Hey, don't pay any attention to *him*. He's a fuckin' nut." And Scheinman pushed that kid, hard, which surprised Tommy, because he'd thought that Scheinman couldn't touch anyone.

"He assaulted me! Officer, you saw him assault me!" the kid said.

Tommy had turned to Scheinman. "I didn't see anything. Did you, Mr. Scheinman?"

Rumors abounded. One had it that Alan Scheinman paid women to cover themselves in plastic wrap and have sex with him. Another, conversely, held that he was afraid of menstrual blood and avoided women altogether. None of it was true.

Alan had come to town about twenty years ago, when he was in his early thirties and still trying to get out from under his fierce, successful father's shadow. His father had been crippled from infancy by polio and had made a fortune as a courtroom lawyer, conquering the world on atrophied legs. He was a man of many accomplishments, and he'd tried to make Alan one of them. Alan had become a lawyer, too, trained at Boston University, because it was his father's alma mater. After about ten years his father decided it was time for Alan to come home to New Bedford and join his firm. But Alan wanted to move to Northampton and become a publisher of fine hand-bound books. He wanted to be connected to an enterprise of beauty that he'd chosen for himself. He couldn't make the choice until, on an August night back in 1975, he drove into Northampton and through his windshield saw an array of shooting stars. Alan didn't believe in God, though his family was religious, but right then he was willing to accept outside help. He believed, not in a divinity behind the shooting stars, but in the effect they had on him. "There are things that override," he said later. "You believe in a thing even though you don't believe in it. It was hard to argue with my father. Even harder to argue with meteors." Looking back, Alan was amused. "A meteor shower is like a horoscope. The message is so general that you can get anything out of it. It's like the fortune cookie that says, 'You're secretly admired.' "

A lot of Alan's hometown, New Bedford, had gone through urban renewal: that is, it had been torn down. He arrived in Northampton during the early days of downtown's restoration. All sorts of people were moving into town, some equipped with capital, most exuding youthful confidence: artists looking for cheap loft space and musicians looking for a scene, American Buddhists who'd heard of an authentic lama living in the area, graduates from local colleges and idealists disillusioned with communes in Vermont, young architects with their heads full of high-sounding phrases about the human need for human scale and quirky symmetries. Some newcomers already knew, and others soon discovered, that they were also entrepreneurs. Alan looked around and he saw all sorts of new enterprises growing up on Main Street: a health food store, a natural food restaurant, new bookstores, an imported-wine-and-cheese shop, arts-and-crafts galleries. Youngish people like Alan were tearing down plaster walls and ripping up linoleum, exposing the brick and wooden floors underneath. Some people were beginning to reinhabit the upper floors on Main Street.

Alan liked all this. Here was a place where his generation seemed to be taking charge. But they faced a lot of obstacles.

The first of the region's malls had opened, in Hadley, across the river. Downtown rents had fallen, while property taxes remained high. Many merchants had grown old and their children weren't joining the family businesses. Alan hoped that restoration would succeed, but for a while he wasn't willing to bet money that it would.

He published several books after settling in town, but the artisans and artists had so little sense of deadlines that they nearly drove him mad. So he set himself up as a lawyer, and then he met Sam Goldman, the Medici of Northampton's little downtown renaissance, a newcomer who above all others had foreseen the possibilities and invested in them. Before Goldman left Northampton, in search of other challenges, he imparted to Alan both a passion for real estate and the craft of making it pay. "Making money on real estate is very simple," Alan later said. "The only mystery was why everyone in Northampton wasn't doing it." The details of an Alan Scheinman deal looked complex only if you weren't Alan.

There was, for example, the four-story building on Main Street that Alan bought from Goldman. The transaction stretched out over years. "That building made me a lot of money," Alan said once, as he walked past. "I love every brick in it." Alan bought it with three partners. Calculations could always be upset, say by the failure of the furnace, and Alan liked to spread the risk. He brought in his law partner, partly to make him indebted, and he brought in a tenant, a bookstore owner already on the premises, because he wanted someone in the building who had a stake in its upkeep. And he asked Goldman to take a share, in the form of a second mortgage, which Goldman granted Alan on extremely favorable terms— if the building failed to break even in its rents, Goldman would defer payments on that second mortgage. Thus Alan arranged to own part of the building with virtually no risk.

Several years later, he perfected the deal. He bought out Goldman and his own law partner, who had by then become his former law partner, and, in one single transaction, he bought out the bookseller and sold him back a chunk of the building, then used that money to pay off the mortgage, which was exactly the same amount he received from the bookseller. He now owned the rest of the building—one storefront and a number of upper-story apartments. He sold most of the apartments, keeping the best and largest, which he easily rented. He sold the other storefront to its tenants. He liked to remember that Goldman had offered to sell them the *entire* building for $200,000, and had been rebuffed. Now Alan sold them a *piece* of the building for $205,000. He laughed, looking back. "It was a lovely thing." That building would have made him money, he believed, even in a stagnant market. In the Northampton market of that time, he made a clear profit of about half a million dollars—and still owned part of the building.

Alan thrived financially during Northampton's recent gilded age, its roaring eighties, an era of booming real estate and expensive partying and, at the town's largest bank, the ironically named Heritage Bank, of phony letters of credit, secret partnerships, bribery, mismanagement. Many of that era's players—they were mostly men and mostly newcomers—appear in a photograph taken at a party at the Hotel Northampton. Alan wore a turtleneck and tweed jacket. He had shoulder-length hair neatly parted in the middle. He was interestingly handsome—fit-looking, with a long nose and full lips, and clean-shaven. He had the sort of face that changes markedly with the light and the viewing angle and what surrounds it—with the length of hair and the style of clothing. A friend, the artist Barry Moser, borrowed his profile to depict Ichabod Crane's severe and bony physiognomy for an illustration in one of the hand-bound editions Alan published. But viewed head-on, his face was sensitive and delicate, almost pretty. He was actually more sedate than many people at that party—he didn't drink a lot and never touched cocaine—but he looked positively debonair.

A lot of funny money helped to finance downtown's renovations, but the place came out of the crash beautified, all in all. Individuals got hurt, of course. One newcomer, who had come to town with zero capital and within a few years had been driving around town in two different Mercedes-Benzes, ended up completely broke and detoxifying from drug addiction in the York Street Jail in Springfield. Alan, who came to town with about $20,000, sold almost all his properties at the height of the boom and emerged about $2 million richer. Of course, he made some enemies, but no one could accuse him of illegal dealing. In Northampton, he felt, he had achieved the sort of stature he'd dreamed of—"a medium-sized fish in a small pond." He had money, and he'd made it all without his father's help. He had made a best friend, in Goldman. He had met a woman, a beautiful, fascinating woman to him, "a stunning woman." And the place itself had taken hold of him. Northampton had some of him inside it now. He could look at downtown and feel he'd played a part in its survival and its sprucing up. When he was driving back from trips away and he came to the rise in the road beside the bowling alley and he saw the old buildings of downtown appear before him, he felt a great, unfamiliar comfort. "The relief of home," he called it. That feeling survived, even when everything else started going wrong.

After Goldman left town, life with the stunning woman became increasingly contentious. Finally they parted. On a day not long afterward, Alan sat in an office at a local bank, at the end of another profitable real estate negotiation. The people at the table stood up and began being pleasant to one another. One of the men offered his hand to Alan. He couldn't remember the man's name anymore. This was just someone in a necktie, perfectly ordinary and presentable. After shaking hands with him, though, Alan felt that his own right hand had become, not dirty, but contaminated. Suddenly all of his attention focused on his hand. It might have just turned purple.

And he realized with what seemed like great clarity—"an insight," he called this, the first of many—that if he didn't immediately remove whatever it was that made his hand feel so alarmingly strange, then everything he touched with it would become contaminated, too, and then all of those things would lie in wait for him to touch them again at a later time, contaminating his hand again. He excused himself and went to the men's room. He stood over the sink and did what one does when one's hand is dirty: he washed it. But it didn't feel cleansed, so he washed it again. And again and again, about twenty times over—all motion and no progress. Finally, he realized, as if from a distance, that whatever had taken over most of the rest of his mind was saying he could stop. He couldn't shake with anyone after that day. For a while he kept up appearances by tying an Ace bandage around his right hand and telling people he'd injured it.

He began having insights everywhere. He walked up to the door of the dry cleaners on Main Street, carrying his laundry bag. He shouldered the door open, so as not to touch the handle, and got in line behind a woman. She delivered a filthy-looking quilt to the clerk, who picked it up and put it in a basket. At that moment another clerk relieved the first, who headed over to another section of the store and started pulling plastic bags over freshly dry-cleaned clothes. And to his horror Alan experienced with what felt like every part of his body and mind a completely logical skein of thought, founded on illogic yet irresistible. "That clerk has been touching these filthy, contaminated, dirty clothes, and now she's touching people's clean clothes and she's contaminating those clothes," he thought, as he stood in line. "Okay, what's going on here is that your clothes are going in here dirty and coming out dirty, and even if they had someone else whose whole job was to pack plastic onto clean clothes and that person never touched dirty clothes, the truth of the matter is that the dirty clothes are given to a man who puts them into a dry-cleaning machine. Now look at that. He doesn't wash his hands after he puts them in the dry-cleaning machine, and he doesn't disinfect or wash the handle of the door to the dry-cleaning machine. So even if he washed his hands after he touched the dirty clothing, which he doesn't do, he'd contaminate his hands by opening the door to take out the dry-cleaned clothes, and then when he touched the clean clothes, he'd contaminate them again." Soon all of Alan's suits and sweaters and sports jackets and slacks lay piled among other trash in his apartment. His former life had ended.

He couldn't wear clothes that had to be dry-cleaned, which meant that he couldn't dress up for court. He couldn't be a lawyer anymore. He couldn't shake hands. He couldn't touch doorknobs. Northampton's banquet was spread before him. There was nothing he couldn't afford to do here. Northampton was beautiful, and he couldn't touch it. In *Paradise Lost* the fallen archangel says, "The mind is its own place, and in itself / Can make a heaven of hell, a hell of heaven." By the mid-1980s Alan would have said that the Devil had a point.

He knew he was a public spectacle. He went outside only when he had to, and he hurried home to his apartment in the tipsy-looking building. The windows were speckled with city grime and the floors were littered, mostly with discarded paper. Inside his rooms, he moved along narrow pathways, between chest-high piles of debris. For years he had watched the rubbish accumulate and for years he had wanted to clean up, but another insight stymied him: "There's no way I can put that stuff in garbage bags without contaminating both my clothes and the bags, and there's no way I could carry them down my staircase without touching the walls, and if my clothes or the bags are contaminated and they touch the walls, then I'll have to spend hours cleaning up the walls and I already have far too much cleaning that I have to do, and besides, once I got the stuff outside, I'd have to deal with the lid of the Dumpster or the incinerator, and both of those are grossly contaminated."

He could still function intellectually, but he had less and less time for anything except his illness. It had progressed to an extreme. He had to spend nearly eleven hours a day in ritual cleaning of himself. Before he could touch his telephone, his only truly functional connection to the world outside, he had to shower for about four hours. He had to wash every square millimeter of his body, and if, when he was almost done, he realized or imagined that he'd missed a spot, or accidentally brushed against the shower wall, he had to start washing all over again. He remembered that when he was a boy he would wash and wax his father's cars and invariably his father would say, "You missed a spot." Alan wondered if there was a connection.

He had to spend about an hour and a half brushing his teeth before they felt clean. Back in Boston years before, he'd had some of his teeth broken in a car accident. The repairs hadn't weathered well, and now he brushed what remained so ardently that he began wearing ruts in them. A dentist told him that decay would destroy his teeth more slowly. But he had to brush for that hour and a half, then clean the spattered mirror and vanity—very carefully, lest he contaminate himself again. If the trash in his apartment had contained food, his only safe place in the world would have become unbearable. So he had to go out to restaurants, hoping someone would be there to open the door for him. At best, that meant sitting in chairs others had occupied. Contaminated by the world outside, his own clothes became dangerous objects. So he had to wash them often, and once he'd washed them, no matter how carefully, he felt dirty and in need of showering once more.

He couldn't let other people inside his rooms. They might touch the few crucial objects that he kept uncontaminated. Maybe that was just as well. He felt beyond embarrassment, not beyond shame. And he was ashamed of his rooms. That was the cruelest side of his illness, he thought. The compulsions that forced him to live in squalor didn't take away his ability to recognize the squalor, or to see that the madness controlling him really was madness.

In later years Alan's illness, obsessive-compulsive disorder, would become quite justly famous, but most people didn't know much about it back then. Alan, always studious and thorough, had learned most of the facts available. He was what clinicians called a cleaner. And he understood with perfect clarity that mastering the proper names of symptoms is far from the same as having power over them. He'd spent time with a psychiatrist back when his symptoms still alarmed him, before they'd become his life, and the psychiatrist had told him there was no cure.

He wasn't completely unhappy. While he sat imprisoned in his rooms overlooking Pleasant Street, his mind ranged far more widely than it ever had before. He had to spend about two and a half hours sitting on the toilet. The time was usually that long, because the moment he felt that he had finished evacuating his innards, he'd feel he hadn't. Unable to leave the toilet, Alan read. He consumed books there, among others all of Edward Gibbon's *The History of the Decline and Fall of the Roman Empire.* In Alan, speech and thought were more nearly identical than in most people. He left enormously long messages on friends' answering machines, messages lengthened by apologies for leaving such long messages. The history of Rome according to Gibbon fascinated him. One of his ruminations went like this:

"As I read *The Decline and Fall,* I had no thoughts about Northampton, but I did have an awareness of changes I saw taking place around me. For example, the fact that real estate has gone from being a long-term investment to a short-term commodity. Western jurisprudence is based on the sanctity of real estate. It's the foundation of Anglo-American law, the ownership, inheritance, and use of real estate. So when you change a long-term, sanctified thing into something like jewelry or cars, that's a huge change in basic values. Now I'm not sure how that comes about, but clearly it represents an erosion. I don't know if it signals the decline and fall of the American or the Northampton empire. Is there a connection with children in Pulaski Park piercing and tattooing themselves? I don't know. But certainly this has been a century of dramatic changes.

"Let's say it's the year 817 and a horde of Vandals is roaming across the steppes of eastern Europe and they come to a walled town and demand that it surrender, and the town refuses, and the Vandals overrun the town and because it would not submit to them, *extirpation* takes place. They leave *no trace* of it behind. Gradually, over the centuries, humanity becomes more civilized. Wars take place between armies and aren't aimed at running over civilian populations. And then in the twentieth century that changes again. Civilian populations are again dramatically affected by wars. Society exists essentially to protect individuals, and if governments can't protect individuals, there's a fundamental breakdown. When people survive the bombing of a city, they tend to feel individually spared. It's the equivalent of going, 'Phew!' That kind of thing heightens your sense of the value of your own life. I think that in this century, because of wars waged on civilian populations, there is a heightened sense of the individual, who wants his voice heard and his influence felt. And that leads to a further inability of society to protect its own from the people who are expressing themselves."

If someone bumped into Alan when he ventured onto the streets outside, he felt very angry, because for him the consequence was five hours of ritual cleaning. He thought it was a good thing he didn't have violent tendencies, or else by now he might have killed one of the careless people who didn't think that bumping into someone else was a big deal. "When I grew up, you would say, 'Excuse me,' and avoid bumping into people, or say, 'Sorry,' if you did. People have no sense of personal space anymore. Or maybe it's just that, because of my illness, I have a heightened sense of this. Maybe I'm just a one-note musician. Maybe reading Hobbes's *Leviathan* had too much of an effect on me. But I think people are much more focused on themselves than on relations with other people nowadays." He wasn't sure, but sometimes it did seem as if he could glimpse connections between the decline of manners, and maybe even the fall of the Northampton real estate market, to the grand, tragic story of civilizations past. At any rate, his reading on the toilet took his mind away for moments from the fact that he was compelled to sit there for hours.

At times he felt something like peace falling over him, descending from despair. "There are certain threads of existence that you abandon. It's just that you come to grips with the fact that you're not going to deal with them." He thought he could have been a monk. "Praying instead of washing my hands four hundred times a day." He'd been only moderately well-read before. Now he lived in books and movies. He used his old rock-and-roll records to summon up memories, where he could also go for a while. His experience was increasingly limited, and it intensified in proportion. He knew periods of great concentration. He escaped into them. Meanwhile, he considered suicide.

Alan had a charming, roguish friend. He'd done a small business deal with him. Ever afterward he would say that this was the kind of guy with whom you'd never want to be in business, though you'd always be glad to meet him for a beer. The friend had been trying to seduce a certain woman, and in order to impress her had taken her to look at some apartments he'd had renovated. He took this woman to the apartment of a tenant who said he'd be away. He opened the door and saw the tenant hanging by the neck. The body had been there awhile. A frightful sight. That very day, Alan's friend had begun a course of psychotherapy.

Alan had sent away to the Hemlock Society for advice, and read their pamphlets thoroughly. For him, he thought, carbon monoxide would be easiest. He had keys to his friend's garage and to one of the cars inside it. One night, he figured he'd get a little drunk and lock himself in there with the car running. He imagined his friend finding his corpse and rushing off again to a therapist, and he laughed in perverse amusement. Alan had a distinctive laugh. It began with an "Ah" and proceeded in an even tempo, "Ha-Ha-Ha-Ha," and died away in a tone that sounded a little sorrowful, as if at its being over.

But he wasn't ready to die yet. He often sat alone at one of his windows, looking down at the street. The sounds of night in Northampton rose up to him, of music, happy voices, arguments. He watched the town pass by below, the friends on their way to restaurants, the drug dealers and swaggering homeboys, the body-pierced Goths, the married couples, the lovers, the lesbian mothers pushing baby carriages, the homeless who rooted through the trash barrels, the staggering collegiates who appeared from the bar across Pleasant Street as night in Northampton began to end. And all of them seemed enviable, because they were alive in the world. He sat for hours sometimes, gazing down with longing.

In nearby cities and towns the name "Northampton" used to be synonymous with the state mental hospital. If a mother told a friend that her son had gone "to Northampton," the friend was apt to say, "Oh, I'm sure he'll get out soon." The hospital was founded in the nineteenth century, in an age less euphemistic than the present one. The Northampton Lunatic Hospital was its first name. But the place wasn't built to imprison what the mid-nineteenth century called lunatics; they were already shunned and tied up in their beds. The hospital was supposed to free them, to get them out into the country, to place them in front of lovely views and in airy interiors, to give them religion and outdoor chores, and thus to relieve them of the greatest imprisonment of all—by curing them. For the working people of Northampton the hospital had meant jobs, of course, but if you looked at its oldest buildings—the inventive flourishes in the brickwork, the elegant dormers at the rooflines, the grand scale of the whole—you knew that the people who built it and worked there and ran it had the best of intentions. Eventually, however, it became a terrible place.

In the 1950s, when she was a student at Smith, Sylvia Plath described it in a letter to her mother.

> We changed then, for the cocktail party, and walked over to the professor's house. On the way we decided to keep on walking for a while longer, and so walked up to the mental hospital, among the buildings, listening to the people screaming. It was a most terrifying, holy experience, with the sun setting red and cold over the black hills, and the inhuman, echoing howls coming from the barred windows.

The hospital the young poet saw held about two thousand patients. Now it lay empty up on Hospital Hill, where the Indians used to bury their dead and where the gallows had stood and where children now went sledding. It was a haunted spot, the kind that makes you feel how small a piece of time the living occupy. The old hospital sat there decomposing, about a mile from downtown, a vast collection of giant buildings, all shut up and moldering, surrounded by enormous trees, like a lost civilization, a gigantic lost cause. You craned your neck beside the buildings, looking toward the leaking roofs. There were vermin in the maze of tunnels that connected all the parts. Some windows were covered in plywood. In others ragged curtains hung, and now and then a passing jogger saw one stir, and was startled, and hurried on.

As the hospital closed down, a lot of patients were offloaded into little old Northampton. A former inmate set fire to a downtown building, and two people died. Then, at last, the state got busy, and a brand-new social service apparatus was erected. Rather quickly, the furor passed and Northampton got accustomed to its new strange characters. When Tommy was a child, playing down by the Mill River with Rick and other friends, he'd hear the siren go off on the hill and, assuming that meant an inmate had escaped, he and his pals would run for home. A couple of years back, a national public-TV show singled out Tommy and some of his colleagues for the firm and kindly way they dealt with former mental patients who were living in the town. Former patients had become a part of the place that Tommy and the other cops routinely patrolled. A lot of the most florid characters were gone now: The Sun Tan Man, who used to stand bare-chested on corners. The Bird Man, who used to go up to people on the street and say, "Suck my cock. Oh, come suck my cock." (Once, when Tommy put him in protective custody, he announced that he was going to take "a bird bath," and started splashing water on his face from the toilet in his cell.) The Hamburglar—named for a cartoon character—a tiny man who always wore a trench coat and got in raucous fights with himself on Main Street. He'd throw roundhouse punches at someone only he could see, then go reeling backward from the counterpunches. Sergeant Bobby Nicol would walk up and say sternly to him, "All right, you two. Break it up." And the Hamburglar would obey.

Samuel Johnson said, "A decent provision for the poor is the true test of civilization." Perhaps an even finer one is the way a place treats the mentally ill. A lot of citizens went out of their way to speak to the town's former mental patients. Some downtown merchants joined the cops in looking after them. Alan Scheinman was a harder test. Normal citizens could see right off that people like the Hamburglar weren't like them. But Alan was a lawyer. He was rich. He'd seemed fairly normal just a while ago. Then he'd changed. If something like that could happen to him, it could happen to you.

"Alan Scheinman is the Tylenol killer," someone had written in the women's room at Packards bar and restaurant. One woman, well connected politically, referred to him as "Alan

Scheincreep." A few clerks called him "the germ-crazy lawyer who won't touch any change." But those were the exceptions. "He has a strange illness which makes him cross the street to get away from you," Mayor Ford said, catching a glimpse of him on Main Street. "He was one of the people responsible for the renaissance of downtown. It's very sad." Judge Ryan made a point of falling into step with him, so that when Alan got to his destination he could open the door for him. Alan could sometimes count on strangers, too. He stood outside a downtown restaurant once—looking desperate, he supposed—and a woman inside with her leg in a cast, a woman he had heard described as a man-hating lesbian, saw him through the window, got up from her chair, hobbled to the door, and opened it for him. Many people were kind, even the notoriously difficult functionaries at the registry of motor vehicles.

The world outside Alan's apartment had turned into a giant obstacle course. His greatest freedom was a car. But to drive one, he had to have it registered. Inside the registry, on King Street, the lines were always long. He couldn't expect to stand in one without someone brushing up against him. The transaction with the documents would be impossible. The clerk wouldn't understand. In a panic, Alan called ahead. "Look, my name is Alan Scheinman. I'm a lawyer here in town." (Saying he was a lawyer sometimes helped.) "I suffer from an illness which makes my behavior seem bizarre. I have to register a car, but I can't stand in line, and I can't touch papers that anyone else has handled."

The clerk's voice said, "Just a minute, please."

Then another voice came on the line. He explained again. He heard that second voice say, "Just a minute, please." He thought this wasn't going to work, but the third voice offered hope. "Come on down, and we'll see what we can do."

Alan stood a little distance from the crowds at the counter, in his usual defensive mode—forearms pressed together, both hands in plastic bags, one hand cupping his chin. From the other, also near his chin, dangled a plastic bag full of documents. "I was a sight," he remembered. He waited there for a few minutes, feeling desperate and helpless, and then a clerk appeared from behind the counter. She looked at him and didn't even seem surprised. She led him to an empty office, took the bag of documents, and returned ten minutes later with all the paperwork completed. She even escorted him out to the parking lot, opening all the doors for him.

That Christmas Alan sent a four-pound box of Godiva chocolates to the registry, along with a thank-you note. He got back a letter signed by the entire staff. Were there tearstains on it? The letter said how very rare it was for them to get a thank-you note, let alone a present. On Valentine's Day, Alan sent the registry two dozen long-stemmed roses, and on Thanksgiving a large fruit basket. He'd sent those presents every year since. He also sent chocolates to his bank. The head teller would fetch a stack of crisp, new money from the vault for Alan. Alan sent his gifts to his auto dealership, too. He couldn't let anyone inside his car. The mechanics allowed him to drive it into the service shed. No one there openly made fun of him, though it was a strange sight, Alan's car aloft on the lift with Alan sitting in the driver's seat.

At the grocery store, Alan would take a box of plastic garbage bags from the shelf, open the box, pull out a bag, put the rest of the box inside the bag, then start moving down the aisles. He'd put each item in his bag. He'd practically empty the shelf of cleaning agents. Sometimes another customer scurried up to the service desk and whispered that a strange man in shorts was shoplifting. One time Alan confronted a would-be snitch. "I hope you feel better," he said to her, thinking to himself, "Oh, Alan, another pathetic comment, out of abject hostility." But the employees were obliging. They didn't make him stand in checkout lines. He went to the customer service desk instead, took each item out of the garbage bag, and read the price to the clerk, who added everything up and called out the total to him. He'd ask the clerk if he still had enough on account to cover the bill, and if she said he didn't, he'd pull some cash out of his shirt pocket, crumple it up, then toss it to her. He sent his gifts to the grocery store, too.

Not many ironies were lost on Alan. Northampton was kind to him, all in all. His wealth helped him to secure that kindness, through what he called "preemptive bribery," and it also allowed him to equip himself for illness—to buy, for instance, the expensive turbo tank that kept the water hot during four-hour-long showers. Wealth and local kindness. Those good things had made it possible for him to spend a decade avoiding confrontation with the demon in his mind.

OCD had its allure. All by itself, it made his parents suffer. He could speak to them through it, without having to utter his thoughts: "So sad. You can't do anything about it now. You're screwed. Gotcha." Of course, the illness wasn't operating on a tabula rasa. It evoked and magnified parts of his former self, like his cunning, and it called on what felt like a deep, inborn desire to have exclusive management of his own life. OCD provided him with what he called "secondary gains."

According to the current clinical definition of the most common form of obsessive-compulsive disorder, the victim engages in compulsive rituals that relieve obsessive thoughts, these rituals and thoughts interfere with the victim's normal functioning, and most victims realize, to some degree at least, that their fears and rituals are inappropriate. They often suffer from other problems—depression is common. But a single illness seems to lie behind compulsive hoarding, checking, cleaning. It may afflict as much as 3 percent of the general population, a very large percentage for a psychiatric ailment. It chooses people of every race and both sexes equally and without regard to position or intelligence.

When the obsession with contamination first crawled into Alan, there was a lot of talk in the news about the herpes virus. Alan worried that he might catch it. But that was just a particular form of a general fear that OCD provokes. Earlier in the century "cleaners" like Alan fretted about syphilis. By the mid-1980s many worried about AIDS. Obsessive-compulsive disorder almost certainly predates the germ theory of illness. Various symptoms were described in medieval times. Martin Luther and Samuel Johnson may have suffered from it.

The ailment has an eerie quality. Accounts of victims' lives often sound familiar, like myths or fairy tales, and their obsessive thoughts resemble what Western cultures now call superstitions—for instance, the belief that things once connected can, when separated, still affect each other, that fingernail clippings or locks of hair can be used to harm the people they came from. Or the belief that thoughts can in themselves cause calamities. The person who knocks on wood after feeling lucky may not be doing something very different from what Alan felt compelled to do when he washed and washed his hands after touching a doorknob.

Freud described a case of OCD and theorized about it, but he was clearly stumped. Current hypotheses about the cause include psychodynamic, chemical, neurological, and neuroanatomical explanations, and there is tantalizing evidence for each, as well as for a genetic predisposition to the ailment. The cause or causes still aren't known. During the 1980s, though, some treatments appeared. Psychotherapy didn't seem to work. But it was now known that a class of drugs called serotonin-reuptake inhibitors—the famous Prozac is one—helped many victims. So did a form of behavior modification called exposure and response prevention therapy. The local psychiatrist whom Alan consulted called him back a few years later with this news. Since then Alan had sent away for information from the Obsessive Compulsive Foundation. He had spoken on the phone to some of the leading experts. And before writing to the Hemlock Society, he'd made an effort to get well. He checked himself into a mental hospital, McLean, near Boston. But a while after he returned to Northampton, Alan said ruefully,

"McLean's works great. But only if you spend the rest of your life living at McLean's."

Americans began to feel ashamed if they lived above a store in an old downtown. As they moved to the suburbs and merchants stopped residing above their shops, upper floors grew seedy in the collective view and, soon enough, seedy in fact. But here in downtown Northampton the trend had been reversed and an old pattern rediscovered: shops, restaurants, theaters, nightclubs at street level; professional offices, hair salons, dance studios on second floors; and apartments up above. Nowadays people paid high rents to live downtown. A few kept veritable penthouses overlooking Main Street. And some of the mystery of the place had been revived—for people glancing up at windows, in their private thoughts imagining others' private lives.

Upstairs in the old tipsy-looking building near the corner of Main and Pleasant Streets, unbeknownst to anyone, Alan had an accident. He got a small cut on his shin. It became infected. The infected leg began to swell. Then the other one did, too. Soon he couldn't get his pants or shoes on. He ordered larger ones over his decontaminated phone. The skin on his shins itched maddeningly. He couldn't keep from scratching. When he saw that the skin had begun to ulcerate, Alan told himself, "I'm dying. And this is a good way to go, because even though it's painful, it avoids the embarrassment of suicide. I'll be dying of a systemic infection." The skin on his lower legs began turning black. It didn't look human to him anymore. His calves looked like the bodies of dead fish, covered with plates of dry dead skin. He couldn't sleep. He'd drop off for a few minutes, then awake in pain. And then one morning he woke up in his fastness over Pleasant Street, and heard himself say, "I don't want to die." He couldn't walk very far anymore. He'd have to find a doctor with a nearby office.

"You don't know who I am, but I'm a lawyer here in town. I

suffer from obsessive-compulsive disorder, and I need to be examined. I know I have a serious infection. I can't take my clothes off. I *can* wear loose-fitting clothes. I *can* pull up my pants legs to show you, but you can't touch me directly. You have to wear rubber gloves. And I can't touch anything that's been on the ground, so you may have to help me put my socks back on when you're done. It's really bizarre. I understand if you're not going to be able to do this."

"Come on over," the doctor said. "We'll see what we can do."

The doctor was alarmed. He confirmed Alan's own diagnosis. "You have cellulitis. You're going to die if it's not treated. The next stage—and I mean within the next two minutes—this goes to blood poisoning, and when the poison hits your organs, you're dead. You're at the point now where it's going to happen. You need to be in the hospital."

That was impossible.

The doctor didn't dare to treat him outside. It would be extremely poor medical practice.

Alan said he'd make up a release and sign it.

Reluctantly, the doctor prescribed enormous doses of oral antibiotics.

Alan was afraid of ingesting pills, but he took these, for weeks on end, and gradually the infection receded. He had saved himself. Afterward, alone in his squalid rooms, he took stock. He had already let the doctor touch his leg. He had already done what the uncontrollable part of his mind had told him was even more awful: he'd taken pills. Alan could not say why pills should seem dangerous when food prepared by others didn't. He didn't make those ridiculous distinctions. His illness did. Contemptibly, cravenly, he'd obeyed its orders for a decade. But now he had actually ingested pills on his own. He called his old psychiatrist at McLean, whom he hadn't spoken to in over a year, and he asked for a prescription for Prozac. "I don't know if I'm ready to take it," Alan said. The psychiatrist sent him the prescription. Alan filled it. For a time the bottle sat unopened on his dresser.

Clinicians who treat victims of OCD talk about courage. You have to understand, they say, that a truly potent set of fears lies behind the bizarre and sometimes comical-looking behavior of a person who starts weeping at the idea of throwing away an old newspaper clipping, or checks the same lock two dozen times, or rushes for the sink after touching a doorknob. Victims who decide to get better do what most people never have to do. In one kind of therapy, they have to expose themselves deliberately and repeatedly to what truly terrifies them. In another, they have to take a drug, an act equally terrifying to some. Hardest of all, they have to begin. Alan poured himself a glass of water and shook out a capsule of Prozac. Then he sat on his bed for a while, just holding the water and the pill, one in each hand, contemplating what might happen if he combined them in himself.

He wasn't thinking, "I'm about to do something brave here." He didn't feel very afraid of contamination by pill just now, as he sat on his bed, staring at Prozac. At the moment his fears were rational. He had read about the drug and knew that it reduced the sex drive in a fairly small percentage of people, and he didn't care at all about that. He'd been celibate for almost a decade. But this little tablet in his hand was powerful, he knew. It would change him. He thought, "If I take this mind-altering medication, I may suddenly feel lost. I may lose that sense of continuity of self, that ongoing, ageless voice that is a sense of self. This may make me function at a lower, or on a different, plane. I don't know if, when I take this, I'll end up barking like a dog."

And then he thought, "Screw it. How much worse can it be, whatever it is?"

CHAPTER 6

Hunting

THE MORNINGS GREW chilly, the great river vaporous. Mist hung in the folds of Mount Holyoke, burning off a little later each day. The natural beauty of Northampton seemed clearest and most poignant now, in the views that opened after leaf fall under north wind skies—the yellow cornfields all laid flat, the river running by, the murmurings of history. The greenness had so recently departed from the streets and southern hills, and in the lengthened shadows on the sidewalks you sensed the many months before greenness would return. Time to look "down cellar," as people from Northampton say, for the storm windows and snow tires, and time for the better-organized to start their Christmas shopping. At Northampton's facilities for the homeless, the waiting lists grew longer.

Throughout its first century, Northampton had paid citizens to house and feed the local poor. But that tightly woven, religious farm town hadn't looked kindly on indigent strangers. At one point the town meeting had even voted to evict about a hundred families who had not properly applied for the right to settle. (No records show how many actually departed, only that some certainly stayed on.) Eventually Northampton established a poorhouse. The one still standing at the end of the nineteenth century had all but rotted away beneath the beds of the inhabitants before it was rebuilt. Nowadays distant governments subsidized about 10 percent of local housing—just about the percentage that the federal bureaucracy deemed proper. State and federal money financed a number of halfway houses for the addicted and variously handicapped, and the shelter for homeless veterans at the veterans' hospital out in Leeds. Many of the people who lived in the city's privately owned boardinghouses and apartment complexes paid their rents out of government stipends. But the state and national social service apparatus was too big and too distant for its local extensions to serve everyone who came to town looking for shelter. To catch some of the overflow, Northampton had established its own homeless shelter, and, to catch the overflow from the shelter, churches set up cots in their basements from late fall until spring. Local charity paid most of the costs.

On the afternoon of October's last Sunday, a banner in Pulaski Park proclaimed, SHELTER SUNDAY. Again this year, several wealthy residents, who preferred anonymity, had each put up $10,000 for the local homelessness programs. Today more than a hundred citizens were out searching for the remainder, knocking on doors and holding out coffee cans. On Main Street, in front of coffeehouse row across from the park, tourist shoppers, coffee drinkers, Sunday strollers flowed around a stout figure dressed in a red blazer and billowing skirt. She, too, held out an empty coffee can. "Hi. Would you like to contribute to our homeless?" Some parts of the current swung wide to avoid her, averting their eyes. Others eddied around her, digging in their pockets. "Good afternoon, Your Honor." "Hi, Mayor! Nice of you to volunteer."

Down on Pleasant Street a very thin black man leaned against a building, huddled in layers of coats. "Jesus loves you," he murmured to passersby. Leaves blew past him in the chill October wind and into the duck ponds at Look Memorial

Park, around the trunks of the great oaks in Childs Park, across the lawn in front of Forbes Library. The wind rustled the informational handouts and tally sheets on the long church-basement-style table set up in the middle of Pulaski Park. The mayor dumped her take on the table—$75.35—and, rubbing her hands to warm them, turned to the *Gazette* reporter who stood by, awaiting quotes. "What I like about Shelter Sunday, besides the money it brings, is that it raises the community's consciousness," she said in a voice high and cheery. She went on, more somberly, "Whatever the combination of underlying causes of homelessness is, they're getting worse. At least in this area."

Northampton's homeless shelter was called the Grove Street Inn. It stood about a mile from downtown, out past the ruins of the state mental hospital's power plant, on a rutted asphalt road—a clapboarded house, like a New England farmhouse, and painted the appropriate white, but not recently. The Inn sat all alone at the bottom of a long hill, its only near neighbor an abandoned house. Residents sat on the front porch on broken-down furniture, smoking—the shelter was a part of Northampton: no smoking allowed inside. The interior rooms were clean but unadorned, furnished with hand-me-downs. It seemed like a place without promise. Residents got only temporary refuge. Three months was the limit.

But when it had room, Grove Street accepted anyone in need. It didn't ask for virtue. Colonial Northampton had warned out indigent strangers. Contemporary Northampton tried to accommodate them. The Inn amounted to a principled, communal gesture. Some citizens grumbled, of course. Set up shelters for riffraff and you'll attract more riffraff, they felt. But once in a while a place like Grove Street could be good for more than the conscience of a place. After all, St. Peter says, "Be not forgetful to entertain strangers: for thereby some have entertained angels unawares."

· · ·

In summertime a few years back, a man carrying a little airline bag shambled up to the door of the Grove Street Inn. He was short and stocky and clothed like many people down on their luck. His jeans hung too low, revealing the cleft of his butt. He had a broad, copper-colored face, not quite handsome but full of interesting things—close-cropped, jet-black, curly hair; a black mustache and a little compensating fringe of hair below his lower lip; mysterious dark brown eyes. He didn't seem to know that when he smiled, his ears wiggled slightly, but it was obvious that he knew he had charm—from the sweet look he'd put on, cocking his head a little to one side, as he listened to what other people had to say. He laughed with a smoker's deep huskiness, in low piratical tones.

Asked for identification, he would produce from various pockets all sorts of paper—business cards and crumpled remnants of letters and, mixed in with the rest, a Massachusetts driver's license, a Social Security card, and a birth certificate. These identified him as one Samson Rodriguez, an American citizen born November 28, 1950, in Puerto Rico. He had been laid off from his job as a loom operator in a factory down in Holyoke. Samson had worker's compensation coming. He stayed at Grove Street on Northampton's hospitality just long enough for his check to catch up with him, then moved to the rooming house at 96 Pleasant Street downtown. A lot of the people at Grove Street were sorry to see him go. Surely this was one of the shelter's best uses, to put up a good-natured blue-collar worker temporarily short of funds.

It didn't take Samson long to feel at home in downtown Northampton. His feelings for the place weren't all that different from those of other recent settlers, the board-certified surgeons and lawyers and people with fancy degrees and well-heeled married couples with children and the many recent graduates of the region's five colleges who lingered on. Like them, Samson was smitten by downtown—its prettiness, its liveliness, and above all its mannerly, safe atmosphere. He stood on the stoop of the rooming house, watching the traffic move through downtown, and it wasn't long before he realized he was listening for something and not hearing it. Down south in both Holyoke and Springfield, the two biggest cities nearby, drivers honked at each other all the time, like a bunch of barking dogs. But not here, Samson noticed, even when the traffic was thick on Main Street. "Check this out," he thought. "No horns." And down in Holyoke and Springfield—in the parts of them where he'd lived, anyway—arguments and fights were always breaking out. Not here. He studied the people walking around downtown. "The people up here, they're, like, mellow," he remembered thinking.

Everyone noticed this peaceable quality, and some had theories to account for it. The demographic explanation was least convincing. Northampton wasn't rich and it didn't have a wall around it to keep out people who'd caused trouble elsewhere; actually, its many social service agencies invited a number of such people in. Jane Jacobs's famous theories about street life had to do with great cities, but maybe some of them applied in little downtown. Like her ideal urban neighborhood, it was used at almost every hour, and this ensured not just liveliness and profit but also the constant presence of "eyes on the street." Because downtown had become a place of many live-in owners, there were always people around with a stake in what went on in public and in keeping up the place. And perhaps downtown proved the theory that the right kind of well-kept surroundings encourage civility.

The place lacked those features that make many urban streets look like little war zones. The shopkeepers didn't cover their windows with steel grates after hours. Indeed, they left things outside that could easily have been defaced— flower boxes by the sidewalks, canvas awnings over storefronts. Fragile things left out at night seemed to declare that the place was safe, and maybe they helped to make it safer.

Maybe people inclined to vandalism and assault usually behaved themselves here, not just because they realized there was a good chance of getting caught, but also because they didn't want to mess up something they, too, enjoyed. Clearly, something like what sociologists call social norms had been set in motion. A resident hesitated to honk at another driver, perhaps thinking, "I might know that idiot's wife." Visitors sensed, as people rarely do in a big city, that the place had a general code of correct behavior almost unanimously endorsed.

Maybe, as Northampton's city planner said, *all* the theories about downtown were correct. Samson, who had grown up in the Latin American faith called Santería, favored a quasi-religious explanation. He borrowed some of his theory from a Christian lay preacher, a boardinghouse reverend, who told him that an angel guarded Northampton from "the malice power," the evil influences that wanted to migrate up the river valley, from the cities to the south and into Northampton's streets. Looking around, Samson decided that geography also played a part, assisting Northampton's guardian angel. From spots between buildings and over rooftops, he studied the Holyoke Range. One cloudy night he saw a reddish glow in the sky above those hills, and his suspicions were confirmed. Those hills were definitely involved. They clearly helped to block the malice power from seeping into town.

Obviously, something was doing that good work. "The only thing the malice power could do here is a light touch," Samson would say. "You know. The gay and lesbian thing."

Evidence accumulated. When he learned that Northampton had a lot of churches and hosts of counselors, psychologists, and psychiatrists, and New Age mind- and body-workers practicing such disciplines as the ancient Chinese art of skin-rolling, Samson felt sure he'd landed in a specially designated place. Clearly, deep forces had chosen Northampton as a place for healing. And maybe it was no accident that he'd been drawn here. He felt he needed some help. In Holyoke, he'd been smoking far too much crack cocaine. He loved and hated the drug. "If you take the best day of your life and multiply by twenty, that's the first stage. If I'm on a run, I don't want to eat or sleep. But by the third day, it's just maintaining." By the third day his thumb would become an open sore, from flicking the abrasive wheel of his lighter over his crack pipe.

Many people ask a lot of a new town. They expect it to change their lives without their having to change themselves. Samson was no different. He couldn't give up crack on his own, but maybe this place would help him do it. In the meantime, he just wanted to be left alone to smoke a little less in this mellow atmosphere and enjoy the change from Holyoke. After his worker's comp ran out, he'd figure out what to do next.

Samson was a pioneer of sorts, or else he was like a seed on the wind. He may have been the first—certainly he was one of the first—to bring crack to Northampton. You couldn't buy it here when he arrived. But it was easy enough to travel down to Holyoke or Springfield, in a cab or a bus or the car of one of his new friends, and carry back some rocks. And his favorite kind of crack pipe was everywhere for the taking in the parking lots, in the form of car radio antennas. You broke one off and turned it into what was called a straight shooter.

Samson had always made friends easily. Soon new friends here had given him a nickname: Sammy. Then a fateful encounter occurred. He was riding a bus back from the mall in Hadley. He had his eyes closed but wasn't asleep. He felt a hand shaking him by the shoulder, and a female voice with a Hispanic accent said he was going to miss his stop. Samson opened his eyes and found himself looking at a short and buxom woman. "This is Hampshire Heights," Samson told her. "This isn't my stop."

"Yes, it is," she said. "You wanta have some coffee?"

Her name was Carmen. Samson moved in with her, and

before long married her, in a civil ceremony. The town was providing everything he'd hoped for then. If you asked other residents, those with families, what bound them to the city, most would say that even though the high school had some serious problems, this was a great place for children, a place where the main thing you worried about was that your kids wore their helmets when they rode their bikes. Samson's Northampton had a different kind of innocence. No one, he figured, would recognize the smell of crack coming from his wife's apartment. And then there were the local police, another good reason for staying. He'd run into a lot of cops in Holyoke and Springfield. The ones he'd met here in Northampton were amazingly polite and affable by comparison. "Like, gentlemen."

Samson shared the common tendency to judge professionals according to the size of their jurisdictions. "The cops up here, they're, like, hicks," he would remember thinking. "Like boneheads."

In his first five years on the job, Tommy was a diligent, enthusiastic, and inflexible patrol officer, the sort who volunteers for every special training course available and who, imagining a cop's true measure lies in numbers of arrests, handcuffs everyone he can. But a gift of gab can be a great asset in detective work, and the members of the department's detective bureau decided to try him out. Rusty Luce, the most senior of them and one of the young O'Connor's heroes, took him aside. "Just because somebody breaks the law doesn't mean you have to hate 'em," Rusty said. "A lot of people out there hate ya, Tommy. They do! They're your eyes and ears out there. If you're gonna be a detective, you gotta learn to cut some slack." Tommy listened. He passed his tryout. A year later he volunteered for narcotics work.

When Tommy was eighteen, one of his best childhood friends turned up dead in a Northampton apartment. Though he'd never know it for a certainty, he *believed* drugs were the cause. He remembered listening to the evening news on WHMP and hearing Ron Hall's deep voice announce the death. Friends from his old neighborhood were not supposed to end up dead at eighteen. In that moment, he would say, he had learned to hate drugs. He could think of plenty of other reasons now, examples of their poisonous effects on other lives and families and places. He'd heard most of the arguments against the so-called war on drugs, and he didn't buy them. He didn't know why anyone would want to legalize drugs. Alcohol and tobacco were bad enough, he'd say.

The local authorities had never worried much about narcotics, at least not openly. The police department had never assigned a detective exclusively to drug work. But in 1992, the results of a professionally administered survey of Northampton schoolchildren hit the papers. The high school seniors were using illicit drugs at considerably higher rates than their counterparts nationally. And not just marijuana, but also the entire range of hard drugs. Even a few eighth-graders reported having used powder cocaine, hallucinogens, and heroin. In no time, Northampton had joined the regional drug task force, which provided money for drug buys and equipment. Tommy used some of it to buy a disguise, the wig and fake mustache now in a trunk at home. He was given an undercover drug car, a small, low-riding Japanese model. He put an air freshener in the shape of a crown on the dashboard to make it look like a Latin drug dealer's. If he took away the crown, the car became a white or Asian dealer's. "The multicultural car," Tommy called it.

Northampton had a lot of users and dealers, and they weren't used to being pursued. A lot of them were amazingly careless. In one month, Tommy made twenty arrests in a single parking lot, behind Hugo's bar on Pleasant Street—most of the culprits were either selling or snorting powder cocaine. He worked with the state drug cops at the D.A.'s office and he often worked alone. Typically, he spent most of a day in court testifying about his arrests and then spent the evening, sometimes most of the night, making more arrests—nearly two hundred in his top year. In the afternoons Tommy headed out in his cruiser, unmarked but an obvious cop car. He was dressed in civilian clothes but with his bald head uncovered and shined up with aftershave. He toured the various places where drugs often changed hands, talking jive to everyone but especially to the people who his informants said were dealing. Then he'd go back to the station, put on his mustache and wig, tie a bandanna around his forehead, and make those same rounds in the multicultural car, looking for drug deals, gathering intelligence. No one recognized him, even though occasionally the mustache came halfway off. He hid in the bushes at the edges of the projects and parks. He skulked through alleys and parking lots. He took off his disguise before he pounced, so that it was always the fast-talking, bald-headed detective who emerged and made arrests.

The idea, Tommy's own, was to make himself conspicuous and frightening. He wanted the users and dealers to wonder how he knew what they were up to and how he managed to keep showing up at exactly the right times. And he wanted the ones he caught to spread the word about him to the ones he hadn't met. For this, he counted on the size of his town—small enough so that many people involved with drugs knew each other—and on the universal tendency to exaggerate, especially pronounced in youth. He wanted to become "almost a ghost figure" to the denizens of the overlapping drug worlds of Northampton. He wanted the dealers and users to think he might be anywhere, on the theory that fear might slow them down, and he imagined that stories about the bald-headed narc might make a kid at the high school hesitate when first offered pot or cocaine or heroin.

Part of the plan clearly worked. Some years later, a young man who had been a member of the high school druggie crowd but had never actually met Tommy said, "Guys were goin' unmarked and then suddenly, I don't know what happened. Cops were coming out of the bushes everywhere." More than once a parent came to the station complaining to the captains and the chief that Detective O'Connor was harassing his child. Tommy told his bosses with perfect candor, "I don't even know the kid." He smiled. "But I'll be looking for him now."

Many times people who could have run away or come at him with a weapon surrendered without even arguing. "It was like they thought the hammers of hell would come down on them," he said. The process had its own momentum. "My reputation. It was almost like they created it for me."

What many people find repulsive in drug work is the cultivation of the snitch. Personally, Tommy didn't like most informants. "Rats. There are very few who won't roll over on friends or family members," he once said. "Nobody takes responsibility for their own actions. You get caught doing something, *you* do the time. Don't rat out your friends." Tommy understood the dangers of giving informants special powers, the importance of keeping them under his control, of verifying their information through other sources. But he had no qualms about making use of them. And they weren't hard to find. He arrested a lot of people who were eager to become informants in return for leniency, and soon every dealer in town who wanted to rat out a rival dealer knew that O'Connor was the person to call. His pool of informants grew along with his outsized reputation. But he still didn't have a high-level informant, one who could lead him to people who dealt significant quantities of hard drugs. And he still had a lot to learn.

The antennas, for example. Several citizens had come to the station complaining that someone had torn the antennas off their cars. "Kids," Tommy thought. The antennas weren't just broken off and left behind. So he figured they must have become a new teenage weapon of choice. Meanwhile, he was mystified by the capsules he kept finding in the parking lots and the alleys behind the rooming houses, little empty vials with screw tops, the sort you might find in auto parts stores holding things like ball bearings. He thought they must be significant without knowing why. Then a cop from Holyoke showed him one of those capsules with a five-dollar rock of crack cocaine inside it. And then someone else told him that crack smokers used car antennas as pipes. Tommy had heard of crack, of course, but he hadn't known it had arrived in Northampton. He was galled. He thought, "Jesus Christ, O'Connor, how many crackheads have gotten over on you?"

The avuncular detective Rusty Luce had taught Tommy the mechanics of a controlled drug buy: how you handled the confidential informant, recorded the serial numbers of the bills, established probable cause for a search warrant. Tommy had also attended a two-week course in drug investigations, taught by agents from the federal Drug Enforcement Administration. Rusty and the DEA had been Tommy's high school. He'd been a detective for about two years when he met his Harvard and his Yale.

The first time he ran into Samson Rodriguez and got his vital statistics—Samson's wife had taken out a restraining order against him—Tommy went to the station and ran a Bureau of Probation check, a "BOP," and then an interstate check. And when Tommy saw that the man's record was virtually unblemished, he said to another detective, "No way this guy is who he says he is."

This wasn't the most pressing of issues, but it sat in the back of Tommy's mind like an unfinished chord, and he felt a little quickening in his pulse when, on a spring afternoon in the early 1990s, he came to work and, looking through the arrest book, saw that Samson had been locked up and then bailed out the previous night for violating his wife's restraining order.

Several times wives had ratted out their husbands to Tommy, usually as last-ditch efforts to get their men off drugs. A wife could be a good way in. Tommy drove to Hampshire Heights in his unmarked cruiser.

For most people in Northampton, this housing project was a secret place in plain view, one they often passed and didn't have to think about. It was built in the 1950s to house returning Korean War veterans. People liked to say there *used* to be no shame in living there, and yet when he was a boy Tommy never went inside the place. He had made some friends in school who lived in the project, but they had always come over to his house to play, never invited him to theirs. Tommy knew most of the current residents. Some of the Hispanic families had given two of their children the same first name, such as Jose. "Hose-A and Hose-B," Tommy said.

He was on friendly terms with many of the people who lived here. Until about a year ago he'd allowed himself to imagine that some of them were friends. But no one had tried to help him the time when he was arresting Danny Cruz on a warrant and ended up perilously close to losing his gun in the fight. A few people came up to him afterward and in effect apologized: "I wanted to help you, man, but, you know, I have to live here." He didn't blame them. No matter how friendly he was, he came to the place only as a cop, preserving the professional distance that makes other people's troubles easy to bear, and he realized he'd expected the residents to respond to him with a deeper commitment than he'd ever make to them. He felt a reciprocal warmth like friendship with most of the children, but it often didn't survive adolescence.

A battered chain-link fence surrounds the Heights, a warren of flat-roofed, two-story buildings. To Tommy all the units had that hole-in-an-institutional-wall look, like identical stables or cells. Outside several front doors, residents had created little gardens, surrounded by miniature white picket fences. On the other hand, Dumpsters stood out front along the asphalt streets, and the snow had melted, uncovering all of last fall's trash, scattered across the scruffy lawns. Carmen answered the door. She spoke with a Hispanic accent. Tommy told her he wanted to get some information about Mr. Rodriguez's 209A violation. Could he come in? He sat on a battered sofa in front of a coffee table littered with beer bottles, an overflowing ashtray, and half a dozen empty screw-topped vials.

Carmen said that Samson did terrible things to her.

"What kinds of things does he do?"

"It's very hard for me to talk about."

Out of the corner of his eye Tommy caught glimpses of empty vials all over the living room floor. "Well, like what, ma'am?"

"Unnatural sex."

"This oughta be pretty good," Tommy thought. Carmen had a fairly long record herself, made up mostly of drug offenses. "Unnatural sex, ma'am?" he asked.

"Yes," she whispered. "He made me have oral sex with him."

He looked in an imaginary mirror, keeping a straight face until the silent laughter slid away. "These vials, ma'am. Tell ya straight out, it looks like someone's been smoking a lot of crack in here."

Carmen said those vials were Samson's. He was a terrible addict.

Tommy said he could well believe it. This was a bad guy. Samson could get her evicted and in a lot of other trouble. She agreed with that. Tommy thought, "Boy, I'm glad she's not *my* wife."

Many people let Tommy search their cars and houses, even if they had something to hide. It was usually just a matter of asking the question the right way, of saying, "You don't mind if I take a look inside, do ya?" amid a bunch of other fast, friendly talk, as if the question were just incidental and rhetorical. As if, once given permission, he wouldn't bother to search. And then, of course, he always searched. Did Carmen mind if he looked around the apartment? She did not. Every room was strewn with empty vials. "Mind if I go down cellar, ma'am?" In the basement, he found two large empty canisters of laughing gas. "Samson's?"

She nodded sadly.

At the door he thanked her for her cooperation. He told her it would be in her best interest to continue it, laying out all the many ways in which this man could harm her more than he already had. She said she would help.

A few nights later Carmen called, and the night after that, Tommy stood in the front door of the station, saying to Samson Rodriguez, who stood at the foot of the steps, "Sammy! What's happenin', man? Come on in. I got your welfare check." Tommy kept up a steady stream of talk as he escorted Samson inside. He chattered away, telling Samson he couldn't allow Carmen to hold the check, not with a 209A outstanding. He said Samson should be careful about restraining orders in a town like this where there was a lot of sympathy for women who claimed to be abused, which wasn't a bad thing but Samson knew the game.

The skinhead detective talked so fast that Samson hardly noticed where they were going. Through the door into the station proper, across a linoleum-tiled floor—shabby-looking under fluorescent lights—and around one corner and then through another door into a room that Samson recognized, but was for a moment too confused to place. The room had a desk and a chair in front of it. "Sit down, Sammy," the detective said. "I'll go get your check."

Samson looked around. There was padding on the walls. He'd gotten booked in this room before. "I might as well relax," he thought. "I'm gonna be here for a while." Then the skinhead detective was back, standing over him and handing him a photograph, a mug shot of a man holding a nameplate under his chin.

"Sammy, you ever see this guy before?"

"Wow. Francisco Sandoval. No, I never met the guy." Samson looked up at the detective earnestly. Tommy was grinning down at him. Then Samson turned into Frankie, and started laughing.

The mug shot was a good likeness but it didn't capture the person, Tommy thought. The man in the photograph looked dour. Now he was howling with laughter, his head tilted back, his hands gripping his jiggling stomach. He was laughing so hard he began sliding off the chair. Watching, Tommy started laughing too—more sedately, of course.

Tommy didn't lock him up right away. He took him to his office and let him put his feet up on a chair. A bunch of fancy-looking hash and pot pipes sat on Tommy's desk, campaign souvenirs. "Nice pipes," said Frankie.

There wasn't time that night for more than the merest sketch of Frankie's life and times. Unlike the fictitious Samson, he had been born in the Dominican Republic, during the reign of the dictator Trujillo. When he was still a boy, his grandmother spirited him out of the country under an assumed name, which she had taught him to think of as his own—his grandfather had been strangled in his own bathtub, probably on Trujillo's orders. Frankie did the rest of his growing up in an Italian neighborhood in Springfield, Massachusetts, learned English by immersion, earned American citizenship, and built up a successful business with his father, the cornerstone of which was a large bakery in Springfield's North End. It thrived until the recession hit in the 1980s. "I was like a Boy Scout until about ten years ago. Then it was like, what's the sense of being a Boy Scout? I'm gonna go for whatever I can get," Frankie said. "That's when the bakery blew up."

Tommy had a copy of Frankie's printed criminal record. Fanned out, it would have stretched across the floor like a wedding dress's train. Parts of the record, the story of Frankie's criminal career, were puzzling, at least superficially. Frankie had served only seven months of his five-year sentence for blowing up the bakery. When he saw this, Tommy thought, "He's a rat." To Frankie, he said, "You did some work for someone, huh?"

"Yeah, but check this out." There was this Colombian drug lord Frankie met at the state prison in Concord. He took a shine to Frankie: "I'm lucky, I guess. Wherever I go, people like me." The authorities noticed. They offered to let Frankie out early, and also Frankie's father—Frankie bargained for his father, too—and in return, Frankie agreed to traduce the Colombian and help bring down his cocaine operation in Boston. He made controlled buys for the cops, and did some drug dealing himself on the side. After a while he asked the cops for a finder's fee, 10 percent of the loot they would confiscate when they finally busted the Colombians. "They say, 'We got you out of jail.' I says, 'Enh-enh. The Colombians are gonna make me look like cheese.'" (He meant Swiss cheese, of course.) " 'You do this or I quit.' " A prosecutor told Frankie he must like jail because he was going back there. At this point in the story, Frankie drew his head down to his shoulders, and his eyes grew furtive. "That's when the chase began."

Frankie bought a well-forged birth certificate from a Venezuelan he met on the docks in Boston, and in no time at all there were two of him again. The rest was fairly ordinary—a common-law wife, a child he didn't get to see very often, a lot of different jobs, a lot of crack, and Carmen. As for the most serious outstanding charges on his record, threat to murder and intimidation of a witness, he'd acquired those because a cabbie in Springfield had helped the cops convict his father of cocaine trafficking. Frankie didn't shoot the cabbie, but he tried.

"It's like a movie, Sammy. Or should I call you Frankie?" There were five different dates of birth listed on Frankie's rap sheet. "So how old are you now?"

"Frankie's forty. Sammy's only thirty-six."

"He thinks Samson is real," thought Tommy. It made a certain kind of sense. A false identity wasn't much good if you didn't believe in it. Frankie clearly thought that Samson was his better self, and he wanted Tommy to know that. True, Samson was Puerto Rican, and Frankie said of Puerto Ricans, "They give us Latins a bad name." But Samson was one of the good ones, better than Frankie, anyway. Frankie had been violent. Samson had never hurt anyone. Frankie had dealt large quantities of drugs. Samson just used them.

Tricks of the drug-dealing trade were mainly what Tommy wanted to hear about, of course, and Frankie was a wealth of information. They talked for two hours in Tommy's office that night.

Frankie savored the conversation for a long time. It may be that only a criminal can truly appreciate an honest cop. The fact that there were crooked ones, who would arrest drug dealers while dealing drugs themselves, the injustice of that, was enough to bring tears to Frankie's eyes. Later, Frankie would say of Tommy, "Oakie's, like, a Boy Scout. They only got like one Oakie in the whole New York department who's honest." Of course, he didn't know Tommy back on that night of his arrest. But he had an intuition that this was a cop he could trust. "He seemed, like, a reliable person," Frankie later explained. And the cop was interested in him, very interested. So Frankie talked freely. What did he have to lose? He withheld a few stories, but he told the detective all the details about how he'd managed to live so long as Samson and a great deal about his days of running cocaine from New York to Springfield. And he imparted some professional secrets. How, for example, he'd prepared large quantities of cocaine for transport in the bakery truck so that even police dogs couldn't find it—wrapping the drugs inside a plastic bag, putting that inside another filled with powdered detergent, then placing the whole inside a box of cookies. And the more he told, the more the cop wanted to

hear. For Frankie, it was like being a teacher, like talking professional to professional. The detective clearly understood the real
meaning of the stories. Frankie could tell that he appreciated
the way he'd duped both the federal agents and the Colombians. "I played double agent, heh heh." Later, remembering
that conversation, Frankie would say, "Oakie was happy, happy.
It was like he caught a *special* kind of fish."

Tommy walked Frankie to his cell. As he shut the clanging
door, the sound echoing in the tiny lockup, he said, "All right,
Frankie. Come and see me when you get out."

Frankie returned much sooner than Tommy had expected.
Frankie had faced eight separate charges, but for some reason
all the serious ones were dropped. Tommy never learned the
reason; Frankie didn't explain and Tommy thought it best not
to inquire.

Frankie had ambled up to the side door of the station and
asked to see O'Connor. He soon became Tommy's favorite rat.
Listening to Frankie's stories really was like going to the
movies, and so was skulking around with Frankie in backyards
and parking lots, Frankie playing what he liked to call "double
oh seven" just like James Bond.

Drug work by its nature encourages both corruption of the
old familiar kind, and also violations of the Bill of Rights. Even
conscientious cops sometimes cross the boundaries that the
Supreme Court sets. Some lawyers specializing in drug work
despised Tommy, but probably in part because his cases usually
survived their motions to suppress the evidence. Tommy didn't
find it hard to keep on the right side of current Fifth
Amendment rules. "You have a right not to be scammed? I
don't think that's what the Fifth Amendment says. You have a
right not to be stupid? I don't think that's what it says. It *does*
say you have a right to remain silent. But who's gonna remain
silent with his friend?" Getting inside drug lairs without
breaching the Fourth Amendment was trickier, but rarely

impossible. He'd part ways with Frankie in backstage North-ampton, in an alley or a parking lot; if they ran into each other on a sidewalk, they wouldn't even make eye contact. Then Tommy would walk up to the locked entry door of a rooming house and press four different doorbells at once. Invariably, one of the four would buzz him in. Then he'd go to the door of the apartment that Frankie had identified, and he'd knock as if he were a friend—"Dump-dump-dedump-dump. Dunt-dunt." Then he'd put his finger over the peephole.

One time Tommy put his ear against an apartment door and heard, just as Frankie had said he would, people smoking crack inside. It makes a distinctive chuffing sound. He couldn't remember who had taught him that. Probably Frankie. Tommy knocked on the door.

"Who's there?"

Tommy made a series of loud, unintelligible cries.

"Who the fuck is it?"

He made the same weird cries more loudly, and eventually the people inside got curious and opened up. He arrested all of them.

When the stakes were larger, and they were chasing substan-tial dealers, Frankie would make several controlled buys; Tommy, and the state detectives he worked with on large cases, would get a search warrant, then raid the dealer's home. Sometimes they staged the arrests in parking lots. Behind the bowling alley was a favorite site. Time and again, Tommy stood beside Frankie at pay phones downtown, listening in as Frankie talked to cocaine dealers. Making gigantic winks to Tommy, Frankie spoke into the phone in his normal tones, low and secretive: "Hey, you wanta come and meet me? My car ain't workin'. Alley Oops, the bowling alley. Yeah, it's just across the line." Frankie made a convincing buyer of drugs, naturally enough. He knew the region's dealers—not the most exalted, but bigger ones than Tommy had managed to find without him. He was remarkably daring and usually reliable. Tommy paid him small stipends and, what was always more difficult and never fully possible, tried to keep him out of trouble.

Frankie said his wife, Carmen, had three different personalities. One was kind and spiritual. Another, Frankie told Tommy, was quite lascivious. "She's into, like, neurotic dancing."

"Frankie, you're a beauty."

The third personality was the problem, Frankie said. She disliked men, and when the money for crack was gone she'd throw him out and make up lies about him. Frankie swore he never beat up any of the three, and Tommy came to believe that Carmen was at least an equal partner in their battles. These often concluded with Frankie in court.

One time she accused him of forcing her to have "kinky sex" on a wet mattress for eleven hours. The judge was an elderly man, one of the last, still-standing pillars of the local Yankee aristocracy, and he seemed a bit puzzled by Carmen's charges. Then he turned to Frankie, who denied everything.

"No wet mattress? No eleven hours?" asked the judge.

"I can't last that long, Your Honor," said Frankie earnestly. That time the judge dismissed the matter.

Frankie wouldn't give up Carmen, in spite of Tommy's arguments. Frankie would shake his head, describing the three of her. Then he'd say, "I'm not complaining. It's very exciting."

Crack and Carmen. Those two habits made Frankie what was called a high-maintenance rat. There was Frankie's mother, too—"Moms," Frankie called her. She often dialed Tommy's beeper number. She called Tommy "Toms." Over the phone, she seemed like a very nice and worried mother. One time Tommy sent Frankie into 96 Pleasant Street to buy some crack, and Frankie never came out. It turned out he'd bought some crack, all right, but had run into Carmen inside the building and they'd simply absconded with the drugs. A few nights later Moms called Tommy. She wanted to go on vacation, but Frankie was back on drugs and he had a key to her house. She had just bought a new TV and VCR and didn't want to lose them. Tommy told her, "Don't you worry. You go on your vacation. I have a place for Frankie to stay." There was an old outstanding warrant for Frankie's arrest, on a minor charge. Tommy hadn't bothered to execute it. A few days after Frankie's absconding and Moms's worried call, Tommy and the state drug cop he often worked with, his old friend Steve, spotted Frankie downtown and invited him into the cruiser. They were driving along chatting pleasantly as if nothing had happened, and then Tommy pulled out a set of handcuffs and held them out toward Frankie in the backseat. "Oh, by the way, Frankie, put these on." That was to teach Frankie a lesson, which never took entirely. Tommy recited the gist of it as Frankie obediently cuffed himself: "You don't fuck with *us*, Frankie."

Once—around Thanksgiving—Tommy was playing in the annual Turkey Day touch football game with a group of old high school friends, some who still lived in town, others who were home to visit family. He was rolling around on the muddy field by the Clarke School for the Deaf when his beeper went off. The screen read, "88. 911," which meant Frankie had to talk to him at once. Frankie wept over the phone. He was supposed to see his son today but he was in the courthouse lockup, about to be arraigned for supposedly kidnapping Carmen. He swore he hadn't done it.

Tommy left the game and headed for the courthouse. He felt a little embarrassed, walking up the stairs in a muddy sweat suit, a bandanna wrapped around his head, and, more than that, about to ask a judge to spring someone charged with a truly serious crime. He'd never done this before. It was crossing a line. But he just knew that Frankie hadn't kidnapped Carmen.

He walked in through the swinging doors of District Court and saw up on the judge's bench the familiar, small, black-robed, gray-bearded figure of Mike Ryan. This was a relief. Usually, it wasn't. Usually, when Tommy walked in to testify in a minor drug case and found Judge Ryan presiding, he could expect not rough, but disappointing treatment. Ryan would reduce the charges, invariably. Sometimes he'd declare Tommy's search illegal and throw the whole thing out. Tommy found ways to complain. He ran into Ryan on the street now and then. The judge would ask him what he was up to, and Tommy would smile and say, for instance, "Oh, not much, Your Honor. Haven't violated any constitutional rights yet. It's early, though." But Ryan would laugh. Tommy had to give him that. The judge had a good sense of humor. Tommy thought a judge ought to be more careful about the company he kept—a judge shouldn't be drinking in bars with defense attorneys, let alone a few stools away from ex-cons. But Tommy's father and Judge Ryan's had been friends. And Ryan was still Mike, approachable even in his robe, in a whispered conversation at the sidebar. Ryan didn't ask too many questions. He took Tommy's word and turned Frankie loose.

Tommy tried to rehabilitate Frankie. Countless times he tried to talk him into leaving Carmen. He helped to get Frankie enrolled in drug programs. He got him real day jobs in Northampton. And many times, after those efforts had failed again, he sprung Frankie from jail or got the charges against him reduced.

He helped Frankie, and Frankie helped him. The first time Tommy applied to be a sergeant, he was passed over, had a tantrum that lasted about a week, then went back to work. Shortly afterward, in the summer of 1994, he started the small case that eventually led to the seizure of two and a half tons of Colombian marijuana in New Hampshire. Big stuff for any drug cop, let alone a local one. Frankie had nothing to do with that case but a lot to do with Tommy's schooling and many smaller cases that were big by local standards. And it was partly because of those that Tommy had received two prizes in 1994: the Major John Regan Award as one of New England's most effective narcotics officers, and his promotion to sergeant.

• • •

Sometimes while working as the town's drug detective Tommy had felt cornered by futility, and wondered if he was doing anything besides creating statistics. According to the latest study, drug use in Northampton's schools was still rising. But then again, the study didn't say what the rate would be if no one were trying to enforce the drug laws. And once in a while someone he had busted stopped him on the street and thanked him. More often, he was thanked by wives of former addicts. They all seemed sincere. He'd never imagined that he could put a stop to drugs in town. But most of the time he'd been able to work wholeheartedly, just as if he could.

Anyway, he'd enjoyed the work, and, usually, Frankie. Tommy had left drug work now, and he hadn't seen Frankie in a while. Sometimes out on patrol on these late fall evenings, Tommy thought about him, and realized he missed him a little. The instructors at drug school had recited the maxim "A rat is a rat is a rat." Tommy figured that if worse came to worst, Frankie would turn on him, but he liked to imagine otherwise. "I take a liking to Frankie," he said. "Mind you, I wouldn't give him my home address." Frankie had been worth all the trouble. For him professionally, and for Northampton, Tommy thought. Frankie had helped him set up the arrests of dozens of users and small-time pushers and of at least eight substantial dealers with records full of mayhem, who had been sent away to state prison. Frankie was, certifiably, what Tommy called a bad guy. But he'd helped to rid the town of many who were worse.

"Frankie's done more for the drug wars in Northampton than anyone," Tommy said one night, telling old stories at the police station. "On both sides."

CHAPTER 7

Sanctuary

LAURA BAUMEISTER WAS a Smithie, an Ada Comstock Scholar, one of the students who matriculated as undergraduates in the midst of adult lives. Some were elderly and looked like grandmothers, carrying green bookbags instead of pocketbooks. Laura was in her twenties, slim, with strawberry-blond hair. Her good looks had unfortunately attracted the attention of a local stalker. A respectable-seeming man. She'd thought of him as just a friend. But soon he started calling her, more and more often. One day he called her thirty times. He said some terrible things. She called Smith College security. They called the local cops. As it happened, Tommy O'Connor was supervising patrol that afternoon.

These days when he went to a house or apartment it wasn't usually to look for drugs, but to sort out an argument. On an average of four out of every five days, domestic life somewhere in town turned into a "domestic." Once in a great while Tommy went to the apartment of a battered husband and maybe once every two years to the home of a battered lesbian. Recently, it was the house of a father and son, battered by each other— they sat bleeding quietly in the living room; they agreed they needed counseling. Usually, of course, the call came from a woman asking for protection from a man.

Domestics came in many varieties. There was the young woman with a bruised cheek, wet with tears. Tommy examined her face, then stared into her kitchen sink, and his eyes grew wide. "Who stabbed all these condoms?"

"I did."

"How come?"

" 'Cause I was mad at him."

"So you stabbed all the condoms?"

"Yeah! I'm not gonna go and cut someone. . . ."

"Yeah, good! That's good. Good for you."

If she'd swear out a complaint, he told her, they'd find her boyfriend and lock him up. Tommy looked at the condoms again, and he blushed, smiling. "Hang them on the wall."

She began to smile.

"We'll call this spermicide."

There was the weeping woman with a blackening eye and a baby in her arms. When her boyfriend saw handcuffs, he began to fight. Some boyfriends went on fighting even after having pepper spray squirted in their faces. Then bodies lurched around living rooms. That was the kind of domestic during which Tommy heard the sound of jangling hardware and creaking leather, like the sounds of wind and water to a sailor.

Some domestics were false alarms—a young couple sitting on a sofa in a book-lined living room, with tears streaming down their faces, the young woman explaining through her sobs, "We called a friend to come over, so we can stop yelling at each other."

And some were repeat performances. Tommy stood, wearing his fierce, implacable stare, in a living room he'd visited two weeks ago. That time the girlfriend had accused the boyfriend of pushing her around, and Tommy had locked the boyfriend up. This time the boyfriend claimed the girlfriend had abused him. She'd scratched him, he said, and he had the marks on his arm to prove it. Tommy stood between them now again, his arms folded on his chest, like the Colossus. He thought he'd like to leave them here to finish each other off, but then he had a better idea.

He said, "I'll tell you what, if I were you guys, you've done about as much as you can with this relationship. I'd call it quits. Now you're *both* goin' to jail."

Northampton was a town of many happy families, whom Tommy had never met. "No one ever calls and says, 'Hey, we're getting along great today!' " he said, as he drove away from the apartment complex in his mobile fortress. "It's just miserable stuff we deal with. And it's fun. It's not happening to me."

Tommy went to Laura Baumeister's apartment with Micker, one of the senior patrolmen. By policy, the supervising sergeant went along when one of his male officers had to call on a lone woman. In this case, Tommy was just a witness. Micker knew the routine, and for a change Tommy didn't do any of the talking. While Micker helped the young woman fill out a request for a restraining order, Tommy stood near the door of the apartment, looking around and listening.

The apartment was situated in an old Smith-owned building at the foot of Bedford Terrace, at the edge of the campus, at the edge of downtown. The furniture in the living room had the worn look of hand-me-downs, but the place was very tidy. Tommy listened, with habitual suspicion, to Laura's story about the telephone stalker. At length he thought he could tell that she wasn't lying. Besides, he knew the man in question, the worst kind of creep because he didn't look like one. He'd harassed other women. He was essentially a coward. Micker would serve the restraining order on him, and that would probably be enough to keep him from scaring this woman anymore.

An evening's patrol usually contained an assortment of brief events. Tommy dealt with local criminals again and again, but when he entered the life of a law-abiding citizen, he rarely stayed for more than a few minutes. Tommy left the apartment with Micker, and promptly forgot Laura's name. As he figured, her problem with the man was over.

Laura had come to Smith several years before. The stalker, as it happened, had been one of the least of her problems.

The mustard jar was empty. Laura stood at the kitchen stove and called to her son, Benjamin. Would he please go to the grocery store across the street and get some more?

The time of her son's independence would be coming soon, Laura knew. She hoped his revolution wouldn't be as long and hard as hers had been, and she hoped that when it came, she wouldn't feel like an old shoe being discarded. Maybe being in a new place, among strangers and without friends, had delayed the moment. Anyway, Benjamin was still in the compliant stage. Sure, he'd get some mustard, if she gave him some money. Laura was in a hurry. She had to get supper out of the way. She had a paper to write tonight. She looked around, and grabbed the booklet of food stamps. Then Benjamin told her he didn't want to go.

Only a few weeks before, Laura had stood in a checkout line at a grocery here, about to use food stamps for the first time in her life, and the moment she'd taken them out of her pocketbook she'd felt mortified. Suddenly, the place was full of eyes. Hurriedly, she handed the booklet to the cashier. The cashier said, in a weary voice, as if talking to a child, "*I* can't tear them out. *You* have to." As Laura fumbled with the things, she could hear noises coming from the woman in line behind her, a sniffing, then an angry-sounding clearing of the throat. So Laura should have understood how Benjamin felt. But she wasn't thinking clearly. She told him to knock it off, just go and get the mustard.

He came back with the wrong kind. It wasn't their favorite brand. It wasn't even honey mustard. She would be calm. Maybe the store didn't have the right one. Was that the problem? He wouldn't answer. He wouldn't look at her. He sat on the sofa with his arms folded across his chest and scowled at the wall. Then she raised her voice. Damn it! What was wrong now?

He started crying, angrily. He'd done what he was told to do! He had brought the right brand, their brand, up to the cashier, but when he'd handed her the food stamps, she'd suggested that he buy a less expensive kind. "I hate it here! I hate being poor!"

"We aren't poor! You can't be poor at Smith College! We're just broke!" Angry scenes played out in Laura's mind. She would go and confront the cashier. "How dare you!" she would say. She rattled pots and pans instead. Benjamin had enough troubles. He still insisted on dressing for school in his West Coast surfer shorts and Vans. Some of his new classmates called him the California kid, sarcastically. The other day she'd had to go to the school because he'd gotten in a fight, and he wasn't a fighter. She had saved and bought him a pair of hiking boots and some flannel shirts, but he refused to wear them. She had brought him here completely unprepared. Herself, too. It hadn't even occurred to her that in New England she'd need a winter coat.

They didn't talk much during dinner. Afterward she sat with him and watched TV, apologizing with her presence. That was more important than trying to write her paper. It might be different for a man, she thought, but a woman couldn't throw herself into anything wholeheartedly until she felt her family was secure. Besides, she didn't know how to write the paper.

The women at the Ada Comstock office had told her that most first-year Adas carried light academic loads. So she'd enrolled in just two courses. One was elementary math, designed especially for Adas. The first lesson was how to understand your phone bill. They'd gone far beyond that now, and she was barely getting by. She'd enrolled eagerly in her other course, English and Irish drama, her kind of subject. The class met in Seelye Hall, a venerable building of brick and stone. The closer Laura got to it, the more ominous it looked. She looked at it as little as possible. The ground was ordinary. The ground was safe to look at.

By now she knew all the cracks in the pavement between her apartment and Seelye Hall. If she caught a glimpse of a passing fellow student who gave her a quick smile, she would smile back. Then for a moment her face was lit by dimples. When the smile faded, you noticed that the little creases on her chin and along the left side of her mouth were actually small scars. Laura kept her hair cut fairly short and coiffed like the feathers of a dove. She wore wide glasses. They made her look innocent and fun-loving and amusingly confused. But she thought she looked out of place. She wanted to keep her face hidden because she thought that anyone who got a good look would see that she didn't belong here.

She sat in class and tried to listen. Very young women, students of traditional college age, said the most amazingly perceptive things. "In this play, I think we hear echoes of Joyce." She wished she could say something like that. This wasn't her, this person who sat so fearfully in class. She was a laugher and a talker. She couldn't think clearly about anything without talking. But if she opened her mouth, everyone would know how stupid she was. Also that she hadn't really done the reading.

She tried to read, up in her apartment, but her mind wandered. While she asked herself, "Have I done the right thing for Benjamin?" words on the page passed by like highway scenery, glimpsed, not seen. The longest paper she'd ever written, back in community college, was just a thousand words. The professor here assigned much longer ones, and expected her to write three of them this term. She made up an excuse and the professor gave her an extension on the first. She watched the other students turn in their papers, all printed on computers. Laura didn't own one. She didn't know how to use one. Smith had computer centers, and people at them who were paid to help you. She got as far as the doorway of a computer center, then turned away and walked home. Smith also had people who were hired to help you write your papers. All you had to do was ask. They had made it sound easy during orientation. But any fool knew that they probably kept track of the students who came in looking for help. And if they found out how much help she needed, they'd probably go to the Ada Comstock office and talk to the director, Mrs. Rothman. "There's an Ada who came to us for help the other day. She doesn't have a clue. Frankly, Mrs. Rothman, she doesn't belong here."

Laura had found it easy enough to write the application essays for Smith. Smith hadn't seemed real, it was so far away from Mendocino. She hadn't even known what state it was in. When her father had called her and said he'd seen a show on national TV about this special program for older women at Smith College, Laura had wondered, "Where is that? Is it near Harvard?" She knew about Harvard, from the movie *Love Story*. She asked around. Most people shrugged. "Smith?" But her favorite professor at the College of the Redwoods told her, "Laura, that is a very old and very prestigious women's college. And, Laura, this is something that you *need* to do." She got right to work on the application. Describing her life in a formal way made her feel as though another person had lived it. She wrote about her troubles as if she had put them all behind her. As she wrote, she started to believe this. One question on the form asked, "Why do you wish to enter Smith College?" Laura had her answer ready:

> There is an image that epitomizes my feeling for Smith. It is a picture of two women, one about fifty years old, and another, half her age. They are walking; their faces turn toward each other in expressions of genuine interest; their books are cradled confidently in their arms. They look like energetic, joyful women, sensitive and intelligent. Their feeling for one another seems to be one of mutual respect and caring. The discrepancy in their ages adds a special note of humanity to the simple portrait. It is

an appealing and encouraging characterization of what Smith
College means to me.

Actually, this was an accurate description of a photograph in
the Smith brochure. "That's so *cool*," Laura had thought, when
she'd seen it.

When she got her acceptance letter, some months later,
Laura jabbed the air, just like those football players whose
sport she feared and despised. *"Yes!"* She skipped around the
halls of the community college, telling everyone. Once the surprise wore off, a troubling thought crept up, like someone
whispering in her ear: "They made a mistake." But people at
Smith had to be very smart. They had to know what they were
doing. And then again, all her life people had somehow gotten
wrong impressions of her.

Laura remembered a school in a suburb of Portland,
Oregon, and the day in fifth grade when she was sitting at her
desk and saw her teacher walking toward her, carrying a brand-
new length of rope. She could still feel it. It was the soft, not the
scratchy, kind of rope. The teacher tied one end around Laura's
waist and knotted the other to the back of Laura's chair. She
remembered the heat and tightness in her cheeks and how
hard she made her jaw, as she sat there tied to her desk all that
endless day, repeating to herself, "I'm not going to cry." It was
many years before she could work up any sympathy for that
teacher. But now it seemed clear that the woman must have
been sorely tested to have done a thing like that. Laura thought
she must have been an impossibly unruly child.

Not everyone had misunderstood her. Her sixth-grade
teacher let her spend most of a school year sitting on the floor
in the library, reading. Laura read *every* book there. It was a
very small library. What she remembered best, though, was
years of school days during which she felt both antsy and
afraid.

It seemed as if, looking back, she'd awakened to the world

around her crib with insistent questions in her mind. In adult paraphrase, they ran: "Why are we here? What are we doing? Where are we going?" Soon they took the form of worries, attaching themselves to her mother. Her mother was a drunk. Laura still felt disrespectful saying that. Alcoholism was an illness, she believed. She preferred to say her mother had been sick, though when she did, she'd think, "It's true, but that's not why you say it."

Laura wasn't sure where she picked up the rudiments of religion. She hadn't been taken to church. But she lay in bed cutting deals with God. She'd be a good, good girl if He would make her mother stop drinking forever. She spent most days at school worrying about home, fidgeting in her chair, jumping to her feet when the pictures in her mind became alarming. She imagined dire tragedies, her infant brother suffocating in his crib while her mother lay dying in the wreckage of her car. And she couldn't sit still, unless the teacher roped her down. She made up excuses to go to the principal's office and call home. She listened, hardly breathing, for her mother's voice to answer. The way the voice whispered, "Hello," told Laura at once if her mother had been drinking. If the word was slurred, Laura spent the rest of the day like a caged wildcat around her desk, desperate to go home. If her mother sounded sober, she acted much the same, giddy with the residue of worry and relief.

Her mother would sober up. Laura would think her prayers were answered. Then she'd come home from school and see no lights on, hear no movement in the kitchen, and smell alcohol. It had become the smell of fear to her. She'd run to her brother's bedroom, then look for her mother, and usually find her passed out on her bed. She would take over her brother's care and feeding. She'd get her mother under the covers. As she grew older, she began to think, "I'm very good in a crisis." A dangerous thought for her, since she had also grown adept at creating crises of her own.

Laura got thrown out of three different high schools. She

remembered the last of the exit interviews—the premature ending of her time at a boarding school, a place she didn't want to leave.

"Laura, we're heartbroken. You have so much potential."

"What's the *big deal*?" she thought. "I'm not a criminal."

Forever, it seemed, people in authority had said to her, "We don't know what to do with you, Laura."

And she'd shown them her chin, while thinking, "I don't know what to do with me either."

She understood her mother now. The woman had been terrified when she'd seen her own costliest traits reemerging in her daughter. Their fights had never really ended until her mother's suicide. As a grown-up, Laura would tell friends and new acquaintances: "I was grounded from the time I was ten until I got pregnant."

She liked her last high school—a home for adolescent girls, in an Oregon farmhouse. But she turned up pregnant there, and a kindly woman told her she could have an abortion or leave the school and live as an adult. Laura became a mother at sixteen.

On Super Bowl Sunday, 1980, she was sitting at a bar with her child's father and some friends. She thought they were all having a good time, but evidently her drunk boyfriend imagined she was flirting with some other guy. She remembered seeing him stagger back from the men's room. Then everything went out of kilter. She was being pulled off her stool by the hair. He dragged her out to the sidewalk and punched her. She ran to the car. He got in, too, and really beat her up. She threw open the door and ran out into the middle of the street, waving her arms at oncoming cars. She still wondered why no one stopped. But she must have looked frightful—barefoot, her dress ripped, her hair wild. She ran away from him the next day, to Los Angeles.

When she thought back to her years of living alone with her young son, she felt she'd drawn more strength from him than he had found in her. From an early age, Benjamin had given her reassurances that he and she were different. He seemed to know things that she never had. The time, for example, when he was five and Laura's mother had just killed herself and, in something like terror, Laura turned to him in the backseat and asked, "Benjamin, do you have anyone you can talk to about your feelings?" He said, with great self-assurance, "I know about feelings, Mom. If you don't get them out, they stay inside and turn into monsters."

She thought she'd often been lucky. She got in a serious car wreck. The doctors at the L.A. County Hospital, to whom she was just a Jane Doe, could have done a much less careful, much less artistic job of repairing her face. She'd been a stranger to the women in the support group whose name she found in the phone book and called, asking for help, from a fleabag hotel in Portland. A different woman took her home every night and fed her, until her hands stopped shaking and she felt strong enough to live on her own again. An old Polish woman kept Benjamin during that time, until Laura could manage motherhood again.

For a while after she moved to Mendocino, Laura thought she'd found her place. From the classroom windows of the College of the Redwoods, she could watch the dark northern Pacific roll in. In Mendocino she was never far from the sound of the waves, and it was as if for once she'd found another soul to commune with, one as turbulent as her own. She got straight A's, except for a C-plus in psychology from a latter-day hippie professor. His usual commentary on the material was, "Oh wow!" She sat in the back of the room, making sarcastic remarks a little too loudly.

Mendocino had a white-steepled church, which Laura liked. She liked the town, but it was, as she began to see it, a place of newcomer artists and third-generation blue-collar workers, riven in two by competing philosophies—"Earth Firsters against millworkers," she said. Benjamin was happy. He was in love with baseball and music, and Little League baseball was run wisely there, and the school had a great chorus, which won statewide competitions. But she worried about his prospects. "I knew I didn't want him to work in the mills." And she had done all she could at the community college. She'd have to go elsewhere if she wanted to continue her education. She thought perhaps she wouldn't bother. She worked at a hospital as an admissions clerk, usually for the emergency room. She liked the drama of the ER. She liked the other clerks, especially an elderly woman who had worked there twenty-three years. That woman's retirement party was a turning point, one of the real answers to that question on the Smith application. Listening to the testimonials, Laura wondered, "How did she do it?" Laura didn't want to be a snob. She liked this woman. She respected her. But how could anyone settle happily for such a life? That sensation of not being present washed over her. The party went on but it had become her own retirement party, after thirty years as a clerk at an emergency room. A lot of her old friends had gone on to college. They were getting interesting jobs. She talked to some of them now and then, and she envied them.

So she left Mendocino, bound for Northampton, on a day late in August. She drove a small Chevrolet, a gift from an old man she'd helped take care of. After a few days on the interstates, she realized she was keeping company with several other cars, cars full of young men and women with college stickers like coats of arms on their rear windows, and she thought—it was a revelation to her—"This is something people *do*." Other people were driving east to college, as she was. People must do this every year. But the people in those other cars were young. They were doing something that they had either done before or had expected all their lives to do. She was a twenty-seven-year-old woman with an eleven-year-old son beside her, with a frying pan wedged under her seat and a housecat prowling the back.

They started the journey with $600. It seemed like enough,

but it was almost gone after four and a half days of gas and tolls and motel rooms. And what would she do when they got to Northampton? Her thoughts got away from her, gathering momentum in a frightening, familiar way. She and Benjamin would land in Northampton unable to afford even toilet paper!

Laura had cut herself off from her father and stepmother, but they'd reentered her life recently. Smith was their idea. They'd encouraged her to do this. At a rest stop near Baltimore, she went to a pay phone, out of sight of Benjamin, and called her father in Oregon. She wept into the phone. "I don't know how I'm going to buy toilet paper!" Her father told her that she had to trust herself and this enterprise. "But what if I can't buy toilet paper?" To say out loud how she felt was a relief, of course, but his consoling words changed nothing. She remembered a conversation they'd had many years ago, when he was driving her to junior high. "Why do you feel that way, Laura? You're pretty, you're smart." He'd meant well. He always did the best he could for her. But the words he'd intended as reassurance had only upset her more. If she was pretty and smart, then something really must be wrong with her, because she dreaded encounters with the junior high cheerleaders and wanted to cry when they called her Four Eyes. Now at the rest stop, after placing what her father would later christen "the toilet paper call," Laura knew she wasn't equipped for this great opportunity. Other people thought she was. So she still wasn't what she ought to be, and she was going to let them down.

In every place there are people too preoccupied to see what lies around them. They think it doesn't matter where they are, or that they should be somewhere else. But maybe the best refuges allow a person not to notice them.

The Smith campus is an arboretum designed by Frederick Law Olmsted, the genius behind Central Park. The place reminds you of an old and polished piece of silver. All but a couple of Smith's new buildings fit the old. Wood-framed ones had been left standing. There were gardens everywhere, and the whole place was a museum of trees. The little metal plaques on their trunks read like a catalogue from an emperor's far-flung holdings: London plane tree, Japanese snowbell, hop-hornbeam, dawn redwood, Japanese pagoda tree, Chinese fringe tree, Kentucky coffee tree, devil's walking-stick, Dahurian larch, California incense cedar, Tatarian maple, Amur cork tree. There were more than 150 different species. But Laura didn't see them, not individually. She didn't want to see them.

Smith's loveliest prospect is from the hill overlooking Paradise Pond. Huge hardwoods surround the still waters; a little island floats out in the middle. In the fall, the water reflects all the colors of autumn burning in the trees. Now the leaves were falling. Soon they would cover the pond. But Laura didn't go there. She walked straight to class and straight back to her apartment, dressed now in the parka that her father had kindly sent her, and more than ever she kept her eyes lowered. Her apartment had a bay window with a view—downtown's rooftops, the First Church's steeple, the turrets of city hall, the cupola on the ancient fire station, and behind them, rising up, the wooded slopes of the Holyoke Range. But Laura was used to the Cascades and Sierras. When she first heard someone call those hills out her window a range, she felt like laughing scornfully. She missed the huge dark ocean off Mendocino, and when she looked out her window, the memory of sea sounds made her weak all over. Everything here felt small and confined. "It's so *quaint*," she said sarcastically to herself, hating the place for having her in it, and for the downward tugging in her stomach, which, she thought, must be what "homesick" meant.

She knew she shouldn't feel this way. Back in California, after she'd gotten her acceptance letter, a lot of people had told her she wouldn't believe how beautiful fall was in New

England. Now she could see from her apartment windows that it was almost over. One day she set her jaw and told herself she had to get out into the countryside. "You're going to do this, Laura." She drove alone, without any plan, heading northwest into the foothills of the Berkshires.

In Northampton, the settlers built their houses close together and divided up the rich, flood-prone fields by the river. In the hills that Laura drove through, farmers had settled down beside their land, far from one another. Many of the fields and woods they'd cleared had returned to forest now. The beautiful old stone walls beside the roads made her wonder—all that abandoned labor. Every five or ten miles she'd come to a village center, a bunch of houses and a church, practically every building clapboarded and painted white. "*Cool*," she thought. She was smiling now, actually smiling. She was driving slowly through the outskirts of one of those old-timey places when she came upon a vision. It was real enough, and it was homely—yet another white clapboarded house, with a yard full of leaves, and out in front a woman raking.

The woman seemed ageless. "She could be anywhere from fifty to ninety," Laura thought. She didn't see her for long, but she told herself she was going to remember this picture: a woman in a man's old brown fedora and rubber knee-length boots, wielding her rake adroitly, neither hurrying nor slacking. Laura drove on, and imagined a life. "You can tell she's physically strong. She's also alone. She's, like, a solitary. This is what she does every year, at this time of year. It's one of the many jobs she does. Each season has a corresponding job, and so it's really *her* land. She's just so humble, and she looks perfectly peaceful out there raking her leaves." On the West Coast you didn't see women like her. "Everyone out there seems to be obsessed with how they look and what they have. They're always getting new things. That woman's hat and boots, they must be thirty years old, at least."

As she drove back to Northampton—a long drive; she was

lost on back roads for half of it—she thought, "I want that. That's what I'd like to be when I'm old. Like that woman." She said to herself, "Oh, I guess I'd really like to stay here in New England." Then she felt very sad, because it was probably too late.

She'd gotten by so far without being found out. She didn't have any midterm exams. Her English professor had granted her still more extensions on her papers, no questions asked. She was still squeaking by in math, and all the way up to Thanksgiving, she kept thinking she'd soon figure out how to write her English papers. But when classes resumed after the holiday, she didn't go to hers anymore. She told herself she'd been given one chance and she'd blown it. People had expected too much from her—her father and stepmother, her teachers back in Mendocino, the people at the Ada Comstock office. She couldn't face them. She retreated into her apartment. She stopped answering the phone.

A couple of long weeks passed before her so-called "big sister," the veteran Ada assigned to look out for her well-being, knocked on her apartment door.

"Go away. Leave me alone," Laura called through the door.

"No."

The knocking resumed.

After a while Laura opened the door. Her big sister said, "I'm taking you to see Ellie Rothman."

"No, you're not!" said Laura. Laura remembered the first time she'd met Mrs. Rothman. It was a very hot day and Mrs. Rothman, who was probably about sixty years old, was wearing a very fine-looking dress and nice jewelry and pumps, but no nylons, and Laura had thought, "That's just so cool." Mrs. Rothman would not maintain a rigid dignity at the expense of being sensible and comfortable. That was real dignity. Talk about a confident woman. Everyone referred to her as Ellie, but the last time Laura tried, she choked on the name and ended up saying "Mrs. Rothman." The woman looked you right in the eye. Laura imagined that she always knew what to say, and always said exactly what she thought.

"I'm too scared," Laura said.

"You *need* to go and talk to Ellie Rothman," the woman answered softly. If she'd yelled, Laura might have been able to refuse.

It seemed like a long walk, up Bedford Terrace and down Elm Street, past the art museum, which Laura hadn't visited, to a side entrance of College Hall. Windows set in lancet arches lend it an air of the sacred. The building came at Laura in a blur. Three flights of beautiful old creaking stairs led to the Ada Comstock office on the top floor. Entering, Laura noticed again the collages of photos of Adas on the walls. Those pictures had already upset her. All those women smiling. All those confident, happy faces.

Mrs. Rothman ushered her into her private office and closed the door. She said she wanted an account of Laura's academic progress.

"I haven't written any papers," Laura said.

"Do you have finals?"

"Two."

"Can you do this work, Laura?"

"Yes, I can, if I can get more extensions," Laura said. She sounded as if she meant it, and she thought she did.

"Ellie's so kind," Laura remembered. "She believed me. She said, 'Okay, you'll have the extensions. All you have to do is write the papers and show up for your finals.' "

As she left, all false smiles, it occurred to Laura that she had often put herself in impossible positions, and hadn't known what she was doing until it was too late. Walking back down the stairs, she figured that she'd just made everything worse. She had wanted to avoid another expulsion and had cut herself off from any help she might have gotten, by lying to a person who trusted her. She had missed too many math classes to catch up now. There was no way she could write three papers in the last week and a half of the term, and if she didn't write them, there would be no point in studying for exams, and no point in taking them.

Benjamin had gone to school, unhappily as usual. Laura sat by the window in the kitchen, smoking a cigarette and gazing out at nothing. She listened to the footfalls on the staircase just outside her kitchen door, the sound of other Adas passing. They were going to exams. Their footsteps sounded serious and sober. She didn't hear any voices. She was still sitting there two and a half hours later, when she heard much louder sounds outside. Her fellow Adas were returning. They were running up the stairs. She heard shouts and laughter through the door.

"I want to die," she thought.

"You have so much potential, Laura." "We don't know what to do with you, Laura." She would be asked to leave. That was what happened when you failed. She decided to withdraw gracefully. She called the Ada office and asked to speak to Mrs. Rothman. But Ellie was away. She wouldn't be back for a week, said the woman on the phone. She told Laura not to make any decisions until Ellie returned. Laura felt calmer. At least this ordeal was over. She spent that week planning to make plans. Then she found a letter in her mailbox, from Mrs. Rothman. It read:

I am puzzled and distressed by your failure to contact me on Friday 12/20. . . .

Because you did not call or come in, the extensions have been negated. You are therefore in a very difficult position. . . .

Please call to discuss this if I can clarify it for you, and good luck.

Again Laura trudged up to the imposing façade of College Hall. She trudged up the stairs to the Ada Comstock office and into Ellie Rothman's office. "I lied to you," Laura said, when

Ellie closed the door. "I was in your office a while ago, and if I'd been honest I'd have told you I knew I couldn't do the work. I didn't go to my finals."

"I know," said Ellie.

"I understand if you have to kick me out," said Laura.

Ellie raised her right hand, the palm facing Laura. "Wait a minute. You're going too fast. No one has said anything about that."

Ellie was businesslike. Laura listened in astonishment as Ellie took charge, saying, "If you give me your permission I will go before the Academic Board and plead your case."

If you screwed up in school, you got kicked out. "But she's saying that I'm someone worth helping," Laura thought. She had never felt quite this way before. She thought, "What I'm having is what James Joyce would call an epiphany." She looked at Ellie. "*Will* you help me?"

"Yes."

Laura started to cry.

Remembering that day, she said, "I didn't fling myself across her desk or anything." She cried quietly, and Ellie, looking at her sternly, said, "Laura, you are going to be on academic probation, and you're going to meet with me once a week."

This seemed like a brand-new, brilliant strategy. Even she could be a student one week at a time.

CHAPTER 8

Too Cold for Crime

Winter came early this year. On November 28 the police found a body near the railroad tracks behind the lumberyard on Pleasant Street, a very thin black man in layers of coats. He lay near a portable toilet, a "Sani-Can." To the cop at the scene it looked as though he'd lived in it. There was no question of foul play. He'd clearly died of exposure.

The man's name was Ben. He was a former mental patient. He'd come from the eastern part of the state, and had hung around Northampton for a couple of years. The town stirred at the news. Tommy had a little interest in the case. He used to see Ben on the nighttime winter streets downtown and call to him from the cruiser, "Hey, you want a ride to the cot shelter?" But Ben never accepted help from him. Local social service professionals called Ben another terrible example of someone who had "fallen through the cracks." It might have been more accurate to say that Ben walked out the door, but you knew what those people meant, and of course they were right. Northampton had more people on boards that worried about homelessness than it had beds for the homeless.

Some of the people who had known Ben a little, and others who felt his life should be marked, arranged a memorial service at the Unitarian church. A good-sized crowd attended, reporters included. At the service one of the speakers said of Ben, "He was such a sweet and gentle person." Another said he'd seen in Ben's eyes "softness and sweetness, an incredible love." Ben had changed his life, that speaker declared. A musician had composed a song. It was called "For Ben." Another eulogist said that while he and Ben had never actually talked, they had communed. "We spent a lot of time reading newspapers together in the laundromat. I miss him." Several people told the *Gazette* reporter that they used to buy Ben coffee.

Tommy read the newspaper accounts of the memorial service with mounting irritation. The reported speeches reminded him of Frankie, who often said that he meant well. "I'll put that on your tombstone," Tommy told him once.

The first substantial snowstorm hit early, too, on November 29, but Northampton's winter always arrived before the solstice, sometimes with snow and invariably with the unhoused taking desperate measures to get indoors. Old-timers remembered when the ancient county jail was situated near downtown, and how Sheriff Boyle, God rest his soul, used to run it like a shelter. A lot of reprobates made sure to get arrested at this time of year. Judge Ryan remembered, from his days as a probation officer, the autumn day when a judge tried to sentence a drunk to probation instead of jail. The drunk yelled at him, saying he was entitled to a sentence of ninety days. One night in late fall a few years ago, a man stole a bus and drove it to the police station on Center Street, so the cops would have no choice but to give him a bed for the night. And now, sure enough, one dark cold morning, Ron Hall's voice announced, with the pregnant pauses that had filled the morning air for going on forty years: Last night the glass in the front door of city hall was. Kicked in.

One of Tommy's officers found the culprit sitting on the steps of the Castle, evidently waiting to be arrested. He came from Peru. He didn't speak much English. Tommy told him that he could make his phone call. The young man tried to call his mother collect from the Booking Room, and she hung up on him. Tommy saw to it that Northampton treated him better, and gave him a bed for the night behind bars.

Notoriously, the holiday season spreads despair to people who feel they have nothing to celebrate. The Christmas season and the river often claimed a Northampton resident or two. This year, on a December afternoon, some people driving over the Coolidge Bridge saw a young man climb the railing and jump off, the body falling feet first toward the icy waters of the Connecticut. The lighted Christmas tree was moored out there again, on a float in the current south of the bridge. Christmas lights winked from evergreens beside ranch houses in the suburban neighborhoods. White lights made halos in the trees downtown and arches over Main Street, where a man from St. Kitts played yuletide tunes on his steel drum. The old place looked dressy and rather pleased with itself.

Early in the morning two days before Christmas, a van traveled through Northampton with a Santa Claus in the back, his head out the window, his white beard flowing in the wind like a dog's ears. He was bellowing and throwing candy canes. He threw one at a startled pedestrian—"Too much caffeine will make you jumpy, young lady! Merrr-eee Christmas!" He threw one at a jogger—"Merrr-eee Christmas, young man! I'll get you a skateboard!" He threw one at a mailman—"Oh, Charlie! You're a hardworking postal employee! Here's something to suck on!"

Inside the van, the lieutenant of detectives said, "Careful, Tommy, don't hurt yourself." Jean, who was sitting on Tommy's lap because the rest of the space was filled with presents, shook her head, cast her eyes upward, and smiled, a little wanly. She looked especially small on Tommy's knees. She had her hair pulled back in a ponytail, which made her look younger than thirty. Then again, when Jean was sixty, she'd still probably look young, and her eyes would still look serious.

"Everybody likes Santa Claus. If people knew it was me,

they'd flip me off," said Tommy. The startled pedestrians looked angry enough to do that anyway.

Earlier, while they were passing over the Coolidge Bridge to get the candy canes at the mall, the image of this year's river jumper and the floating Christmas tree out there in the frigid water conjoined in Tommy's mind. "The last Noel," he said, by way of acknowledging that the festive mood in town wasn't universal. His own was made of nervous hope. Jean might be pregnant. A couple of weeks ago the doctors in Boston had said the chances were only three in ten, but now the odds had risen. Jean had just told Tommy the news. The latest reading of her blood was "low positive," which meant she was precariously pregnant. Confident thoughts might jinx their chances, Tommy felt, and so might negative ones. So he had to entertain both. Underneath his beard and bellowings, Tommy was scared, Tommy was excited. High expectation and anxiety. He let it out on Northampton. He was a public nuisance for a morning.

They passed a pedestrian with a stogie in his mouth. "Merrr-eee Christmas, Harold! You should give up those cigars!"

They passed a well-known drug dealer. Tommy tossed a candy cane at him, and called back as the van sped on, "Merr-eeee Christmas, Johnny! I've been checking my list and I'm checking it again right now! Ho ho ho! Merrr-eee Christmas!"

Every Christmas he dressed as Santa and distributed some of the presents that local charity assembled for poor children. One year, up at Florence Heights, the door to a unit opened and before him stood a man he'd been trying to find for weeks. Tommy had pulled off Santa's beard. "Ho, ho, ho," he said.

"Oh, shit!" said the wanted man.

He and Jean spent the morning carrying gifts to the children inside the apartments at Hampshire Heights. This year he made no arrests.

Jean's face lit up at moments, when the children screeched in the crepuscular doorways at the sight of burly Santa and the presents, Tom bellowing out his "Ho, ho, ho!" But she was generally withdrawn, as if listening to other voices and not liking what she heard.

Tommy met Jean when he was still molting adolescence. He saw her at a party, he liked the look of her, and he showed it by making a hostile remark as she was leaving: "Hey, little English girl, where you goin'?" She walked off haughtily, saying it was none of his business. He thought she was stuck-up. Some people still made the same mistake. Jean could seem severe and full of disapproval. Sometimes she seemed shy. It took a while to get to know her, because actually she was reserved, which came with being a Yankee, Tommy supposed. The first time she had dinner at the O'Connor house she'd been shocked into silence and indigestion. Six kids all trying to talk at once, all arguing with what seemed like great intensity. She'd felt in triple exile. "I was English, Protestant, and from a Republican family. But, I did the dishes."

Jean's fantasy of true delight, she once told Tommy, would be to jump out of the basket of a hot-air balloon, free-fall with a bungee cord tied around her ankle, then parachute to earth. She looked back with nostalgia at her years as the daughter of farmers. "I wouldn't trade it for anything now," she said. But she hadn't forgotten the hard side of that life. In the era of her childhood, New England hill farms had grown scarce. The ones that remained had to struggle for survival. Her family couldn't get away for a vacation. For Jean downtown Northampton was far away, as Florence was for Tommy. The difference was that Jean came to adulthood yearning for travel.

It seemed like a long time ago when they first started trying to have children. After a year or two with no result they'd started talking about adoption. Tommy kept running into candidates. He found a man and woman smoking crack in a Northampton motel room while the woman's baby lay on the bed, its bottle empty, its diaper unchanged for at least a day. He arrested the man and got the woman into a rehabilitation program. She got cleaned up and then relapsed and asked him if he'd take the baby for a month or so. But Jean said she could imagine the moment when they'd have to give the baby up. She wanted one for keeps. Then there was Felix, the handsome little Puerto Rican boy who used to get in trouble just so he could hang out at the station. Tommy would look at him sitting on the wooden bench outside the Booking Room, swinging his feet from side to side, and he could imagine Felix his son. Also the child named Brownie, whose mother was addicted to crack; Brownie used to steal bikes that were much too big for him to ride, so that the cops would pay attention to him. They seemed to be the only adults who did. Tommy looked at him and thought, "I should take you home." But he didn't act, and now he thought it was just as well. Little Felix had grown up to join a gang. Recently he'd turned state's evidence in some nasty shootings. And Brownie had gotten arrested elsewhere for molesting a child. Maybe they'd already been damaged when he met them, maybe irreparably, Tommy thought.

Jean thought they should adopt a Chinese girl. She talked to him about the plight of baby girls in China. Tommy had been getting comfortable with that idea, gazing at Asian children on his rounds, when, on a winter night in 1993, he was called to a unit at the Meadowbrook apartment complex. The largest cop on hand kicked in the apartment's door, the others spread out through the rooms of the apartment, and Tommy headed for the bedroom. He looked in from the doorway and for a moment he froze. A woman and a child with Asian features lay on the rug at the foot of the bed. Both were covered with bloody wounds, dozens of them. A wooden-handled steak knife stuck out of the young woman's cheek, below her right eye. It was buried to the hilt.

That case was easily solved. The woman's common-law spouse and the child's father, a man named Sean Seabrooks, confessed that he had hacked both of them to death in the midst of an argument about child support and baked potatoes. In the aftermath, several of the officers who had been at the scene said it left them deeply troubled. Rick was one of them. He had brought up Seabrooks again when he'd talked to Tommy about the reasons for his drinking problem. Tommy accepted this. The other cops' feelings belonged to them. Tommy assumed they were genuine. He had tried to describe his own to a reporter shortly after the murders. "There's no training, no preparing yourself for the worst, that can prepare you to see what I saw," he was quoted as saying. "It doesn't go away after you get off shift. It's times like this when you wish you'd become a teacher." The words looked wrong when he read them in the paper, not inaccurate, but a little self-serving, as if he were trying to take something for himself that rightfully belonged to the victims and their relatives. He still regretted saying that much. Out in the air, some thoughts spoiled. They also became vulnerable, out where other people could mess around with them. When others told him how he must have felt, he thought, "Sure, it had an effect on me, but it's not the one they want to make it." He didn't talk much about the case again, until he testified at the trial. He got some satisfaction from helping to send Seabrooks off to Walpole for life without parole. "If there was a door to hell, I'd gladly push him through."

Tommy would say about that case, "If you work at a grocery and the fruit spoils, you deal with it. It's part of the job. You do your job. You deal with it." But inadvertently he ensured that the case would invade his private life. By law, a detective had to attend a murder victim's autopsy. Tommy volunteered to attend the child's. Volunteering was a habit, formed during his Police Explorer days. Besides, all the other detectives had children of their own. He figured the postmortem wouldn't bother him as much. So he ended up standing, in gown and rubber gloves, inside the grubby little abattoir in West Springfield, staring down at the waxen face of a cute little boy with slightly slanting eyes.

Jean worried about Tommy out on duty, and never more than during the aftermath of the Seabrooks case. "Not that he won't come home," she said. "But his seeing too much of things." He wouldn't have thought that possible himself; ever since he was a boy he'd imagined himself dealing with nefariousness. But he rarely forgot a face once he had seen it. Faces just accumulated, like stuff in a garage. A day, maybe two after the autopsy, he drove through one of Northampton's housing projects, he saw an Asian child walking with its mother on the sidewalk, and on the instant he was looking at the image of the Seabrooks baby, laid out on a steel table, blood blossoming under the coroner's knife, superimposed on the living child. This kept on happening. He lay awake many nights with the lights on. He didn't talk about his nightmares to anyone but Jean. He was afraid they sounded like the invented stories he sometimes heard from arrestees, the ones who claimed to have flashbacks from Vietnam, even though they'd been in diapers when that war had ended. Jean remembered, "I was afraid he'd crawl into a little shell and never come out." She worked on him until she got him to shed some therapeutic tears. But when she brought up the idea of adopting a Chinese girl again, Tommy said he couldn't, just couldn't, adopt an Asian baby.

They had turned to technology. The doctors couldn't find anything wrong enough with Jean to account for infertility. Tommy got checked, too.

Superstitiousness asserted itself. He imagined he was being punished for a sin he had forgotten. Or maybe all the hours he used to spend running a radar gun had left him sterile—the motorists' revenge. He sat in the gynecologist's waiting room, surrounded by pregnant women. He knew half of them from high school, and they knew him, of course. They smiled at him and went back to their magazines, and then they all must have looked up again—he felt the weight of many eyes behind him—when the receptionist called out in a loud voice, "Tom O'Connor for a sperm-washing."

He went to the counter quickly. Maybe she'd lower her voice if he stood close to her. But she didn't.

"Mr. O'Connor, you didn't put down when this sperm was produced."

She might as well have gone around the room and whispered to all the pregnant ladies, "Do you know what Tom O'Connor did in the bathroom just a while ago?"

He stared at her. Then he looked at his watch. "Oh, about five minutes ago, ma'am."

He wasn't sterile, it turned out. He almost wished he were. Then at least he and Jean would know the cause.

They continued with technology. High, then higher, and now, for the past year, highest—trips to Boston, more Latinate terms, and shots that Tommy had to give Jean in the butt. A heroin addict would have been better prepared for this, he thought. He didn't know anything about hypodermic needles. The first time he used one, upstairs in their house, he accidentally blunted the tip. Jean yelped, and, without thinking, reverting to one of his boyhood means of self-mortification, Tommy ran out of the room and down to the kitchen. He cowered in a corner, until Jean came looking for him and he had recovered enough to wonder at the strangeness in himself. Frankie might have understood. But if the psychotic tough guy who had told a rat of his, "I don't mess wit' O'Connor. He's a *wrangler*," or any of the homeboys, felons, and drug dealers who thought the same, could have seen him then, hiding in a corner because he had inadvertently inflicted a little pain on a woman . . .

Unlike some colleagues' wives, Jean had never asked him to work the day shift. She knew he hated Days. They tended to be dull, he disliked the lieutenant usually on duty then, and the shift had several cops who seemed to have gone, whining, into on-the-job retirement. "Boy, Jean's tough," Tommy often said. And this was truer than he knew. He figured she had to be lonely, in their house at night with only their dog, Murphy, for company. But he didn't know how lonely, because she didn't tell him. She'd only said she'd rather he worked Evenings than Midnights, because at least on Evenings he got to see some people who were normal. And she never complained about the trips to Boston or the surgical procedures or the hormone shots.

Because of their mismatched schedules, he often had to give her the shots at the police station. He'd find an empty room with a door that locked, always a shabby-looking room, because those were the only kind the station had. It was more humiliating for her than for him, the open surreptitiousness of the procedure, the backseat-of-a-Chevy air it had about it. Through the window in the station's side door, he'd see her walking toward him, carrying her little bag with the needle and the drugs in it, like a toy doctor's bag. If she'd asked him to sign up for Days, he probably would have then.

Jean loved Christmas. The other day she dressed up the dog in his Christmas necktie and took him to the mall in Hadley, where Murphy sat on the lap of a department-store Santa. As usual, she had their house decked out with ornaments and lights and figurines and a toy New England village, cottony white cloth representing snow. The only thing missing was a child to enjoy it. They held the O'Connor Christmas party at their house this year, the usual raucous affair. Tommy had a fine time. He always did. After everyone went home, Jean told him she'd miscarried. She'd mourned the death inside her silently, because she hadn't wanted to spoil the party.

As usual, Tommy tried to hide his disappointment and to cheer her up. He got control of his face, put on his wild, grinning look, and said, "Hey, you've still got some eggs in Boston, right? Think we oughta send 'em Christmas cards?"

Once when they were dating, he made her laugh so hard she sprained her stomach muscles. But as Rusty Luce once said, "O'Connor can wear ya out. He can." This time Jean said to him, "Don't make a joke out of everything. Just let me get through this."

• • •

Tommy wanted a child, ardently. He also felt he was expected to have one. He'd begun hearing that message from other cops years ago. He'd let it drop around the station that he and Jean were trying to have a kid, and after a while some of his colleagues started in on him. "Hey, Tom, want me to give it a try?" Cop humor. He had to smile through it. At one point Rick jumped in: "Hey, Tom, we'll pass a cup around the station." He couldn't always count on Rick when other people were around, but when they were alone, and they got serious the way they had as boys, discussing the adult world while making models years ago, Rick asked him why he and Jean didn't see a fertility expert. Rick and his wife had, and look how well it had worked.

He'd told Rick that they were seeing more fertility experts than he could count. Right away Rick had apologized. He was an anxious person, just as Tommy was. Tommy simply covered up with more congeniality. But Rick wasn't cruel. He'd been completely sympathetic since that time when Tommy let his anger show.

All but one couple among their married friends had children now. While their friends' kids were small, not much changed. But eventually, the kids got into sports and dancing lessons and their parents spent more and more time driving them around, and through the children they met other parents, and soon their social lives were entirely organized around the kids. Jean's best friend confessed that the last time she'd gotten pregnant she hadn't wanted to tell Jean. At parties where all the others talked about their children, Tommy and Jean would end up talking to each other. She felt defective, without having done anything to deserve it. He'd bring home stories of women who spent their pregnancies smoking and drinking, even taking drugs, and then gave birth successfully. She didn't drink while trying to get pregnant. She even gave up coffee, which she missed much more than alcohol. It all seemed so unfair.

More and more often, jaw-flexing anger seized Tommy when couples at parties started telling cute stories about their babies, when he ran into old acquaintances back in town to visit family and they asked him how many kids he had. Then sometimes he'd think, "Is that the only accomplishment in society? Having a kid? I got the Major John Regan Narcotics Investigator Award. Did you?" Reunions and the stories told by people who had moved away made him envious. Family was the best of all his reasons for having stayed at home. Without a child, he felt the weight of all he might have done. Everywhere around him in Northampton, people he'd known for years were moving on in life. Now in the winter, in the aftermath of Jean's miscarriage, he felt as though he'd come to a dead halt.

One afternoon Tommy swung the cruiser into Hampshire Heights, with his window down and the heater on. A girl he knew slightly came up to his window. He got out to talk to her. She wore a winter coat, so he couldn't tell that she was pregnant until she said, "Guess what!" and spilled the news.

"How old are you?" asked Tommy.

"I'm thirteen."

"What are you doing for your kid?"

"I got these pills from the clinic."

She handed him the pill bottle. He looked at it and handed it back. "That's good."

Then she lit up a cigarette. He snatched it out of her mouth and ground it under his boot. "Don't be smoking!" She cowered at his stare.

Tommy drove away, muttering. "I'll go out on a limb and say that I think our population of idiots has increased. And a young kid like that. It really irritates me." Then his voice grew quiet, musing: "Kids having kids, and we can't seem to have one."

For years commonplace encounters like that had seemed designed to cut Tommy. On winter evenings now, they seemed sharper, as if the town itself were reproaching him. It wasn't possible for Tommy to go through a whole shift feeling dour. But he was beginning to wonder if he was obsessed. He kept gazing at small children and imagining them his own. If one of them were, he'd dig in that trunk at home and watch the kid grin when he pulled out the wig and mustache. When the boy—a tomboy would be acceptable, too—was old enough, he'd show him the old neighborhood, all the backyard spots, the path down by the Mill River, the old hiding places on the Smith campus, White Rock across from the defunct state hospital. They'd walk up to the kitchen door of his father's house, and he'd say, "Grandpa and his friends did some pretty goofy things. Ask him. I'm pretty sure he'll tell you all about them." He and Jean would save up. They'd make sure their child had the opportunity to go away to college.

Being full of his own childhood, the winter landscape became the playground of his absent child. Less often now, but occasionally, he stopped at a favorite spot and reminisced—at the foot of Hospital Hill, for instance. He looked at it through the side window of the cruiser. The sledders had gone home. The steep white hillside lay in shadows. But he'd bet he could still find the spot where he and his friends used to build their toboggan jump, voices hooting and hollering, toboggans flying. They'd land in heaps in the snow. The only things cold were his ears.

Tommy remembered playing out there on many winter days. Who would have been with him? he wondered. He started a list: Morker, Ethan, Bobby, Lisa, maybe Jimmy—Jimmy was probably one of their gang by then. And who else? "Oh, yeah. And Rick." He turned away, put the cruiser in gear, and drove off.

He and Jean had decided to try again next spring. It seemed as if he'd been waiting forever to become a father and a real adult. He wished he didn't have to wait to be installed as detective sergeant, which would be some kind of change at least. But it didn't seem as if he had much choice except to wait some more. He'd just have to clear his mind of everything that shouldn't be in it, and hope some bad guys acted up.

"Goo-ood morning. This is. Ron Hall. It's twenty-two degrees. Russ Murley is. Here! With the forecast." There was snow in it again.

Tropical air full of moisture comes up from the south, while cold masses descend from Canada. They meet over New England, and in some winters produce a sequence of snowstorms. Northampton was built for this. The town in a winter without snow was like the tropics without palm trees. The place never looked cozier than when everyone was booted and bundled up and the residents looked more alike than not and all had something in common to discuss at the post office, the barbershops, the ubiquitous hair salons. It was not too far-fetched to imagine that in the town's most private places, Northampton's many psychologists and their patients took a moment off from therapy, that most self-regarding of pursuits, to talk about the weather. Settled under snow, Northampton looked united, simplified, full of fellow feeling.

On a street near the college, inside his ancestral home, Judge Ryan lay in his sickbed, and stared out the window. On a day earlier this winter, he had been presiding over district trial court. A jury had just filed in, and as usual he had begun to stand, in order to greet them. The next thing he knew his head was lying on the bench, and he was listening to worried voices around him.

He'd had the precursor of a heart attack. He was operated on in Boston, in a novel procedure, much less intrusive than the usual bypass. The news had made the local papers, and even *The Boston Globe*, which had described his operation in great detail. So the judge's friends, who were legion, knew what had happened. He was spending a lot of his recuperation answering the phone. The doctors had taken out one of his ribs. For a couple of weeks now he'd been telling well-wishers over the phone that he might become a scientific—if not biblical—puzzle for the future, if some anthropologist dug up his body.

The judge was only forty-nine. He was mending well and quickly, but, lying alone in his house, he had long thoughts. He'd imagined that he would live here in Northampton to the ripe old age of eighty-three, just as his father had. Now he wondered. He gazed out the window at the falling snow.

Inside the police station, Tommy came up the stairs from the locker room in a leather jacket and a furry black hat. He looked like a Russian commissar. "Okay, it's dat time, men," he announced. He paused a moment to model his hat for the patrol officers in the Ready Room. "You know what's good about storms like this? They make everybody friendly. It's something everybody's got in common," he said, and added, for the benefit of his officers, "I don't know why anybody would stay in the station in a storm like this." He stopped on his way out to hold open the door to the parking lot for a man who had spent the night in jail in protective custody and was being released. Evidently, he hadn't fully sobered up. He staggered past Tommy, out into the snow. "And good luck to you, young man," said Tommy. He whistled a snatch of a tune as he cleaned snow off the supervisor's cruiser. When he climbed inside, the radio dispatcher was announcing an accident on Pleasant Street. Downtown was a muddle through the openings the windshield wipers made, a white construction site, storekeepers shoveling, the city's big road grader bumping and rumbling up and down Main Street.

Some time ago Tommy had begun to notice a recurring pattern. He would be out on patrol, a remembered face would swim into his mind's eye, and just moments later he would encounter that face in fact. This gave him an eerie feeling, as if he had been singled out for clairvoyance. Then again, he rarely forgot faces and there were only so many in town. Ones in his mind were bound to match up with ones on the streets now and then. Not so often downtown, though. "Downtown isn't used by natives much. I can work Downtown and not worry about stopping an old friend," he was saying as he pulled up to the accident.

A little Japanese car with its front end mangled sat at the curb. It was pointed south on Pleasant Street, toward the road to Holyoke. Pieces of bumper lay in the snow. Tommy waded up, opened the driver's door, and his eyes widened. *"Jackie?"* he said.

A vast distance separates a teenage boy and a beautiful girl a year or two older. It makes the boy wonder if he'll ever grow up. Her face was still unravaged, beneath the blood around her mouth and nose. But her tongue was thick. So was the smell of alcohol inside the car. A man sat next to her, another familiar face.

"Get Sergeant Tommy O'Connor down here *right now,*" said the man. He slurred the words.

It was one of his old rats. Tommy leaned around the woman and snarled at him. "You must be cocked, because you're looking at him, you idiot. Shut up."

This kind of incident often devolved into scenes reminiscent of junior high, with pupils dressed in adult bodies. The erstwhile narcotics informant standing unsteadily in a snowdrift on the sidewalk, crying out, "I'll take all the blame! 'Cause I'm no good!" Tommy directing traffic around the wreck, yelling over his shoulder, "Get back in the car!" The rat picking up a piece of bumper, holding it as if it were a knife, glaring at Tommy, who noticed, of course, and turned around and stared.

The rat dropped the piece of metal, and started wailing again. "Leave her alone! Take *me* in, 'cause I'm no good!"

When a patrolman arrived, Tommy extracted his high school classmate from the driver's seat. She used to be a runner. He remembered her in gym clothes, her long and shapely legs. She was too drunk to stand on them right now. He rarely put suspects in his cruiser without cuffing their hands behind their backs. But he didn't cuff this old friend of his youth. He took her by the arm as if she were an old woman, and put her in the cruiser, then drove back toward the station through the snow.

"How'd you hook up with *him*?"

"Jesus fucking Christ." She was weeping. "Because my husband's beating me."

"How'd you make friends with *him*?"

"Through AA."

"Through AA." He made a face. "That didn't work too well, did it? Were you taking him to Holyoke?"

"He's like a really hard person to deal with."

"Oh, Jackie, a lot of changes in eleven, twelve, fourteen years, huh?"

"I know." She put her face in her hands. "I was married to a transvestite."

"What?" Silence, except for her sobbing. Any other noise was preferable. "Sounds like you could end up where you are just from the stress of it."

He led her toward the side door, then turned her so she faced him. "You were on your way to Holyoke for him."

She nodded.

"So he could pick up a couple vials of crack, I have no doubt. He played you like a fiddle, Jackie."

A couple of patrol officers took over, one of them a woman. A moment later the patrolman poked his head out of the door of the Booking Room. "Tommy, good search," he said sardonically. "We just pulled a razor out of her coat."

Tommy sat down in the Report Room. "I couldn't even give her a field sobriety test." He put the drunk-driving form into the typewriter. "We could lose this case. I don't care if we do." Another native casualty, another from his high school years.

But a good priest believes in hope. He began to type. "Maybe we could get her some help."

It was snowing again, a blizzard, and the wind whistled through the opening Tommy left in the cruiser's side window, like breath across a bottle top. He parked beside Augie's rooming house downtown. One of the patrolmen stood in the doorway waiting for Tommy. The manager had called the cops to demand that they roust a pair of legendary local drunks, trespassers in a tenant's room. "If they're cocked, we could PC 'em," Tommy told the younger cop. "It'd be a nice thing to do for 'em." He snapped his fingers. "Hey, what's his name? Ben. I hear his Sani-Can is up for rent. Great thing everybody bought him coffee so he could live high on the hog. Why isn't anybody worrying about Joe and Michelle? They're still alive."

Joe and Michelle were sitting on the wooden floor of a room under a bare lightbulb. Michelle had a girlish face and dead-looking teeth. She said, in her liquor-thickened voice, "Hey, Tommy, I got a joke for you. It's really terrible. What did the duck say to the waiter? 'Just put it on my bill.' "

Tommy smiled. "Okay, you've been trespassed," he said and left them there.

"Love through the bottom of a bottle," said Tommy when he got outside. "We did our job," he explained to the young patrolman. "We told them to leave, but we left first. What the hell's the point of throwing them out in this shit?"

It was getting dark. Tommy was driving through snowdrifts, chortling, when the dispatcher called. A teenage boy had been playing football with friends at the Meadowbrook apartment complex. The boy had fallen down and wasn't breathing. Tommy grimaced. He had no good memories of incidents like this. The cruiser's siren sounded muffled in the falling snow. The car seemed afloat, drifting sideways around corners. He managed to take a sip of his coffee. "Something to throw up when he pukes in my mouth." It was a white-and-black scene in the twilight, a crowd looking on, silent, except for the mother. Tommy moved her away, while she screamed in Spanish over his shoulder. An off-duty cop, who'd happened to be driving by when the call came in, crouched over a small, quiet, supine figure. Tommy ran back through the drifts in loping strides and took a turn, kneeling down, rocking back and forth, compressing the boy's chest. Then the medical technicians took over with machines. "Tom, get the suction, the board, and the stretcher." And soon, with methodical haste, the cops and technicians were wading toward the ambulance, carrying the stretcher. They looked like pallbearers, but the boy was breathing again.

In the cruiser, driving slowly toward the hospital, Tommy beat his hand on the steering wheel. "That's what it's all about! That's all of it! I'm all for go out and catch the bad guys, but if you can save a life!"

He stood in the hall outside the emergency room, his face flushed, chatting with the emergency technicians. Their faces were flushed, too. One said, "If it works, it's my first time."

"When I worked Midnights, they called me the angel of death," said Tommy. He turned to shake hands with the head technician.

A nurse came out. "Nice for a change, huh?" she said.

"Hey, now I'm one for twenty-one!" said Tommy. He stopped in the waiting room, where the parents were sitting. He hadn't paid much attention in high school Spanish class, but he knew a few phrases. *"Buena suerte."*

"Gracias."

He drove toward Forbes Avenue for his forty. A lone figure waded through the snow, down the sidewalk near his father's house, a scanner buff, one of those who liked to listen to police calls. "Wannabes," some other cops called those people, but occasionally they were useful. "Besides," Tommy said, "I wannabe, too." He stopped and rolled down the window. "Did you hear that call? No? It was a good one."

"Hey, Dad, a fourteen-year-old kid playing football in the snow." Tommy stamped his feet on the mat inside the kitchen door. "He dropped. He was dead and he's up at the ER now, and he's doing well. I'm one for twenty-one."

Bill was puttering in the kitchen. He smiled. "Really, Tom? That's good, huh? That's very good."

They sat down to supper, and Bill began. Perhaps tonight he took his cue from the story Tommy brought in from the storm, but it was impossible to know. Bill might have been answering a question that Tommy had asked him decades ago, a question like, "Dad, how come I'm superstitious?"

"But you know my mother got very nervous if a bird landed on the windowsill," Bill said. " 'Mom, what are you so upset about a bird for?' " Bill's voice slid into an Irish lilt, like his mother's. " 'What's the matter with you? Don't you know it's *death*?' My mother never dodged a question. 'Mom, I saw shadows behind the windows of the Polish church.' " He did her voice again: " 'Oh, yes, yes. That's the priest who died two years ago, that's who that is. He's comin' back to say mass. Now, Billy, what that is, that priest had so many masses to say and they gave him so much money to say them he *has* to come back.' "

There was an old-world quality about the elderly man, an elegant detachment. He seemed to stand looking back at the land of irreversible time, calm and amused. He rarely took a direct route, but he never rambled. He always seemed to know where his thoughts were heading, and he was the only one who did, until he reached familiar ground. Bill sighed. He said he'd been remembering his own mother's passing.

"The ice cream headache, right?" said Tommy. And he laughed softly.

"Yes," said Bill. "She said, 'Oh, it's nothing but an ice cream headache, Billy.' It was a hot day. 'I'll get you a cold drink, Billy.' She poured the soda on the table."

The walls around the kitchen were like a family photograph

album. In them you could follow the ontogeny of Tommy. It was just as Jean said. Sitting beside his father, he did look like the fresh-faced, smiling boy of ten or so on the wall. Except for the lack of hair and the fact that the boy in the picture was still surrounded by immortality. Boys of ten don't stare at their fathers so intently, lips moving slightly, as if silently reciting.

"The next day I was waiting for the doctor to come," Bill went on. "Two Irish ladies knocked at the door. 'Billy, we heard your mother's sick. Can we go in and see her?' I sat in the rocking chair, thinking, thinking. They came out and the two of them t'rew their arms around me. 'Don't you worry, Billy. She's gonna be all right.' Then they went out. I went to the screen door and they were going down the stairs. I heard one of them say, 'Where do ya think she'll be waked? Hulbert's or John B. Shea's?' Well, I went back in the bedroom. I sat down next to my mother. 'God, I wish I could wake you up,' I said. 'You would enjoy this one *so much*.' "

Tommy plowed slowly down Elm Street toward the station through the snow. "I try to remember some of the stories, in case something happens. So if, knock on wood, Jean and I ever have kids I can tell them who their grandfather was." It had been a boy's night on Evenings. He planned to nominate everyone involved for lifesaving citations. "I was looking forward to coming in tonight. On a night like this, there's nobody else out. You see what nobody else does." He jerked the wheel to the left and put the cruiser in a half spin on the empty, snowbound avenue. "Plus you get to slip and slide around in this stuff."

Mrs. Levi Shepherd, née Mary Pomeroy, the daughter of the town's most famous Revolutionary War hero, wrote of her sixty-first winter, the winter of 1804: "The snows have often been repeated . . . and at this day, the snow is 4 feet deep, where there has been no travelling." Northampton had seen many snowy winters. This had already become one of the snowiest.

Frankie was in winter storage, back in jail for violating one of his many probations. The longer Frankie's record got the harder it was to disentangle him from the system. Tommy had tried to help this time, but only a little. He had to set a limit. Dealing with Frankie, he had to remind himself which team he played for, since Frankie played for all of them.

Sunsets came early when they came at all. Many gray afternoons simply faded into black. The wind blew over frozen snow and propelled lone figures down Main Street. The kids wore their pointy-topped hooded sweatshirts under coats. Through the cruiser's windshield, they looked like packs of elves. It was hard to tell one from the other. "It's too cold for crime," said Tommy. But he had ways of getting through a winter. They'd always worked before.

In between calls these slow winter nights, he relived old stories as if he were being transported from one episode to another, from one handcuffing to the next. He remembered the day when he was still brand-new and found himself outnumbered and almost overpowered by two drunks in a pickup truck. An off-duty state trooper stopped and rescued him. "He got out and waffle-stomped the other guy, and I realized that if I was gonna do this job, I'd better learn some things." How if a person with a knife comes at you from as far as twenty feet away, you don't have time to pull your gun, so you have to learn the proper way to move and make it instinctive. How to get handcuffs on a suspect before he starts to fight . . .

So much past had collected in this place for him that it was always present, and often just up the street ahead. Near dark Tommy turned the supervisor's cruiser into the parking lot of an apartment complex, and, scanning the landscape as usual, he spotted a middle-aged couple walking arm in arm toward one of the buildings. Tommy drove up beside them. "How are *you*?" he asked the man.

Tommy studied him—neatly dressed, clean-shaven, evidently sober—and thought, "A hundred and eighty degrees." When this man used to get arrested in nearby towns, he'd tell the cops he was Tommy O'Connor's brother. Three years ago, Tommy found him lying in a filthy sleeping bag in a corner of the abandoned grocery store on King Street, amid empty liquor bottles and used hypodermic needles. In a sleeping bag next to him lay a corpse, an elderly drunk who must have died several hours before. The man now standing in front of Tommy had lain with his back propped against the wall, as if sitting up in bed, chatting away to the corpse. Tommy took him to the diner across the street, got him halfway sobered up, then started in on him. "You're gonna end up like that guy you were talking to." Tommy went on and on. Finally, the man had started crying.

"Good, Tommy, good," the man said now. His eyes moved away. He smiled toward his shoes. It might have been a grimace.

"Are you Tommy O'Connor?" asked the woman. She held on to the man's arm, held on to it hard, it seemed.

"Yes, ma'am."

"God bless you," she said. "God bless you."

Tommy smiled, but in a moment said good-bye. If he let her go on and started feeling too smug, he might regret it—if, a month or a year from now, a cop from Amherst or Hadley called and said once again, "We got your brother locked up here. What do ya want us to do with him?"

It snowed again, the skies cleared, and for an afternoon the city and the country roads looked freshly painted. By the next evening they were grimy, gray, and sandy, and the whole town looked to Tommy like a graveyard. Then it snowed again, another whistling near-blizzard. He decided to drive around the rural parts of town. The cruiser's headlights bored into wind-driven, sharply angled snow. Frosted tree limbs hung low over two-lane country roads. Tommy drove hunched over, peering out into the swarming snow. "This is a good thing to do on a night like this. In case someone's wife is stuck out here."

He tuned one of his radios to the Holyoke police frequency.

Maybe one of their car chases would end up in Northampton. They were always busy down there, too busy. He turned Holyoke off. "It's too cold for crime," he said again. Then his eyebrows darted up, slashes of color against pale winter skin, and his face opened up, and he cried, "But, hey! There's always spring!"

It kept on snowing, though; every few days, it seemed. Tommy used to love a good snowstorm, just a while ago. He'd planned to ski on his days off this winter—the mountains to the north lay deep in snow, deeper than in any year he could remember—and yet he'd gone only a few times. He didn't know exactly why. Only halfway to the vernal equinox, and already a general mood of exhaustion had seemed to settle over the town, the kind of exhaustion that comes from waiting for an end that looks too far away. Maybe, he thought, the mood was catching.

He was tired of snow, tired of wet floors, tired of reaching out his window and snapping ice off the cruiser's windshield wipers, tired of listening to police calls in Holyoke as if he were no more than a wannabe scanner buff. He couldn't re-member a winter that made his town seem so gloomy. At the door of Dunkin' Donuts one of the local undertakers told him, "Twenty funerals in a month and five suicides. I'm sick of it."

"Me, too." He drove away from D&Ds in silence. Then he said, "All right, I'm gonna get myself out of my hole."

If only the chief would hurry up and install him as detective sergeant. The delay grew embarrassing. People kept asking him, "So when are you going back in the bureau?" Any day now rumors would start, saying that O'Connor must have done something wrong. He probably beat up a prisoner or stole some drugs. It was hard not to care what the town thought. Around here gossip could turn into something like an inquisition.

And a detective always had some cases to work on. "See, if I was back in the bureau, I could be doing something now, instead of driving around aimlessly in this shit. But I won't let it bother me, so that I hate my job."

. . .

Nothing much happened at the start of the shift, on a cold clear afternoon already sinking toward twilight when Tommy headed out from the station. He stopped a carful of boys who had obviously been smoking blunts, but found only stems and seeds of marijuana and a pipe, and sent them away with the usual advice about wasting their time on drugs, and with the usual parting words: "Stay out of trouble." Then one of his old informants beeped him, to say that a certain woman was trying to sell him cocaine. The woman was another informant, who was actually trying to set up the informant who'd beeped him. Rats ratting on rats. It was amusing, also a good way of checking up on them.

Around dusk Tommy pulled into the lot outside Dunkin' Donuts to get his coffee. He turned in his seat, reaching for the door handle, and there was Rick, standing at his window.

Tommy rolled it down. "How ya doin'?"

"As well as can be expected."

Rick crouched down by the door, a graceful and athletic movement. "Guess what my wife did? All the presents I sent to the kids, she gave them to the D.A.'s office and they opened all of them. Who the hell do they think I am?"

"It's like you grew a third eye or something," Tommy said.

"It's the nineties equivalent of leprosy," said Rick.

Tommy looked away, and wet his lips. For a moment neither spoke.

"You gettin' to the gym?" Tommy asked.

"Every day."

"How are your parents?"

"My wife's position is that there should be a child care person there when my kids visit my parents."

"Jack was home," said Tommy. "Did you see him?"

They talked awhile about their families. Then Rick said, "My wife's having an affair."

Tommy looked at him sharply. "How far has that gone?"

"She's given him my computer, and our camcorder. I ran

into him. I said, 'I understand you have a camcorder of mine.' He said, 'You're going to have to bring that up with your wife's attorney.' I said, 'Fine. I just thought I could save my wife some money.' "

"I wouldn't try to save her a penny," said Tommy.

Silence came between them again.

"And it's going to trial?"

"Oh, *yeah,*" said Rick. "They're offering me anything I want if I plead out." But Rick wasn't going to do that. His voice was full of irony. "Oh, and the D.A.'s office has made a motion to intervene in my divorce."

The pause was longer this time.

"I don't know what to say, Rick. It's a *lot*, huh."

"Oh, well."

Tommy laughed. "Keep up the exercise."

"Hey, no body fat. Five months of sobriety."

"Well, I gotta go up to that candlelight vigil, Rick. I'll see you at the gym. I'll be going there in the mornings again."

Tommy drove back toward the station, without coffee. "What do you say to him? That's why I don't call him too often. What am I supposed to say? 'Oh, that's too bad'? . . . Well, maybe he didn't do it." That line about the leprosy of the nineties. What was Rick saying? That Tommy was avoiding him, that he'd noticed?

He drove the rest of the way to the station in silence, went inside, put on his round policeman's hat, then walked up Center Street to the front of the First Church. A small crowd had gathered there, a crowd in heavy coats, all holding candles. Their collective breath rose in the air beneath the streetlights, far below the great stone spire and the city clock. Tommy took a candle. When the TV cameras arrived, they all went inside.

The grand nave of the old church had a yellowish tint, like golden twilight. Up on a table by the pulpit stood a studio-type photograph of the victims in the Seabrooks case, a young woman and a smiling little boy, their faces side by side.

Tommy glanced at it. It was on this night three years ago that he had found their bodies. He didn't feel upset. He remembered feeling upset. He believed in ceremonies like tonight's memorial service. The family and the town were trying to make something good out of something evil. They should try to keep the memory alive. But personally, he wouldn't mind forgetting the whole thing. The other day, anticipating this ceremony, he'd said, "There's a lot of things you can do with a beautiful little kid like that. Besides kill it."

Tommy sat down in a pew. The minister and Chief Sienkiewicz and the district attorney and a glamorous-looking female TV anchorperson from Springfield all came up to the pulpit and gave speeches. The woman from the TV station started out by saying it was so cold outside her lips felt frozen. Tommy smiled. "And wouldn't a lot of guys here like to warm 'em up," he murmured. Then he composed his face. This was a Protestant church, but a church nonetheless. The speeches were all on the same theme. The anniversary of these two deaths must become the beginning of an end to domestic violence. Good would triumph over evil. No new recipes for pulling off that feat were offered. But they were worthy, hopeful speeches, saying all the things that should be said. They weren't hard to listen to, except for the last one.

The dead woman's sister ascended the pulpit. "How could a father do those things to his wife and a son?" she said. "I wonder if I can explain to *my* son. If I can understand. I can't! What screams they must have endured the last moments of their life." There was an undercurrent in her voice, like sobbing in the background. "We can't carve a pumpkin face, can't remove a knife from a dishwasher, can't watch certain TV shows, and can't take the air out of a blow-up toy, without thinking of them." Tommy lowered his head a little, and raised his thumbnail to his teeth. He scraped it, looking up at the woman from the tops of his eyes. She was tall and thin, and looked taller than she was, from where Tommy sat, down below the pulpit in his pew. She looked like someone who would ordinarily keep you at a friendly distance, and now it was as if she were opening the door to her boudoir. Inside, she and her dead sister were getting dressed: "When we collected her belongings, there was a single pearl barrette. I thought, 'Oh, my God, she just put her hair up.' Who knew it would be for the last time? I cannot put on a barrette without thinking of her. The smell of soap brings her back, the act of shaving my legs and giving myself a facial, acts we did together."

The service ended. Mayor Ford bustled past Tommy, wiping her eyes with a tissue. She patted Tommy's arm. He headed back toward the station. His voice echoed off the tall stone wall of the church, at the top of Center Street. "Well, this has been a banner evening so far." Then the sour look departed, and Father O'Connor returned. "But the sister did a good job, huh?"

PART III

CHAPTER 9

Tearless, Eager and Longing Eyes

In the household of Tommy's youth, everything was tinted green. You absorbed Irish history just by living there. Looking back, Tommy had the impression that even his Polish mother had come to feel she was Irish. He felt impatient with the current tendency for ethnic labeling. "I think we've put too much into names," he said. But it wasn't as if ethnicity didn't matter to him. "I think it's great that someone's proud of their heritage. I certainly am. But don't kill it with names."

About halfway up Hospital Hill, a huge oblong stone stands upright on a pedestal, like a big tombstone. No one in town seemed to remember who put it there, or when, or why. Some local people assumed it marked the site of Northampton's gallows. Eleven years earlier, at any rate, it had become a memorial to the town's most notorious hanging. One day Tommy parked his cruiser and climbed up to the stone. A plaque was fastened to it. The inscription read:

DOMINIC DALEY
JAMES HALLIGAN
EXECUTED 1806
EXONERATED 1984

"One of the arguments against the death penalty," said Tommy, looking at the plaque. He didn't agree with most of those arguments. Reminded that execution was not a deterrent to murder, he'd reply, "It is for the person who gets executed." But this was a place for longer thoughts. "Like I say, in 1806 being Irish was a crime. Just like today—whoever's on the bottom of the totem pole gets blamed." He stood there for a few minutes, the old buildings of the defunct state mental hospital behind him, the town's favorite sledding hill off to his left. He looked downhill to the east, over the Smith playing fields and riding stables. "I don't know if this is where they were hanged or not. Nice place to hang somebody, if it was."

On November 10, 1805, a young traveler named Marcus Lyon was found murdered, a bullet in his chest, his skull caved in, some miles south of Northampton. The body lay in the shallows of the Chicopee River near Wilbraham, then part of Hampshire County. Northampton was the county seat, so the case became in part Northampton's. Caleb Strong, the governor of Massachusetts and a favorite son of the town, was running for another term. He posted a reward of $500 for the murderer of Lyon, an extraordinary sum back then. A posse rode out of Northampton, and on the twelfth arrested two Irish Catholics, James Halligan and Dominic Daley, who were about to board a boat for New York City. The suspects claimed they were innocent. They languished for about five months in the county jail downtown. The transcript of the trial, informally compiled by an anonymous "member of the bar," describes a vigorous prosecution. The state's attorney general came from Boston to perform it. He was running for governor against Strong.

The old courthouse was too small for the occasion. So the authorities repaired to the town's largest public theater, the Old Church on Meeting House Hill. The crowd filled every seat.

The overflow peered in the windows. The judges and the lawyers sat on a stage hastily erected in front of the pulpit. None of the chroniclers describes the defendants' location. Halligan was twenty-seven. A witness to the events remembered him as short and "robust," and claimed he was illiterate. Daley, thirty-four, was "well-educated," and of a more refined appearance—"rather tall, a well formed athletic man." Daley also had a little child and a "fine looking" wife.

The town had erected this church in 1737, after the upper gallery of the previous one had fallen down during Sunday services. No one had been injured, but seventy years later the town's faith in balconies remained shaken. One eye-witness to the trial of Halligan and Daley wrote: "In the afternoon, just as the writer, then a small boy, with his father, reached the top of the gallery stairs, a cry was raised that the galleries were falling." A number of people jumped out the windows. "But the alarm soon subsided, when it was seen that it was false, and the trial proceeded."

The prosecution proved that Halligan and Daley had traveled swiftly after they passed the murder site. They showed the jury that pockets had been sewn inside the Irishmen's long overcoats, pockets that would have nicely accommodated pistols, such as the one they must have left behind in pieces near the body. The prosecution offered no proof that the pistol was theirs and no other evidence worth mentioning, except for the testimony of a boy from around Wilbraham. He identified the two Irishmen. He said he'd seen one of them put the victim's horse in a pasture, and that the other Irishman had stared at him, giving him a dirty look.

The trial lasted all one day and well into the night. The judges—there were two—had given the defense attorneys only a few days to prepare. The defense produced no evidence or witnesses. The court would not allow Halligan and Daley to testify: until 1866, criminal defendants in Massachusetts had only the right to remain silent. There were four defense attorneys. Three don't seem to have tried very hard; maybe they were worried about the future of their practices. But one of them, a young lawyer named Francis Blake, made a long and eloquent closing argument. Eighty years later, when they were old men, boys whose fathers took them to the trial still remembered Blake's address.

"That the prisoners have been tried, convicted, and condemned, in almost every bar-room, and barber's-shop, and in every other place of public resort in the county, is a fact which will not be contested," he told the jurors—all men, of course, sturdy burghers, solemn-faced. Blake reviewed the evidence, pointing out that Halligan and Daley might indeed have murdered Marcus Lyon—and so might many others on that dangerous public highway. Blake's oration makes it clear that in Northampton anti–Irish Catholic bias was not so thoroughly ingrained that it was invisible. He told the jury: "There is yet another species of prejudice, against the influence of which it is my duty to warn you. I allude to the inveterate hostility against the people of that wretched country, from which the Prisoners have emigrated, for which the people of New England are particularly distinguished."

Blake spoke until around ten o'clock that night. Then the presiding judge addressed the jury. He told them that if they believed the boy from Wilbraham, they must convict the prisoners, even though, on the face of it, his testimony didn't prove much. The judge also described the boy's testimony as "consistent," even though the record shows it wasn't. Then he sent the jury off to deliberate. According to one contemporary newspaper account, it took them "a few moments" to find Halligan and Daley guilty. Several days later, before another packed house, the presiding justice addressed the convicted men. He spoke to them about the wickedness of their crime, "a crime so horrid and so abhorred by every pure and virtuous mind." He remarked on "the humane indulgence of our laws." Then he said, "It now only remains that we . . . pronounce against you the sentence of the law, which is, that you Dominic Daley, be taken . . . to the place of execution, and that you there be hung by the neck until you are dead, and that your body be dissected and anatomized." He said the same to Halligan. Then the judge raised his voice, apparently: "And may God Almighty have mercy on your souls!"

The convicts languished in the jail again, for months. The high sheriff, General Mattoon of Amherst, made preparations. He spent, in all, $92.80. Hezekiah Russell built the gallows. The cost for that and for "ropes and cords" was $9.17. Daley's wife had come to Northampton. She suffered what one chronicler called "convulsions" the night before the hanging. And in the region anticipation mounted. Northampton was a town of only twenty-five hundred then. A crowd of men, women, and children, which may have numbered fifteen thousand—about half of Boston's population at the time—crammed itself into downtown. It was a fine June day. The atmosphere was festive. Daley, the literate one, had written to a Catholic priest, pleading that he come and give them their last rites. The priest was John Louis Lefebvre de Cheverus, later bishop of Boston and later still cardinal archbishop of Bordeaux. He cut an exotic figure in that dirt-street Yankee town. Northampton was still a very religious place, with a single church. Its citizens grew up believing that the pope was an agent of Satan. The keeper of the local inn, Asahel Pomeroy, refused Cheverus a room. Pomeroy's wife later said that she "would not have been able to sleep a wink under the same roof with a Catholic priest." Cheverus appears to have stayed with the prisoners in the jail for several days.

It is almost certain that no Catholic had ever preached in Northampton before. A Protestant minister was hired to deliver the customary sermon to the prisoners. But Cheverus insisted on his duty. On the morning of the hanging he mounted the pulpit in the Old Church and began to speak in what one witness remembered as "a stern voice." Apparently, some windows had been removed, "so that a crowded house and a vast multitude outside could hear him." A huge and, one assumes, mostly hostile audience surrounded the priest. The text of his sermon has been preserved. He said, in part:

> Orators are usually flattered by having a numerous audience, but I am ashamed of the one now before me. Are there men to whom the death of their fellow-beings is a spectacle of pleasure, an object of curiosity? But especially you women, what has induced you to come to this place? Is it to wipe away the cold damps of death? Is it to experience the painful emotions which this scene ought to inspire in every feeling heart? No, it is to behold the prisoners' anguish, to look upon it with tearless, eager and longing eyes. I blush for you, your eyes are full of murder. You boast of sensibility, and you say it is the highest virtue in a woman: but if the sufferings of others afford you pleasure, and the death of a man is entertainment for your curiosity, then I can no longer believe in your virtue. You forget your sex, you are a dishonor and reproach to it.

Some accounts say that most of the women on hand decided not to go to the hanging after all. One wealthy woman of the town, who did not attend the priest's sermon or the execution, wrote in her diary that Cheverus was "a remarkable Mild Man." He got some other good reviews and was actually invited to preach a few more times. A prominent citizen named Joseph Clark entertained Cheverus in his own home. But one history has it that when Clark's wife died prematurely a few years later and lightning struck his house and burned it down, all of Northampton knew that God had punished him for putting up a papist.

After church, the hanging. A rumor may have spread that Irishmen were coming to liberate the prisoners. In any case, the sheriff took precautions. "The high sheriff came over in the morning on his parade horse, with his aids, [*sic*] all armed with pistols hanging by their saddles, and presented a very imposing appearance," wrote one of the men who'd been a boy back then. Probably the prisoners walked on the dirt roads in front of the sheriff and his men. A company of artillery and a detachment of the militia, all in uniform, followed, raising dust. The parade went uphill from the Old Church, up Main Street and out on what was then called Welch End Way, now West Street, and finally up to the top of Hospital Hill, then known as Gallows Plain or Gallows Hill. There must have been a military band, because one witness remembered there was music and that it was the Death March.

Much of the crowd ran on ahead, vying for vantage points. The spectators covered all of Gallows Plain. "An immense multitude had already congregated on the Plain," wrote one of the witnesses. Men and boys climbed trees to get a better view. "The pines on the west side of it were filled with spectators. . . . The writer has seldom seen such a mass of human beings together since that day, all the events of which he perfectly remembers. The infantry were drawn up around the gallows, the poor condemned culprits were allowed to say their last words."

Daley had written out a short speech. He read it aloud to the multitude.

At this awful moment of appearing before the tribunal of the ALMIGHTY; and knowing that telling a falshood, would be eternal perdition to our poor souls,

We solemnly declare, we are perfectly Inocent of the Crime for which we suffer, or any other Murder or Robbery; never saw, to our knowledge, Marcus Lyon in our lives; and as unaccountable as it may appear, the boy never saw one of us, looking at him, at, or near a fence; or any of us either leading, driving, or riding a Horse, and we never went off the high road. We blame no one, we forgive every one; we submit to our fate as being the will of the Almighty; and beg of him to be

merciful to us, through the merits of his divine Son, our
blessed Saviour Jesus Christ.

Our sincere thanks to the Rev. John Chevers, for his long
and kind attention to us, as likewise every other friend, that
served us, and comforted us during our long Confinement.

When Daley finished, according to one account, he handed the
written speech to the high sheriff, who then leaned from his
saddle and "with a heavy knife or hatchet" cut the rope that
held the drop. "... And as the platform fell, one fell much
below the other having been allowed more rope according to
his request, that his neck might be broken so that he might
have a speedy death. His body was dissected a short distance
from the present residence of this writer."

The town seems to have quieted down by the following day.
Probably it just cleaned up, as after a party, and went back to
life as usual. But the story survived through many generations,
and, as Irish immigrants acquired local standing, it grew and
changed, from a story that two killers got what they deserved to
a story that two young Irishmen were in essence murdered
here.

One hundred and seventy-six years after the event—in 1982—
a crowd much smaller than the one that watched the two men
die gathered around the monument on Hospital Hill. The little
party included a retired fireman of Irish descent who was trying to get the governor to pardon Halligan and Daley. Bill
O'Connor was there too, still county treasurer then. And also
one Popcorn O'Donnell, who got his nickname as a youth
when his date at the Calvin movie theater slipped away while
he was fetching popcorn.

For decades Bill O'Connor's generation of Northampton
Irish had dominated local politics. They had routed the Yankee
Republicans, and were on the way out now themselves.
Popcorn had been both an ally and an enemy of Bill's. But the

attempt to exonerate Halligan and Daley was one of the last great acts of the old tribe, and Popcorn belonged in the picture. He was fat, florid, and doddering now. Looking at him, Bill O'Connor thought, "Popcorn's had a few." Bill told him to get a grip on the stone and hold on tight. Then he turned to the local TV anchorperson. "Take the picture quick," said Bill. "Because he won't last long."

Bill had arranged the publicity so that Popcorn and the retired fireman would get the limelight, and so that certain others wouldn't. Some of the new Democrats in town were Irish, among them Mike Ryan, who was the district attorney back then. Ryan had wanted to be part of the ceremony. He'd wanted to have his picture taken at it, Bill figured. Bill was afraid that Ryan and another Young Turk would try to hog the credit. So he told them that the TV cameras would arrive at noon. In fact, he'd arranged the ceremony for eleven. The picture-taking was all over when Ryan and the other young Irish politician came running up the hill from their cars. "Oh, Jesus, you're late," Bill told them, sorrowfully. He gestured at the TV crew, who were packing up their gear. "They came early."

Actually, Judge Ryan had a legitimate claim to a part in the ceremony. As a young man, he'd written a play about the trial, dramatizing its egregiousness. Moreover, up in the attic of his house, among his dead father's papers, he had found correspondence and research notes on the case. According to one version of the old story, Halligan and Daley weren't just tried unfairly but certainly were innocent. No actual evidence of that had ever surfaced. Ryan's father, Judge Ryan the elder, had spent a lot of time and effort trying in vain to find some.

Odd how an episode like that hanging can become a source of satisfaction. Distance is the crucial thing. It allows you to look back with horror, and to forget that if you had actually been there, you might have climbed a pine tree, too, to watch with eager eyes. At the right distance, injustice looks thrilling.

So much of American history, and particularly New England history, gets absorbed in a storybook sense of colonial days and of the early years of the Republic that modern times can seem like little more than a falling off. The world seems to have been better then, in ecology, landscape, architecture, manners, moral staunchness. Travelers praised the Connecticut River Valley of the early 1800s for its bucolic calm and the levelness of its communities. In 1789, George Washington himself described the region this way: "There is equality in the People of this State—Few or no oppulent Men and no poor—great similatude in their buildings." And yet less than two decades after Washington rode through the valley, a court as prejudiced as any modern-day totalitarian tribunal summarily condemned two human beings, and a huge percentage of the people of the region flocked into town to watch them die. A comparable act of communal barbarism was never impossible, of course, but it did seem unimaginable just now in Northampton.

These days Main Street saw only mild eruptions, times of demonstration and speeches. Once in a while the issues were local. Most of them would have seemed small in a big, angry city. Northampton afforded its residents many luxuries, and one was the chance to exercise their moral faculties in calm surroundings. Some events looked like sessions of moral jogging. Last August, for instance, seventy-five women and children had gathered in front of the old courthouse. A number of the women sat on the steps breast-feeding their babies. They were angry, and tenderly protesting the actions of a local court officer. He'd ejected a woman from a district courtroom because she was breast-feeding her baby there, but he was no enemy of breast-feeding. "They don't know me," the court officer said afterward, of the people who denounced him. "I'm not against that. My mother did that for me. No way I'm gonna be against that."

Judge Ryan quietly intervened. The officer thought he'd been carrying out the judges' wishes. Ryan made sure that the man didn't get punished, and no harm was done all around.

Sometimes when Judge Ryan was supposed to preside in the local District Court he was called away at the last moment, and another judge would appear from chambers. If you were sitting among the defense attorneys then, you might hear a few groans, pitched low enough so that the replacement judge couldn't hear them. One of the defense lawyers might mutter very softly, "This isn't the judge we want." And, conversely, if it was Judge Ryan who came out and mounted the bench, wearing his small, crooked smile, only partly concealed in his beard, you'd see the defense attorneys smiling, too. Especially some of the female ones, one of whom on one occasion kept up a running commentary on the judge's performance—whispering words like "compassion" and phrases such as, "He's *so* kind."

On the wall, to the right of the elevated bench where Judge Ryan usually sat, hung a photograph of his father, the former presiding District Court judge Luke Ryan—"Luke Hang 'Em High Ryan," as he'd been admiringly called in law-enforcement circles. In the photo, the elderly judge looked unpleasantly surprised at what his son was up to. Perhaps, for all his expressions of filial piety, Judge Ryan liked to express the philosophical differences between himself and his dead father.

Judge Ryan the younger was beloved by courthouse workers, and generally disliked by police. He'd made some intemperate remarks in the past. Speaking disapprovingly of the state police uniforms, he'd once told a reporter, "If you dress 'em like Nazis, they'll behave like Nazis." Mainly, though, the police objected to the judge's leniency and his out-of-court behavior. "The drinking judge," one waggish lawyer called him. Both slanders contained some truth.

He stopped being a judge when he left court. If a stranger on a nearby bar stool asked him what he did for a living, Ryan would say, "Oh, I have a government job, cleaning up small messes at the courthouse."

As for his leniency, a friend once accused him of harboring great compassion for many defendants, and the judge replied, "I think it's something stronger. I think it's more like identification."

He didn't like sending people to jail, because he didn't like jails. He thought they disimproved most people. He often felt he could invent better punishments, like the one he once imposed on a troubled boy who had stolen scratch tickets from his employer, a stationer in Florence. The store owner confronted the boy in court, saying, "I treated you like a son!" He had bought the boy a New England Patriots cap before he'd discovered the crime. Now he held it out and said, "Take it!" The boy cowered at the sight of the cap. Seeing this, Judge Ryan felt inspired. He ordered the boy to pay restitution and to wear that New England Patriots hat *whenever* he went outdoors. The sentence was derided in several newspapers, including one as far away as Philadelphia. But it was a serious sentence. If you understood Ryan, you understood that he imagined the boy would think of his crime whenever he put on his cap. Ryan was trying to turn that homely object into an agent of remorse. He was trying to sentence the boy to penance.

He had a theory that every group of people, every society that had occupied Northampton from the Puritans on down, created boundaries in law that invariably excluded about 10 percent of its members. Thus each society identified itself by identifying the enemies within. From an early age, he had been mindful of the excluded. He once wrote a poem about two of Northampton's castoffs whom he'd seen as a boy from his childhood home. It was the 1950s. The siren at the state mental hospital across the Mill River had sounded; as usual, his parents had ordered him and his siblings indoors. Mike stood at a window, gazing out at his family's backyard, and in a moment a woman in a hospital gown appeared. She began picking dandelions. From behind her, walking stealthily toward her, came a couple of men in chino pants, with keys dangling from their belts.

He remembered as vividly gazing out a front window at another lone figure, the locally infamous Smith College professor Newton Arvin, harried and denounced for being a homosexual. Mike's father had arraigned Arvin on that charge of possessing indecent pictures. The professor wasn't violent or likely to flee. Many judges would have released him on his own recognizance. Old Luke had demanded that Arvin post bail. He had told Mike that the professor was dangerous. Gazing out the window, watching the professor walk by, Mike felt puzzled. The man was reading a book as he walked. He didn't look dangerous to Mike.

Judge Ryan the younger had a temper. It flared up occasionally in barrooms. In court, he sometimes shouted at lawyers who didn't listen to his advice. He said he thought of his court as a classroom, and he wanted everyone to leave his classroom better. He believed in progress, and as a student of Northampton history, mindful of episodes like the hanging of Halligan and Daley, he believed that his town had made some. In the community center in Florence one evening, a group of residents had gathered to hear about plans for a statue of Sojourner Truth, the famous black abolitionist, who had lived in Florence for a while. The meeting began with high rhetoric; a member of the statue committee said: "A statue to someone ignored and neglected by history can mean everything, to your entire community, to American history." One of the audience dared object to the whole idea, and then angry words flew. Hearing an account of the contretemps the next day, Judge Ryan grew thoughtful. "I think I'm one of the few Northampton natives who would be in favor of the statue," he said. "A lot of people are upset about newcomers coming in and taking over, about national magazines calling Northampton the lesbian capital of the world. But I think there's something wonderful about a community where a thing like a statue gets people excited. Not drive-by shootings or gangs, but whether a statue of Sojourner Truth should be put in a little park in Florence."

It would have been hard for anyone to disagree. What a far better place Northampton was, where babies were nursed as expressions of outrage, than the town that had made a holiday out of hanging two immigrants. A place can't function or improve through compassion alone, but it can't become a good place without it. Over the years many people had added to the sum of kindness in Northampton. Judge Ryan, a student of human frailty, was one.

CHAPTER 10

Plain
Miss Smith

WHEN SHE FIRST entered Northampton, Laura sensed she'd landed in a historic place, and this had been another way in which she'd felt that the town reproached her. Downtown and the campus made her feel that she had lived with scarcely any history at all. The old buildings reminded her that no one could even find her mother's parents when she died.

On a winter night soon after she got her reprieve from Mrs. Rothman, Laura went walking on the campus. The students were still gone for the holidays. The air was cold, the place as empty as the limbs of its exotic trees. Laura found herself standing in front of Seelye Hall, the site of the past fall's worst disaster. Even while she'd sat inside one of its classrooms, silently flunking her course in Irish drama, Laura had liked the innards of this tall brick building—the way the stairs creaked and especially, as the weather grew colder, the irreverent knocking sounds the old steam radiators made, in the midst of her professor's lectures. When the radiators had started knocking, like rude sounds of indigestion, she'd wanted to laugh, but hadn't dared even to smile. How droll, she thought now, looking up at Seelye Hall, that a building should have its own, ancient sounds.

She walked around the empty campus, down the asphalt

paths, looking all around. "It's as if I'm seeing it for the first time," she thought. It was glorious. It had an old, settled kind of beauty, lodged in the buildings and trees. "There's this history with this place and it makes you very much aware of your own smallness," Laura thought. "But now I belong."

It was obvious that the past had enriched Northampton. All you had to do was look around at the things the wealthy had left behind. It would have been a different place without them.

Real estate agents trying to sell Northampton to prospective settlers liked to drive them past the cows that grazed in the green, sloping fields of the Smith Vocational High School Farm. Look, the agents would say, we have it all right here, a farm and cows within a mile of our lively piece of city. A country squire named Oliver Smith had left the money to start that school and farm, and had created Northampton's Smith Charities. Other gentry had bequeathed the Academy of Music, Look Park and Childs Park, both managed and maintained at no cost to the city, the famous Clarke School for the Deaf, the People's Institute on Gothic Street, the Hill Institute in Florence, where nursery school and adult education classes were held nowadays, and Forbes Library, the town's public library, both the grand stone edifice and also some of the money that still ran it.

A lot of present-day Northampton would have felt uneasy about the sources of some of those gifts. Judge Charles Edward Forbes, for instance, created the town's library to fight the religion immigrants were bringing in—like smallpox to the Indians, he seems to have believed. In his will Forbes wrote that the knowledge stored in his library would be Northampton's best defense against the doctrines of the Catholic church, against "the progeny of the Purple and Scarlet clad Mother." But within a couple of generations of Forbes's death, Irish Catholics were running Northampton, and the library was none the worse in the 1990s for the piece of paper buried, so to speak, beneath its cornerstone. Childs Park across from the high school was once the estate of a Christian minister who owned a thousand slaves in Georgia, but the land wasn't poisoned, and anyone could walk there now. The principle of noblesse oblige was a part of Northampton's heritage. It had served the town better than no sense of obligation at all.

Smith College represented the most important of the legacies, and not just for Northampton. From Smith's sacred grove, many strong, accomplished women had emerged into the wider world—important bankers and lawyers and editors, media stars and notable feminists and poets, even a couple of influential first ladies. The college no longer adhered to every provision in the will of its founder, Sophia Smith—for instance, this command: "that the Holy Scriptures be daily systematically read and studied in said college, and, without giving preference to any sect or denomination, all the education and all the discipline shall be pervaded by the Spirit of Evangelical Christian Religion." But for over a century, for many students, the college had certainly fulfilled the will's most eloquent, most often quoted statement of intent—"to furnish for my own sex means and facilities for education equal to those which are afforded now in our Colleges to young men."

Interest in Sophia had revived at the college. She was just now being rediscovered as a woman far ahead of her time, with an independent mind, whose own vision had created Smith. The evidence for this portrait was scant. It was far more likely that Sophia's pastor, John M. Greene, a country Congregational minister, did most of the inventing. Sophia got credit mainly for listening to him and, with enthusiasm, putting up the money. In any case, almost everything known about the founding comes from Greene. There seems no way of knowing if he exaggerated his role, though more likely he did the opposite. After hearing one of Greene's glowing eulogies after Sophia's death, another minister who knew her wrote to him, "I fear you have overestimated our plain Miss Smith."

Sophia was born in the late 1700s. She lived and died in Hatfield, a very sleepy little farm town near Northampton. If Greene had been a self-aggrandizing Svengali, he might have tried to talk Sophia into leaving Hatfield a cathedral-sized Congregational church. Sophia, too, might well have acted differently. Most of the money she left to create Smith came from her brother Austin, by virtually all accounts a nasty, pathologically miserly man. He was once quoted as saying that not even God would get his money. If she had resembled him, Sophia might have refused to make a will at all. Or she might have acted like her uncle Oliver. He had a larger fortune than Sophia, but he encumbered his will with instructions and prohibitions. He made it a dead hand of the past, and by now his legacy had shrunk to insignificance beside Sophia's. Compared to Uncle Oliver's, Sophia's will reads like a love letter to the future.

Sophia never married. No evidence has yet turned up that she ever had a lover, male or female. In middle age she was, in the words of a fellow townswoman, "short of stature, plain in face, limping in gait, with a partial deafness." She came into her fortune late in life, after everyone else in her family had died. On December 26, 1864, when she was sixty-eight years old, Sophia wrote in her journal: "Sunday morning. In the house all alone. Oh how solitary is this home! I look forward, but it looks more dark. I only see old age in the distance, and sickness and death. Backward all these ties broken that connected me with them and with life." She had become almost completely deaf. Greene was one of the few people whose speech she could decipher, fortunately enough.

They were frequent companions, and it is pleasing to imagine the two of them dreaming up the college, in the parlor of her family's farmhouse, Greene speaking to her through her ear trumpet. Perhaps he talked about how college education would make women better wives, especially wives for ministers; he is known to have harbored that theory. Perhaps it was Sophia herself who came up with these lines for her grand bequest: "I would have the education suited to the mental and physical wants of woman. It is not my design to render my sex any the less feminine, but to develop as fully as may be the powers of womanhood, and furnish women with the means of usefulness, happiness, and honor, now withheld from them." Words embarrassingly tentative to sensibilities at Smith today. But Sophia lived in the eighteenth and nineteenth centuries. She didn't think that women ought to have the right to vote. Most likely it was just a good impulse of her heart that led to this wonderful college. But there is wisdom in a simple generosity like hers. For one thing, it avoids the often costly error of trying to imagine the future in great grasping detail.

As recently as a couple of decades ago Smith College might have seemed vaguely familiar to Sophia and her pastor. Not now, not at ten P.M. on the night before exams, called Primal Scream Night, and not at Convocation or at Rally Day, when a few students were bound to show up wearing only bras and britches. And certainly not on National Coming Out Day, when some of the lesbian students chalked messages on asphalt paths all over the campus. Recently, a student found herself giving her parents a tour of the campus on that day. She spent the whole time frantically pointing up at trees, hoping to keep her parents from looking down. One chalking declared:

I FUCK WOMEN

Another said:

I'M A VAGITARIAN

Another looked like this:

> TOP 5 REASONS
> TO ♡ ♀
> 1. SMARTER
> 2. BREASTS
> 3. CUTER
> 4. BETTER IN BED
> 5. NO DICKS

No one alive in Northampton in 1870, when Sophia signed her will, could have imagined the Smithies who wrote those naughty words. Sophia could not have conceived of a college that admitted a grown woman who arrived with a child instead of a lady's maid, wasn't even married, didn't go to church, and smoked a brand of cigarettes called Kools. Sophia couldn't have imagined Smith. She couldn't have imagined Laura.

CHAPTER 11

Total, Mindless Joy

IT WAS GOING to take a while for Northampton to notice the change in Alan Scheinman. As always, he scurried in shorts down the snowbound streets, following his theory that being cold in the morning kept one warm the rest of the day. But Alan was taking steps to rejoin the contaminated world.

He hadn't realized how much time and energy he'd consumed by being depressed, until his depression lifted. He had begun to attack his compulsions. His psychiatrist came up with the general plan, and a behaviorist suggested that Alan keep track of the time he spent at each of his cleaning rituals. He took this on as assiduously as he had once prepared law cases, searched titles, devised real estate deals, as compulsively as he had decontaminated his world for the past ten years. He made up charts and hung them on his wall. He had to beat the charts, just had to. And what a pleasure of accomplishment it gave him to see the hours he spent at showering and tooth-brushing diminish. He stared at the charts. The pattern was dramatic.

His father had died about two and a half years ago. The old man hadn't left him any money, only his favorite treasures—

three very costly Patek Philippe wristwatches and a powder-blue Rolls-Royce, the only Rolls in Northampton. Alan often thought about his father now. He felt proud of the way the old man had departed, refusing to be kept alive on respirators.

Several times every year, and always before he went on a trip, Alan's father used to visit his own mother's grave. He never spoke about it, and never took Alan with him—he wasn't a demonstrative man, except in the courtroom. On a drizzly, dismal-looking day, Alan drove to the little Jewish cemetery in Connecticut where his grandmother was buried. The place contained about three hundred headstones. As he searched for his grandmother's, Alan noticed that the dates on many stones were old, and that no one had left pebbles on them. "There's no one *alive* who would have known these people *ever*," he thought. "*No one alive* would have known these people." When he found his grandmother's grave, he began to speak out loud to her, to this woman whom he'd never met. He told her that her son had died and wouldn't be coming to visit her anymore. He didn't imagine that she could hear him. He didn't imagine that she couldn't. He simply felt obliged to deliver this news to this place. And once he'd done that, he thought again of all the other people buried there. "No one alive is likely to have ever mentioned their names. Ever said their names." He walked from one stone to the next, in the rain, and read each name aloud. There was no one else around, but he felt as though he were repopulating the place. He felt as if he were shaking dust off all those names.

He still had a horror of things that touched the ground, but now, back in Northampton, he put on rubber gloves and began to clean ten years of trash out of his apartment. It filled about two hundred large garbage bags. He lost count. Perhaps he used three hundred. While cleaning, he found about $3,000 in soiled currency on the floors.

One day, as he drove alone across the state, heading for his psychiatrist's office, Alan put on a tape of old rock-and-roll tunes. Over the Rolls's sound system came the song "Angel Baby," by Rosie and the Originals. The lead singer had a high, tinny voice. "It's just like heaven bein' here with you." It took him right back, to Friday night record hops at the Y in New Bedford, all the girls on one side of the room and all the boys on the other, the boys standing around discussing the things they knew least about, such as women. When that lovely, sexy girl Donna and her lovely friend Elaine walked in, in their Ivy League button-down shirts and tight, knee-high sheath skirts, everything would stop, and the boys would stare and the girls would make catty remarks, and Alan, socially one of the least of the boys, shy and retiring, not popular enough to be dating anyone, would gaze longingly at Donna until he finally worked up the nerve to ask her to dance. He wouldn't dance with anyone else, and back then he wasn't coordinated enough to manage anything faster than slow dancing. Back then slow dancing was a clinch, the girl's arms around the boy's neck, the boy's arms around her waist, every square inch of the fronts of their bodies pressed together. It was the closest thing to sex he ever had with Donna. He didn't talk to her before they danced, while they danced, or after they danced. He did get to drive nice cars to the record hops, and sometimes Donna would let him drive her home in his father's T-Bird or Lincoln, and sometimes they'd stop at the Orchid Diner for a toasted Danish, and they would talk a little but not about much. He was aware even then that he had no real control over his future and assumed that she didn't either. He would follow his father's program, while she would probably become a hairdresser.

Driving along now, Alan could feel Donna in his arms—he was plastered to her again, swaying to "Angel Baby"—and he had what felt like a compulsion, like the one he'd felt in his grandmother's graveyard, to let her know that he possessed this warm memory of her. "I don't want to get together with her, I don't really want to know what she's been doing for the last thirty years, I just realize how grateful I am to her, to dance with this kind of geeky guy, this nerdy guy, and what a thrill it was for me."

Back home above Pleasant Street, once he'd decontaminated himself and could use his phone—rituals he still had to perform—Alan spent a long time tracking down Donna's mother. She told him that Donna had gotten married and divorced and had gone back to college. The mother was hard to talk to, though, and Alan quickly realized that she would never give him Donna's phone number or address. So he said, "I'd like to write a little note to Donna. If I do that, would you forward it to her?" And, of course, the woman said she would.

So Alan wrote a letter. Before he sent it, he decided to add a touch of glamour to it. From his Tiffany's catalogue, he bought a little sterling silver heart-shaped perfume bottle, perfume included, for about $85. He enclosed it with the letter, and in due course he received a note, not from Donna, but from her mother, saying that Donna was much moved by the little remembrance he'd sent her. Alan laughed, imagining the mother dabbing perfume on her neck as she wrote the note. He'd wanted only to thank Donna. A typical performance, he thought afterward—to get obsessed about having contact with another person and to act in a way out of all proportion to the circumstances. To overdo it. On social matters, he was out of practice.

In Northampton he dressed so raggedly sometimes that newcomers mistook him for one of the town's street people. Standing in conversation, he would fold his arms on his chest in a fidgety way and rise up on tiptoe, and these seemed like signs of a self-consciousness that doesn't know it's visible. But he was not an unappealing dinner date. He could dress up again. He didn't have to wear rubber gloves every time he went outside. He talked at immoderate length sometimes, but he also conveyed a genuine curiosity about the people he talked to, and the stories he told were frank and interesting. If you looked at him carefully, you saw he wasn't bad-looking at all. And he drove a Rolls.

Alan went out on a few dates. He grew quite fond of a certain woman, a little but not very much younger than he. It seemed there might be hope for a real relationship with her. But he let her slip away. "There's a certain expectation of intimacy after you've gone out with someone a few times," Alan explained. And intimacy was something that he still couldn't manage.

Alan understood the theory of what is called exposure and response prevention. In this clinically proven therapy, the patient is deliberately exposed to a fearful thing and is not allowed to respond with the usual anxiety-relieving rituals for at least forty-five minutes. A cleaner, for instance, might have to plunge his hands in dirt and refrain from washing them for most of an hour. After repeated sessions, most cleaners begin to relax in spite of their contaminated hands. The process terrifies the patient, but the great majority eventually become "habituated." That is, the compulsion to perform the ritual diminishes greatly. Alan, who had rejected this approach earlier, now decided to employ it, but in his own way and for an unusual purpose: "to reacquaint myself with the female geography," he said.

Northampton didn't have a strip club—imagine the uproar, if it had. But there was one nearby, called the Castaway Lounge. It was situated in a rural town, right next to a small swamp, Alan noticed, with a lot of pickup trucks in the parking lot. A banal sort of place—a barroom that contained a raised rectangular platform with a linoleum floor and a low counter running all around it and cheap swivel chairs set up beside the counter railing, the inner walls of the counter strung with what looked like Christmas-tree lights. On the runway, to the strains of loud contemporary music, a naked young woman was doing what was called dancing, which meant striking poses—draping herself over the counter, lying on her back on the grimy linoleum floor of the runway with her legs spread, then kneeling with her naked buttocks lifted high, all the while wearing on her face, Alan noticed, a look of studied indifference. All around the counter lay dollar bills.

The discriminating part of Alan's mind didn't find the entertainment sexy. It wasn't even raunchy. It was gynecology in a flophouse. But gynecological exhibits were what he came for, the first times he entered that dingy place and sat down in front of a counter scarred with cigarette burns, in a vinyl-covered chair that looked truly contaminated. He felt frightened of the place, and more frightened of his reactions to the sights one purchased there. He had his hands covered with plastic bags again. He kept his chair several feet back from the edge of the runway, just in case. It was a little scary sitting there, a few feet away from a naked young woman, who was looking at him upside down from between her legs. But he didn't want to get up and run away, as most people do in their first anguished sessions of exposure and response-prevention therapy. These were, after all, the first naked female bodies he had seen in years.

So he sat there by the runway with his hands covered in plastic bags, his elbows against his chest, his wrists against his neck. He'd pull, not dollar bills, but fives from his shirt pocket, lay them down on the railing, then return to his defensive posture and watch.

He became a Castaways regular, and his self-designed therapy created odd scenes. On a typical late afternoon in that dim room, he sits on a stool at the far end of the runway and orders an astronomically overpriced drink. Nearby, a middle-aged man leans his elbows on the railing, wearing a rapt expression. If he were a cat, he would be purring as he gazes through half-closed eyes at a dancer. She sits naked on the linoleum runway floor, facing that other man, earning his dollar bill by caressing her breasts, while she chats with Alan, over the noise of slow New Age wind-chime music.

"Are you still working at the restaurant?" Alan asks. He helped her get a job at a Northampton restaurant not long ago.

"Yeah!"

"Are you waitressing or hostessing?"

"I'm waitressing now and hostessing on Sundays. It's been really tough, though. I incurred so much debt because I was taking time off from here, so I had to come back here."

"I know you hate it," says Alan.

"Yeah," she says. Absentmindedly she runs a finger around a nipple. The man sitting nearby wets his lips. "And, like, during the days at the restaurant it's pretty slow. It's tough. I mean, I love the place and I love the atmosphere." She lifts a breast, eyeing the other man, then bends her head and licks her nipple. The other man leans forward a little. He licks his lips delicately.

Alan doesn't look half as strange as many of the other patrons. He talks to the stripper about her jobs, her dreams, her grades in school, her boyfriend; finally, she stands and lets the other man run his dollar bill up and down her leg, then stick it in her garter. Alan puts a five on the ledge. There is no question of his touching her garter belt. She murmurs thanks to Alan, and moves off on her high heels to attend to the other men, saying to Alan over her shoulder, "The only thing I'm scared of is that I won't be able to handle both jobs during the semester, and I might have to choose this one over the other one because this is the one that, I can pay my bills."

Alan grew weary of the Castaways. It had served its purpose. It had allowed him to relearn the female geography. In retrospect, this hadn't been very difficult. "After all," Alan later said, "it's pretty obvious."

He graduated to photography. Primitive Leathers, a tiny but well-stocked erotic-gadget store, lay just a few blocks south of Alan's building. He began to shop there, buying paraphernalia for his photo shoots—feather boas, platform shoes, leather mesh bikinis, chains. He set up a studio in his apartment. Word spread fast in the quasi-underground world of erotic catering. He paid well for models, always careful to make sure they were over eighteen, always getting signed releases, and letting them strike the poses of their choice. One wanted to do elaborate S&M tableaus. Alan had a carpenter construct an apparatus in his studio, like the framework of a tepee, from which a model, if she chose, could hang by chains. Nothing dangerous, just exotic. He didn't like the idea of seeing anyone get hurt. He worried a little about the rumors that were bound to spread through town, and what they would do to his reputation. Then he thought, "Well, it's a little late for that." He stayed behind the camera, treading on the brink of real engagement.

Many of the things poets have said about love—love distills desire upon the eyes, love brings bewitching grace into the hearts of those he would destroy, love is more cruel than lust—could be said of Alan's experience when he at last fully reentered the contaminated world of Northampton. He met a beautiful twenty-nine-year-old woman who was living in town and working a respectable but low-paying job there. Her name was Suzanne. The first time he saw her, drinking coffee at a table on Main Street, she took his breath away. He asked if she'd let him photograph her. She said she'd think about it. He persisted. Finally, she told him no, and he stopped asking.

A few weeks after that, feeling a bit lonely and sad, Alan stopped at the Castaways for the first time in months.

When Alan Scheinman approached her, Suzanne thought, "He's probably far from a photographer." Not that she objected in principle to being photographed with her clothes off, which was what she suspected Scheinman had in mind. But she didn't think she wanted anything to do with him.

Suzanne grew up in an old working-class New England town. She went to the Polish church because her mother was the organist. Suzanne had a good voice and she liked to sing; eventually she gained enough poise to do it in front of a microphone. When she was fifteen, the priest asked that she take part in the Lady of Częstochowa Holy Mary Mother of God procession. "I had a long white dress like a *bride,* and a veil and all these little children who grabbed the veil. It was something even more gaudy than a first communion, because we all wore white linen and there was incense in front of us and behind us, a procession of virgins or something, and, of course, I'm like squirming and blushing, because I'm like smoking joints and drinking rum and doing everything but screwing with my boyfriend. And, oh my God, why couldn't it be a *black* veil? Standing up and selecting the lilies and putting them around the statue and reading whatever was the psalm of the day. And the only way I could justify it—I was a student of the classics, of Latin. Five years. The only way I could justify it, I was a vestal virgin. I was like chosen by the high priestess. I just kept having this illusion that this was just a modern-day version of that. That I had *power* because I was in that position, even though I felt really humiliated."

She left home and childhood full of potential and, she felt, unequipped to use it. She still didn't know why. She had energy. She was adventurous. She had gotten excellent grades in high school and she got excellent ones in college, first at Boston University, then at the University of Massachusetts. "I had something going, I was really good, as an English student. I did really well. I was told by a professor, 'You wrote the best paper I've ever read by an undergrad.' And I thought it was a pretty large compliment to be paid, you know, and he said, 'I assume you're going on, aren't you?' And I just said, 'No, actually I'm not. I'm going to New York City and hang out with my boyfriend and try to get into the film industry.' I mean, that's what he was doing. And, you know, I was just trying to ride on someone else's wave, really, and at the time that was more important to me? Love was like the number one thing for me in my life, being loved by somebody, and I seemed to have kind of a deficiency and so I based my decisions on that, rather than my own career."

She spent her twenties in furious action, which, she felt, led nowhere. She acted with an experimental theater group in Boston, and made some cash delivering what are called strip-o-grams. She'd arrive in a gorilla suit or French maid's uniform, or—one of her favorites—a bag lady costume, and she'd dance as she unzipped them. She never jumped out of a cake. She worked on a small newspaper, which opened and closed during her tenure. She wrote some stories, but didn't save her clippings. She described her philosophy this way: "Live for the moment, work your butt off, but you're not going to amount to anything." She got married, but it didn't last. Her husband, she said, "objectified" her. With him and most other boyfriends, she felt adored, even worshipped, and left without room to breathe. The young Arab who wanted to possess her in a tent he set up in his living room was only one extreme example. A man she'd thought was just a friend ruined her friendship with his wife by propositioning Suzanne. She didn't think she'd encouraged him.

She had lived in Northampton as an au pair during her last year at the University of Massachusetts, and she loved the town. She thought of it as "Cambridge West." It was, she felt, a very safe place for a woman, and lively enough for her besides. She returned and began to look for a job. She didn't find much. Northampton's new prosperity, so apparent downtown, depended largely on a corps of young men and especially young women who would work for low wages as clerks and waitresses just for the privilege of being here. She had to compete with thirty other people to land a minor managerial position that paid only $20,000 a year. It was a better job than many, but rents were high in Northampton. She ended up sharing a small house with a couple of other single people, one of them a young woman who, Suzanne noticed, kept strange hours. The clues accumulated. Finally Suzanne asked her if she was a stripper.

"It's at this really surreal club," her housemate told her. "It looks kind of like something in a David Lynch movie, out there in the country on Route Five. Come up and see me there some time."

"Well, I need some cash," Suzanne said. "And some play money, too."

She kept her night job a secret from colleagues at her daylight one. Most weekend days downtown she'd see three or four of her fellow strippers window-shopping and having coffee, and she'd wonder, "Are we the women of the scarlet letter around here?" Not that she was ashamed. She thought she performed a service. Some of the men at the club said things to her that they probably couldn't say to their wives or girlfriends. Or maybe some of them *had* said those things at home, and now the only way they could get a glimpse of a female body was if they paid for it. But better for the wives and girlfriends that those men should have a place to go. And the money was good. She could earn $200 to $300 in about five hours of working the runway and doing table dances. She was older than most of the others—twenty-nine—very fit, thin and muscular, and unlike most, she enjoyed the work. "I'm a good dancer, and a frustrated performer also." Most of the men who came to watch her and laid their dollar bills on the ledge of the runway were pathetic, but for once it wasn't the men who were in charge. Not when she was up on that linoleum stage. "It's actually part of my therapy," she thought. "There's a certain power that I'm reclaiming, and maintaining, and experiencing."

Unlike some of her colleagues at the Castaways, Suzanne actually did dance and she actually did strip sometimes—that is, she started out with some clothes on. She planned her performances. She gave some thought to her music and her costumes. Tonight, a Saturday night, she planned to try out some new music—"Liz Phair, and she's like quote unquote feminist, and it's a little country-sounding." She'd wear one of her good costumes—"This very demure kind of a little farm-girl milkmaid's outfit." It was still evening when she climbed onto the runway, dressed in a blue-and-white checked miniskirt, a little white shirt, not buttoned but tied above her navel, and a straw hat with flowers on it. She had just started strutting around and stripping, aware of the faces gazing up at her but, as always, distant from them, like an actress, when she saw Scheinman—the bushy mustache, the odd, quick, nervous-looking mannerisms—come in the front door.

It occurred to her that she might leave the stage and hide out in the dressing room. "This is a moment of truth," she thought. "Am I a professional or not?" She could tell he hadn't noticed her yet. He was standing alone near the bar, looking around, as if he might be thinking of leaving. She kept watch on him from the corners of her eyes, as she paused to let a patron slide a bill under her garter. Then she saw his face turn toward her. Then he started squinting at her. She thought he must have recognized her. Then she thought he hadn't. He came to the runway, still squinting up at her, and sat down at the far end. She was naked now, except for her milkmaid's straw hat. Turning away from Scheinman, she tilted it forward a little, so that it would cover some of her face.

She'd planned to fling it off at some point. Maybe she'd just keep it on, keep her back to him and her head tilted down for the next twenty minutes. But that wasn't possible. "All right," she thought. "I'll just give the bastard my best show."

She worked the entire crowd with special vigor, all the while keeping half an eye on Scheinman. He looked mesmerized, she thought. He didn't seem to be looking at her face anyway. Finally, she moved to the end of the runway and squatted down in front of him. She had kept the hat on for this moment. She pulled it off and leaned her face toward his. With all the irony she could put in her voice, she said, "Surprise."

They talked later that evening. Since he'd found out her secret, she decided she might as well let him photograph her. He said he'd like to take her out to dinner first.

Soon Alan had begun to get his teeth repaired and to purchase a new wardrobe. Eventually, he shaved off his mustache.

Without it, he looked ten years younger. But of course he could never look as young as Suzanne.

Alan often breakfasted at Sylvester's, a historic spot on Pleasant Street, the renovated former home of Sylvester Graham, a vegetarian who invented the cracker that bears his name—though the commercial version doesn't much resemble his. Graham proselytized for twelve-hour-old whole-wheat bread, for opened bedroom windows, for cold showers, and for the reform of courtship. Ralph Waldo Emerson described him as "the poet of bran bread and pumpkins." Graham influenced American diet profoundly, it is said. Once, during a lecture in Boston, he dared to discuss sex publicly, and on top of that suggested that for the sake of health, it should be carefully regulated—that, in effect, women should have the power to decide when to have sex with their husbands. And that shouldn't be more than once a month, he felt. A near-riot ensued. Graham spent his last years here in Northampton. The place didn't treat Graham very well. A local newspaper article of 1851 made sport of the elderly man: "The people of Northampton were amused one day last week by seeing this philosopher of sawdust pudding trundled on a wheelbarrow from his house to the barber's house." Perhaps Graham's greatest offense was to go before a town meeting and say that because of all he had done for the world he shouldn't have to pay taxes. Children sometimes threw rocks at him.

Alan liked the feeling of a historic place. At another time he might have thought it amusing that he should eat his breakfast here, in what had been the last abode of the former oddest man in town. But he was entirely preoccupied these days with what he called "the relationship."

He reviewed the facts of his recent return to the world. "Initially it was just a complete, total, mindless joy," he said. But now he had calmed down enough to look at matters clearly. He'd gone into a tunnel for ten years and come out in his early fifties, more mature. "All the things that I took for granted for years and years and years, like sex. It was like starting all over again, but not as an adolescent. I had already realized what it meant to be alone and what it meant to miss the touch, the loving or lusting touch of another person, or to have a loving or lusting touch or both toward someone. It's been like the first time every time. I don't think it's going to wear off." He added, "Not to say I'm a model of mental health now, but I do enjoy things now."

He had learned how to live more entirely alone than most hermits. Now it seemed he would head into the future accompanied. Suzanne had beauty, intelligence, and energy, and hadn't yet figured out how to make the best use of them. He'd given her money so that she could quit her dead-end day job, and see a therapist regularly. Eventually, they'd launch some sort of enterprise together, with his money and experience, her energy and imagination. Was she in this for the money? Of course, he'd posed that question to himself, and he'd pulled the thorn from it by offering the money before she could have asked for it, and also by giving it to her in a lump sum. "So that if things don't work out between us, she's not caught in the middle." And if money were all that mattered on her side of the relationship, she wouldn't have told him his teeth made her uncomfortable or asked him about the bizarre rumors she'd heard about him. And she would have agreed to let him retire her from stripping. But she had refused to quit. He didn't like that, but he could live with it.

"She'd walk naked through the streets of Northampton if it was at all possible," Alan said. "That's her. I mean, she's completely unfettered in her mind. She's just frustrated that she can't do all the things she wants to do. So I don't know. That's very threatening in a sense, but what's good about her and what makes me much less threatened is that I can tell she's serious about the relationship, because she puts things on the table." He had never met anyone quite like her. All that vast potential wasted in a sordid little strip joint. All she needed was opportunity. He could provide that, then stand back and watch her fly. "She's not quite successful yet, but she's heading that way. I'd love to see her do that. I can't do it for her. I don't have the skill, and no one can do it for her anyway. I don't want to make her my tool. I just want to lay out a smorgasbord in front of her. Let her make her own decisions. She's a person who can't be controlled, and I don't want to control her."

Now when Alan laughed, the sorrowful sound was gone. "I can survive the relationship with her and I can carry my end of it. I feel pretty confident. I don't know if I can keep her completely satisfied, because she's a very juicy woman, very passionate, and I have moments of passion, but I don't sustain passion. I'm a grinder, though I'm highly opinionated and I certainly have a well-developed ego. There's part of me that's coldly dispassionate about her and the relationship. Which isn't to say that I'm not involved with her, but I'm *clearly* not losing myself in the relationship. I'm *clearly* maintaining myself strongly from this relationship, and I'm encouraging her to do the same thing, though she needs less encouragement than I do. I would have a tendency to throw myself in. I'm trying to throw myself in, trying to entertain all sorts of possibilities, but maintaining a sense of self. I'm not certain that it's entirely possible. When I said this to my shrink, he smiled a little bit, but he said, 'Well, sounds like everything's proceeding as well as it possibly can right now. You seem encouraged and I think you oughta be.'"

People used to say he looked like a rodent, scurrying across the streets. The furtive, harried look was gone now. He still wore shorts and ragged sweaters at times, but at other times he actually dressed up. He sat at breakfast with careless-looking ease, silk shirt opened halfway down his chest. When he smiled now, he looked like a boulevardier.

The relationship lasted about four months. At Sylvester's, he reported its crumblings and revivals many times. They had the first argument in which they raised their voices, shouting at each other terms such as "commitment" and "exclusive relationship," which was what he wanted, and "ambivalence," which was what she said she felt. Several times he called her answering machine and said he thought their romance was at an end, that she had lost interest. She agreed, and then again she didn't. Some return messages said that she couldn't live without him. In his journal Alan wrote a poem:

> Love, dark insight opens mind
> Closes heart. Lover closes door,
> Uttering words of love and regret
> With sad sounds of tsk tsk

They started to talk on the phone and Alan said he couldn't talk directly to her; she should hang up, and he would say what he had to say to her answering machine. The next day he planned to finance joint projects with her. The next he told her the relationship, the romantic part, was over, and she agreed, and he made a couple of dinner dates for the weekend, and then she called and said she missed him, so he canceled his dates. Then he went into Thorne's Marketplace, to the science store, and purchased some symbolic items: a 15-million-year-old shark's tooth, a 175-million-year-old piece of amber with a stingerless bee trapped inside it, and a piece of a meteor, billions of years old. He left these in a gift-wrapped package at her house, with a note that read, "Put your troubles in perspective. You need time, but we have just a tiny bit of time." It had been a short, elegant note, but then, he said ruefully, he kept adding things to it.

A thought was blossoming in him, he said: "I'll use her for everything I can, and when I'm done, I'll dump her." He had to say this to reject it. He remembered that when he'd arrived at McLean, the very first day, he'd been told he must prepare himself for the day that he would leave. It was time to do that now with her.

His last conversation with his psychiatrist had left him feeling that he'd harmed the relationship, that all his gifts had placed "unspoken demands" on her and that she was bound to feel "overwhelmed" and bound to express a need for "autonomy." It pained him to think that he, who was a good negotiator and businessman, was least adept at handling what mattered most to him. "I'm just so totally inept when it comes to relationships. When it comes to personal emotional stuff, what's appropriate is *so* unclear to me, that as soon as I have feelings for anyone, I'm over my head. Everything gets blurred."

He said this to a friend, who told him, "You're being too hard on yourself." After all, Alan had only just emerged from ten years of solitude. He was bound to be rusty at relationships.

"Yeah. Except that I wasn't any good at them before."

He laughed, the kind of laugh that seems to hurt. A person with broken ribs would laugh like that. "How can I be so confused as not to know when I'm aspiring to too much? Did I make too much of my relationship with Suzanne? Was it just inappropriate? In some ways in retrospect, it was extremely inappropriate. At the time it just seemed okay. But it seemed okay in the context of a guy who has *no* idea of what 'okay' is. I mean 'okay' in the sense that if I see someone who is attractive I don't rip their clothes off and say, 'Let's fuck.' If I see someone attractive, I don't say, 'Gee, I find you attractive. Let's go out to dinner tonight.' "

He paused. "Actually, I have said that."

In the middle of the night years ago, Tommy parked his cruiser near a dirt road to the Meadows, and in a moment, to his surprise, a prominent citizen, an older man, appeared out of the dark, walking east toward the great river. Tommy called to him. Tommy knew him well enough only for hellos and weather conversation, but the man stopped and climbed into the cruiser and started talking. On and on he talked, about nothing that seemed very important to Tommy, but, his radio being silent, small talk seemed as good a way as any to pass the dead hours of the night. Tommy thought he sensed a hint of urgency in the man's voice, but then again this guy was known to be a bit eccentric. He talked to Tommy for almost two hours. The next day he showed up at the station, handed Tommy his rosary, and said, "You saved my life last night." Then it all seemed clear. The man had planned to drown himself in the Connecticut. Just by chance Tommy had intervened. He knew it for a certainty.

At times like those it seemed as if there really was design in the intersecting lives of the town. For Alan, the place seemed just big enough to hold out the promise that he would find the right person in it. He still thought he had found her. The place was also small enough to keep her in his view, now that he had lost her.

Alan took long walks through downtown and its surroundings. He knew the landscape well, all the alleys and the hidden spots, such as the dry riverbed that he occasionally traced through backyards toward the Connecticut. He often felt as though he lived, as he put it, in the third person, observing both other people and himself. He was a watcher, an especially intent one now. He'd driven to Suzanne's house to drop off some books she'd left at his place. A car he didn't recognize was parked outside. He knew from their last conversation that her roommates were away, so the car had to belong to someone visiting Suzanne. Alan noticed cars. "It was a distinctive car. It was a very attractive car. It was a British-racing-green Chrysler product with a tan convertible top."

Alan drove away. He didn't want a scene or even a conversation. A few hours later he returned to drop off the books, and the car was gone. Later he saw Suzanne on the sidewalk on the other side of Main Street, walking with a man. No matter how crowded downtown was, she stood out for him. Seeing her, and unseen by her, he studied the other man. He looked young—

younger than Alan, anyway. He was casually and conservatively dressed. Maybe he was the engineer she'd mentioned. Alan remembered, from a time that now seemed long ago, her telling him that she'd met a "mellow guy" and was going to the movies with him. His heart had sunk in expectation of her telling him, as she had a few days later, that she was going to this guy's house, because he worked with computers and would teach her how to surf the Internet. She'd told Alan where the fellow lived, an apartment house downtown. Watching from a distance now, Alan saw the man climb into the British-racing-green Chrysler. A few days after that, he went out walking on Pleasant Street and spotted the green car again, turning down a side street. He stopped and peered after it. The car turned in to the lot of the apartment house where Suzanne had said the computer expert lived. QED.

He felt relieved, he said. "I have to admit that as much as I would rather have a good relationship with her—although I'd rather have none than a bad relationship—that I do take some comfort in knowing that she's with someone who, who is anchored in the real world. I do take some comfort. In that. I don't think that this is necessarily a deep romantic relationship. I think that he's more like her than I am, a more familiar element. And I think that's part of it. I think when she was talking about, complaining that I wasn't good enough turn-on material to have as a steady boyfriend—she was saying it in those terms, but I think it was a more global thing. It was like, 'I think you're too old for me.' She would say things to me like, 'You're a pretty good dancer, but I don't like the way you dance. You don't dance the way I do.' Of course, I dance in the sixties style, and she dances in an eighties and nineties style. And she'd say, 'We dance so differently.' And she'd say, 'I can usually tell who's going to be the most satisfactory lovers for me, from the way they dance. People that dance more like me.' And so. Which expands from the notion of, whether or not I'm really a satisfactory lover to her, to whether or not I'm a satisfactory relationship for her. And a person who's more like her age, like this guy . . ."

Soon, from a stripper friend, Alan heard Suzanne was moving. A few days later, he saw her car go by, filled to the roof with stuff. That afternoon he walked through town shying away from people on the street, now and then bringing his forearms to his chest. But the fit passed. He called Suzanne's old number and the recording gave him a new number. The prefix signified that she'd simply moved a few miles away, to a neighboring town.

CHAPTER 12

I Could Do This Stuff

Snow fell yet again on March 8. Thirty-five trucks of various sizes with fifty-one men aboard plowed through the night. The revolving yellow light on the roof of the big sander truck looked like a beacon on a mobile lighthouse in the driving snow. At the controls, young Rich Parasiliti of the DPW glanced at the windows of the passing houses. In them TVs glowed. Fireplaces flickered. Rich smiled. "We'll see how many babies are born nine months from now." Obliged to work all night inside a roaring, lurching machine, Rich was a lot more cheerful than some citizens at home. One storm ago, a citizen had hurled his snow shovel at the windshield of the snowplow just ahead of Rich; the man had just finished clearing his driveway when the plows had arrived and buried it again. Here and there tonight, homeowners put barricades of lawn chairs across the mouths of their driveways to try to block the plows. Around midnight a figure appeared in Rich's headlights, facing the oncoming plow, holding his shovel at port arms, defending his driveway against the public interest. Rich laughed and drove around him.

By the time the storm ended, the season's cumulative total had reached 109 inches, the most snow ever recorded in

Northampton. The local travel agencies were swamped. All over town, residents muttered that they might just leave this place for good. But then, as if appeased at last, the weather relented.

Coming out of an apartment building—another routine domestic sorted out—Tommy stopped in his tracks amid melting snow and turned an ear skyward. "Geese. The geese are back." The last snow fell on April 10, but it didn't amount to much. Out on his rounds, Tommy tuned the cruiser's commercial radio to the Red Sox on WHMP, to hear the sound of bats on balls, the sound of new-mown grass. Here the grass was just beginning to turn green. Good citizens swept the sand off it beside the roads in Florence. He spotted lacrosse nets on the high school playing fields and paused to watch the boys practice. He sniffed the new air that came in the cruiser's windows. He could smell the town again—the earthy smell of the brimming river; the sewage treatment plant, odorous on lower Pleasant Street. Jonquils bloomed in the gardens beside the tidy houses in the historic district of Elm Street. Down below in the Meadows, tractors inched across the fields. On the sidewalks he caught glimpses of faces he hadn't seen in months. The town had come out of hibernation. Now at last enough was going on outdoors to override unquiet thoughts. Moreover, Tommy knew a secret. The wider world of criminality was coming for a visit.

When Tommy's old friend Steve had gone off to the state police some years ago, Tommy had wanted to go with him. But he hadn't done quite well enough on the state police exam. That was an odd thing about Tommy. He welcomed danger and feared written tests. Back when he worked as a young security guard at the Hotel Northampton, he used to get bored and jumpy in the dead hours before dawn. He'd climb to the roof and walk up and down the narrow ledge of the building's triangular pediment. Balancing precariously over King Street far below, he replaced all mundane anxieties with one that he could master. Several years ago, he'd arrived with just one other officer at the site of Northampton's last adolescent riot, and the moment he waded into the fighting crowd, bottles flying past him, he felt completely calm. But he'd felt very nervous every time he sat down at a desk to take a professional exam. Questions that he could have answered anywhere else left him stupefied.

A few years back he and Steve had worked a great deal together, Steve as a state drug detective and Tommy as the local one. They'd learned the devious trade as partners, with a lot of help from Frankie. They still did their Christmas shopping together—they'd buy a present, have a beer, buy another, and so on. But professionally, they'd parted ways. Steve went on to bigger things. While Tommy spent this past winter patrolling Northampton, searching for something to do, Steve worked for a state and federal task force, posing as a drug dealer who supplied cocaine to a Connecticut chapter of the Diablos, a large motorcycle gang.

The task force planned to trap the bikers at Northampton's little airfield in the Meadows. Steve would land in what looked like a private plane, carrying a briefcase filled with drugs. He'd hand the briefcase to the bikers, they'd hand him the cash, and then, once Steve had walked slowly away, FBI agents would come out of hiding bristling with guns. They'd emerge from bulletproof Kevlar boxes, constructed for the occasion and strategically placed around the country airfield. It was Steve who suggested Northampton as the site. The airport was remote from the populated parts of town, so the area was fairly easy to control. And, maybe most important, Tommy worked in town. The bikers would bring guns. For some moments Steve would have his back turned to them, as he walked off with their cash. The last thing he wanted was for something untoward to happen on the periphery, for a civilian or a local cop to blunder in. He wanted someone he trusted absolutely to take care of security and local logistics—to make sure an ambulance was ready, for one thing. He also knew that

Tommy felt a little restive. Northampton had a shortage of serious criminals acting up just now. So Steve imported some for him.

In the midst of the preparations for the bust, Jean was implanted with fertilized eggs again. Tommy drove her to Boston, then drove her home, and, feeling guilty and excited, left her there and went down to the airport to watch the FBI agents rehearse. On the appointed day, an hour or so before the sting, he sat in a room in a motel out near the highway. He had his pistol in his lap. He sat amid half a dozen other cops and agents, watching a video screen. The Diablos, three of them, were in the adjacent room. The FBI had wired it for sound and video. Watching the video screen, Tommy saw one of the bikers, an enormously fat man named Nino, walk to the door between the rooms. It was locked, of course. The gigantic biker rattled it. The cops looked at each other, all holding their breath. Tommy thought, "If I were him, I'd kick it down." He was also thinking how much fun this was. The video camera in the other room was lodged in a piece of furniture. These federal guys had toys he'd never even dreamed about.

On the screen in their room, the fat man, Nino, turned away. Then, through the hidden microphone, he offered his assessment of Northampton. "This is the wrong part of Massachusetts. They're all fags here."

The bikers left for the airport. Tommy followed at a distance. The bust went off almost exactly as planned, and with no shots fired. Tommy was in charge of transporting the prisoners afterward. He reserved the gigantic Nino for himself. Nino was so big Tommy had to link together three pairs of cuffs to secure his hands. "Nino, I've got leg irons for ya. You gonna run?"

"Yeah, I'm gonna run across the parking lot and have a heart attack."

Tommy put Nino in the backseat of the cruiser, then headed

for the station. "You know, I used to be a biker myself," he said over his shoulder.

"Oh, yeah?" said Nino.

"Yeah, I used to be pretty much known in my neighborhood as an outlaw. On my Raleigh three-speed. *Ching, ching, ching.*"

"Man, you're crazy."

"And don't you forget it."

They chatted all the way to the station. "You guys shouldn't be worried about us," Nino said. "You should be worried about the blacks."

"Do you work, Nino?"

"Nah. I'm disabled. The doctor said I'm retarded."

Tommy helped Nino don an orange prison jumpsuit. "You look like a pumpkin, Nino."

Nino laughed.

Later on that night, he drove Nino to the Hampden county jail in Ludlow. Tommy hadn't slept for about twenty-four hours by then. Exhaustion often worked on him the way dangerous situations did. Objects became sharply etched, like clouds on the north wind. Meanwhile, thoughts came at quickened tempo and in a higher register.

"You Diablos have a gang sign?"

"No. That's just for Puerto Ricans."

"I'll think one up for you."

Nino was processed and locked away. Tommy went to say good-bye. He stood outside Nino's cell. "I've got it." He made his fingers into a pair of little horns on either side of his head and wiggled them. Nino's gigantic frame shook with laughter. "Nah, that's no good, Nino. It would look ridiculous with a helmet on. That's another reason to repeal the helmet law."

"Tom, you're all right," Nino said. But then he looked glum.

"Hey," Tommy said, through the bars. He felt as if he were talking to a sad-faced child. He really meant to buck him up. "Remember when your mother said, 'Nino, we're sending you to camp,' and you didn't want to go? And it turned out you kinda liked it?"

"Tom, this ain't camp."

"Hey, Nino, it won't be all that bad."

"Whaddaya mean it won't be all that bad? I'm goin' to prison for forty-five fuckin' years. I'm gonna die in jail."

"Well, when you put it that way," said Tommy, not unkindly.

When he was a young patrolman working Midnights, and the bars had closed and his radio grown quiet, Tommy used to sit in his cruiser and play the harmonica. Sometimes a fellow cop who had a harmonica, too, would pull up alongside and they'd play duets in the dark. Sometimes Tommy would sit in his cruiser outside the picture window of a night owl's house in Florence and, unbeknownst to the man inside, watch movies with him, killing the time until dawn. Then he'd get his cup of coffee and drive to a good spot, sometimes up to Turkey Hill and sometimes down along the edge of the eastern Meadows, past the airport and the last of the houses where the road turns to dirt and gnarled trees are draped with twisted vines.

His town was lovely down there at that hour. Most big-city cops, he'd tell himself, probably drank their morning coffee beside the hulks of burned-out buildings. In the distance to the west, the steeples of downtown rose over the elevated Interstate. Standing by the river, its waters roiled brown and steaming like his coffee on those early spring mornings, Tommy gazed south across the yellow fields, all covered with the flattened stalks of last year's corn, like gigantic mats of straw. In the distance, in the gap between Northampton's little mountain ranges, the red lights on the smokestack of the Mount Tom power plant were blinking. He had imagined that on one of those mornings, he would see another set of blinking lights appear. A small plane would materialize against the wooded hills, swoop down over the runway, and eject a package. In his fantasy, based only on old rumors, the package would contain kilos of heroin or cocaine, and he would be waiting for the big-time dealers when they came to pick it up. The airport bust came close enough to his old fantasy to seem like its fulfillment.

A cost-conscious bureaucrat might have yelped when he saw the bill. Northampton had been well protected. Forty FBI agents and a host of other people had been deployed. A helicopter and fixed-wing plane had circled the operation. All to round up three armed bikers. Of course, Tommy didn't look at it that way. At one point he asked Nino if he thought of using his gun when the FBI agents came out of hiding. Nino said, "Yeah, I thought of usin' it. To shoot myself." Nino added, speaking of the agents, "Those guys were slick."

Tommy had watched carefully as the federal agents had rehearsed. Their techniques were sound, a few seemed novel, but none differed fundamentally from the ones he taught at the police academy. Watching them, he thought, "I could do this stuff." After it was over and the prisoners all put away, one of the agents said, "Hey, Tom, come on down with us to Springfield for a drink." He couldn't. It was long since past the time when he should have been getting home to Jean. But earlier, during one of the rehearsals, an agent told him that the FBI was hiring cops these days. Tommy should apply, he said.

Everyone lives somewhere, and sooner or later the suspicion that somewhere else is better disturbs the peace of home. Over the years Tommy had felt tugs from the wider world. Thirty-three was old to be feeling them grow stronger. But for a while he wasn't sure his own job would ever feel the same once the FBI packed up their amazing gear and left and he went back to routine patrol in little old routine Northampton.

He wondered if he'd have a chance of getting into the FBI. It was the highest law-enforcement agency in the country. From here it looked like the pinnacle of his profession. He could picture himself an aging local cop, staring out the door to the parking lot and wondering if he could have been a federal agent. In a few years he'd be too old to try.

He sent away for an application. The information packet said that over fifty thousand people applied each year, and this year the FBI would accept only about nine hundred for training. He thought he'd have a better chance of getting into Harvard. He read on. "Prior to employment, all candidates must complete a rigorous application process. Successful completion of written tests and . . ." Tommy thought he might as well stop there. He left the application in his desk at home, among other souvenirs.

One night around this time, the chief invited Tommy into his car for a talk. In the car, Russ said that he wished he could clone Tommy and have one O'Connor supervisor of evening patrol and the other the detective sergeant. He said he was doing all he could to get Tommy back into the detective bureau, and it wouldn't be long now. It was almost as if the chief had read his mind. Anyway, that news was good.

In retrospect, it seemed as if most people who got a chance to leave had taken it. Recently, for the first time in several years, Jean had talked about moving. She said, "We're going to be old and alone and in the same place." But where in the world would being childless feel better? "We'd have to find an island where they don't allow kids." He knew that if one night he told Jean he was ready to leave, the next morning he'd wake up surrounded by suitcases. But just having entertained the idea of applying for another job, another life, made his own seem much more complicated than it already was. He could imagine selling their house and packing up their possessions, and it gave him a sick feeling on top of a sick feeling. "Christ, I'd still be in my parents' house if Jean and my mother hadn't moved me."

Bill was getting hard of hearing, and a disturbance of the inner ear made him dizzy sometimes. Tommy and Jack, back on a visit last winter, had grilled the doctor. He'd said it wasn't serious. Bill certainly didn't look sick. He was making supper.

"Hey, Pop, how ya doin'?"

Bill turned and sadly shook his head. "This morning I was feeling very blue. I was fightin' it. Coming down the stairs, I was talking out loud. I said, 'There's an old man lives in this house. And he's old and he lost his wife, many years ago.' Of course, that put me way up." Bill made his great laugh, then went on, sadly, "But he comes down the stairs very slowly now, not with a jump the way I used to."

Tommy smiled. "Well, think of something else to say to yourself. Something a little more lively."

So Bill told a Tunker Hogan story. A complicated tale in which Tunker falsely accused Big Jim's Republican opponent of endangering the nuns at St. Michael's parochial school.

Over dinner, Bill said he was going to visit Tommy's mother's grave. The next morning Tommy drove to the cemetery down in Holyoke, to make sure things were ready. It was the start of a very bad day. He sank almost to his knees in the dirt surrounding the grave. He searched out the cemetery's caretaker. "My mother was buried two years ago, and last year my father practically sank into the grave and today I did, too." The maintenance man said he'd take care of it soon. "No, no, no," said Tommy. "My father's coming over. You'll come and look at it with me now."

Then he went off to give Jean a shot, and just a few minutes afterward, the call came saying she wasn't pregnant. The doctor hadn't bothered to look at the results of her last blood test until then. The shot had been unnecessary.

Once in a while Tommy seemed like a dangerous person. You knew that anyone who hurt Jean would probably pay a dreadful price. He came to work fuming. "Here she's had two surgeries for the fifth time and because some bonehead doctor who's making a million doesn't read the results right away, she has to get a shot. That's because they don't give a shit about the little people." He said to the doctor far away in Boston, *"Do your job."*

CHAPTER 13

The Witness List

JUDGE RYAN HAD returned to the bench. He wiped a hand downward over his gray beard, as if wiping the defense attorney's argument off it. "Your client's testimony was incredible to me," he growled at the lawyer.

Tommy sat in the gallery, waiting to testify in another case. He spent most of that day in Judge Ryan's court, then went back to the police station, looking bemused. In the hallway he ran into a fellow officer. "I was in court today? And Mike Ryan sent *two* guys to jail," said Tommy. "In that case of mine, he gave the guy ninety days direct, and he said if he wasn't there tomorrow to start serving it, he'd do a year."

"*Ryan?*" said the other cop, in a voice of utter disbelief.

"I know," said Tommy.

But the judge hadn't changed. He still described himself as "a liberal libertarian." He still handed down lenient rulings and made special allowances for unemployed musicians and especially for immigrants—"If the Irish can become law-abiding, anybody can." He felt, as always, that if society must have jails, then it ought to reserve them for people who had truly injured others, for defendants such as the two men he'd sent to county jail today. One had terrorized a woman for the second time and the other had robbed a paraplegic.

And the judge still liked working in what he called the vulgar court. For one thing it connected him, on a long, meandering line, with the frontier town of the 1600s, where, records suggest, the issues judges dealt with weren't all that different from today's. Except for spelling: "Obadiah Miller complaynes against Joane his wife for abusing him with reproachful tearmes or names as calling him foole toad and vermine and threatening him," reads the transcript of one case from the western Massachusetts frontier court. Like his distant predecessors, Judge Ryan spent a large part of his day sorting out the problems that surround human sexuality. One time a husband and wife stood before Judge Ryan and the husband said that his wife had plugged up his penis with Krazy Glue while he was sleeping on the sofa, and the wife cried out to Judge Ryan, "He ain't usin' it anyway!" On any given day, a visitor to the judge's court was apt to enter in the midst of proceedings that were vulgar in two senses, Judge Ryan sitting behind the bench with his gray-bearded chin on his hand, eyebrows just slightly lifted, as a red-haired female prosecutor cross-examined the defendant: "And she asked for intercourse, she specifically asked for intercourse, and you indicated that in the middle of having intercourse you stopped, and after that incident she was quite hostile to you?"

Life had returned to normal now, since his heart attack. At lunchtime on a fine spring day, Judge Ryan, looking dapper, dressed in suit and tie, headed with a jaunty step down Main Street toward the railroad bridge and TJ's Sports Bar just beyond it. The establishment belonged to John Smith, one of Northampton's bad boys, a good-looking, dark-haired fellow in his forties, one of the judge's best friends. They'd met years ago, when the judge was a probation officer. Out of curiosity John had come to Ryan's office with a high school friend who was on probation. John was the son of a tough, hard-drinking bricklayer who had eight children and threw the boy out of the house. John spent one summer of his high school years sleeping on the roof of the Hotel Northampton. He told Ryan that life on the roof wasn't so bad, and that his girlfriend joined him there.

That John had managed to graduate from high school seemed remarkable to the judge. Even more remarkable, he had managed to become a modestly successful businessman. The judge liked to say that Northampton was the wrong-sized town for a person like John, small enough that everyone heard the bad stories about him but too large for most to know of his good qualities. His generosity, for instance—he employed some people down on their luck, and fed some others for free. It was true, though, that he had a terrible temper. One time the judge said, "John has been in seventy fights in his life. He never backed down, and he never won either." And John earnestly corrected him, saying that there was one fight he did sort of win.

A few years ago the judge went to Key West with John and some other local sports, and the judge took second place there in the Hemingway storytelling contest. He told a story about John in Northampton. In the version Ryan told for the contest, John has a tumultuous relationship with his girlfriend. She picks fights with him when he comes home late. He complains about his girlfriend to his bookie, who advises him to put his foot down and not come home until two in the morning. Then, says his bookie, his girlfriend will be happy to see him when he comes home. That night, a winter night, Ryan is driving home and sees John walking back and forth on Main Street, slapping his hands together, trying to keep warm. He explains that he's teaching his girlfriend a lesson. Ryan tells him this is absurd, he's going to freeze to death. Ryan gives him a ride home.

An hour later John calls, from the police station. When he came home, he found his girlfriend in bed with his bookie, and there was a terrible row. He had thrown a chair through a window and had just picked up a bag of flour when a cop who lived in the building appeared in the doorway, wanting to know what was going on. Moments later the cop was covered with flour, and soon after that three policemen were, with difficulty, subduing him. They put him in a cell down at the police station and he proceeded to destroy it. He ripped the bunk off the wall and the toilet out of the floor and had begun to tear down the ceiling when officers entered and prevented him. So Ryan goes to the station and bails John out, and because he can't think of anywhere else to take him, he puts him in the St. Vincent de Paul clothes box outside St. Michael's parochial school.

The story continued. John's girlfriend goes to live with his bookie. Thus, said Ryan in Key West, he has lost both his bookie and the love of his life.

The truth wasn't all that different from the judge's prize-winning confection. The bookie hadn't been so clever as to talk John into coming home late; John merely caught him sleeping with his girlfriend. Ryan didn't put John in the St. Vincent de Paul box; he spent the night in jail. And on the morning after he had ripped apart his cell—"If they gave me another hour on that ceiling I'd have gotten out," he would say, telling the story himself— Ryan came down to the police station and had a chat with the old chief. They agreed that John would leave town for a while. He had no shoes, so Ryan, who was a defense attorney then, had to carry him piggy-back from the door of the station across the snowy parking lot to his car. He went on a tropical vacation with his unfaithful girlfriend, and about three weeks later called Ryan to see if it was safe to come back to Northampton. Ryan told him over the phone, "You owe me big time."

John's most recent trouble had been splashed all over the Northampton section of the Springfield *Union-News*. He owed the city a considerable amount in property taxes. Now, as the judge approached TJ's, fresh from a morning at court, the door swung open to receive him, an old friend holding it. The judge handed the man a dollar bill in payment for this service; the man handed it back to the judge, who walked to the end of the bar, slapped the bill down in front of John Smith, and said, "Here, John. Pay your taxes."

John turned around on his stool. "Did you see the article in the paper? There are a hundred and sixty other offenders." Some establishments—a nursing home; an apartment complex—owed far more back taxes than he did. "I went from being a draft dodger to a tax dodger."

"Just remember, John," said Judge Ryan, "this country was founded by people who didn't want to pay their taxes."

The lunchtime clientele at TJ's was polymorphous as usual, as at District Court, though there was a higher percentage of respectable clients here—local business folk having lunch at one of the last downtown bars that served decent food but wasn't fancy. Besides, at TJ's, the smoking ban was ignored, which recommended it to a lot of local entrepreneurs, including some who didn't smoke, and also to the judge. He was feeling very well again, and a cigarette or two at lunch was a delicious guilty pleasure.

A garrulous former mental patient also sat at the bar, wearing what looked like a woman's wig. And seated at the far corner of the bar, drinking beer after beer and smoking unfiltered cigarettes, was the blind poet Woody.

The judge sat down at the bar, amid this mixed company, and ordered a diet soda and a sandwich. He was thinking about a woman he'd spotted in the gallery in court today, a defendant's daughter, a truly beautiful young woman. "I want her for a daughter-in-law. I'll find her father innocent if we can have an arranged marriage."

A local businessman sitting nearby started fulminating about the smoking ban. "You know what we've lost? The concept of free enterprise."

"Never mind free enterprise," said Judge Ryan. "We've lost the concept of freedom." He said that his sister forgot to pay a parking ticket and ended up having her registration revoked and her car towed. "Outrageous!" said the judge.

Then, down at the end of the bar, Woody began to recite a poem he'd written. John Smith called out for silence, and turned off the radio behind the bar. Woody had a deep and very raspy voice. He held a hand on his thin chest as if to steady himself. The poem was called "The Hour of the Wolf." "Money talks and animal manure stands silently in the gutter. . . ." It went on for a few minutes, and afterward everyone applauded.

The judge said softly, "That wasn't too bad. Whitmanesque." Then, back on his earlier theme, the judge began quoting Oliver Wendell Holmes, Jr., on the subject of unenforceable laws, and Woody, hearing Holmes's name, said, "He wrote good poetry."

"I thought it was lousy," said Judge Ryan. "There was more poetry in his decisions than in his verses."

"Are you a lawyer?" asked the blind man.

"I used to be," said Judge Ryan. "Then I took a state job. You get older, you want to do different things."

"All I want to do is make money," said the poet.

The judge said, "I was never that interested in that. Sometimes I wish I was. I'd have more of it now."

In fact, Ryan had once gone into private lawyering in order to make money, for his four children's college tuitions. But, as one member of the local bar explained, Ryan never did make much because he kept on representing indigent clients for free. He'd managed to put his kids through college, though, and he made a good salary now—nearly $100,000, about twice what the mayor got paid. He didn't really wish for more than he had, not in any department.

Judge Ryan headed back to court. The air was softening, the trees along the sidewalks in bud. Passersby kept greeting him—friends of his parents; former teachers and coaches; former schoolmates and political allies and rivals; old girlfriends; kids he'd coached in soccer, now grown up. Outside the courthouse, he ran into a small group of men and women—members of the local bar, in suits and dresses—just as one of them was delivering sad news. A native Northamptonite, an old ne'er-do-well, had died yesterday. "He gave us a dog one time," the speaker said to the judge. "Turned out it was stolen."

Judge Ryan smiled. His smile enveloped his face. He would

have been glad to be alive anywhere. He was very glad that it happened to be here.

NORTHAMPTON WAS CALLING on Tommy again. The kids in Gothic dress, like cartoon caricatures of evil—spiked collars, torn black clothes, mascaraed eyes—were spreading trash and graffiti around Pulaski Park, intimidating citizens, and they needed hassling. Tommy trolled what he called his favorite fishing holes, talking to skateboarders and homeboys, old friends and enemies, reformed and recidivist drunks and drug dealers, new acquaintances like the man who used to be a cop in Bosnia and was now bagging groceries in Northampton. Driving through town, Tommy said, "This is life! People are out. People you can talk to. It's like a reunion. I love reunions."

On an afternoon at the end of April, the air turned summerlike. Down in the locker room before his shift, Tommy put on a short-sleeved uniform shirt.

The sergeant of the day shift was sitting at the desk in the gloomy-looking Ready Room. He looked up at Tommy.

Tommy lifted an arm, modeling his uniform shirt. "Short sleeves. It's that time again."

"The witness list for Janacek's trial just came out," the other sergeant said. "I'm not on it. *You* are."

Tommy nodded, and looked away toward a window. The light was very bright outside.

Driving away from the station the next afternoon, Tommy saw an unmarked cruiser in the courthouse parking lot. He pulled up beside the driver's window. A state police detective, an old acquaintance, sat inside. He worked in the D.A.'s office.

"Am I on the witness list for Janacek? I heard I was."

"I don't know, Tommy. I can ask."

Tommy shrugged. "No. That's okay."

He shouldn't have bothered to ask. Of course, he would be on the witness list. Any prosecutor would jump at the chance to have a defendant's oldest friend testify against him. That was how the game was played. Too bad. So sorry. If he were the investigator on this case, he'd expect the prosecutor to do this. He'd be angry if the prosecutor didn't.

The state detective talked about the case—no details, just the gist of it—saying, at length, "When a person says, 'I might have,' ninety-nine percent of the time he did it." Tommy listened, gazing out at nothing, nodding now and then.

Around five, he headed for his father's house. Buds were sprouting on the small trees along the sidewalks and high up in the maples on Forbes Avenue. Everything living seemed to be straining for the sun. Its light has great intensity in New England springtime, especially at evening. No leaves had opened yet to shield the sidewalk. Driving down Forbes Avenue, Tommy was half-blinded by the glare. He pulled into his father's driveway, then turned and saw a red Saab pull in behind him. It seemed to have materialized from behind a curtain of dazzling light. Rick got out, smiling. "Hey, Tom."

Both Tommy and Rick wore sunglasses. They shook hands. They stood together on the sidewalk. Rick looked as if he'd just come back from a hiking trip, tan and lean.

A small, flower-scented breeze came down the street, and on it the voices of children. A few houses away, a young mother was shepherding two toddlers down the sidewalk. They were churning the pedals of plastic tricycles, moving slowly toward Tommy and Rick.

Rick seemed fidgety in spite of his smile. "You and the chief are the only Northampton cops on the witness list." In a moment his voice turned vehement. The D.A.'s office wasn't giving him all the reports they should, he said. They were playing around with the trial date.

"I think you're making a mistake if you think they're out to get ya," said Tommy. "You were a cop in this town a long time. I think they'd like this to just go away."

They hadn't talked in a while. Rick had a lot of news stored up. He said his wife had told him she wished he'd commit suicide.

"Well, you know," said Tommy. He looked squarely at Rick. "If you believed the accusation, you can see where she'd be pissed. Right?"

Rick looked squarely back at him. "Hey, Tom, those two weeks before I saw my daughter's interview, I had the comfort of knowing there was a loaded thirty-eight in the next room."

"I know," said Tommy. "That's why I stayed in close contact with you."

The mother and children on the sidewalk had finally arrived. Tommy turned to them gratefully. He bent down toward the little boy and girl. "And what are your names?" He looked especially shiny and enlarged in his uniform in this light. The two children looked at him big-eyed, and shied away.

"I'm not that scary-looking, am I?"

Rick laughed. "Hey, Tom, looked in the mirror lately?"

Tommy smiled. "Yeah, I know. I looked in the mirror the other day and I thought I was looking at Spellicy." In memory, the physiognomy of all drill instructors remains ferocious. Spellicy had been their drill instructor at the police academy. Tommy used to study Spellicy's head while standing at attention. Spellicy, too, had been bald all over.

The mother and children continued on down the sidewalk, and the conversation resumed, and then, apropos of nothing that had gone before, Rick asked, "You haven't been making any new statements, have you?"

"No, I haven't."

"I know. I would have seen them if you had."

Rick started talking fast and angrily, about the D.A.'s office again, and the most recent deal that they had offered.

"Look, you gotta decide what's best for you," said Tommy.

"What about the truth, Tom?"

"Right. Only you know the facts."

Rick looked angrily around. "I used to believe in justice. I used to believe in all that stuff."

It was time for supper. How often had they parted here, heading home for supper? Rick put a little laugh in his voice. "You're not wearing a wire, are you?"

"Hey," said Tommy. His eyes looked surprised, the whites very large, their innocence offended. "I'll just testify to what's in my statement."

Rick's voice was serious again. "You're not gonna lie. That's one thing you and I have always had in common."

The blessing of the job in springtime was that something else usually lay around the corner. Later, after supper, Tommy was driving down Main Street, trying not to think about his chat with Rick and what it signified and what was coming, when he suddenly yelled, "Oh, Jesus!" and pulled over.

Frankie was mounted on a moped and weaving around in traffic on Main Street.

A few weeks ago Tommy had at last met Frankie's mother, Moms. It might have been better if he hadn't. Moms told him some of Frankie's history: How he'd had a nanny back in the Dominican Republic who had made it possible for him not to learn to tie his shoes until he was eight years old. How his grandmother used to take the spoiled little boy on carriage rides through Santiago. Tommy had turned to him and exclaimed, "Frankie! You were a rich kid!" And later, in the car, on the way to drop him off at the Grove Street Inn, where Frankie was staying again, Tommy had given him a look, a sidelong look, a look of fresh appraisal, which carried no amusement. "So you were a rich kid, Frankie. So pretty much you ruined your life with cocaine."

"Yeah," said Frankie very softly. For a moment he'd looked chastened. Then he'd declared, "That's how come I work with you and Pete." He was saying something about helping to keep the poison out of other people's lives. And Tommy, not looking at him then, had nodded—not in agreement, it seemed, but as if in answer to a thought in his own mind.

But now he was chuckling. Frankie looked like an overgrown kid on the little moped, like a Shriner in a miniature car, like a hefty caballero on a donkey. He was decked out in a white helmet and a black tank top that stretched tight over his ample belly, and he was grinning as he created havoc in the traffic. Then he spotted Tommy. He made a breathtaking U-turn across Main Street.

Tommy put his face in his hands, so as not to see the crash, and said, "What the *fuck*?"

When he looked up, Frankie stood beside the window, straddling the moped. "How do you like my Chebbie? Ah hah hah!"

"Whose is it?"

"A friend's. It's licensed and everything. It's legal."

"*It's* legal. *You* aren't, Frankie. You don't have a license."

"No," said Frankie. "It's a mopad."

"No, you need a license, Frankie."

"Oh, okay," said Frankie, his voice turning soft and sweet. Then he declared bitterly, "I can't even ride a bicycle because of you guys."

"Frankie, you are one of the most difficult people I know to keep out of trouble."

Not long ago Frankie had been arrested by some of Tommy's officers for driving without a license. The car wasn't registered, either. It bore an inactive plate, which Frankie said he'd borrowed. Now he said, "Oakie, you could fix up everything. Why don't you just give me back my license?"

"Frankie, it's your Samson Rodriguez license." Tommy was smiling. "Look. When you go to court, Luce is gonna see you, and this motor vehicle shit you got into here is gonna go away."

Frankie thanked him, and walked off, pushing the moped.

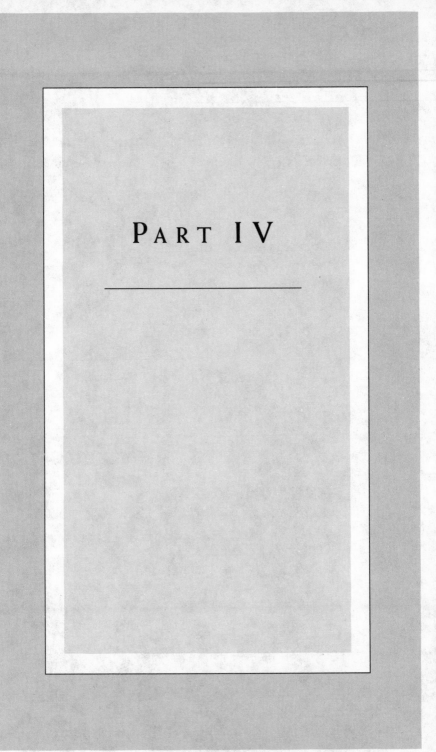

PART IV

CHAPTER 14

Public Works

THE SKY BEGINS to brighten, and the birds of summer chatter in anticipation, but dawn is still a long way off, and in its colorless first hints the lighted sign above the door of a little building back of Main Street still stands out:

$$W_{1400}^{HMP}$$

Inside, a gray-haired man—slightly stoop-shouldered, dressed in shorts and sandals—moves quickly between his desk in the glassed-in studio and the adjacent room. He makes the coffee, scans the newsprint that spills out of the wire service printers, calls Russ Murley up in Maine and records the day's prediction—"Hot and hazy with evening thundershowers"—studies the local section of the *Union-News* and rewrites a few news stories from it on an old typewriter, records the feed from the network, checks the studio's thermometer. "Seventy-eight degrees? Can that be right?" Typing, flicking switches, he listens to the police scanner. There's a fire in progress in a town up north. In a moment he picks up the phone and calls the fire department there.

Half a lifetime doing this and he has never overslept, not

once. He grew up in a Connecticut River town to the north. "So, I guess I found my niche right here in my native area. I always liked radio and news," he says. "I'm one of the lucky people." And blessed not just with the instinct for punctuality but also with distinctive vocal cords. He glances at the clock on the wall and leans toward the microphone.

Out toward the apartments and houses and the cabs of the trucks of early-rising tradesfolk, out toward the brightening ether above the Holyoke Range, goes the deep dark voice. "It's a warm night. Or morning. Now. Seventy-eight degrees. Russ Murley calls for showers. Goo-ood morning. I'm. Ron Hall. There's a big fire in Turner's Falls. . . ."

On Main Street, on the stone steps of city hall, a lone, seated figure emerges out of the gloom, a young man with a handlettered sign that reads, 48 HOUR VIGIL FOR WORLDWIDE LIBERATION. He comes from Hampshire College over in Amherst. He has sat here on the steps of the Castle all night long, his only occasional company one of the cops on Midnights.

Her Honor Mary Ford, the incorruptible mayor of Northampton, often goes to meetings in the early morning. Sometimes she completes her toilette in parking garages while standing in front of the opened trunk of her car—it's a Ford; she bought it used; it now has a crack in the windshield. Mirror in one hand, compact in the other, she adds some color to her pale, pale cheeks, then rummages around in the trunk, saying, "I have to find the notes for what I'm supposed to do today. I'll comb my hair after I get there. Oh, I forgot my watch." She keeps her black hair short so she can comb it quickly. She wears practical shoes, and dresses and skirts to vie with the suits of male politicos. She feels she ought to watch her weight. She eats, she says, to celebrate victories and to console herself over defeats. But she doesn't have time for much exercise or sun. She is no longer youthful, but she still has energy. She gets up early and works all day and at night she goes to meetings, more than any mayor before her. She is rarely late and almost always on the verge, always bustling down hallways, with a pocketbook as large as a saddlebag slung over her shoulder, huffing and puffing at the tops of staircases, and smiling when she arrives.

The mayor spends much more time taking care of the town than of herself. She seems to feel it needs her attention more. Brown water occasionally comes out of Northampton's faucets. Building inspectors condemned the fire station decades ago. In recent years only one boys' room functioned in the entire high school. When Mayor Ford was first elected and assumed command of Northampton's bureaucracy, many departments didn't talk to one another and a lot of arithmetic was still done by hand. The new computer system she had ordered might well become obsolete before all the bugs were fixed and all the clerks knew how to use it, and in the meantime, citizens would probably go on receiving, once in a while, tax bills saying that they owe nothing.

But not far from anywhere in the country, not far from Northampton, the plumbing and heating don't work at all. Broken sewers and rats in children's bedrooms guarantee despair in the housing, danger on the streets. Northampton, by contrast, has decent, if flawed, public accommodations. Only a very small number of residents lack telephones and complete bathrooms and kitchens. All in all, the town's underpinnings work well enough to soften local inequalities.

Northampton contains 152 miles of paved streets and 15 miles of unpaved streets, 70 miles of sidewalk, and 22 bridges. It owns 4 cemeteries, 120 acres of playing grounds (and many more acres are privately endowed for public uses), 2.6 miles of bicycle path, and one public beach. The town has 3 reservoirs that connect to 140 miles of water mains; 60 miles of storm sewer for emergencies, as well as 3 flood-control dikes; 90 miles of sewer mains, all leading to the sewage treatment plant, Northampton's Cloaca Maxima. Twenty-four hundred manholes let workers down into all that plumbing. Enough people to fill a regiment keep the equipment functioning. They fight among themselves, of course. No doubt there will be other winters when a mayor's street won't get plowed.

A vast external bureaucracy and a small local one regulate the town's biology and mobility and many of its pastimes. The printed rules would fill half the shelves in Forbes Library. In Mayor Ford's office upstairs in the Castle, voices rise over terms such as "surplus overlay," "enterprise funds," "chapter 61b rollback taxes." Statements begin in the imperative and conclude as questions: *Know that the funding piece is kind of unique, Mary, so that, in terms of leadership, we need to bring stakeholders to the table to strategize, not in a sort of bootstraps way, but, based on a quantified understanding, proactively?* To try to run Northampton, you would think, is to risk permanent befuddlement. But not for Mayor Ford. When people talk like that, she knows exactly what they want—to form a new committee, usually—and usually she agrees. She can toss off references to chapter this and chapter that with the best of the state and federal bureaucrats, and she has a fecund mind. It bursts with ideas. Sometimes too many flow out all at once. One time she got an audience with the Massachusetts Senate president and asked him a question about educational funding that went on for seven and a half minutes. The senator smiled and said, "Could you repeat that?" And she did, in a slightly different way, which took only five minutes. She is also capable of avid listening. At the most recent meeting of the Massachusetts Municipal Association, after half a day of speeches, she hurried into something called a financial tools seminar, and when the speaker intoned, "Municipal incentive grants can be used for *visioning,*" she could hardly contain her excitement. She made a little, throaty exclamation—*"Oh!"*—and quickly scribbled a note to herself.

The mayor quit her education a dissertation short of a Ph.D. in sociology. She is married to a college professor. She came here more than twenty years ago and has raised three children in the town. Oddly, she isn't very friendly to some of the city's workers. A lot of them dislike her. She doesn't always say hello when she passes the clerks in city hall. But that's the way the mayor is, shy in private and full of feeling out in public, and if you watch her for a while, you know that both sides of her are genuine. She came to this office with dreams of doing socially important things. "I'm an old human services junkie," she once said. But she's had to spend most of her best energies looking for ways to eliminate that $3 million deficit. She still whittles away at it. For her pains, even some allies have begun to call her a "bean counter." It isn't fair. She has not abandoned her causes. Lacking money, she has given herself— to the DPO last fall, to public education, to the local committee on racism, to homelessness in town. "No one should be sleeping under bridges and on grates in a place like Northampton," she declared around the time of her first election. She remembers those words as "a vow." And she has lobbied ardently to shake some money loose from Boston to help finance the local homelessness programs.

Any mayor with an eye to the whole town's best interests is fated to make enemies. Stay in office long enough and the sum of enemies inevitably grows to 51 percent. Mayor Ford was unbeatable when she ran for her third term, but maybe only because she was unopposed. There are signs her popularity is waning, but not for lack of conscientiousness on her part. She spends most of her days working upstairs in the Castle, in the office that looks as if it was furnished from the local Goodwill store. Perhaps she keeps the blinds on her window shut so she won't be reminded of how fast life can slip away, so the travels of the sun won't dim the happiness she feels when she sits here working, scheming, talking.

Great mounds of paper still cover the mayor's desk. Paper here is Sisyphus' boulder. Her assistant Corinne pokes her head around the door and says, sotto voce, "Mary, the Bank of Boston folks are here, for their meet-and-greet."

"For heaven's sake!" says Mary, after a while, to the suspendered, suited banker. "Isn't that interesting!"

She gives half an hour to an elderly couple from Northampton, England, who want a snapshot of themselves standing with her. "I'm delighted you stopped by. This is fascinating."

She gives up more time, almost an hour near the end of a busy day, to a homeless man who walks into her office. He wears dirty blue jeans and cowboy boots, a necktie with a picture of the Mona Lisa on it, a large wooden cross, a handlebar mustache, a ponytail. He tells her, "I'm an adopted Lakota Sioux who started out as a Jewish kid from Brooklyn." He wants to give her an Indian necklace. "I have a plan for rebuilding the economy of Massachusetts," he says, as he fits it around her neck. "My probation officer thinks I should go into politics."

Meanwhile, every day she and her budget analyst snip at the deficit, and she thinks wistfully of ways she would use more money: to combat homelessness and teenage drug use; to provide all-day kindergarten and reduce class sizes at the schools. The farmer at the Smith Voke Farm can't seem to stay within his budget—her latest crisis; some of her oldest allies blame her for the threat to Northampton's cows. The high school simply has to be replaced, as does the fire station. At least last winter she prevailed upon the council to take out snow insurance.

She likes to say she was elected mayor of every resident, including those who won't vote for her no matter what she does. As she also likes to say, she usually leaves the front door to her office open. A building contractor once complained that he knew he didn't get a good hearing from her because she didn't close that door while they talked. Her office has another door, a back door with a chair in front of it, usually closed, rarely used. But by late afternoon on a long day, she feels as though her face is about to slide off the weary muscles underneath. The mask of a face would lie at her feet, still smiling. Corinne pokes her head in the doorway. The boy on the front steps outside, the one keeping a forty-eight-hour vigil for worldwide liberation, waits in the outer office. He wants an audience.

A moment later, Mayor Ford opens her back door, and a moment after that, clerks looking up from their desks see Northampton's chief executive hurrying down the hall, casting backward glances, heading for the stairs.

The fact that machines actually work, a philosophical engineer once said, proves that God exists. But divine wisdom left it up to people to invent the machinery and keep it running. Committees that the mayor appointed now meet regularly to plan a new fire station and an improved high school. The town is revamping its water system, along with its treatment plant. Former generations of functionaries acted similarly, enacting improvements that would outlive them. When managers recite the old joke "The graveyards are full of indispensable people," they mean that anyone can be replaced. But in a town where things function most of the time, the irony falls away. The saying is literally true. Northampton's graveyards really are full of indispensable people. So is the town of the living.

For example, the shy, big-hearted, thoroughly competent, imaginative, and garrulous mayor, who works an average of twelve hours a day on behalf of the town. And the civil servants like Rich Parasiliti, who spent the winter cheerfully performing what he calls snow-fighting and now looks after Northampton's grass and playground equipment. Also the town's many volunteers, only some of whom are rich enough to be suspected of atoning for it, who seem to feel it is a privilege to go to endless meetings and be denounced by some in town, all so they can serve Northampton without pay. The mayor's office keeps lists of people waiting for spots on the town's twenty-three permanent boards and eight *ad hoc* committees—the Skateboard Task Force and the Waterways Committee, the DPW board and the Board of Health, the Fire Station Site and Building Committee, the Arts Board, the Council on Aging, the Committee on

Disabilities, the Fair Housing Committee, the Northampton Housing Partnership. Just recently the mayor got a postcard from a Peace Corps volunteer in Africa, offering his services when he returned.

Many members of the town make smaller contributions: the renters raising flowers beside dilapidated porches on lower Pleasant Street; the person who planted pansies in the scraggly ground beside a pair of public steps; the youthful anarchists who retrieved the stolen plaque from the front steps of the First Church; even, perhaps, the man who goes out early in the morning and tears down the posters illegally attached to light poles, mailboxes, and other public property.

Northampton has a constructive role for every willing resident to play. Not all are quite the same as service on the mayor's *ad hoc* committees.

CHAPTER 15

Meaning Well

Over at the police station, inside the Detective Bureau, Peter Fappiano, the drug detective, peered at the rap sheet of a new Northampton resident, a man named Tyrone. He lived in an apartment over Hugo's bar on Pleasant Street. The rap sheet spilled from Peter's hands onto the floor. It listed seventy-six arraignments, Peter said to the veteran detective Rusty Luce, who was sitting at his desk. "He has an FBI number. He has a huge out-of-state record, too. Aggravated assault and battery with great bodily harm, out of Florida." Tyrone was driving a truck for a local food distributor, and, according to Peter's sources, selling crack to about half the people in one of the local rooming houses.

"Let me see that," said Rusty. He was a round-faced, stocky man with thick-fingered hands, which fellow cops likened to paws. Rusty the Dancing Bear, they called him. Rusty read the rap sheet, and started talking to himself. "He did three years of an eight-year sentence. *For?*" Rusty peered at the page. "For rape. This guy has a *bad* record. He's not good. He's not good. We don't need him around here."

"You know what?" said Peter. "He's on parole. We could bring the parole officer and when we hit the place, he could be violated on the spot."

But before they could hit the place, they had to get a confidential informant to buy some crack from Tyrone. No question who was the best person for that job. The problem was that Frankie had to go to court this week to face his outstanding motor vehicle charges. Rusty shook his head. He'd always thought that Frankie was more useful to the town out of jail than in. Northampton cops had arrested Frankie and charged him. Now Rusty would have to undo what fellow cops had done. Rusty chuckled. "What a system."

Rusty and Frankie stood in a corner of the hallway outside District Courtroom 2, conferring in soft voices. Frankie was dressed up. He wore a pair of wrinkled jeans, a blue windbreaker, a wrinkled white shirt with a button-down collar, and a regimental necktie. He also wore his sweet, boyish smile, his I'm-on-my-best-behavior smile.

"Where you livin' now, Frankie?" Rusty wore a necktie, too. His sport jacket was unrumpled.

"I'm still at Grove Street. I'm waiting for a subsidy."

Rusty looked at Frankie and the tip of Rusty's tongue came out. A merry little smile half-concealed his eyes. Rusty never used the usual epithets for criminals—"maggots," "assholes," "mopes," "scumbags," and the like. Half the people Rusty had hired to help him build his own house were ones he had arrested. He'd had to delay construction until one of his helpers got out of jail. Now Rusty's tongue withdrew. He frowned at Frankie. "I'm trying to help you out on this case. But no more fucking up. How many times can I do this? It makes me look bad, Frankie."

"It was just transportation," said Frankie. "See, those cops didn't have probable cause to stop me."

Rusty didn't bother to say so, but Frankie was a walking case of probable cause. And there was no telling what might happen if Frankie made an argument like that before the judge on duty today—an elderly man, not as easily amused as Judge Ryan.

Rusty eyed him sternly. "When you get before this judge, don't say *anything*. He's a tough judge."

"Oh, okay," said Frankie.

The prosecutor walked up and said to Rusty, "What I can do is recommend that these charges be continued for six months, on a general continuance on a guilty plea." He turned to Frankie. "That means if you get in further trouble, these charges can be brought back and you can be tried on them."

"Okay," said Frankie.

"For some reason the Northampton Police Department speaks very highly of you."

Frankie looked at him with great sincerity. "I mean well."

"I remember a few things from some years ago," said the prosecutor. "But that was long ago."

"I been, like, a Boy Scout ever since," said Frankie. He had his hands folded in front of him, like an acolyte. "Thank you, sir."

"Well, keep up the good work," said the prosecutor.

"I did that heroin case last year."

"Sounds like *Columbo*," said the prosecutor.

"I'm trying to represent for my bad deeds, you know?" said Frankie.

He sat most of the day in the gallery, waiting his turn before the judge. The gallery was relatively unfamiliar territory. In recent years he'd often gone to court handcuffed, because he hadn't shown up on his own. "Procrastinating," he explained. His therapist had warned him about this tendency. "My home away from home," Frankie said, looking around the courtroom. He knew a lot of the people in the courtrooms of the region, both lawyers and defendants. A young Latino man stood before the judge. He was charged with possession of cocaine. He asked for an interpreter. "This guy speaks English," Frankie whispered. "When you say you can't speak the language, you get more time to figure out a strategy. It's perfect if you want to act dumb, too."

Watching cases come and go, Frankie chuckled softly. "It's a drive-through court system. It wasn't me. I didn't do it. Motion to suppress. Okay, next." The day in court wore on. At one-thirty in the afternoon, his name was finally called. He folded his hands in front of him as he stood in the well of the courtroom. Up on the bench, the judge read Frankie's record. He scowled at it. He scowled down at Frankie. Then, with obvious reluctance, he let him go.

"It's boring," Frankie said, walking out, a free man on probation. "Imagine doing that for fifty-one cases."

Frankie already knew Tyrone. They'd spent some time together at the county jail—Camp Hamp, most inmates called it. In fact, he had Tyrone's beeper number. Peter didn't bother to ask Frankie how he got it. They went to a pay phone on Strong Avenue. Peter listened in on Frankie's side of the conversation.

"Hey! This is Frankie. Can you hook me up? I need some rock. Yeah, yeah. I need a twenty."

They went through the usual procedure, which Rusty had taught Tommy and Tommy had taught Peter. Frankie could have taught it, too. Peter searched Frankie, so Peter could testify in court that his informant had no drugs on him beforehand. Peter recorded the serial number of a twenty-dollar bill—bills don't have to be marked, because they already are. He gave the bill to Frankie, who ambled off alone and stood on the sidewalk on lower Main Street outside the Italian restaurant there.

Peter and another detective, Bobby Dunn, sat in an unmarked car across the street. In a little while, they saw Tyrone come around the corner on a bicycle. Frankie—stocky, smiling, pants adroop—sauntered up to him. The two men shook hands. Tyrone dug in a pocket, then held out an open hand. Frankie looked around as if to make sure they weren't being watched, then bent down and scouted around with his index finger in the palm of Tyrone's hand, as if he were sorting through a handful of jewels, as if he wanted to make sure he picked out the best-looking rock of crack. Frankie could have been a method actor. He could have been a lot of things. He handed Tyrone the twenty-dollar bill, they shook again, Tyrone rode away on his bicycle down Pleasant Street, and Frankie sauntered across Main. As he passed the cruiser, he gave Peter and Bobby a gigantic wink. They met up in the alley behind the pizza shop. Frankie handed Peter the rock of crack. Peter searched Frankie again, then gave him another twenty-dollar bill, which was Frankie's pay.

To get a search warrant that was certain to stand up in court, they had to make several controlled buys. Frankie made two more, both in Tyrone's room over Hugo's. It was a living. Frankie was nowhere around, of course, when, a few days after the last buy, four cops burst in on Tyrone early in the morning. They found twelve rocks of crack and $1,500 in cash in the room, including the bills that Frankie had passed to him. Tyrone's parole was revoked, and he was sent out of town and back to jail to finish up his sentence, with another year tacked on for selling crack.

If they only knew, wouldn't every citizen of Hamp applaud Frankie's work on their behalf?

The assistant director of Grove Street, a young Ph.D. candidate at the university, was writing his dissertation on homelessness in Northampton. "There's so much of an effort to fix people," he said. "But I don't think the problem's with the homeless person so much. A person will stop drinking, for instance. They're still poor, they still have no family or community support. They leave Grove Street and go to a rooming house and start drinking again. So I think it's a lot more than just looking at the individual. I don't see any movement towards housing as a right. Drug testing comes up every six months or so. Does it mean if someone is using, they shouldn't be allowed to stay in an emergency shelter?"

The young grad student went on: "Instead of trying to provide support, we ask what's wrong with Frankie. How can we fix them." He said, "In Frankie's case, whether he's disabled or not, he's considered disabled, and he can't afford a place to live on his income from that. Not even a rooming house. But what kind of job is he going to get at this stage? The joke is every time he leaves the house, the police hook him up for something."

Actually, just now Tommy was trying to figure out how to keep Frankie from getting hooked up again and going back to jail. Frankie had some more outstanding charges pending. He'd been caught buying crack in Holyoke a while ago. Frankie had said he was "doing research." Tommy had made a call and gotten him released until the case came up in court. Then Peter had called a prosecutor down in Hampden County, who had said, "All right, we'll do something with him. But if he fucks up again, we just throw him away." So concessions would be made, perhaps for the last time, when Frankie went to court again. But someone would have to make sure that Frankie went to court. Meanwhile, Frankie's unregistered car was still impounded, locked up in a fenced-in lot at a gas station in Florence. Frankie had been pleading with Tommy to get it back. On a summer evening, Tommy sat in the Detective Bureau discussing the problem of Frankie with one of the state police drug detectives.

Tommy was wavering. Maybe they should help Frankie retrieve his car, his latest "Chebbie," then try to get him re-licensed.

"It's the worst thing we could do," said the state detective. "If he gets that car, he'll get more charges and more charges. He'll get in so deep we'll never be able to use him again. And he owes the world for parking tickets in nineteen different jurisdictions. It would take an act of God to get him licensed again."

Tommy nodded. He picked up the phone and called Grove

Street. He turned on the speaker so the state detective could listen to both sides of the conversation.

"You know what, Frankie? I don't think we're gonna get your car out. It's gonna get you in more trouble. Here's what I think we should do. Work on getting your license back. I mean, I like ya, Frankie, you know that."

"Why don't you just give me back Samson's license?" said Frankie.

"Frankie, it expired in 1992. But you could probably go down and renew it, you jerk. How 'bout the license plate? Where'd you get it?"

"It came with the car."

" 'It came with the car'? Frankie, it doesn't work like that."

"Come on, Oakie. It's got all my stuff in it. It's got my crutches."

"Your crutches? What were you doin'? Jumping out a window to get away from the police? So it's best if we just leave the car."

"Come on, Oakie! If you leave it there, I'm gonna lose my Chebbie."

"We'll get your license back and get you another car."

"That's gonna take three years!" Frankie paused. "Now I'm depressed. I'm gonna go get some Prozac."

"When we get off the phone, I can imagine what you're gonna say about me."

"I can't. Because I can't tell anyone I know you."

"That's right." Tommy started laughing.

"I'll go upstairs and bite on my pillow."

"And don't do anything stupid," said Tommy. "Like go and get the car yourself."

"I already checked," said Frankie. "They got dogs."

Tommy shook his head. "You know, Frankie, if you weren't older than me, I'd adopt you."

"Yeah! I could be, like, your older brother."

Tommy laughed again.

Frankie must have thought he'd softened him up. "Okay, Oakie, let's go get the car."

"If we get your car back, you're gonna drive it."

"No, you can keep the key. I can't drive it without a key."

"Do you know how to start a car without a key, Frankie?" Tommy asked.

Actually, Frankie was a skilled automobile mechanic. He was good with his hands. He'd held a lot of jobs around here. He'd worked as a mechanic and in construction. He didn't mind working. One time Oakie got him a job at a local factory and the boss liked Frankie so much he even gave him a raise. But then Carmen got him in trouble again, and by the time those charges were dismissed, someone had taken his place at the factory. He was on the dole now. Better here than in some places, Frankie thought. The people in the social service agencies were nice to him up here. He fit into a lot of categories for getting help and it was easy to adapt himself to fit some others. He was having trouble getting into subsidized housing, where priority went to the elderly, disabled, and people with dependent children. But he didn't usually mind Grove Street. He got fed, and the social service system supplied him with a regular doctor, for an old injury to his foot, which was a blessing, because it brought some disability money and didn't actually bother him much. A psychiatrist and a therapist were also provided. One prescribed drugs for his depression. The other was trying to help him get off the other drug, his beloved and hated crack, which, he'd come to realize, was the main cause of his depression. This had come to him as a revelation, part of a larger one, which had arrived in stages.

When Frankie had returned to Northampton after his last stop in jail, he'd told his therapist, "I feel miserable when I'm not high and when I'm high also. I'm fed up with life, fed up with drugs, and I haven't shot myself in the brain because I'm waiting for an answer."

The therapist told him, "You're suicidal because of the massive amount of drugs you've been taking."

"And it hit me, pow!" Frankie remembered.

That was when everything started to make sense. While in jail he'd met a nun, a volunteer, who had instructed him in meditation and theology. She'd told him, as he recalled her words, "You meditate to get healing. To become whole. That's what we're here on earth for. And after you're whole, you try to become holy." The only good thing about jail was the time it gave him to think. In the long hours of doing nothing, Frankie pondered the nun's words, until he thought he understood. "There's a natural magnet, name it anything you wish, God, Buddha, infinite intelligence, the Supreme Being. We're all part of Him and there's a natural draw. Eliminate vices that get in the way, the pleasures of the flesh, which I'm guilty of." It followed that there was a reason for his crack addiction. That was the Supreme Being's idea. "That's all to block the natural pull of the Supreme Being. It's like a test." Frankie felt angry, though. "Why do you put me through all this, you asshole?" he asked the Supreme Being. He didn't feel this kind of talk was dangerous. "He's got the kind of sense of humor, you can call him an asshole," Frankie said. "So I'm defying the Supreme Being by calling Him a jerk and an asshole." And, as he told his Northampton therapist, he was waiting for an answer.

Then he met a woman. At the time he and Carmen were estranged again. He was walking north up Pleasant Street and this other woman, who had just driven into Northampton from the West Coast, was walking south, both of them heading for the same pizza joint. The place was closed. They got to talking at the door. The annual Indian Pow Wow had convened at the fairgrounds. He and the woman went to it together. Frankie said something about the dances being religious ceremonies, and she asked him if he had an interest in religion, and he poured out his whole story to her. "Tears were coming down my eyes, which is hard for me to do with a female," he remembered.

The woman listened. Then she said, "I never heard such a crock of shit in my life." She went on, "This is just a bunch of whining. There are no victims, Frankie." Then she told him about karma. "Deserve it or not, that's where karma comes in. Basically it gives you what you need. To purify yourself." The idea reminded him of an ad for the marines he'd seen on TV. "It's like a sword heated and pounded," he thought. "All for you to evolve and learn from."

Frankie felt that forces far beyond him had answered his angry question, first through the nun, then through the therapist, and finally through the woman from out west. She was clearly a messenger. "This is a meeting from three thousand miles away," Frankie said. "I don't believe in accidents." Northampton was a place of spiritual power, just the sort of place the Supreme Being would choose. Everything had come together now. He had his answer. "There is a reason for this bull, and maybe I'm supposed to pass on the word. God has a terrific sense of humor. Life doesn't stink if you look at the whole picture. I'm a poor, worthless piece of shit right now, but I have a little contribution to make." Working for the cops as a drug informant, helping them arrest a man like Tyrone, was part of the divine plan for him.

But it is one thing to believe you are being tested, and another to endure the tests themselves. Frankie had to struggle to keep the picture focused. Peter and the state drug cops and especially Oakie, who was one of his oldest friends in town, could certainly have treated him better. They seemed to think they'd done him a great favor by getting him breaks on the motor vehicle and crack charges. But how was he supposed to stay connected to the drug world if he didn't have a car and if he didn't buy some crack now and then? True, he had intended to smoke the crack he'd bought in Holyoke, but he really had been doing research, too, so he could help them bust the dealer later. "They've been playing me. My life is at risk. There are twelve to fourteen people who would love to put a bullet in me for the cases that I did. The cops get what they want. Cases, pats on the back, promotions. What do I get? What did I ask for? My car and my license. That's nothing. These guys in blue, there's just black and white to them. But there's a thousand different colors we don't even know about."

On the Supreme Being's test, however, Carmen was the toughest question. After she'd filed her latest charges against him, he had filed some against her, and she had been very nice and loving toward him while the ones he'd filed were pending. The day he dropped them, they were supposed to go to the social service agency on Pleasant Street for marriage counseling. She said to him, "Never mind that marriage counseling. I never want to see you again."

"So you were only nice to me so I'd drop the charges," he told her. "You know something? I'm tired of this roller-coaster ride. I'll go along with anything you want." He got some divorce papers typed up. He brought them to her. "Do me a favor. Sign these papers."

Relating this story, Frankie said, "I used to cry and stuff, but this time I didn't do the wimpy stuff."

A few days later she called him at Grove Street. He should meet her at Pulaski Park. She would sign the papers. Then Frankie realized they'd need a notary public as a witness. He had no money at all. He stopped in at the office of a lawyer he knew, who said she'd notarize them for free. He walked back to the park. Carmen was sitting near the Academy of Music in the summer morning, drinking vodka.

"And she has an appointment for alcohol counseling!" Frankie thought. But he didn't criticize her. He felt sentimental, on the brink of this final act of their marriage, and he said a few sentimental words as they started walking toward the lawyer's office. They were walking down the alley beside the police station when she started calling him a mama's boy.

"Okay!" he yelled. "Divorce this mama's boy!"

They stood there shouting at each other, and after a while one of the higher-up cops—maybe it was the police chief himself—came out. "What's going on here?"

"I'm getting divorced," said Frankie.

"Well, you guys please quiet down. I'm trying to read."

He arrived at the lawyer's office with Carmen trailing after him, yelling, "Mama's boy!" And then she wouldn't sign the papers. The secretary in the lawyer's office started laughing. "Damn!" said Frankie, holding a thumb and forefinger half an inch apart. "This close to getting divorced." He followed Carmen back toward Main Street. They passed a construction site. The workmen stopped to listen in. They started laughing too. Carmen kept yelling, "I ain't signin'. I want some money."

He followed her all the way back to the substance abuse agency building, pleading with her. "Carmen, I want to get on with my life." He followed her inside, to the little cafeteria at the agency. He got a cup of water, and suddenly, feeling overwhelmed by his karma, he threw the water in her face. Carmen was threatening to file new charges against him when one of the agency's therapists appeared, and Frankie had to explain himself. "This is an oxymoron type of thing. She wants to get rid of me, and she won't give me a divorce. She loves me, she hates me, she wants to see me, she doesn't want to see me." He left the place still married.

He still craved cocaine. His car was impounded. He owed about a thousand dollars in parking tickets and couldn't get a license until he paid the fines. He had to go to court in Holyoke in a few weeks, and the cops down there would demand that he do some work for them for free. And he was broke and living in a shelter. One day a bag of donated clothes arrived there. Rooting through it, Frankie couldn't find any men's clothes, just women's. He took some of them, and put them on. "Just for a joke," he insisted. "I don't have any tendencies." But the effect surprised him. "I felt like a different identity. I'm not Frankie anymore. Frankie had enough pain and suffering." He went to his room in a skirt and blouse, lay down, and slept all day, his first sound, peaceful sleep in a long time.

Afterward, though, he felt worried. "What's happening?" he asked his therapist. "Am I changing or something?"

His therapist reassured him: "No, you just needed a break from being Frankie."

The only problem was that Carmen heard about it. "Hey, you got a boyfriend, Frankie?" she said the next time he ran into her in the park.

"Anything to hurt me," Frankie said bitterly.

He was about to lose his disability, his only source of income now. But the temporary change in identity and the summer weather seemed to have restored his spirits. He took a break from sitting in the park to stroll around Smith College, mostly emptied out for summer. Shambling across the Neilsen lawn, passing under the giant London plane tree, Frankie thought of the Smithie he had met this spring. "Her father's rich. She's Mexican with blond hair and blue eyes, a gorgeous little thing. I met her in the laundrymat. But check this out. Can you believe it? I was too shy to call her." He ambled back to Pulaski Park. Small, buxom Carmen was sitting there with her new boyfriend. Frankie went up to them and shook hands with the boyfriend, then walked over to a bench some distance away. "That's the guy who took my place. In his dreams. Ever see anybody so glad to meet his wife's boyfriend?" Frankie laughed and laughed, half slithering off the bench. "Fuck it. It's America. He can have her. Just divorce me, please."

A man in casual, respectable dress—oxford shirt and khakis—came down the sidewalk. It was Frankie's regular doctor, and he greeted Frankie with a smile. Frankie wanted to show him the papers he'd received, notifying him that he was being taken off disability. He rooted around in his trouser pockets, producing as usual fistfuls of business cards and rumpled court papers. The doctor looked at the notification. "Well, we'll just have to start over," he said. He walked on.

"He's a real humanitarian doctor," Frankie said. "Best I ever had."

Frankie languished around town, laughing, trading stories with other unemployed people in the park, killing time. And then the test resumed. He got evicted for a week from the Grove Street Inn. He walked in smoking a cigarette, and one of the workers there reminded him that this was against the rules. At that moment he was feeling gloomy about walking into a homeless shelter, remembering the days when he was flush with cash, and he said, "Go fuck yourself." He was banished and wouldn't leave. The management on duty called the police. Frankie said he wanted to get his windbreaker from his room. A friend, a fellow resident, said he'd get it for him. In the meantime the cop arrived. Standing outside, Frankie saw the cop's reflection in the window of the front door. The cop had intercepted the friend and was searching the pockets of Frankie's windbreaker. Frankie watched as the cop found both his crack pipe and the nip of vodka he'd left in the pockets. So he was ready when the cop came out, carrying the jacket.

"This yours?" the cop asked him.

He denied it was his jacket, and the cop let him go. But it had begun to rain, and now he had no jacket. He spent most of the night in Pulaski Park and most of the next day wandering around town while his clothes dried out. He was tired. Tonight he'd have to find a place to sleep. In the evening, he ran into a friend from Grove Street who told him to go to the emergency room at the hospital. "Act like you're real depressed." His friend said that had worked for him. Emergency Services had put him in their "respite bed," available for people in desperate straits, said Frankie's friend.

So around nightfall Frankie hiked up Elm Street to the hospital, about a mile away. He went in and told the nurse that he had tried to kill himself last night, by overdosing on his antidepressant. "I hear there's, like, an asbestos bed for things like this," he said. The nurse and a doctor questioned him and they did blood and urine tests, but no one from Emergency Services came. He languished in the waiting room for hours. Finally the nurse came out and told him, "They don't have a bed available, but you're going to be all right."

"I coulda told you that three hours ago," muttered Frankie.

He walked back to town, to a rooming house, and knocked on the door of a man who used to be a friend. The man let him in but said Frankie couldn't stay, because he was trying to get off drugs, and they argued, and the man called the police. So Frankie started walking again. He headed out of downtown toward Florence. The agency Service Net had recently opened a renovated apartment building for the needy there. Frankie had tried to get a room in it, but had been turned down. "They picked a pot dealer from the shelter instead," he reminded himself indignantly. It was almost dawn when he arrived. Someone he didn't know let him in, and he went into the building's common room and stretched out on a sofa. He had just fallen asleep when yet another cop arrived and rousted him. He could smell himself now, an odor like rotting fruit. Frankie walked back downtown. To the rooming house at 96 Pleasant Street, the place where he'd lived as Samson before he had met Carmen. Some old acquaintances were loitering outside the front door. "The cops've been all over the place, lookin' for you," one of them said.

"Holy shit," Frankie thought. "Somebody who looks like me did something." He was irritated with the cops in general. He had his pride, but then again he wasn't about to call Carmen and ask her to hide him. There was only one thing to do. "All right. I'll call Oakie."

"Where are you?" Oakie's voice was loud. Frankie had to

hold the phone away from his ear. He was too tired for loud noises.

"I'm not tellin' you," said Frankie. "What's goin' on?"

"Nothing. Just don't miss your court date down in Holyoke."

Frankie thanked him. He was greatly relieved. "I can tell it was all right just the way he said it."

This was like an omen. That very day he met another woman, overweight certainly, but sweet. "Anyway, I'm not into that physical shit," Frankie said. And she had an apartment at River Run. He moved in with her. But Frankie didn't go to his court date in Holyoke—he didn't have a car now and that morning it just seemed too hard to go by bus. And Oakie, of all people, had him arrested on the default warrant. He spent a week in jail in Ludlow, which he hated, partly because he couldn't smoke in there. Then Peter made a phone call for him—anyway, that was what Peter and Oakie said. He came back to town, and returned to the woman's apartment, only to find some other men there. He got into a fight, which he lost. Being broke and homeless can be an exhausting business in itself.

Then he got lucky again. A local woman had a boyfriend at the county jail, who had begged her to smuggle in some cocaine. The woman went to a friend of Frankie's, an old Northampton rooming-house friend, and he went to Frankie, who knew just what to do. They sold the woman a bag of baking soda for $500, and split the proceeds. When she realized she'd been burned, the woman confronted Frankie's conspirator. He blamed Frankie. She said she wanted Frankie killed. His friend said he'd do the job. She gave him $300 in advance. The man split that money with Frankie too. So now Frankie had $400. He used most of it to get back together with Carmen, figuring that if he had some money, she would take him in. She was living in a neighboring town. For three weeks he partied with her and her boyfriend, and, while he partied, he waited for revenge. They used up his money first, mostly on crack; then they started cashing the stolen checks that her boyfriend had. Her boyfriend wasn't very cagey. Frankie made sure that he didn't forge any signatures himself. The night the money ran out, Carmen got angry. There was a fight. The neighbors called the cops. Frankie left the apartment just in time. He was standing outside the elevator with his shoes in his hands when the police arrived. They arrested both Carmen and her boyfriend, charging them with possession of crack cocaine and Carmen with assault besides. Frankie also told them about the stolen checks. They let him go.

Things were looking up. After his last short stint in Ludlow, he had gone to Springfield, borrowed some money from his father, and gone to the Mardi Gras, a Springfield strip joint, or, as Frankie put it, "a tit bar." He had spent the whole afternoon there, drinking and recuperating from his week in jail, and who should walk in but an old friend and business associate, a man he'd met years ago in Northampton. Frankie's old friend had gone straight—he swore he had—and was living in Springfield now. He owned both some apartments and a small home-renovation business, called Hearth 'n Home Construction. He offered Frankie a job and an apartment in Springfield. Carmen, meanwhile, had started making overtures of reconciliation. After all, Frankie would be the only witness against her on the pending assault and cocaine charges, and she'd been evicted from her last apartment. It seemed as though, at last, a better life was beckoning.

Archeologists surmise that portions of humanity stopped wandering when they began to make graveyards and other fixed investments in a place. But the traveling instinct has never been fully suppressed. It remains as powerful as the nesting one, especially among Americans, a famously peripatetic people who get misty-eyed over the idea of home. Some try to reconcile this paradox by saying they carry home with them wherever they go, and this was true of Frankie if it was true of anyone. He didn't find it hard to imagine leaving Northampton. He still liked the town, its mellowness, its lack of blaring horns, but the comfort had gone out of it for him. It had grown too small. All the cops knew him and his unlicensed driving status. Besides, at the Mardi Gras that day, he'd discovered new opportunities elsewhere. On an August afternoon, he sat in the bar of the old Bay State Hotel, saying good-bye to Northampton. An old Claudette Colbert movie was playing on the TV. An elderly man sat alone at the bar. Frankie, drinking beer, sat at a table from which he could keep an eye on his new car.

It was a used and rather battered American car. "I got it for a deuce. It runs good." He had found a license plate for it at a junkyard, and a 1996 registration sticker to put on the plate, which he'd found in a parking lot—crouching down behind a properly registered car and carefully peeling off the sticker.

He felt he had to reequip himself for driving. "See, what Oakie doesn't understand, there's a gray area. I don't want to be driving, but I got no choice, if I want to work. Look at the risk. I'm out on ten grand surety and if I get caught I won't see bail. But if I'm not working, I'm out here selling drugs. Which is worse? I heard about a Cinderella license, where you can't drive after dark. I could get back into, like, the productive mainstream. A lot of guys in Springfield say, 'Hey, you want to sell?' For what? I want to get out of that hole. It ain't easy." He figured that if he didn't break any traffic laws, he wouldn't get stopped. Except here in Northampton. "I'm scared when I drive around here now. It stopped being fun. I get this knot at my solar plex. Oakie said even if he's here, he can't stick up for me. Outside Northampton, I'm relaxed when I drive."

He had a job and an apartment in a Springfield suburb now. He had invited Carmen to live with him there. He had felt compelled to take her back. "She's a challenge. It's like getting a Ph.D. in psychology. I don't know. She's a challenge." He had few illusions, he said. He had tried to get her into a program called "anger management," but she wouldn't go, and she was still on drugs. "She's not straight. I'm not either, completely. But I met these guys from the past and they're straight now. It's like a message, like proof you can do it. And I like the challenge. She'll be doing drugs and taking my money. That's a challenge and a half. I think of it, like that's my cross. Nothing can get me down except that thing, the stuff and her." The nun he'd met in jail had told him that after becoming whole, then holy, one became immortal. He remembered her saying, "Think of it as a caterpillar. We're in the caterpillar stage. Then it turns into a butterfly." Pondering those words in the quiet barroom, Frankie said, "So if I pass that test, I'll probably graduate to something."

He figured that when he dropped his charges against Carmen, she'd turn on him again. But her court date wouldn't come up for a while: "I've got her on a string until then." Saying this, he assumed the stance of a deep-sea fisherman, leaning back, pumping an imaginary rod, reeling in a big one.

It was time to leave. Outside the barroom doorway, Frankie paused and glanced furtively up and down the street, Strong Avenue, named for Caleb Strong, that eighteenth-century local boy made good—state governor, member of the Constitutional Convention. Then Frankie got in his falsely licensed car and drove away, very slowly. At the stop sign on Pleasant Street, he looked both ways.

CHAPTER 16

The Caretaker

I̶T'S A SUMMER evening and the blood is hot. Tommy turns south on lower Pleasant Street. In the vista framed by the cruiser's windshield, a dark thunderstorm sky that won't come this way hovers over the Holyoke Range, lit from the west, a wall of green rising up to meet dark purple sky. For human eyes, there is ferment where the colors meet.

Tommy turns around and heads back toward downtown. He glances at the little storefront of Primitive Leathers. "Whip me, beat me, make me feel cheap!" cries Tommy. He passes by. "I think cops here have to be a little more open-minded than they do in a lot of other places." He adds, "Sometimes I think Northampton is the four corners of everywhere. Maybe every place is, but I think we have a little more. Maybe it's all those psychologists' shingles."

So many towns this size look sadly out-of-date on a summer night. But what an imaginative-looking place Northampton is on shirtsleeve evenings, the old buildings rolling by—the one over there with a rounded end like the stern of a Pullman railroad car, and that one with a turret on the top that looks as if it belongs in a fairy tale, and all those others with their window sashes painted cheery colors.

The cruiser turns down Crafts Avenue, past a graffito on the brick wall of an alley: ROMANCE IS NOT SEXY. So much for champagne and candlelight. But on the sidewalks that surround downtown's churches, on any given summer evening, the attractions of the natural world, the human hunger for each other, right now, right here on earth, are all visible in the pictures framed by the cruiser's windows: Northampton roués making their moves in Birkenstocks; women draped in colorful Third World fabrics. In storefront after little storefront plumage is on sale, in dress shops and jewelry stores, and in boutiques that sell incense and exotic robes and sexy underwear. One hawker hands out ads for Self-Esteem Electrolysis, another for a show tonight at the Fire and Water Café, where a moonlighting college professor will perform an original one-woman cabaret entitled *Conceptual Orgasm*. Quick, darting swallows disappear beneath a gutter over the awning of a shoe store, as if birds, too, have secret assignations. A buxom transvestite ambles across Main Street. "Look at the rack on that guy," says Tommy. "But, hey! This is America." A pair of women in short shorts go jogging by. "I better get out of here. I'm having impure thoughts."

Shortly after dark, Tommy parks his cruiser behind the Castle and sneaks around behind Memorial Hall. Standing in the shadows, he surveys Pulaski Park. He's looking for teenagers dealing drugs and drinking. Instead, he sees a female couple on a bench, locked in heavy petting, like a single figure with the several arms of Shiva. He turns away and heads back for his cruiser. In the parking lots behind Main Street, he glimpses a familiar sight: girls whose parents won't let them out in immodestly short skirts crouching behind their cars, changing into their dancing clothes.

He drives to the upper deck of the parking garage to render advice to one of the young officers, who has come across an awkward situation—a young woman's battered car parked beside her boss's Mercedes. When the patrolman shined his flashlight into the more expensive car's backseat, the couple were about to be in flagrante delicto. No crime in that, but the woman's car is improperly registered. Tommy confers with the officer. "You have every legal right to take her plate. *Or* you can cut them some slack." Tommy drives away. "I guess she's trying to move up in the world," he says. "When the weather gets warm it's amazing where people will fuck. It just proves that people are part of the animal kingdom."

In the perfumed night, under the lights on Main Street, the town looks all paired up, like Noah's ark. The supervisor's cruiser passes by the coffee shops. The day's last meeting of Alcoholics Anonymous has adjourned, and what some locals call "the Hell's Angels' coffee klatsch" has begun—tough-looking men and women in leathers, sipping coffee and licking ice cream cones beside a fleet of motorcycles. Nearby on the sidewalk, Alan Scheinman stands alone. He's dressed in hand-tooled cowboy boots and a silk shirt unbuttoned almost to his navel. Sipping iced coffee through a straw, Alan stares intently at the passing crowd, looking for her.

One day while Alan was riding down the bike path, he saw another bicycle coming toward him, and a vision sprang into his mind. "A metaphorical image," he called it. One person comes riding along, trailing all his "issues" behind, like cans tied to a newlyweds' car. That person meets another similarly encumbered, and a terrible tangle ensues.

The other bicyclist passed. He nodded to Alan. Alan said hi and rode on. Then another image surfaced. This time two strangers meet without their baggage being visible. But all of it is there, a huge pyramid of other people underneath each of them, a mile-high construction made up of their ancestors, their parents, the doctors who delivered them, their baby-sitters, the people who had looked at them in their baby carriages and pulled their little earlobes—a huge invisible crowd gathering when two strangers meet casually and glance at each other and one says hi. These thoughts amused Alan, and they left him no further from despair.

He toyed now and then with the idea of going back to work. He'd long imagined developing the back side of Main Street. He made fast tours of a couple of buildings and talked to the owners, but his interest kept waning and reviving and waning again. He said, "I try hard but I suffer from indecision. One of my fears is that I'll get started on something and be stuck, or not achieve some announced objective." He seemed to be waiting for something to happen to him, like another meteor shower.

Then one day, at the end of a long walk, he resolved to act. "I'm not exactly a prime candidate for huge changes," he said. "But at the very least I could start with the thought that I kept telling Suzanne: that if you don't do anything, nothing changes." By the time he got back to his apartment, he had made up his mind. "To have a more rewarding relationship I'm going to have to let go of a number of things."

He'd been, he said, "the patron saint of strippers." He'd stop hanging around with them so much. "And maybe I'll stop taking pictures of the kinds of things I've been photographing." He began the next day, in his apartment. He sorted through piles of photographs. "Someday I'll either have a show, or when I die people will find this huge body of moderately pornographic material." He gathered up the many props he had acquired for photographing fantasies that he and his models had concocted: leather bikinis, a red latex bodysuit, feathery masks, garter belts and outlandishly high-heeled shoes, black leather vests and collars. All these he now deposited in boxes, which he sealed and carried downstairs to his storage room.

For years he'd saved a box of letters from his first real girlfriend. He threw them away.

The odd wooden contraption still stood in a corner. It looked like a piece of sculpture now. Birdhouses dangled where once young women had hung by the arms, posing for his camera. "Gosh," said Alan, looking at it, "I went out with so many kinky girls I can't even remember which one wanted me to make it."

. . .

"I have a date Saturday night," Alan said about a week later. "She's on welfare, has two kids, goes to community college. She has a goal. She's kind of pretty. The problem is, there's this huge socioeconomic gap between us, which I'm more sensitized to than ever." She lived in a Northampton housing project. He had never visited one of those. On their date, they were going to Boston with her kids. He fretted over whether to take them in the Rolls, which would be comfortable, or his other car, a battered Honda. "When it comes to human beings as opposed to numbers, I'm totally hopeless. Things exist in reality in a much tinier form than they do in my mind. I'm probably a person who should have had an arranged marriage. Just one bad experience after another. It's almost safer to ruminate on Suzanne than to go back out on the street again. I'm *really* scared about this date." He chose the Honda.

The next week, heading off to the project on his motorcycle, Alan said, "I'm on the road to another adventure." He said of the new woman, "She has had probably as many bad relationships as I have."

Alan's prospective new girlfriend had come down with the flu. While she slept, he took charge of her children, one three, the other five. He squired them all over downtown, buying them treats. He watched them cavort on the playground equipment in Pulaski Park. "It was nice," he said afterward. "I got a chance to be controlling and parental with actual children, instead of thirty-year-old women." He liked the housing project. It seemed like a real community, a place where neighbors helped each other out.

He hadn't slept with her. He wasn't sure he wanted to. He was awaiting what he called "chemistry." He had paid for dancing lessons for her daughter. And he was very worried about doing too much this time—of making this woman feel he was trying to buy her, of letting her know there were a lot of things that he could buy. "I'm trying to be careful, but I think she spotted me in my Rolls."

He rented a movie, a Hollywood production, not especially risqué, and brought it to his new girlfriend's place. They'd been watching only a few minutes when, the actors on her TV screen having fallen into a clinch, she said, "This is too racy for me." He left her apartment disconsolate.

From time to time errands took him out of town and north past the Castaways, and he'd always look for Suzanne's car. He hadn't seen it there or caught a glimpse of her downtown in a long time. He decided she had moved. The thought smothered him. One night he went down to the office that he rented out on the floor below his rooms and called her number. He let it ring a couple of times and then, in a panic, hung up. Almost immediately the phone in the office rang. The person on the other end, Suzanne presumably, must have used the call-back option. He got out of there fast. He walked across Main Street to the Hotel Northampton, and at the pay phone called her number again and again hung up, and again the phone he'd used began to ring immediately. He felt wretched. Some nights later he saw her profile reflected in the glass of a door he was about to enter. He hurried away, taking refuge around a corner.

Reflecting on her time with Alan, Suzanne said, "It just really felt like he was making the moves for me and living my life. He'd breathe for me probably, if he could. I'd mention something so *casually,* an author, or something I was thinking of doing, and next thing I knew there was a package at my door or on my table. It was nothing that I was going to be able to really pursue, I felt like. On my own. He'd do it for me too much." She thought it poignant. "But it's not enough to weave this sort of tapestry of love. I think there has to be, I think you have to be maybe partners more, and, a little more equal. It's a thing I have trouble with, too. My sister calls me the blonde who makes the plans."

Her psychiatrist had told her that what lay behind her stripping was an obstacle in her life, and she agreed. She remembered his telling her, "You think you're earning a decent amount of money right now. You have a certain amount of independence where you don't have to work five days a week nine to five and you can take three weeks off if you want to and travel, and you can make this much money. But if we get through this, you can make as much money, you can have the same freedom and everything else." She had remained skeptical. "I feel in a way that I'm still the wounded woman or something. I see a lot of that, in the women I'm working with, that I'm stripping with, women with great potential but with something wrong." She said, of her therapist, "He's like, 'We need to spend two years on this, so you can get this out of your system and out of your way.' " She had quit going to him now, only partly because of the expense. "I think I can find things out in another fashion. I don't want to try to exhume things. I like the mystery, anyway."

So she was still dancing. She needed the money, and she insisted she still liked the work. "I do! I really do! I like being the center of attention. I like making people feel good. I like the whole challenge of that, and the turnover that's involved in that, too, and a crowd, you know. I can get a following and everything else, you know. I don't think I could get that in a lot of other jobs. You know, a lot of people say, my gosh, you're really a dancer and a comedienne, because after a while if things are getting really dry and slow, I'll just do something, just do something funny and just do my best to be Jay Leno or something up there on the stage, and it usually works."

She wasn't tired of the work, but she *was* sick of the Castaways. "I need a change. I need a challenge. I need to move up. I need to challenge myself and go see a dance coach, and develop a new routine, and feel like I'm a little more invested in it. It's too easy just to cruise through. And the money hasn't been good at the Castaways lately. People are saving money, whatever. I've just heard that the business is down. So I can't afford to have that happen." Alan had told her once that if she had to do that kind of work, she ought to do it at a place like Saint-Moritz, not a grubby little joint in western Massachusetts. She didn't feel ready to go that far. But the region contained larger, better strip clubs than the Castaways.

ALAN HAS DECIDED to go out slumming with some friends. They'll have a few drinks, some good conversation, a mildly picaresque adventure. In the afternoon, Alan's party arrives in downtown Springfield, in front of the Mardi Gras.

On the windows, multicolored blinking lights outline a cartoon painting of a naked reclining woman and a champagne glass. The windows are all painted over: no free looks inside allowed. The vista up the street, of gray, half-demolished city blocks, hardly looks inviting, but the doorway even less. Almost anyone would feel a qualm when entering a place like that in daylight. To leave a nighttime street for a dingy bar or strip joint is one thing. It is different on a sunny afternoon. The daylight is reproachful, a reminder that a choice is being made, again, to waste the daylight of a life. So the atmosphere seems just right for slumming. Alan and his friends enter laughing through the turnstile; no cover charge is levied at that early hour. The crowd inside is small, but a couple of women are performing on the stage, one lying on her back in gynecological position, another rubbing herself against a pole that reaches to the ceiling. The elevated stage has those same blinking Christmas tree–like lights around it. Alan says he thinks electricians probably have a special name for them. Then he sees Suzanne.

She is between sets, dressed in high heels and a black string bikini, which leaves to the imagination only a few square millimeters more than the bodies writhing on the stage. She might be a picture of the universal nightmare, in which one finds oneself in underwear in public. It is like Suzanne, however, not to grab a robe. For Alan, both the splendid and the terrible in her.

They stand beside a round table a little distance from the stage, bathed in dark orange light. Alan stands as close to her as a person can without making contact, his pale blue eyes fastened on her face. She looks squarely back at him. It is inevitable, of course, that they should meet this way again.

Alan approaches his friends, who are sitting by the stage, and says they have to leave. In the car, he tells them, "Suzanne said to me, 'Isn't it funny? We first broke the ice at a strip joint, and now we're meeting in a strip joint again.' " He says they made a dinner date for tomorrow night. He says, with a question in his voice that asks whether he is understood, "My heart is like a bell that's stopped ringing but is still vibrating?"

On Main Street a boy is practicing the craft of panhandling. His clothes are clean. His pants have a brand name on them. "Got any spare change?" he calls to Alan.

"Yes, I do," says Alan, walking past.

"Well, can I have it?"

"No."

Alan is prone to charity but discriminating. Even at the height of his illness, he used to keep a lookout for the interestingly needy. He had loved Northampton most in the days when the state hospital had first begun to empty onto Main Street. He loved to watch the man who walked along holding an opened book at arm's length in front of him. Suddenly he'd stop, and stand rigidly, as if he'd just read an arresting passage. Alan studied the man's battered shoes. Alan had walked all over town carrying a new pair, looking for him.

Alan had angrily refused to participate in last fall's memorial service for Ben, the homeless man. He'd known Ben at least as well as anyone else in town had. Ben had greatly admired Alan's Rolls. Alan couldn't let anyone inside the car back then, so he'd started giving Ben copies of the quarterly Rolls-Royce owners' magazine, and Ben would wander off toward his home by the railroad tracks, studying the glossy photos of polo matches and picnics in the Alps. Alan gave him money regularly. One time he offered Ben a job, but Ben just walked away.

American Christmas can be painful for a Jew. But for Alan, it was an exciting potlatch. He'd study his friends' children, then go shopping. He'd buy toy trains and drums for the boys, art sets and wristwatches and fourteen-karat gold chains with pendant amethysts for the girls. A couple of years ago the four-year-old daughter of a friend made a book for him. He bought her a small gold chain with an emerald on it. Every year thereafter another book had arrived, and Alan headed out for downtown's jewelry stores, laughing happily, saying, "I could be in trouble for a lot of years. Until she reaches her twenties and decides all this is stupid." Alan thought the cause of his gift-giving lay in his childhood home. He couldn't remember hearing the word "love" used there, and presents from his father were usually the result of arduous negotiations. Maybe the array of wants and needs and stratagems gift-giving served could be subsumed under a term like "control." But it would have been as accurate to say that acts of largesse gave Alan chances to act in the world with some visible effect.

A psychologist at Smith—he'd never met Alan—had for years conducted clinical research on obsessive-compulsive disorder. He'd begun to think that many victims shared the most civilized of traits. These weren't obvious, but dig beneath the bizarre behavior, then down below the crippling fears, and, he said, you'd often find a kind of thinking that looked out on the world with great concern. "It's like having the world in your head," the researcher explained. "And it's your responsibility to keep the world safe, to fix it." Believing that their own thoughts had power, obsessive-compulsives tended to try to worry theirs toward harmlessness. Some—so-called checkers—fretted endlessly over the fear that they might have done somebody harm. They seemed like model citizens gone mad with conscientiousness.

Alan's political philosophy was libertarian. He'd voted against the Domestic Partnership Ordinance because he felt it granted too much power to the city government. The power to license various kinds of cohabitation implied the power to forbid them, he thought, and he wanted none forbidden. But if it had been even remotely possible, Alan would have taken care of the world, one needy individual after another. He was especially susceptible to youth, and to pretty waifs. In town, rumors abounded that Alan hunted little girls, but this was untrue. He had asked young women to pose for him, but he'd always made sure they were over eighteen. He imagined having an affair with one of them but, sensing that she wasn't interested, he'd lost interest, too. And then for a time she became virtually his ward. "I feel another subsidy coming on," he said happily of her a while back. She needed help, unquestionably. "I want to be someone, I guess. I don't want to be just another statistic," she told him once. She said, "I think a lot of teenagers go through a stage of feeling rejected, feeling really awkward. Sometimes I still feel like I've grown an extra arm or something." He helped her go back to school. He counseled her relentlessly. But for some reason that Alan couldn't fathom, she attracted truly psychotic young men. Worse, she was attracted to them. She had a brief affair with one young man who soon afterward was sent to a mental hospital, and Alan thought, "I hope she never hooks up with him again." Then she did. Alan told her over the phone, "One of these days one of these people is going to do you great harm."

"Well," she said, "why are people always telling me I'm about to ruin my life?"

In the end, he had to give up trying to help her. He lay awake nights worrying about her, and the worries began to feel familiar.

There was an odd nobility, a knight-errant quality, about Alan—in his willingness to suffer for the sake of life itself, in his tendency to view himself under harsher light than he would turn on others, in his impulsive generosity. Alan wasn't about to divest himself of his fortune on behalf of the interestingly needy, but he was prepared to divest himself of a sizable percentage for love.

Suzanne had come back now, and his life was exciting again. "Without her in my life, my life would be okay. I would go to Sylvester's every morning, read the paper, do the crossword, schmooze, shop, read, watch TV, maybe have a date or do some photography. Take a trip here and there. That would be my life. That isn't my life with her. I'm out learning about computers now. I bought one. It's capable of editing film." They were going to make videos together, designed for foot fetishists. "I would never have been *interested*," he said. "It's like hitting passing gear. We run our separate lives and talk about people we're seeing. Whether we have a hot, exclusive romantic relationship or not, we'll have a hot something." He said, "If I walk away from this minus fifty thousand dollars, with all that I'll have learned and the excitement, you know you can't buy that for fifty thousand dollars."

But the new relationship, what Alan later called round two, followed much the same course as the old. Suzanne got into a scrape with some people she met at a strip joint. She told Alan about it. For the first time since he'd met her, he heard fear in her voice. He felt greatly moved. He gave her $10,000 so she could quit stripping. But then an old boyfriend came to town, and round two ended. Round three began some months later, when she called him from a police station. She'd gotten caught in the middle of a fight between two boyfriends. In due course, Alan put on a jacket and necktie and made a brief return to his lawyering past. She'd done nothing wrong and he easily got her off. Not long afterward he heard her say, "I met this really mellow guy." Alan told her, "Don't call me again, unless you're interested in an exclusive romantic relationship." Several months later, she called.

When Alan talked about the relationship now, his tone was weary and determined and fatalistic. "I have to say that in my own demented way I did love, I still do love Suzanne." In part he felt indebted. "Suzanne represents for me, if not hope, the willingness to strive, to try something different, to keep moving on. She opened doors for me I would never have opened myself." He'd house her in a separate apartment, replace her dying car, call in an old favor and get her a job, pay for her therapy. "I'll be there, be a rock for her," he said. He didn't sound happy or unhappy. He seemed to feel this was an obligation, not a burden, that fate had settled on him. This, he thought, had become his job. (Not the most productive line of work, though it was interesting to imagine a Northampton in which every resident with means felt compelled to assume obligations of that sort.)

Alan continued to visit his old psychiatrist, the one he'd met at McLean. Alan liked him. The man was wry, judicious, openminded. From time to time he uttered prophecies. One afternoon Alan sat in the psychiatrist's office relating the latest episode in the relationship. It was failing again, and this time it was Alan who planned to end it. He talked on and on, and then finally had no more to tell.

A pause ensued. "I have good news and bad news for you," the doctor said at length. "You haven't heard the last of her."

CHAPTER 17

The Application

Tommy had an office in a basement room at home. Jean called it "Tom's shrine." On the walls around his desk hung the plaques and citations he'd received, and various mementos. A framed letter from a little girl—he'd caught the burglar who robbed her family's house and took her piggy bank. A photograph of Tommy taking target practice, dressed in a T-shirt that read, NEVER QUESTION AUTHORITY. A snapshot of a man lying on his back on Elm Street—he told Tommy he was trying to contact people from outer space. Another of some automatic weapons he once found at Hampshire Heights.

A sticker on his locker at the police station read, HAVING FUN AT OTHER PEOPLE'S EXPENSE. He'd put it there years ago, where fellow cops could see it. It expressed one way he felt about his job. This room expressed another, privately. The souvenirs in here were like the pieces of a story that he told only to himself. Read backward, it went from the citations and photographs to a snapshot of the days when he had hair and was marching in the department color guard, then to a portrait of his police academy class, then to the bookcase behind him where in neat array sat many little models of police cars, a collection of policeman figurines, a couple of dozen old badges. At the beginning, on the wall to his right, hung a framed reproduction of a Norman Rockwell print—a uniformed cop leaning down from his cafeteria stool to befriend a child.

Tommy got two days off out of every six. On one of them, several weeks after the airport bust, he went down to his basement office and took the FBI's application form out of his desk drawer. The heading read: "Preliminary Application for Special Agent Position (Please Type or Print in Ink)." Tommy stared at the form. He read over the attachment to the application again. "To qualify for training as an FBI agent, a candidate must be: 1. a U.S. citizen 2. between the ages of 23 and 37 when entering on duty 3. hold a bachelor's degree obtained in an accredited four-year resident program at a college or university, and 4. have three years full time work experience. . . ." The sheet listed other hurdles—the written test, an interview, a lie-detector test, a physical, a background check. But he had the preliminary qualifications. This part of the process would be easy. The form was only five pages of simple questions. They asked only for his age and Social Security number and a few details of his education and experience.

But he paused over the first question, in the box in the upper left-hand corner of the first page: "Name in Full: (Last, First, Middle, Maiden)." It suddenly seemed to be asking for more: What did it mean to be Thomas F. O'Connor?

Things changed and changed again. That was the lesson of this past year. If he filled out this form and Jean got pregnant or he found he simply couldn't leave, he could withdraw the application. Even if the FBI accepted him, he told himself, he'd probably turn them down. Chances were he'd fail the written test, but he'd never know if he didn't try. In the meantime, he didn't have to tell anyone he'd applied, except for Jean. She hadn't talked him into doing this, but he knew she hoped he would.

After a while, as if all by itself, the first box was filled in:

O'Connor, Thomas Francis

• • •

On a day in early June, a friend at the D.A.'s office told Tommy that Rick's trial had advanced onto the Superior Court's schedule. It would probably start sometime in August. That night Tommy had one of his jail dreams. He was sitting in a cell. He was guilty, though of what he didn't know. The walls around him were painted a pale gray-blue, like the walls in the lockup at the station. He stared through the bars in his door down a long cellblock. Then he saw a jailer leading Rick in. He woke up to the sound of his own voice yelling, "Run, Rick! Run!"

The dream hung around him until the following evening when he went to work. Then action dissolved it. The dispatcher's voice on the radio announced "a family fight" at Hampton Gardens. "Gonna be busy tonight, eighty-three," the dispatcher added.

"Praise the Lord and pass the ammunition," Tommy said into his microphone. He hung it up and turned on his siren. He wore a manic grin. "I feel like I should have a bag of popcorn."

Summer nights passed quickly, as they always had. But many shifts still started slowly. On a hot afternoon in July, Tommy drove into Hampshire Heights and found the streets all but empty. A teenager came up to his window.

"Can I play with the siren?"

"No, Angel. You're too old for that now."

Tommy drove away. "Boy. You know you've been working in a place a long time, when you start to deal with the kids of people you arrested as kids."

The radio was silent. He had some time to kill. He headed west toward Northampton's countryside. The transition was so quick, from the Dumpster-adorned project, where tar was melting in the heat, to wooded roads, that the trip seemed dreamlike. He listened for duty calls on the radio, but drove as he sometimes did in his civilian car, slowing down to look at a house where he used to play, taking a turn to pass a piece of woods where he'd made an interesting arrest. In theory, a drive like this could go on almost forever, the landscape held so many remembered scenes. When Jean was in the car and he got sidetracked this way, she'd indulge him for a while, then say, "Stop driving around aimlessly, please." Now, in the cruiser, he decided he should have a destination. On his way to work, on the outskirts of town, he'd noticed a newly bulldozed dirt road. When something new was built in Northampton, he liked to know it.

He drove down the dirt track into a woods. The hot air coming in the cruiser's windows had a sudden vein of coolness in it, falling from the foliage, all that green water suspended overhead. Then abruptly, as if the cruiser had just passed through the dark entrance of a cathedral, the view expanded and Tommy was looking out across a huge clearing, surrounded by trees, a brand-new opening in Northampton's forest, soon to be another subdivision. Right now it looked like a wasteland. The ground had baked to a light brown. He drove across it raising dust and stopped beside a tall, fat mound of loam. Weeds sprouted from it here and there. It was just a dump truck's sculpture, its value to the adult world calculated by its price per cubic foot and the quality of lawns to come. Tommy stared at it, remembering. "We'd have *loved* this."

He smiled. He thought of Rick and his other friends gathering on Forbes Avenue on hot summer mornings. "Let's play Grunts and Gorillas." "No, let's go to the dirt mounds." Mounds like this were always temporary things, of course, but they could usually find some. This one would have kept them busy for a week, sliding down it, burrowing into it, constructing forts—unless the contractor showed up and scared them away, as sometimes used to happen. "You never have friends like you did when you were twelve," Tommy said. Then his expression turned sour. "Yeah, sure, until he goes and ..." Tommy put the cruiser back in gear and drove away.

These western parts of town didn't get patrolled much.

Tommy could always say that out here aimless driving wasn't aimless, that it was his duty to check this quiet territory now and then. The radio remaining silent, aimless driving continued. He turned north on Sylvester Road, and in a little while the cruiser was bumping up the dirt road toward the place he called Turkey Hill. He couldn't remember the last time he'd driven up here, it had been so long. "There's a zillion-dollar place up at the very top." He stopped before the house came into view, as he always had on those mornings long ago when he'd come up here to watch the sunrise. He got out and looked around. The trees had grown, as trees will. He craned his neck, but only a narrow vista remained. There wasn't much point in standing there staring at leaves, so he headed out and drove around aimlessly for a while longer, a twisting, turning route that eventually led him back toward Main Street.

In the first week of August, Tommy and Jean went to the Cape for summer vacation with Steve and Jane. They were the last of their childless friends, but were about to be childless no longer. Jane was very pregnant. Tommy and Steve dug a belly hole in the sand, so she could sunbathe comfortably. Every year he and Jean would come to the beach and Tommy would imagine that next year they would have a child with them. He'd dream of how, in a few years, the kid would discover beach glass and learn how to get mauled safely in the waves, as he himself had done on the O'Connor summer camping trips. He was glad for his friends, but sitting on the beach, staring out to sea, he felt again as though his life had come to a dead stop.

At night in the cottage, he studied math, for the FBI's written test. He didn't enjoy the studying, but it let him feel that he was trying to create some progress in his life. Besides, he didn't have much choice. Jean tutored him, and none of his old schoolboy ruses worked on her. She'd tell him to knock it off and get back to work. He returned to Northampton and his uniform a week before Rick's trial. The date for it was fixed now. Jury selection and hearings would begin on the fourteenth of August, and the trial proper on the fifteenth probably.

On the evening of the eleventh, Tommy was driving in the cruiser south of downtown, when the dispatcher called him over the radio, saying in a slightly elevated voice, "Eighty-three, we have a report of an individual pointing a gun out a window, over Main Street Cleaners."

"Yeah, sure," said Tommy. He unclipped the microphone from the dashboard. "All right. I'll check it out."

Old South Street rises steeply toward Main. Tommy stopped at the intersection, at the crest of the hill. Main Street was packed. Before him lay a typical summer evening scene. Women being led along the sidewalks by their dogs—notable how many dog owners Northampton had—a young woman in the crosswalk blowing bubbles through a little bubble-blowing wand, wobbly, rainbow-colored spheres rising in the air. There was the usual human background of ordinary-looking couples, some with ice cream cones, strolling down the sidewalk past the cleaners, and also, above the cars and crowd, leaning out a second-story window, the figure of a thin young man with dark hair. He held a black object in his right hand. "Jesus Christ!" yelled Tommy, leaning forward toward the windshield. His eyes looked almost cartoonlike, as if bulging at the sight.

Tommy grabbed his binoculars from their place beside his seat. He focused them on the boy in the window. The kid was holding what looked like a black automatic, the size and shape of a Lüger. He was moving it from side to side as if it were a paintbrush, over the strolling crowd below.

Tommy put down his binoculars. He glanced at the traffic, waiting for an opening, then gunned the cruiser through it, driving with one hand. With the other he unfastened the safety strap on his holster. He slammed the cruiser into park at the foot of the sidewalk, and jumped out. The boy in the window couldn't have noticed him yet. The boy had his pistol hand extended and was sighting at the back of a man walking on the sidewalk below. It was hard to believe that what this looked like could really be happening on Main Street.

Several weeks ago Tommy had dreamed that he was on a staircase and a suspect pulled a gun on him. It was a familiar dream, one that he believed his mind brought up for a purpose. When he had it, he always dodged the bullet. This time he got shot. "That's telling me I'm getting careless," he'd thought. So he'd reviewed street tactics in his mind and done some target shooting. On the perimeter of sleep, he had often warned himself against doing the wrong thing at a time like this. Then in his imagination, and in his jail dreams, came lawyers, court, a liberal judge who disliked cops, the view from the inside of a cell, and a funereal empty feeling that he deserved what he was getting, for killing someone he didn't have to kill.

He would give the young man in the window one chance. He'd draw the kid's attention away from the people on the street and toward himself. If the kid in the window turned the pistol Tommy's way, Tommy might have time to duck behind the cruiser and then shoot. He had one hand on his pistol. It was still holstered, but he had his finger on the trigger guard. He put two fingers of his left hand into the corners of his mouth and whistled, a piercing sound he'd learned to make long ago as boss of the O'Connor Detective Agency. Then he bellowed, *"You!"* Up and down the street, startled faces turned. The young man turned, too. He looked surprised. His mouth fell open. Then, very quickly, he lowered the pistol and pulled his head and torso back inside.

"You get down here *now!*" Tommy yelled toward the window.

The door at street level let into an old wooden staircase. At the top, a door opened, and the young man appeared, no longer carrying the gun. "Show me your hands!" yelled Tommy. His face was bright. He bounded up the stairs two steps at a time, grabbed the young man by the arm, and took him back inside the apartment. "Where's the gun?" It lay under a pillow on the sofa. Tommy turned the black pistol over in his hands. A pellet gun. Tommy checked the chamber. It wasn't loaded. He made very sure of that. By now a couple of his patrol officers had arrived. Tommy held the pellet gun in his right hand, by his side. He'd bring it back to the station as evidence.

The kid told the other cops that he was a student from UMass. He said, "I was just having some fun."

Tommy's face got redder. "What kind of a moron are you?" he said through his teeth.

"It's just a toy."

In one swift, leather-creaking movement Tommy backed him against the wall. He pressed the barrel of the empty pellet gun against the young man's forehead. *Does this look real to you? Does this look real to you?*

He lowered the pistol and took a deep breath. The patrolmen led the boy down the stairs in handcuffs, the make-believe Raskolnikov saying, "I'm a moron. I admit it."

By the time Tommy got back to the station, half a dozen people had come in to report that a man with a gun in a window had threatened to shoot them. Tommy sat down to write his report. He regretted the aftermath then. He shouldn't have put the gun to the student's forehead. It wasn't smart. It wasn't professional. He couldn't remember the last time he had felt so angry. But it was over. It would never happen again.

He went back out in the cruiser. There were no bodies on Main Street, no young student slumped over the windowsill above the cleaners, no ice cream cone melting on the pavement beside a corpse. He wasn't facing an investigation. His world had reassembled. On the corner of Old South and Main a crowd surrounded a belly dancer. A little farther down the block, the steel drummer played "Danny Boy." Tommy smiled. "Summertime!" he said.

CHAPTER 18

The Trial

Tommy HAD THE next night off. He unfolded his pop-up trailer in the driveway at home, so that he and Jean could pretend that they were camping out. He often proposed that they spend summer nights in the trailer. Life with Tommy could be exhausting, but it was rarely boring. Jean went along with her pillow, amused.

The air was cooler out there, behind walls of mosquito netting. They lay awake in the trailer talking for a long time that night. Jury selection would begin the day after tomorrow. Rick was an inescapable subject now.

"He's such a jerk," Jean said once again. "I'm so angry at him."

"I'm angry at him, too," said Tommy. But this time he went on.

Anger was only part of what he felt, he told her. All this past year, when old memories had surfaced, he'd tried to make repairs in them by omitting Rick. It never worked. Every little reverie was still intact, but every one now had another ending. He couldn't shake the feeling that, through Rick, his childhood was now accused of harboring a dirty secret. "It's like everything is poisoned," Tommy said. And when Jean spoke in an icy way about Rick, she wasn't just denouncing an old friend of his, but something else that he cared about, something that seemed like part of who he was, like his religion or his Irish blood.

Jean said, "I understand."

He thought he did too, finally.

The next day Rick's prosecutor asked Tommy to come to his office so they could review his testimony. The prosecutor— David Angier, a dark-haired man with a quiet, confident manner—asked him how he felt about being a witness.

"If I had my druthers, I wouldn't be involved," Tommy said. "And I tried to avoid it. But I don't have a problem with it. I wouldn't lie for him, or anybody."

They talked for about an hour. Angier described a lot of the case against Rick. Among other things, the child. After months of psychotherapy, she had said much more than in her first interview, and apparently would testify without ambiguity now, if there was a trial.

Tommy had worked with Angier before. He trusted him. He trusted the state police officer who had led the investigation. Sitting there in the D.A.'s office, he thought the case looked strong. His own statement seemed relatively unimportant, but, in context, damning.

Angier also said there was a fifty-fifty chance that Rick would accept a plea bargain. Tommy thought he hoped Rick would.

He felt nervous out on patrol that evening. If Rick was going to kill himself, he thought, he'd probably do it tonight. "Now's the most critical time. And I can't reach out to him. It wouldn't be appropriate." But no call for a suicide came in.

Jean was asleep when he got home. He was very tired, and he quickly dozed off. He woke up in the middle of the night and lay staring at the ceiling, waiting for his dream to leave him. It had been another jail dream. This time he was a guard in a decrepit jail, like Northampton's former county jail. He'd just walked up to the door of a cell and was standing outside looking through the bars at Rick, when he woke up.

He stared at the ceiling. The dream lingered, like something interfering with his breathing. He must have sighed, because Jean stirred beside him.

"You all right?"

He could tell from her voice she was still half asleep. "I just did a cell check on Janacek," he said.

She rolled over and was gone again. He turned on the light and read until the words began to blur. As soon as he turned the light off, he felt wide awake. He heard himself sigh. So he coughed to cover the sound.

"You all right?" said Jean's voice thickly. "Something in your throat?"

"No. Same thing."

R ICK HAD A lawyer, of course. A reputable, experienced trial lawyer from Springfield. On August 6, he had written a letter to Rick. "After our several meetings and conferences, I thought it appropriate to make my recommendations in writing," the letter began.

First the lawyer laid out the prosecution's case. Rick's wife would testify that he often drank to the point of insensibility and that he had "allowed for the possibility" that he could have abused his daughter while in a blackout. A host of other witnesses—fellow cops, including the police chief himself, and doctors and social workers and psychiatrists—would all testify that Rick had allowed for that possibility. His wife would also testify as to what their daughter had told her over the past year about the alleged abuse, and this would amount to a more detailed description than the girl had given the state police investigator in her initial interview. The investigator herself would take the stand, of course, and describe the interview. And the girl would take the stand as well. "Your daughter . . . by all accounts, is able and willing to testify to acts that constitute the crimes of rape and indecent assault and battery against her by you," Rick's lawyer wrote. "Your daughter will be confronting you in open court with the most serious allegations of sexual misconduct." She was an articulate child. It would be hard to make the jury doubt her, especially since she had "no apparent motive" for making up the charges. "This, in substance, is the Commonwealth's case," Rick's lawyer wrote. "It is formidable."

Then he turned to the strategies he'd considered using in Rick's defense. He had consulted an expert on cases like these, and the expert had examined the evidence. The expert could point out to the jury that Rick's repeated, voluntary concession about blacking out might well have been nothing more than a confession, innocent and honest, about his alcoholism. But the expert had found no reason to attack the substance of the prosecution's case, no evidence to suggest that the charges against Rick had arisen from "undue or extraneous influence." The lawyer thought that the expert probably wouldn't help Rick's case, and might even harm it. He felt the same about the other possible defense witnesses. All hope for a successful defense would rest on Rick's own testimony. But if Rick took the stand, he'd be subjected to tough cross-examination on "vulnerable issues"—the fact that he himself had said he thought his daughter might well have been molested, the fact that he'd made those repeated, if limited, concessions about possibly being the culprit himself, the fact that he couldn't explain why his daughter would make up the allegations, except to say she was "confused" or was blaming him for what someone else had done.

The prosecution's long-standing offer remained on the table, Rick's lawyer wrote—a suspended sentence, probation, and mandatory counseling, if Rick would plead guilty to a single count of indecent sexual assault and battery. And the prosecution might be willing to accept another kind of guilty plea, one that would allow Rick to stand firm in his insistence that he couldn't remember abusing his child, even while accepting the weight of the evidence against him. A trial was the alternative. In his opinion, the lawyer wrote, they were likely to lose. If they did, Rick would almost certainly be sentenced to jail. The judge who would preside had a reputation for meting out stiff sentences. A former law-enforcement officer convicted of abusing his own child was a perfect candidate for one of those. "If the conviction were on the rape charge, a state prison sentence is likely."

It was a long letter. It had qualities not always present in the arguments of lawyers—calm yet insistent, measured yet relentless. It ended, "We have explored all of these matters and others previously in great detail. You have indicated your preference is a trial. I remain most concerned for you. I urge you to re-evaluate your position. Time is short. I will be available for further discussion at your convenience."

But Rick wasn't about to give in, evidently. The preliminaries began as scheduled, on the morning of the fourteenth. All the potential witnesses were barred from the courtroom that first day. By noon a jury had been selected. For most of the rest of the session the lawyers argued over defense motions. What seemed like the most important of these had to do with a card that Rick had sent his wife, some days after she'd confronted him with the allegations. The D.A. described the card to the judge: "It's a picture of a penguin in a prison outfit that basically says—the gist of it is, I'm sorry for what I did. I'm guilty. Can I get early parole?"

Rick's lawyer stood and argued in a forceful voice: "The problem is, Your Honor, is it makes no reference to the complainant. It was sent to the mother. She had separated from him, indicated and actually begun the process of filing a divorce. They had attempted a therapy session. A letter was sent with the intent to attempt to apologize for the effect of alcohol on their personal relationship. . . . And it depicts someone in garb that just sends an erroneous—totally prejudicial and erroneous message to the jury. This had nothing to do with the minor child. . . . This is not directed at any conduct involving the child."

"Well, that's what he says now," Judge Ford replied, "but couldn't the jury draw the inference that it came within a week after the allegations were made, that it was a response to those allegations?" The judge said he'd let the jury come to their own conclusions. "I think it's a direct admission, or it's very close to being a direct admission."

The day's last event was a hearing on the question of whether Rick's young daughter was competent to testify. Rick's lawyer had requested that this be done. Probably he hoped the girl would perform badly or be moved to recant once she saw her father—for the first time in almost a year, seated at the defense table. If so, it was a sound and proper strategy, but it didn't work.

She was a beautiful blond child, in a dress. As she walked across the carpeted floor of the courtroom, Rick turned in his chair to gaze at her. His face was alight. He seemed to be chuckling, noiselessly. Then he simply grinned. But his wife—a thin woman with delicate features—was escorting the girl, and she whisked her up to the witness box, keeping herself between Rick and his daughter. The girl didn't even look at Rick.

"Hello there," said the judge. "Hi. What's your name?" He leaned toward her, his hands clasped on top of the bench.

She told him her name and she said he could call her by her nickname. She said she knew he was a judge, and that she was seven.

"Seven years old. You're a big girl. Do you go to school?"

She did. She told him her teacher's name and last year's teacher's name, that she could read and do figures. She proved it by adding three plus three, then four plus five.

"Very good. You're very smart," said the judge. "What's your favorite play thing, your favorite game?"

"My favorite board game is Parcheesi."

"Parcheesi? That's a tough one."

"Uh-uh, not to me."

"It's tough for me," said the judge. "Is that where you roll the dice?"

"And then you have like little circle things that are that big." She made a circle with her hands. "And you get to pick a color . . ." She explained the game to the judge as though he were the child, or perhaps a potential playmate. And she told him she watched only a little television and had just had a birthday and had received "tons" of presents. "I got a really, really soft stuffed animal." Also an ice cream cake. "I only had a half a piece because they were like that big."

"It sounds wonderful," said the judge. "Now, do you know why I'm asking you all these questions?"

"Because you never met me and you just want to, I don't know, like get to know me or something?"

"I just want to know something about you. You know what I want to know?"

"What?"

"I want to know if you know the difference between telling the truth and telling a lie. Do you?"

"Uh-huh."

"What's the difference? Can you explain it to me?"

Angier had told the judge that he'd already questioned the girl, to determine her competency. Clearly, she'd already learned her answer to this question, but it seemed like hers alone. "If someone has a red shirt on, and the guy in the blue shirt said to the guy in the red shirt, 'You're wearing a blue shirt.' That's like a little lie, and a big huge lie is when you did something really bad, and then you say you didn't do it."

"Now," said the judge, "if you talk to some people in this courtroom tomorrow about things that may have happened to you, do you promise me that you'll tell the truth?"

"Uh-huh."

"Do you know what happens to people who don't tell the truth?"

"No."

"All right. What happens to you around the house, like with your mom even, if you tell lies?"

"When—if she knows about it, she sends me up to my room for a time out or something."

"That's how she punishes you for telling lies?"

"Uh-huh."

"All right. Well, in the courtroom, I'm in charge of dealing with those types of issues. And I punish people who lie. Do you understand that?"

"Uh-huh."

"So it's really, really important that if you testify in this case, that you not tell any lies. Do you understand that?"

"Uh-huh."

"Do you promise me you won't tell any lies?"

"Uh-huh."

"Now, you know the difference between real and pretend, is that right?"

"Uh-huh."

"Can you tell me something that you know about that would be a pretend thing?"

"When like little girls give a pretend tea party with their dolls."

"Okay. Now, you say that you don't watch *Sesame Street*, but do you know who the people are on *Sesame Street*?"

"Uh-huh."

"For example, do you know who Big Bird is?"

"Uh-huh, the big huge bird."

"Do you think Big Bird is a real bird?"

"A fake," she said.

"He's a fake bird?" asked the judge.

"He's really somebody who's dressed up in a costume."

"Very good," said the judge. "Is there anything else you think I should know?"

"I know the big elephant," said the girl. "But I forget his name."

Indulgent titters had rippled through the gallery during the girl's testimony. That last line brought on more. The judge was smiling, too. It wasn't hard to imagine a jury's reaction to this child. After a little more questioning, the judge let her go. Rick's gaze had never left her. At moments when she was speaking, his shoulders had bobbed, as if he had hiccups or were sobbing. Now he beamed toward her. He looked expectant, but his wife had come forward and, once again, she whisked the girl away. Rick turned in his chair, gazing after the child, until the courtroom door shut behind her.

Then the judge declared the girl to be "a very, very intelligent and verbal child." He intoned, "I find that she has the ability to recall the events accurately and to articulate her memory of those events. I further find that she understands the difference between fact and fantasy, that she understands the difference between right and wrong, that she recognizes the duty to be truthful in the courtroom and that she understands, in a general way, the concept of punishment if one is not truthful in a courtroom. Under these circumstances, I find that the Commonwealth has established that the child is, in fact, competent, and I will permit her to testify at the trial of this matter."

Architects and builders are sometimes blessed by their mistakes. The Plexiglas windows in the vestibule outside Superior Court had grown discolored over the years, but they improved the afternoon sunlight. They turned it a deep shade of gold. Court had recessed for the day and all the parties and spectators had departed, except for Rick and one of his sisters. He sat in the vestibule on the wooden bench outside the empty courtroom, with his face in his hands, and he wept and wept. His sister sat beside him, her hand on his bowed and heaving back, bathed in golden light.

The LIEUTENANT WAS away. Tommy was stuck in the station tonight. He was the officer in charge, the OIC. He and the chief, Russ Sienkiewicz, leaned against opposite walls in the hallway by the side door. The door had a window. Now and then they'd glance through it, at the red Saab in the parking lot, Rick's car. Tommy had been excluded from today's preliminary hearings, but the chief had been called to the courtroom briefly for one of the motions, and he'd heard accounts of what had gone on in there. He'd also heard that Rick had sat outside the courtroom weeping for a full half hour.

"They literally had to mop up the floor."

Tommy grimaced and glanced out the window.

"His lawyer took him to his office for a sitdown," said the chief. Stories of the girl's interview by the judge had circulated. The chief shook his head. "I think Rick might plead tomorrow. If he doesn't blow his brains out tonight."

Old anxieties may fade without quite being outgrown. Tommy would not let his feelings show in front of the guys tonight, not even in front of the chief. "I told Rick to his face, 'If you're gonna do it, don't do it in Northampton.'" Tommy smiled at his boss, the same old manic-looking smile that he used to wear in the presence of a disturbing corpse. "Well, Chief, I'm OIC, and I'm not going out."

The chief stared at him, one of his sphinxlike stares, which always made Tommy wonder if he'd said something stupid.

Tommy looked away, out the window again. "No," he said softly. "I'll go."

They both stared out the window at the red car for a while. "The longer it's there, the more talking he's doing with his attorney," said the chief. "I don't want him to go to jail. He's the one who's doing that."

"I've had a headache for three days," said Tommy. "It's going away. It's not the only thing that's going away."

The chief departed. Tommy went back to gazing out the window toward Rick's car. He murmured, "I feel like I'm putting a nail in his coffin."

Other cases were in progress around the station. There always were. Life went on out in his town, but he couldn't supervise it tonight. He was stuck inside. He wandered around the station, then returned to the hall by the side door, to check on the red car. Still there. "Nine o'clock tomorrow, that'll be fun," he said toward the window. "I'm not gonna be anywhere to be found. I'm not gonna sit with the families. I'm just gonna go in and testify and get out of there. Jesus, Mary, and Joseph, what did I do?"

Jean appeared in the window, walking toward him across the parking lot, carrying a paper bag, his supper. He opened the door for her. She looked at his face, and said, "Are you crabby again?"

"I'm in one of the worst moods of my life," Tommy said in a cheerful-sounding voice. Then he looked serious. "I don't mind doing what I have to do, but I don't want to walk in front of Rick and his sisters and his mother. I feel like I'm putting a nail in his coffin."

"He put his own nails in," said Jean.

Tommy told her the news he'd heard. "Something may happen tonight. They literally had to mop up the floor where Rick was sitting after the hearing. His lawyer took him to his office for a sitdown." He told her he was watching Rick's car now. "I'm onto it like stink on sh—"

"You get in this building and that word just comes out," said Jean.

"I don't use it at home, though. Do I? You bet your ass I don't."

A while later, two small children appeared at the door. When she spotted Sergeant O'Connor, the little girl did a hop and said, "Goody!"

He was glad to see them, too. The little boy asked him, "Do you know our daddy?"

"Yes, I do." Tommy knew him very well. A brawler so tough it was impossible not to admire him, but with an unfortunate habit of smoking crack. Tommy had said of their father once, "Does he get violent on crack? Jesus Christ, he's violent on oxygen." He was in state prison now. Tommy had helped to put him there.

"Have you seen him lately?" the little boy asked.

"No," said Tommy. Then he changed the subject. He thought the children might like to look at all the lost bicycles stored in the station's basement.

At some moment after nightfall the red Saab disappeared. Tommy was away from the window, and the next time he looked out the car was gone. Later, Rick called the station and spoke to another officer. Tommy didn't get on the line, but he stood facing that other cop, mouthing these words emphatically: "Tell him to plead! Tell him to plead!"

O LD-FASHIONED NORTHAMPTON woke up to bad news about one of its own. A Northampton police officer. Was going on trial in Superior Court. Today.

A few hours later, Tommy walked across the courthouse parking lot, carrying his briefcase, and inside it the statement he'd written almost exactly a year ago. The morning was merely warm, but Tommy felt sweat trickling down his back under his white shirt. He had been dieting. His features looked sharper, but his skin looked scrubbed and pale against his gray court suit. He felt, not exactly weary, but as if he had rejoined a dream. Later, he remembered thinking that he would have to concentrate to get through this day. In his mind he gave himself directions. "You walk past the metal detector. Okay, now you go up the stairs."

Two flights lead up to Superior Court. The first lets out on District Court rooms, and the treads are well worn. The second flight is used a lot less often, and as he mounted it, the muffled hubbub of District Court receding, Tommy felt dizzy. At the top, he opened the door to murmurous voices. There was almost always a hush in the vestibule outside Superior Court. People standing there waiting for trials usually talked more softly and dressed better than on the floors below, in direct proportion to the stakes, always larger here. This was the topmost floor, the aerie of justice in Hampshire County. A couple of dozen people stood in clusters in the vestibule, a few reporters, the chief, some of Rick's wife's family. And there on the bench, among some of Rick's sisters, sat Rick's elderly mother. Tommy looked at her and he was a little boy. She was feeding him snacks, talking about her relatives, out on the porch overlooking Forbes Avenue.

The thing to do was clear. He walked straight for her. Bending down, he said, "Mrs. Janacek! How are ya?"

She smiled up at him. They chatted a bit about family. She said, "You're in a tough spot."

"Oh, awful." His voice was loud. He wore his game face.

Tommy turned away and walked over to the chief. There was news. The lawyers had worked out a plea bargain. The judge had agreed to accept it. But Rick was holding out, apparently. In a moment Rick's lawyer appeared from around a corner. He walked up to Tommy and said that Rick wanted to talk to him in private.

Tommy turned to the prosecutor, Angier, who said, "Do what you can."

Tommy understood, and he felt surprised. The lawyers wanted to send him on a mission. They wanted him to talk Rick into pleading guilty. His first instinct was to utter his Explorer Scout's response: Yes, sir. I'll fix this right away. But then he paused: Should I? Do I want to be the one who finally persuades him not to fight? But every choice looked bad. A plea still seemed like the best of them. "Okay," Tommy said.

Rick sat alone in a little room just off the lobby. He was crying quietly when Tommy came in and closed the door. Tommy sat and talked with him for nearly half an hour. He said he didn't think Rick was entirely to blame for what had happened, and that a lot of the other cops in the department thought Rick really didn't know what had or hadn't happened. He was trying to speak consolingly, in the spirit of childhood memories, thinking, "When you were a kid and did something wrong, it was easier to stomach it if your buddies knew it and didn't think it was too bad. It's not as big a thing in your mind anymore." At the same time, he was thinking, "He might confess to me right now." If Rick really was guilty, that would be best for everyone. There would be an end and after it maybe new beginnings. In a little while, Tommy moved his chair closer to Rick's, and, reaching out, he touched Rick's leg.

The trick didn't work this time. Maybe it couldn't.

So the other chore remained. In his mind Tommy wondered if he himself would plead out to these charges, if he was innocent. He believed he wouldn't, not under any circumstances. But he knew another person might, given the alternative that Rick faced. If Rick refused to plead, he'd be tried, not just for sexual misconduct, but also for rape of a child. If he got convicted, he'd be sentenced to state prison for a long time. Tommy couldn't imagine his old friend at a place like Walpole. Rick was too good a person to learn to live by its savage rules. And he'd be a pariah in jail, not only a convicted child molester but also a former cop. He wouldn't survive. On top of that, if he went to trial, his daughter would have to testify against him and maybe grow up believing she'd destroyed her father's life.

But Tommy felt torn. All this past year he'd held on to the possibility that his old friend might be innocent. Since his talk with Angier two days ago, that hope had all but vanished. Rick could perhaps restore it now, but only if he did the self-destructive thing, and, in the face of terrible threats, insisted on a trial.

Tommy had volunteered for the wrong thing. He hoped Rick would plead out and save himself and get this over with, and he hoped that Rick would not.

He began to make his argument. "If there's any possible way

that something could have happened, you've gotta deal with it and get past this. I know you, Rick. You would not do well in state prison. *I* would not do well in state prison. Not in 1996. Inside those big walls at Walpole is a hell of a lot different than these walls up here at Hampshire County."

Rick cut him off. "I know *that*."

Rick said he'd already decided to accept the plea bargain. He'd wanted to talk to Tommy before he made the act official, but he wasn't looking for advice. "I just wanted to laugh a little first," Rick said.

"You're doin' the right thing," said Tommy.

"Yeah, right," said Rick. "I'm throwing my life away. I wish it wasn't necessary." Rick said he'd heard a song this morning— "Evil Woman." He said it had made him think of his wife. She had forced this case to a false conclusion, Rick seemed to say, and left him no choice but to plead out and spare his child. Tommy wished he could believe that.

He smiled at Rick. "I'll come and visit ya."

Rick smiled at him. "Will you bring me a file?"

Tommy had closeted himself with Rick at 9:05. At 9:27, the small crowd in the vestibule heard laughter coming through the heavy oak door to the little room. Eight minutes after that, Tommy emerged, his face flushed. He walked over to the chief and Angier, who stood together near the courtroom door. "He's gonna plead. I got him to laugh. I should go on the circuit."

One of Rick's sisters stood nearby. Tommy turned to her. "Rick said he wanted to laugh a little bit. He said, 'That's why I asked you in here.' He had already made up his mind. I told him to do it. There's no way around it. It's over."

Chief Sienkiewicz lowered his brows, a wary look. "Until he gets on the stand and answers the judge's questions . . ."

Tommy stayed to watch. He'd planned to leave, but he was hoping for an end, and if he wasn't there, whatever happened wouldn't feel like one. He sat down in the gallery. He watched as Rick walked toward the witness box. He thought he saw a smile cross his lips. That was Rick. Still proud on the outside. He looked good, Tommy thought. Rick wore a blue blazer and he sat very erect in the witness chair. He faced the judge, his classical profile framed against the windows behind the judge's bench.

Tommy knew this courtroom well. He'd testified against dozens of people here, and he'd sat through many more plea bargains, watching cases he'd worked on come to their conclusions. The room seemed a shade darker than the ones in District Court, but maybe only because the cases were. The furnishings were modern, made of unpainted hardwood and severely geometrical, all right angles and parallel lines.

The judge was questioning Rick. "So you understand that the recommendation, joint recommendation of both your attorney and Mr. Angier is a sentence of two and a half years in the house of correction with six months to serve, the balance suspended in favor of ten years probation with the condition that, number one, you are to have no contact either direct or indirect with your children unless specifically ordered by the Court and that, number two, you are to undergo whatever counseling or therapy probation may deem necessary. Do you understand that?" The judge might have been a pharmacist explaining a prescription.

Tommy watched Rick's face, framed up there against the windows. He saw it change. Rick's face reddened. "Yes, I do." Suddenly Rick's voice cracked. His shoulders heaved.

"He's crying," someone nearby in the gallery whispered.

"It ain't a good day for him," Tommy murmured in reply. His voice had a mordant edge. He leaned forward over his knees and scraped that old football-injured thumbnail against his teeth, caught himself, then did it again.

The judge's voice resumed. Rick's shoulders had stilled. Did Mr. Janacek understand that by pleading guilty he was giving up his chance of ever working as a police officer again, and that he was also surrendering many legal rights?

The questions and answers went on and on, like a responsive reading of a sacred text, the judge asking the question, Rick answering, "Yes, sir."

Rick was taking an *Alford* plea. The judge briefly explained its provenance—"a famous U.S. Supreme Court case known as *Alford* versus *North Carolina*." In his even voice Judge Ford described the gist of the *Alford* doctrine: "that a defendant who is charged with a crime may plead guilty to that crime even though he is unwilling or unable to acknowledge or to admit the facts which constitute the offense are true." Plea bargains had long been the main vehicle of criminal justice in America. *Alford* made bargains more palatable for defendants. An *Alford* plea didn't ask as much of a defendant's conscience even as a plea of nolo contendere. A defendant pleading nolo simply chose not to dispute the charges. When the prosecutor and judge allowed an *Alford* plea, the defendant didn't have to make even a tacit admission of guilt. Under the *Alford* doctrine, a defendant could plead guilty even while claiming to be innocent.

Tommy knew what must have happened this morning. At the last moment, the prosecution had agreed that Rick could take this plea. In return Rick would have to do six months in the county jail. He had been offered no jail time at all, in exchange for simply pleading guilty to the lesser of the two charges. So he had chosen six months in jail in order not to have to come right out and say that he'd abused his daughter. Maybe he'd done that on principle, maybe out of pride. There was no way of knowing. Maybe *Alford* represented the best solution all around. But it didn't clarify a thing. Watching in the gallery, Tommy thought, "This leaves everything right where it was." At least the first act was over.

The judge told Rick to leave the witness box. Angier, tall and solemn, took center stage and presented a brief précis of the state's case, its case on the lesser charge. This was customary and, to Tommy, as familiar as Catholic mass. Angier spoke about Rick's heavy drinking and the statements he had made to Tommy and the chief. Tommy listened with his head bowed, worrying his thumbnail again. When he looked up, the lead investigator, the female state trooper, was walking to the witness stand. Tommy exclaimed in a whisper, "She trained Rick!" The trooper began to describe her interview with Rick's daughter, adding images to the words that Rick had asked Tommy to read many months ago. "I interviewed her in the backyard. We were sitting under a tree in the backyard. . . . She was very articulate, easy to talk to about general things, and she appeared to be somewhat guarded with respect to her father. . . . She indicated that she had to touch her father's penis, and I asked her to show me how she did that. And she first used one finger and then two fingers in a motion similar to this." The trooper lifted an index finger and drew it horizontally through the air. "Back and forth. I asked her where the touching happened, and she said it happened in the shower and in the big room, which is their living room. I asked if her dad ever touched her, and she said, yes, with his fingers. And I asked her how did that happen, how he did that, and she demonstrated using a stroking motion with one finger and then two fingers in the air. . . ."

Tommy could see the scene then, a female detective and a little girl sitting under a tree on a summer day over a year ago. But who was this whose acts the trooper was describing? "The guy up there is not the guy he's being made out to be. He's the guy playing Talking Football, making models." Everyone here probably looked at Rick and thought, "Child molester." But they didn't know him. The scene in front of Tommy was afloat, entirely familiar and entirely improbable, like a dream except that dreams relent.

"Did you form any judgment as to what she felt about her

father at that time, whether or not she loved her father at that time?" the prosecutor asked the trooper.

"Clearly, she did."

"And was it difficult for her to say those things to you?"

"That's correct."

Rick's lawyer stood up. "You also elicited from this girl and corroborations from the family that there were occasions as very small children that they showered with their parents," he said to the trooper. "With the knowledge of the other parent?"

"That's correct," said the trooper.

Soon Rick was summoned back to the witness stand. He walked across the courtroom with his shoulders erect. Watching him, Tommy saw again that hint of a smile. He knew what Rick was feeling, he knew Rick so well. Inside, Rick was struggling to keep his outside looking strong. That little smile, that flash of pride—there was more pain in it than in the sobs Rick had heaved a while back.

"So I want to be clear as to what you're saying now, sir," the judge said to Rick. "You're saying you have no reason to question what your daughter said happened on the night in question; is that correct?"

"That is correct," said Rick.

The judge asked Rick's lawyer to explain why he thought this plea was in his client's best interest. The lawyer rose and said that he believed the prosecution's case was "most substantial," and the plea bargain "eminently fair." He added that Rick "at no moment desired to have his child, despite his inability to recall, come into this court or, in fact, any other member of the family, and go through these proceedings. And that has played a substantial part as well."

Tommy watched Rick's shoulders begin jerking up and down, puppetlike. Rick was crying again. Tommy thought about the many times he'd seen defendants sit weeping in that chair. Often their families wept too, and he sat out here in the gallery thinking he could feel their eyes on him, and hear their voices asking him, "How could you do this?" Usually he'd felt glad when a defendant pled out and ended matters quickly and he could get out of court and back to work. He remembered wondering what it would be like to be the person in that witness box, pleading out, being sent to jail. "A living hell," he thought.

All the trials and pleas he'd witnessed in this room had to do with someone else's problems. This one came from three doors down the street. This was what could have happened to him, if he had shot that boy downtown the other evening. If he had, maybe he'd be sitting there, where Rick was.

The judge was questioning Rick again. "Did you just hear what your attorney said to me?"

"Yes, sir."

"Do you agree with him?"

"Yes, sir."

"You would acknowledge to me, then, that in your judgment, the Commonwealth's case against you is a strong one?"

"Yes, sir."

"Do you think that your defenses are tenuous at best?"

"Yes, sir."

"And do you believe it is in your best interest to offer an *Alford* plea of guilty?"

"Yes, sir."

"All right. Thank you very much. Now are you pleading guilty willingly, freely, and voluntarily?"

"Yes, sir."

"Has anybody forced you to plead guilty?"

"No, sir."

"Has anybody threatened you or promised you anything to make you plead guilty?"

"No, sir."

"Have you had enough time to fully discuss your case, including your rights, your defenses, and possible consequences of this guilty plea, with your attorney?"

"Yes, sir, I have."

"Has your attorney explained to you all of the rights and choices that you would have in the event you chose to have a trial?"

"Yes, sir."

"Do you think that your attorney has acted in your best interest?"

"Yes, sir, I do."

"Do you think you've been fairly and competently represented by your attorney?"

"Yes, sir."

"Are you confused by any of my questions?"

"No, sir."

"And so, as I understand it then, you are pleading guilty because you think it's in your best interest to do so and for no other reason; is that right?"

"That's correct."

The solemn process of the law had become like incantation. Right before his eyes, Rick was being officially transformed into a confessed child molester, a convicted felon, an inmate of the county jail. For most of the people who were sentenced to serve time there, the place was just an extension of their former lives. Like another rooming house. Of course, they weren't free there, but they could count on being surrounded by acquaintances and friends. But the Rick he'd known did not belong in jail. An intelligent man who had lived in a fine house he'd built with his own hands, with a hot tub, with a wife and children. "And he has to live with what he did, and whether he did it or didn't, he'll probably have to live next to a little worm he would have arrested last year. Watching TV all day. That's gotta be hell." Staring at Rick, Tommy thought—as he remembered later—"Six months in this county jail is not a long time. But six months' incarceration with those mental midgets that I put in there, I'd take the pipe. As my mother would say. Oh, I wish my mother was alive today."

The clerk, one tier below the judge, was standing now. He intoned Rick's name and asked, "How do you now plead to Count Two of Hampshire County indictment number ninety-five-dash-zero-seven-eight, charging you with indecent assault and battery on a child under fourteen?"

"I plead guilty."

Tommy watched as a court officer walked up to Rick and snapped handcuffs on him, shackling Rick's hands in front of him. It gives a person a prayerful look. Then it was like a wedding. The heads around Tommy in the gallery turned. He turned too and watched the uniformed court officer escort Rick down the aisle. Rick held his head erect, tears streaming down his cheeks.

Out in the vestibule, as Tommy was leaving, the chief patted him on the shoulder and said Tommy was the man who had endured the worst today. Tommy liked the chief. More than anyone else, he thought, Russ deserved the credit for the department's transformation. But Tommy didn't like the pat or the sad-looking faces that turned toward him. "Don't make me into some kind of victim," he wanted to say. "If you want to feel sorry for someone, feel sorry for Rick. Feel sorry for the kid."

He walked over to the station and signed out. Then he went to Jake's, the coffee shop across from the courthouse. Most of the legal establishment ate lunch there, or went there for coffee during delays in court. The place was nearly empty now. Tommy sat down at a table by a window.

He thought back to his conversation with Rick a couple of hours ago, in the little room off the Superior Court vestibule. He remembered that Rick had told him, in words like these, "You know, the last time I went out and drank a lot was with you." Had he been saying that Tommy was partly responsible for what had happened? If so, Tommy had an answer for his old friend. He uttered it aloud in the coffee shop. "Let me tell ya, Rick, your problem, if there was a problem, took place in the shower, and I wasn't there."

Tommy's face had hardened. He glared out the window as if glaring at the town, and his voice sounded fierce. He seemed to be talking to Northampton. "What's right is right, what's wrong is wrong, and the state of your *internal being* doesn't matter," he declared. He'd never read philosophy, but at this moment he was reinventing Kant. "You do what's right, even if it makes you feel bad."

His face relaxed. A gray weariness seemed to fall like a shadow over his pink cheeks. In the end he hadn't had to testify against his friend, but in effect he had, in every way that mattered. "The right thing is the honest thing," he said, cradling his coffee cup, staring out the window. "And if I wouldn't have done well by an old friend of mine, I still did the right thing."

In a while, he got up and went outside. He felt very tired now. The coffee hadn't helped much. Maybe tonight he would sleep, and tomorrow he'd feel better. He stood on the sidewalk, waiting for some cars to pass before he crossed King Street and headed home.

The great advantage of plea bargains is efficiency. The court had disposed of Rick in less than a morning. The August sun was high. To the south, a green patch of the Holyoke Range stood in the frame of Pleasant Street. Tommy was surrounded by old stomping grounds—across the way, the tall façade of the Hotel Northampton, the D.A.'s office tucked into a corner of that building, the courthouse annex just beyond, and right behind him the old Calvin Theatre, its windows papered over. The message on the Calvin's drooping marquee, TEMPORARILY CLOSED, had lost most of its letters and now read TEMP C O D. It seemed unlikely that the town's capitalists would let it languish, but for the moment the building looked like a vision of what downtown might have become and, who could say, still might. He'd watched movies there for most of his life. A year or so before the theater closed, he quit going to it because kids he'd arrested would sit some rows behind him and Jean and shower them with pieces of candy. There were only a few public places left in town where he felt comfortable in civilian clothes, having a meal or a drink or coffee, and even in those he'd try to sit with his back against a wall in a spot where he could see the door. And there was hardly a place in sight, a place in town, where he hadn't dealt with a corpse or a criminal, a domestic battle or a citizen in trouble.

The other day he'd sat down in Jake's and the waitress who brought his coffee had said, with a meaningful look, "I got a phone call the other night." Cryptic remarks like that fell immediately into a gigantic structure in Tommy's mind, like a genealogical chart. It had assembled itself over years. The waitress's remark fitted into a small corner of it, a section composed in part, only in part, of the following: The waitress's daughter was going out with a well-known scammer's son, who had recently been in trouble. The son had a child by a woman whom Tommy liked, though he'd arrested her brother for robbery once, and had also arrested her brother's son, who had slashed someone with a knife. The son also had a brother who was a good friend of Tommy's young friend Luis, "a good kid," who in his childhood had been a close friend of Felix, the boy Tommy once thought of adopting. The other night Felix's pregnant girlfriend was wearing a gold chain, which Felix had bought from a boy whom Tommy had arrested many times. Judge Ryan had ordered that boy to sell that chain to pay his fines for beating up a girl, and he'd obeyed, then taken the money to Holyoke to buy marijuana, and had gotten mugged there. That boy's mother was one of Tommy's high school classmates . . . The skein of associations seemed endless.

The chart in Tommy's mind was the human chart of North-ampton, the part he dealt with anyway, sometimes connecting to parts he didn't want to deal with as a cop. It came with his map of the geographic city, which contained all the escape routes and hiding places a criminal might use, both the places where he and Rick used to play and the junkies' lairs. Both chart and map had been very useful. The advantages of familiarity had always seemed to outweigh the liabilities. But he hadn't been amused the other day when he took his best court suit to the dry cleaners and the young female clerk said, "Your name's O'Connor, right?"

"How do you know?"

"I just do."

"That's not good, is it," Tommy had said.

It turned out he'd arrested her boyfriend. Not all that long ago, Tommy would have laughed. Now the thought of encounters like that made him think, "I'm sick of this." He found it harder and harder to write tickets. As often as not, it seemed, the driver turned out to be the son of a teacher he had liked, or the girlfriend of an informant with whom he had to maintain good relations. He didn't care much about traffic tickets, but more and more he found himself feeling slightly reluctant to arrest people for more serious things, because he'd arrested them before, or their fathers, or their mothers, or their brothers, or their sisters.

Rick had pled guilty. Ron Hall would announce it on the news tomorrow. Maybe by then Tommy would feel better. It was just another downtown morning, but nothing in the landscape that he saw around him was as large as it had been. He was standing on a sidewalk in a shrunken town.

CHAPTER 19

Milton

Aᴜᴛᴜᴍɴ, ᴀɴᴅ ᴛʜᴇ faces of young women, nervous and expectant, could be seen looking out at Northampton through the back windows of their parents' cars—here and there a Mercedes or a limousine with diplomatic plates, more often a station wagon. Families emerged onto Elm Street, lugging pieces of households down the sidewalks toward the Smith College dorms.

This was the most hopeful season in Northampton, the time of the return of the Smithies. For Laura, this fall seemed especially hopeful. She would graduate next spring. A commencement speaker might say that finishing college wasn't an end but a beginning. Laura had a better set of lines in her head. She'd been reading T. S. Eliot. She walked around downtown and the campus, reciting in her mind: "We shall not cease from exploration / And the end of all our exploring / Will be to arrive where we started / And know the place for the first time."

The amended will of Sophia Smith required that the college be situated in Northampton, but only if the town put up $25,000. That was just a fraction of Sophia's $400,000 gift, but a handsome sum back then, about half the cost of the college's first thirteen acres off Elm Street. Soon afterward, the trustees had asked the town for $75,000 more, and after a lot of decorous argument, the town meeting had done what democratic governments find easiest and forever tabled the proposal. In an unsigned letter to the *Gazette,* dated March 11, 1873, one citizen listed seven objections. The second read, in part: "This is not a town school, and we are not called upon to appropriate this money to educate our own children, as we do when we vote money for our public schools, because the institution is a college, designed for the use of people in every state in the Union. Why should one town vote its money to aid all other towns?"

Smith nowadays dispensed roughly $50 million a year in salaries, about half of that to people who lived in Northampton. It had become by far the city's largest employer, since the state hospital had closed. To a degree unusual among private colleges, it opened its classrooms to the town. It paid Northampton more for sewerage and water than the real costs of the services. It had pledged $75,000 toward a new fire station. (Perhaps the amount of the pledge was ironically calculated. If so, the joke was, like most items of distant history, lost on most of the town.) Some professors served on city boards and committees. Some students and some faculty did charitable works in town. Officially, relations were cordial. But when the mayor was trying to get some money out of Smith, as she did periodically—and why not, when she was chasing money everywhere and Smith had a big endowment—she could count on at least one city councillor to say for her indignant words about elite institutions that live tax-free in towns with crumbling firehouses and underfunded public schools.

In 1842, some years before Smith's founding, a group of people, most of them from elsewhere, attempted to establish an ideal place inside Northampton. They bought a bankrupt silk mill in what later became Florence, and set up the Northampton Association for Education and Industry. It failed four years later, mainly for lack of capital. The name "utopian community" is usually applied to that early commune and the many others like it that arose in America around that time. But the term, connoting certain failure, applies only in retrospect. The members of the Northampton Association—over two hundred of them at one point—didn't think their dreams impossible. They were abolitionists. Some were active in the Underground Railroad. Many were religious, but at odds with the convenient doctrines of established churches. They dreamed of sexual, racial, and economic equality, and they wanted to show the world that a society built on such principles could thrive materially as well as spiritually. William Lloyd Garrison and Frederick Douglass visited. Nathaniel Hawthorne considered joining. Sojourner Truth was a member.

Mainstream Northampton didn't have much truck with its short-lived radical community, but the community had left some marks on today's incarnation of the town—effects still traceable through some of the equipment left by nineteenth-century philanthropy, and less tangible effects, like those of distant ancestry. The utopian community had contributed to a continuing tradition here, a tradition of secularized virtue that fed on dreams of ideal places. Meanwhile, Smith had endured and grown. It had become that ideal place within a place. The college's first female president, Jill Ker Conway, described her introduction to the campus in 1974 this way: "I could spend months at a time at the University of Toronto without hearing a female voice raised. Here the women were rowdy, physically freewheeling, joshing one another loudly, their laughter deep-belly laughter, not propitiary giggles. The muddy afternoon games on the playing fields produced full-throated barracking. I was entranced." The case for female education made itself. "I realized that this was a real alternative society, a place of true female sociability, where women ran things for themselves."

This seemed true enough for most students. Residing in that arboretum on the hill, most didn't have to notice what was obvious to a town resident who drove up Elm Street or down the road overlooking Paradise Pond—to Hispanic boys from Hampshire Heights looking for a party to crash; and to people whose grandfathers used to earn some extra money by carrying the steamer trunks of heiresses up dormitory stairs; and to residents whose daughters went to state schools but were just as smart as any Smithie, only not as lucky. Within its safe confines, protected by their own police force, Smith students could imagine themselves in a world of a more perfect equality than any world outside. Unless they were on welfare.

Smith, personified, was like the rich elderly person who is both spendthrift and cheap, both indulgent and utterly insensitive. It had corrected some of its former snobbishness. It sought out minority students and had programs designed, on the surface anyway, to make them feel at home. It searched for what Jefferson had called "youths of genius from among the classes of the poor," and gave them scholarships. And it spent about $3 million a year on its Ada Comstock scholars.

Not that Adas were a complete financial loss. They had become some of the college's best advertisements. The administration constantly paraded them before alumnae to tell their sad, inspiring stories. Smith's endowment now approached $700 million and was rising fast. The college spent lavishly on its grounds. And yet it had rules it wouldn't bend, rules that obliged some impoverished Adas to go on welfare or forget their dreams of coming here.

Shortly after she'd arrived in Northampton, Laura had gotten in her little car and driven toward the welfare office in Florence, smoking Kools incessantly. When she saw the sign MASSACHUSETTS DEPARTMENT OF WELFARE on the door, and the linoleum-clad waiting room inside, she felt she'd left another life behind.

The caseworker told her she'd have to bring in documents—car registration, rent receipts, electric bills, statements from the college.

If she did, would she get welfare? Laura asked.

They'd have to wait and see, the caseworker said.

Laura imagined a room far away, and in it a committee of disapproving faces peering at her documents. Her laugh, which wrinkled up her face, camouflaging the little scars around her chin, her way of reaching out to touch the arm of the person she was speaking to—all the warmth she sent out seemed to dissipate before it reached the caseworker. Laura found herself gazing at the woman's mouth. "She doesn't like me," Laura thought. She was surprised. She was happy that Smith had accepted her. She thought others would be happy for her. What were Laura's "career plans"? her caseworker asked. Months went by before Laura felt there was more than formal curiosity behind the question. No one ever said so directly, but after a while she felt she was being told that a person on the dole should go to a community college, not Smith. In America's precariously, contentiously maintained social welfare system, there are officials and petitioners, and petitioners are not supposed to surpass officials. But Laura had never been on welfare before. And she didn't imagine she was breaking any unwritten rules at first, because she really didn't feel she had surpassed anyone.

About a month after she began receiving welfare benefits—the food stamps, cash grant, and medical insurance were worth about $10,000 a year—she got a phone call saying that someone from the department was coming over. "For a home study."

She cleaned her apartment twice on the appointed morning. The man from welfare looked large in the doorway. Then she noticed his yellow work boots. He didn't wipe his feet. He left a trail of mud on her white carpet remnant. She told herself not to stare at it. It wasn't impossible, she thought, that he'd come to arrest her.

He was businesslike at first. He looked in all the rooms and the closets. Laura guessed he was searching for evidence of a man who might turn out to be the father of her son. Then he filled out a form and handed it to her. It stated that he'd found no evidence that she was hiding anything. She sat down on her sofa, and signed the form gratefully. She gave it back to him. But he didn't leave. He settled back on her sofa, an arm, the arm closer to her, draped over the back of the couch, and he started chatting. In her twenty-eight years Laura had done a lot of research on men, much of it painful. She felt she knew the difference between friendliness and flirtation. He told her, "One way to get off welfare is if you can find yourself a sugar daddy." He laughed jovially.

Laura's head began to throb. She glanced at her soiled little rug. She wanted to clean it right now, and he kept on talking. In her mind she kept asking him to leave. Didn't he have any other appointments? He stayed for over an hour.

She scrubbed the rug, but the patch in front of her sofa came out looking gray. She tried some bleach. Finally, she threw out the rug and used part of her next welfare check to buy a new carpet remnant.

One day at the supermarket, pushing her cart past the checkout lines, Laura noticed that a woman, trailing infants, was paying the cashier with food stamps. She stopped and watched. In the line behind that woman, heads moved side- ways, necks craned. It was obvious: everyone felt entitled to see what a person with food stamps bought. What a vast difference between getting help from family or friends and being on wel- fare. To be poor on welfare was to be poor publicly. It had never occurred to her before that privacy and money were inextricably connected.

That wasn't as clear in her other world, at Smith. A friend she'd made invited her to tea at one of the houses. They didn't have teas at her Smith-owned apartment building, but Smithies had been having tea parties for at least a hundred years, she'd heard. "Do they wear gloves?" she wondered. She tried on a dress. "No, that isn't right." She pulled out some clothes she used to wear as admission clerk at the hospital in California, a tan pair of pants with a crease in the legs and a blouse. She got there right on time. She looked around. She thought, "I could have worn sweat pants, but only if they said 'Smith' on them." She thought she might save up for a pair of those. She looked at the refreshments and she was astonished: silver trays and silver teapots, pretty sugar bowls and cream containers. And the cookies! There were shortbread cookies, plain cookies, cookies covered with sugar sprinkles, cookies with tiny dollops of jam in their middles, cookies with one end dipped in chocolate. "So tidy the way they're arranged, and they're nice, too." There were miniature cakes decorated with icing. "I'm pretty sure someone did that by hand." She didn't take anything until she'd watched a few young students and had an idea of the right procedure. She took one of each variety of cookie. And finally, she realized that no one was watching her.

She listened to the voices of the young women around her. They talked about boyfriends and soap operas. In a little while she found herself in a lively discussion about one of her courses. She relaxed, but still she wondered which students were on scholarships. Maybe she'd know which were wealthy if she lived in a dorm and knew their last names. She wondered if anyone could tell she was on welfare.

Laura often felt as if her place here wasn't exactly real, especially when she found herself at college functions at one of Smith's grand ceremonial places, where chandeliers glistened and she could see her face in a silver vase or pitcher—was that really her, reflected in silver, a gilt mirror over her shoulder?—where, peeking into the kitchen, she saw uniformed men and women moving fast and quietly, preparing feasts. It was disconcerting afterward to find herself in her car, which was beginning to make ominous noises, with her pack of Kools on the dash, her outfit altered to jeans and T-shirt, which felt more natural and also safer on those errands, making the short drive out past the houses of Elm Street and the hospital and the Smith Voke fields, then walking into that blank-looking building in Florence, and the clean and barren world of the welfare office lobby. She brought Benjamin with her to that office once and sat there wondering what had possessed her to do so.

Two men sat nearby, in dirty, shabby clothes, leaning over their knees, looking at the floor. One glanced up and she saw Benjamin smile at him, and the man looked surprised, then looked away. A girl, a literal girl—she'd learned not to call regular Smithies girls, but she couldn't help it sometimes—played with her baby on the floor. Benjamin, the chatterbox, was silent. He looked as though he were having long thoughts. He wore his favorite shirt—red with stripes—and suddenly she noticed he had entered that time of life she'd heard described as "arms-legs-teeth." She wondered, "Where have I been while he was jutting out? Those teeth. Where will I get the money for braces?"

Laura stayed in Northampton that summer, after her first year at Smith. She worked for $6.50 an hour as a receptionist at a local realty office. She neglected to tell her caseworker about the job for a couple of weeks, instead of within the prescribed ten days, and received $200 more than she should have from the state. But she wasn't trying to trick anyone. She reported all her income, thinking that it would be deducted from her cash welfare payments. She discovered that, as a general rule, the state also deducted one dollar more than she had made. Was that supposed to make people want to get off welfare? Or the opposite? She heard someone on the news call women on welfare "bon-bon-eating gimme girls," and felt personally insulted. She was making friends now, some at Smith and some in town, mostly other women, some of whom she could call up late at night and read a paper to. One of her town friends was studying to be a social worker. This friend talked passionately about the rights of welfare mothers. The state intended to institute "workfare"—to require that people on welfare perform community service—and Laura's friend had learned that some of the state legislators planned workfare hearings at the county courthouse. The public was invited to testify.

"Laura, your story is great. You're articulate, you're intelligent. It would be very empowering for you to do this," her friend said. Laura guessed she should. When she visited the welfare office and when she saw fellow citizens examining the contents of her grocery cart, she often felt guilty, and angry afterward. "Wait a minute. I have a right to have certain things," she'd think. And then she'd tell herself, "It's not just about rights." She had read Aristotle back in community college. "For each right there is a corresponding duty," he had written. But the process didn't have to be humiliating. She planned to talk about that at the hearing and about the disincentives in the system. She wondered if it wasn't arrogant of her to talk about welfare publicly, as if she were an expert. "I wasn't raised on welfare. How can I claim to have authority about welfare?" But she went.

The state legislators sat beneath the judge's high bench, at a long table in the well of the old courtroom. Senator Therese Murray from Plymouth, the chair of the Subcommittee on Welfare Reform, caught Laura's eye. She looked tough. She sounded tough when she announced, "Each speaker will be allowed three minutes to summarize their issue." Citizens, mostly women, filled the gallery. Laura sat near the back, beside the friend who had talked her into coming.

One of the first speakers, a woman from an organization called the Alliance for Economic Justice, sat down at the microphone and said, "I have been abused and terrorized and starved in this country with my children for twenty years." She told the legislators, "We still have a tremendous amount of misogyny in our country because the white men who live in it sent all the jobs out of it." She declared, "Poverty is hereditary because wealth is inherited." She said that a woman who succeeded in America was merely lucky. "Her husband didn't beat her, didn't pee on her, didn't shoot at her." Evidently, she was telling some of her life story.

"Good for her," thought Laura. "But I wish she didn't seem to be enjoying this so much."

Up at the speaker's table, that woman was saying to the legislators, "I will let you know what is wrong with the welfare system as soon as I let you know what is wrong with *you*."

Laura had a familiar feeling, of wanting to grow smaller.

"I believe you're racist, I believe you're classist, okay?" the woman said. "That's all."

Some of the audience applauded. They applauded every fiery speech. Laura looked around and saw her own caseworker sitting in the audience, on the other side of the gallery. Her caseworker wasn't applauding.

As the speeches went on, Laura realized she was waiting for someone who resembled her to take the microphone, and then a welfare advocate, not a recipient, sat down and read a letter that sounded like Laura's speech. But the advocate explained that the welfare mother wasn't here to testify because she was afraid of what the department might do to her. She wouldn't even let her name be mentioned.

"I don't think I can do this," Laura whispered to her friend.

"Oh, yes, you can. You just go up there and you just be honest."

Laura wore a skirt and a sleeveless blouse. She fidgeted with her hands, wringing them as she sat before the microphone. "My name is Laura Baumeister. I'm a student at Smith College and I've lived in Massachusetts for a little over two years. I've been on AFDC for two years as well. I have a fourteen-year-old son. I had never been on AFDC until I moved here to go to school, at Smith College, and I, uh, I have a lot of mixed feelings about AFDC and welfare because I'm very grateful for it and yet countering that gratitude is I guess some embarrassment and some shame. I know my son feels it." She lifted her hands toward herself and, at the mention of her son, burst into a smile. "When I shop with food stamps, he walks ten paces behind me."

Laura told the legislators that, unlike a lot of speakers, she didn't have any problems with *her* welfare worker. "She's great." But in everything else, Laura took her friend's advice and was completely honest. She merely shortened the speech she'd planned. She put on what she hoped was a winning smile. "Um, I, uh, I guess that's all."

She was turning in the chair, about to stand, when she heard Senator Murray, in a very pleasant voice, say, "Can I ask you a question?"

Laura turned back to the microphone, smiling.

"Were you a resident of Massachusetts before you moved here?"

"No, I wasn't," said Laura. "I was a resident of California. I moved here specifically to go to school, and I had always worked, and when I came here it was recommended to me that I go on AFDC, and . . ."

The senator interrupted her, her voice a little different now. "*Who* recommended that to you?"

"The school where I applied."

"The school did," said the senator.

Laura knew something was wrong, but the thought confused her more. "I know," she said. "I know many other women at Smith College who are on AFDC as well."

"Thank you," said the senator. She smiled slightly.

Laura heard a smattering of applause, as she retreated to the gallery. She was about to sit down, when the senator called to her, "I'm sorry. Are you in the Comstock program?"

"Yes, I am."

The senator made a note.

When Laura appeared in Ellie Rothman's office, fretting about the mistake she'd made in testifying, abject, apologetic, Ellie told her that she'd gotten some calls but that only a few were negative. This was true. Ellie didn't say that those few calls carried a lot of weight.

One had come from a state senator. "I think that you should know that one of your students spoke at a hearing we held in Northampton and it's causing a lot of trouble. The commissioner is really angry that you're bringing women into the state and telling them to go on welfare." Looking back, Ellie said, "It was devastating. It's not good to roil up the commissioner. He has a lot of power." In the end, Laura's testimony inspired the commissioner to issue a new edict: any person who came to Massachusetts in order to go to college would never be eligible for welfare. The policy affected a couple of new Adas, though Ellie was able to get the bureaucrats to reverse their position on one.

Ellie had learned—the hard way, as she put it—that she could not become more than friendly with Ada Comstock scholars. For one thing, friendship cost her credibility when she had to plead an Ada's case with administrative colleagues and professors. But she'd had to smile the day when Laura had burst into the office saying that she'd gotten an A on an anthropology paper. And she couldn't avoid the hug that Laura had suddenly administered, a fierce and thorough hug that revealed both how thin and how strong she was.

Laura had told her that even though she was passing everything now, she'd like to keep meeting with her every week.

"Well, maybe once every two weeks," Ellie had said.

Laura wasn't one of those Adas—there were always a few—who arrived at Smith shy and brimming with gratitude and a few months later decided that they knew much better ways to run the Ada Comstock program. And it is, of course, a compliment when a student puts herself in your hands, a compliment to your trustworthiness, which success enriches. A couple of times last spring Laura had come in asking Ellie to intercede with professors and get them to give her extensions on papers, and Ellie had refused, and later, Laura had actually come back to the office and thanked her. On top of that, not long ago, Laura had called the office saying that she was in a class with an Ada who seemed very troubled. "Bring her in," Ellie had said, and she'd thought, "So there's another side of her to like."

Ellie would have forgiven Laura anyway. Laura was an innocent in front of a Massachusetts politician. She reminded Ellie of the pretty waifs in Charlie Chaplin movies. Ellie figured that the welfare issue would have gotten aired sooner or later. Laura didn't need to know about the trouble she had caused. She was having a hard enough time already.

One day not long after the hearing, Laura went to her mailbox expecting to find her welfare check inside, and it wasn't there. Every day she hovered downstairs in the lobby, waiting for the postman. After she made several worried calls to the welfare office, her caseworker finally explained: the local office had decided that the vendor payments Laura got from Smith should be counted as income and deducted from her check. She would have to wait for Boston to rule on the matter. It might take six weeks before she got another check.

Ellie got her some small loans. The welfare office chipped in with a $50 voucher, which Laura could use to buy groceries. You couldn't get change when you used a voucher as you could with food stamps, so Laura had to buy exactly $50 worth of food. She went down the aisles of the supermarket, trying to keep a running tally, something she found difficult to do. She was always losing track of money, getting a haircut when her car was almost out of gas. The risk with a voucher was that you might end up with more than $50 worth of groceries and have to take things back to their shelves, while people in the line behind you waited, watching, making noises.

The weeks dragged on. The money ran out. Finally, in desperation, Laura drove out Prospect Street to the Northampton Survival Center, a private charity. It wasn't far. She had enough gas to get there and back. You could get free food there only once a month, she'd heard. Laura told her story to the woman at the door, a small Hispanic woman, a volunteer and very friendly. Laura was about to burst into tears, but the woman said that she could get food weekly.

She handed Laura a plastic token with a number on it, and Laura joined the line, which was fairly long. In front of her was a couple she'd seen occasionally, staggering together through downtown. She thought you could get drunk on fumes just from standing near them. Not that Laura minded. The woman had a ravaged face that still looked like a girl's. She was telling a joke about a duck, slurring all the words. Most of the people in line looked destitute, but Laura also saw a woman who was better dressed than most and clearly sober, with children encircling her legs. "What's that person doing here?" Laura thought. "She looks like me."

The routine wasn't really dreary. Everyone who worked at the center was polite and respectful. Posted on the wall behind the counter were lists of what a needy family could obtain. Laura studied the one for a family of two—spaghetti and canned sauce and peanut butter and also fresh vegetables from a local farm and day-old bread donated by bakeries and grocery stores. A volunteer worker would also open a cupboard behind the counter, saying, "Is there anything you want in there?" The cupboard contained treats, such as pie filling. Laura looked forward to the moment of the cupboard. Then one day, waiting her turn at the counter, she saw a very familiar face standing behind it: the face of one of her English professors, one of her favorites. He volunteered here, obviously. She wanted to leave before he saw her, but her own cupboards had almost nothing left in them. "I'm an English major and my English professor is about to hand me my food," she thought. "Here I am. It's not a question where I stand on the social hierarchy. This is my life." As she waited for the confrontation, she said to herself, "Pride goeth before a fall. But why can't he be a biology teacher?" She was afraid he might say, "How's the paper going?" He didn't. If he felt uncomfortable, he didn't let it show. He just smiled and said, "Hi," and filled a grocery bag for her.

Boston reinstated her before that year's first snowfall. But then one day she opened up an official-looking letter and read, "You are being investigated for welfare fraud." Her hands began to shake. This had to do with her summer job, the one that had netted her the loss of a dollar. "You may be subject to criminal penalties," she read.

When she went to his office, the welfare fraud investigator immediately closed the door, then held up his badge, and began reciting. "You have the right to remain silent. You have the right to an attorney. . . ."

She was going to jail! What would happen to Benjamin?

She told the man everything, pleading with her voice.

He asked if she was willing to pay back the $200 extra she'd received. As if she hadn't tried to do that long ago.

"Yes, of course!"

Well, he said, in that case, he wouldn't recommend that she be charged. He made it sound as if he were giving her a break. How was she to know that any self-respecting district attorney would have laughed at the thought of prosecuting a case like this?

"Oh, thank you, thank you," she thought. She got up to leave, and she offered him her hand.

He took it. Then he said sarcastically, "Nice to meet you. I was looking forward to it. You're our little TV star."

"I beg your pardon?"

"Yeah, we watched you on TV. We had a good laugh over you." He added, "I'm not with the welfare department."

She guessed he meant that she had made the welfare department look bad, and he enjoyed that. Laura went home to Bedford Terrace. Sitting on her couch, the rooftops of Northampton behind her, she put her face in her hands and wept.

. . .

For a long time, Laura didn't know who she should worry about more, herself or Benjamin. She felt wretched the day she took him, for no good reason, to the welfare office. Driving home, he was unusually silent. Then he mentioned that he recognized one of the men who had sat in the lobby with them. Benjamin said he often saw that man sitting in Pulaski Park, and he wondered where he went to sleep and eat. She told him about Grove Street and the Survival Center, and what a fine public service they performed, as if she were a solid burgher of Northampton. She couldn't bear to tell Benjamin that some of the food he had been eating came from the same source, that they were not so very far from the condition of that man. Later, for a writing class, she reconstructed that day: "After Benjamin and I came home from the welfare office, he had a snack and then went out to play basketball. It was springtime in New England and the days were getting longer and brighter. I had a paper to write and some reading to do; if I sat down and did some work while he was playing we could spend the evening together." She had the fixings of a cake from the treats cupboard at the Survival Center. "We could bake a Bisquick coffee cake. He likes to sift the Bisquick mix and stir it into the egg while I butter the pan. Then he uses a fork to carefully blend the brown sugar with butter into tiny crumbs for the topping. When he was little, he liked to watch it metamorphose into the final product. Occasionally he'd look one time too often, open the door to 'check,' and it would fall. It tasted the same, though. Perhaps we would do that tonight. Sometimes he would ask me if I would make it for him, especially if he'd had a bad day, and I thought that today was a good day for coffee cake."

Living at Bedford Terrace wasn't exactly like being a college student in a dorm, an experience that she had missed and wondered about wistfully. But the building was full of friends, some of them single mothers, some of them lesbians, and they would get together for their own kinds of bull sessions and help each other through their special difficulties. The time, for instance, when Benjamin had to wear a necktie to a dance. Laura had no idea how to tie one. But her friend Mildred across the hall, who ate dinner with them almost every night, arrived just in time. Mildred had learned the art of tying neckties from her brother. Benjamin had friends now, too, which was a great relief.

He would set off in the evening from their apartment dressed in army fatigues, a canteen on his belt. He'd tell Laura he was going out to hang around with friends. She tried to question him, but got only a vague idea of what hanging around meant. Occasionally, she got hints. One night the phone rang and a Smith security cop said, "Mrs. Baumeister, we've just been chasing your son and some of his friends around the campus, and we can't seem to catch them."

Benjamin and his friends went sledding on Hospital Hill. They rode their bikes around downtown. But the campus and its vicinity were their main playground: the Smith playing fields across the Mill River, the vast state hospital grounds beyond, where they played army games, the dirt path they called the Smith Walk, which runs along the pond and then the river, for them a long, backyard trail, like a secret passage from one part of town to another.

They called themselves the Outsiders. They'd meet around nightfall, all dressed in army clothes, and head up for the campus, sometimes on their bikes, more often on foot. One would usually have a box of eggs, another their gang's posters. They'd pass between the Smith museum and art library, pausing to spin the sculpture that was like an airplane propeller and to make disparaging remarks at the Rodin. They'd yell, because that courtyard had a wonderful echo. On winter evenings, they'd sneak into McConnell Hall to get warm, and, before they left, set the Foucault pendulum swinging. They always kept a lookout for the uniformed fig-

ures of Smith security appearing out of the shadows, especially the Hulk Guys. One was black, the other white; both
were huge.

One night they peeked through the windows of the
boathouse, Tom Sawyers who hadn't met their Beckys yet, and
they saw a party going on, college men and women dancing.
They egged the building, then retreated. Another night they
crept down the passageway beside Neilsen Library and then,
when all was ready, pulled open the door of the security office
and yelled inside. And then they ran, hearing boots behind
them. They'd scramble behind the Dumpsters in back of
McConnell Hall and hold their breath as Smith cruisers
passed slowly by—like commandos, just out of reach of the
beams of the searchlights, slapping high fives afterward, saying "Yeah!"

One time Benjamin got caught. Laura bawled him out:
"Don't do that! The campus security police are *not* there for
chasing kids."

Benjamin didn't say so, but she didn't know what she was
talking about. What else did they have to do?

Benjamin never did wear the hiking boots that Laura
bought for him their first year in New England. As for the flannel shirts that were supposed to help him look like he
belonged, she wore them herself now. But she didn't have to
make him go to school, not after the first few months. From
time to time she was called to the principal's office, but the
kind of trouble Benjamin got into was never very serious,
though she always acted as if it were. He liked to say that he was
friends with every clique at the high school. She wished he
were less friendly with some, like the ones who got in trouble
with the Northampton cops. But he never got arrested himself.
He had a sensible girlfriend now.

He loved Northampton, too. He loved the bricks, he said.
He couldn't explain. He just liked the place. He had long ago
outgrown his army uniform and traded it for baggy pants three

sizes too big. "I just like them loose," he said. He wore a Cleveland Indians baseball cap, discolored, its bill molded to an oval and frayed around the edges. "Yeah, it's been slept on, run over, swum in." He looked back across the vast distance of five years in Northampton, almost a third of his life, after all, and said, of his gang's war with Smith security, "The thing is, it was fun. This was how we got, like, high. Messing with them, running from them, and we didn't have any parties to go to. I think we were the first ones who did that stuff."

What Laura would have been wary of in a place like Los Angeles had come as a surprise in Northampton, in a town where no one seemed to worry much about walking alone at night. Northampton could be dangerous in that way, she thought, especially for a very young woman on her own. It had seemed dangerous enough to her. That man who called thirty times in one day alone, for instance. He had said to her, "You're gonna end up dead, just like your mother." The pair of Northampton cops who came to her apartment to fill out the restraining order were very polite. She'd forgotten their names as soon as they left, and soon managed to forget the obligatory trip she'd made to District Court, which she hoped she never saw again. The questions the magistrate asked seemed too personal, but in the end she felt protected in this town. There were other little incidents. Not long ago, she thought, they would have consumed her.

She'd always found it hard to tell the difference between a thing done to her and a thing she'd helped to bring upon herself. For most of her life, therapists had told her she had good reasons to be troubled. "But half the time," she thought, looking back, "I couldn't find my *damn boots*!" Welfare hadn't treated her very well, she thought. For a long time, she felt jumpy when she went to her mailbox on the first and fifteenth days of the month, and she still didn't like to open official-looking envelopes. But she resolved not to feel sorry for herself anymore. And it was easier not to, because she had less to feel sorry about.

Her first year, at a formal function, she'd met a fellow Ada, a woman dressed in a blue blazer. How the buttons gleamed! "What's your major?" Laura had asked. That had seemed like the way to get acquainted here.

"Economics. I'm particularly interested in international finance," the woman said.

"Wow!" Laura said.

Within several months that woman was an art major. The next time Laura saw her she was wearing paint-spattered overalls. She told Laura she really ought to visit Smith's art museum.

Laura went alone. She wandered around the parquet floors, stopping at every picture, every piece of sculpture. "I've never been at a museum owned by a college," she thought. "I mean, this is impressive." The museum was very quiet. She didn't feel as though she took in much, but while she was there her thoughts stopped chasing each other. She came back again and again, whenever she wanted to calm down. She always spent some time in front of the museum's Picasso, *Figures by the Sea.* She thought of it as the blue Picasso. It interested her, figures that looked like survivors of Auschwitz painted in soothing colors. She liked to sit in the little room full of Greek and Roman pottery and statuary. A small figure of a satyr stood on a pedestal. It made her laugh out loud. "They were twisted little guys, those satyrs." She had read the *Odyssey* at community college, and the room made her nostalgic. It reminded her of a place her mind had occupied, when she'd first read Homer in a classroom by the sea. Gazing at the bust of Silenus, then at the statue labeled *The Smiling Faun,* she felt as if Homer and the sculptors were there in the gallery with her. "Amazing that this stuff is, like, *here.* Here at all. And *I'm* here."

In the fall semester of her second year, Laura took a course from one of Smith's most distinguished English professors: "The Reading of Poetry." This was during the period of her worst travails with welfare, when she spent a lot of time figuring out how to get food for Benjamin and herself and fretting about jail. A portion of her mind still saw imminent catastrophe in even small things that went wrong. And the class itself was sometimes daunting. She sat there awestruck once again at the comments other students made. "In this poem, I think we see an evocation of traditionalism and impressionism." In her own papers, she kept writing, "This poem is great!" She felt silly. "I mean, all the poems are great. It isn't a course in how to read *bad* poems." But she couldn't help herself. The poems were wonderful to her, and they made her problems small. She left that class transported. Literature was a timeless place, she thought. Inside it, there was no welfare office, and her life had a context. Her professor gave her an A. She ran all the way to Ellie Rothman's office with the news.

Ellie had an eye for a person's special talents. She'd made Laura one of the guides who gave tours to prospective Adas. At Smith, Laura usually dressed now in her going-to-the-welfare-office clothes, jeans and T-shirt. The outfit showed off her slim figure and her thin, well-muscled arms. Her nails were often painted green. She wore a gold chain around her neck, and little earrings, and the same wide glasses that protruded past the sides of her narrow face; her blond hair now came down just below her ears and then flipped up. The composition seemed calculated to look uncalculated, as if describing how feminine the tomboy guise could be. Laura was an enthusiastic tour guide. Everything at Smith and in Northampton was "the best," she'd tell prospective Adas. She was reassuring, too. Every touree would get in, and everyone would be all right. She always took a prospect into Seelye Hall, and if the woman noticed the old banisters inside, Laura would say, "I know. Aren't they great? They're great to slide down, too." Then she'd laugh, high and hoarse. "If you *so wish.*" Then she'd climb aboard sidesaddle and slide down. "And there's actually a lot of cool internships and things you can do here over the summer," she'd say at the bottom.

She felt at home at Smith and in downtown Northampton. In the welfare office, she never would. The workers there still seemed to think she should be learning a trade. She might have been tempted to be obliging and agree, but at the college everyone around her *believed* in the value of the liberal arts. Ellie Rothman had taken over the Ada Comstock program without any special training in finance or administration. Ellie thought her own college studies in the liberal arts had given her all she needed to figure out how to do the job. "For me, it proves the value of a liberal arts degree," Ellie liked to say. "You will learn how to read, how to speak, how to write and solve problems, and how to keep on learning." The argument wasn't less persuasive for being familiar. But even Ellie didn't fully understand what liberal arts meant to Laura.

A lot of other Adas said they were sick of being poor and planned to use their Smith degrees to get the best-paying jobs they could. When Laura heard herself saying she wanted to be a high school English teacher, she thought, "That doesn't sound very impressive." But that had been her dream ever since she'd taken a survey course called "Great Authors" at the College of the Redwoods. The teacher had looked as if he were dancing in front of the class. She had come in merely curious. He was passionate. She wanted to be him. She had thought, "If I could be a teacher . . ."

Reading had long been transportation for her. She remembered reading Hemingway's short stories as a girl and thinking, "I *am* Nick Adams." Ever since her sixth-grade teacher let her sit on the floor of that little library, reading had been her refuge from the mad portion of her mind. It had worked better than therapy. At community college she had read excerpts of *Paradise Lost*. At Smith the English department had a course that dealt with the entire poem. This seemed like an amazing luxury. Her professor, the same man who had waited on her at the Survival Center, said to the class, "I don't think I'm ever so happy as a teacher as when I'm embarking on *Paradise Lost*."

Laura thought, "He's been teaching here twenty years, and it doesn't get old!"

She read the poem three times for that course. She slogged through it. She had no religious education and had to keep stopping to look things up. She admired the poem. "I mean, it's great." But she didn't really enjoy it. Samuel Johnson had called it admirable and added, "None ever wished it longer than it is." That was how she felt. She wasn't very sorry when the course ended. She got a B, which was all she felt she deserved. Milton lay behind her, a chore completed. But pieces of the poem kept rattling around in her mind. One night during vacation, she went to bed and lay awake trying to remember a line from *Paradise Lost*. Finally, she got up and went to her living room, and took her volume of Milton from the bookcase that she'd borrowed from Smith. At the start of every semester she would make a reconnaissance of the college bookstore and figure out how much the books she needed cost, and then save up for them. Her Milton was pricey—$70. But she'd felt she had to own it. She liked to open it and inhale its smell. She liked its heft and the way the paper felt against her fingers. Now she opened it and found the passage that was keeping her awake. She still didn't feel sleepy. So she turned to the beginning of the poem, and began to read again: "Of man's first disobedience, and the fruit / Of that forbidden tree, whose mortal taste / Brought death into the world, and all our woe . . ."

Reading modern criticism this past semester, Laura had thought, "Milton probably was a misogynist. But so what?" In one course she had a professor who said the so-called great

authors were best understood as creatures of time and circumstance, as producers of "texts," some of which were "hege-
monic." Laura hadn't studied the fading doctrines of the
deconstructionists, but she knew that notion wasn't right. It
seemed temporal to her, tightly bound to the inessential time
of academic fashion, which was exactly what the great books
weren't. She sat on her sofa now and read on and on through
Paradise Lost. She didn't stop to look up anything. She didn't
have to. The poem's majestic, oceanic music carried her so far
off that when she lifted her eyes from the book, she was startled
to find herself in her apartment.

In her living room window, a gray dawn was rising over
the Holyoke Range. From the street below came the sounds
of the day's first two trucks, delivering bread and newspapers to Serio's Market across the street. Adam and Eve were
leaving the Garden. "They hand in hand with wandering
steps and slow, / Through Eden took their solitary way." She
closed the book. She thought, "I just read all of *Paradise
Lost.* I can't believe it." Inside her apartment all was still.
Benjamin, who was on vacation too, lay asleep in the room
off the kitchen, sleeping the sleep of teenagers. "This is
cool," she thought. "There's nobody here I have to explain
myself to." She had read effortlessly, and this time, she
thought, she'd understood the poem to its depths, a poem,
she now believed, that defined a word like "greatness."
Months ago she'd opened to those pages in ignorance and
little by little she'd made her way through. Now she had
come to the end. In the pattern of her earlier life, she committed a reckless act and got kicked out or dropped out or
watched her life spiral downward, without really knowing
why. That seemed like a pattern without natural progres-
sion, like no pattern at all.

"There's a religious thing that happens in literature," Laura
said later. "It *is* religious. Not churchy religious. I mean, we all
want our lives to be important. You read a poem like *Paradise*

Lost and you get your smallness, but somehow it matters. One thing that saddens me about my mother, I don't think that she thought her life mattered, and it did! I mean, she had four children. I don't think her suicide was a momentary lapse of reason. I think she suffered terribly behind what we today would call *low self-esteem.*" She went on, "I had a conversation with my little brother about literature and religion, and he knew nothing, and I could tell him some, and he was so impressed. 'God, you're smart,' he said. He didn't know anything about the Protestant Reformation. You *have* to know those things. Otherwise, there's huge gaps." She laughed at herself. What difference did knowing those things make? "If you don't know any better, I guess it doesn't, but illiteracy scares the hell out of me. And at some level I always knew that the lack of a formal education limited me. I would read things and find allusions and I wouldn't know what they were. It was like living in a world with a language you don't speak. Literature is an alternative to self-destructive things. I think literature is the way out. I mean, books saved my life."

Most of her high school friends had gone on to college. She'd had a baby instead. She had kept up with some of those friends. She remembered one talking about the books she was reading in college. "And I wasn't doing that," Laura thought, with her volume of Milton closed on her lap. "And now I am. And now I am. And it isn't too late and I'm not too old, and I don't have to punish myself for not doing things the way other people did." As the trucks of the Honor Court rattled down Main Street a couple of blocks away, Laura put her Milton carefully back in the bookcase and went to bed. While Northampton awakened, she slept well.

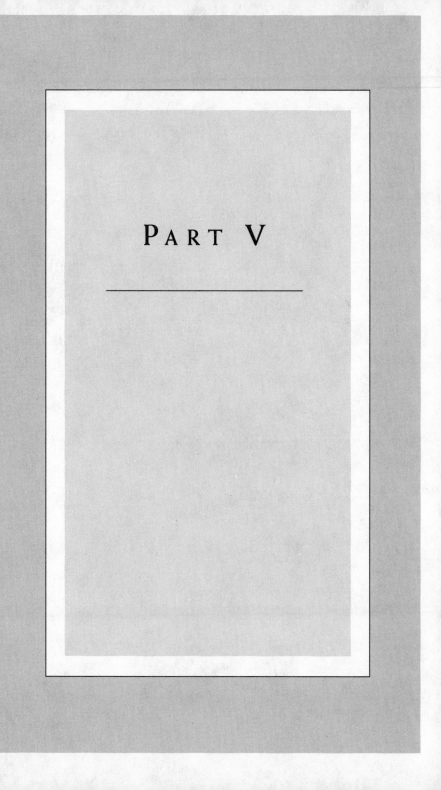

PART V

CHAPTER 20

The Farewell Sermon

A RECTANGULAR PIECE of granite rests, entirely hidden, under a yew bush in front of Forbes Library. It was once a front doorstep, and is all that remains of the Northampton home of Jonathan Edwards. The town has kept some other mementos—a monument to the Edwards family in the old Bridge Street Cemetery; a plaque on the steps of the First Church, noting that he preached near that site. (The church actually named after him, a modern Swiss-chalet-style building, is one of downtown's few eyesores.) A small cul-de-sac near a supermarket bears his name. But the elm trees he planted along Main Street were cut down long ago, and his homestead demolished.

The brownstone steeple of the First Church rises like a tall wizard's hat above Main Street. Both Congregationalists and Baptists use the building now, so "First Churches" has become its proper name. It descends directly from the meetinghouses near this site in which the town's church used to gather, Northampton's only church for almost two centuries. The town built the first two meetinghouses in the 1600s, the third in the mid-1730s, during the first stirrings of the Great Awakening. Jonathan Edwards preached in both the second and third buildings.

It isn't hard to imagine that third church, an ordinary white wooden structure on a dirt Main Street in a small, sleepy town: outside, farmers' wagons and a carriage or two and a great noise coming through the wide wooden doors. Perhaps they stood open, affording a view down the central aisle, past the pews where most of the town sat, to the pulpit where Edwards stood. He wore a bib collar and a periwig, like an English judge's hairpiece. "Tall in person, and having even a womanly look, he was of a delicate constitution," one commentator writes. But Edwards put on a rousing show, the best show in town, the best in the region. The historian Perry Miller conjures up the scene:

> The people yelled and shrieked, they rolled in the aisles, they crowded up to the pulpit and begged him to stop, they cried for mercy. One who heard him described his method of preaching: he looked all the time at the bell rope (hanging down from the roof at the other end of the church) as though he would look it in two; he did not stoop to regard the screaming mass, much less to console them.

Most anthologies of American literature offer only that picture of Edwards, through his fire-and-brimstone sermon "Sinners in the Hands of an Angry God." That one exhortation puts to shame all the rants of TV evangelists, but it doesn't fully represent the man. Edwards felt great solicitude for his flock, and nature could put him in raptures. In frontier New England the Puritans had seen "a hideous and howling wildernesse." In the landscape of the settled Connecticut River Valley of the 1700s, Edwards saw God's beautiful works. He went outdoors to gather inspiration for sermons and dissertations. He had a famous habit of coming back with notes pinned to his coat—"quite literally covered with his thoughts," writes the historian Daniel Aaron. After he'd spent twenty-three years as Northampton's eloquent spiritual guide, the church threw him out.

Scholarly opinions vary on the main reasons, whether they were economic, political, theological, or all of those and more. It's clear that Edwards worried mightily about Northampton's morals. He worried about its tendency toward un-Christian fractiousness. He worried about the decline of family discipline, about the fact that local youth went out walking after dark, wasted time in levity, misbehaved in church. He had exacting standards and he expected the town to hew to them. By this period, the tithing-men seem to have lost their clout. Maybe the town had grown tired of moral goading.

Or maybe the cause lay in the death of his most powerful ally, or in his lack of political savvy. In one incident, some young Northampton men passed around a midwife's manual and made jokes about it in the presence of young ladies. Edwards named both suspects and witnesses from the pulpit, failing to distinguish between them, and some of them were children of the town's leading citizens. His grandfather, the town's minister for almost sixty years, had made it fairly easy to become a member of the single church—an important matter, because membership in the church was equivalent to full membership in the town. After long study, Edwards decided his grandfather's liberal policy went against the word of God. Only those who could say they had experienced a "true conversion" should be admitted, he finally declared. That did it for the parishioners. A majority rebelled and voted to get rid of him.

A long, tangled battle of words ensued. Edwards knew he would probably lose. In a letter to a friend in Boston, he wrote: "If I should be wholly cast out of my ministry, I should be in many respects in a poor case: I shall not be likely to be serviceable to my generation, or get a subsistence, in a business of a different nature." He continued: "I seem as it were to be casting myself off from a precipice; and have no other way, but to go on, as it were blindfold, i.e. shutting my eyes to everything else but the evidences of the mind and will of God, and the path of duty; which I would observe with the utmost care." Edwards stood firm, with magnificent stubbornness. He was not the sort of person who would bend a principle to save his job.

He delivered his "Farewell Sermon" on June 22, 1750. In it, he issued a long and tightly reasoned threat. On Judgment Day, he told the church, they would meet again, and then it would be clear who was to blame for the rift between them. "But they that evil entreat Christ's faithful ministers, especially in that wherein they are faithful, shall be severely punished," he said. That is, some of the people listening might end up in hell for sending him away. He had described hell vividly to them for more than two decades, and now he delivered some frightening phrases—people who thought themselves "the most eminent saints in the congregation" were often, he said, "in a peculiar manner a smoke in God's nose." Northampton was still God-fearing, by and large; reading the farewell sermon, you half expect the people to rescind the church's vote and beg Edwards to stay. It didn't happen.

For many years Northampton's boosters had good reason to feel uncomfortable about the legacy of Edwards. For a long time Northampton was best known to the world as the place that had banished one of the pantheon. But no one cared much about that nowadays. If Edwards had left a lasting imprint on Northampton, it wasn't obvious. He seemed to have become more to the world than to the town.

Perry Miller insists that Edwards's expulsion was a tragedy. And maybe it was, for the town and for Edwards. But not for intellectual history. His Northampton duties claimed a lot of his time and thought. After Northampton, he lived in Stockbridge, on the frontier. There he preached to Indians; evidently, he treated them well and with respect. And there he had time to think deeply and to write his doctrinal treatises *Freedom of the Will, Original Sin,* and *The Nature of True Virtue.* Historians generally regard Edwards as one of the eighteenth century's greatest thinkers. One calls him "America's first systematic philosopher." That part of his reputation rests mainly on what he wrote after leaving Northampton.

But for all the vehemence of his farewell sermon, Edwards felt attached to this place. "How often have we met together in the house of God in this relation!" he said to the people of Northampton. "How often have I spoke to you, instructed, counseled, warned, directed and fed you, and administered ordinances among you, as the people which were committed to my care, and whose precious souls I had the charge of! But in all probability this never will be again." Toward the end of the sermon he offered them advice, rather tenderly. They should stop fighting with each other, he said, among other things, "and by all means in your power seek the prosperity of the town."

One small contingent remained loyal. They tried to persuade Edwards to start a new church in Northampton. He did not want to leave, but he refused. He believed the town should be unified. In the letter to his friend in Boston, he had written: "I am now comfortably settled, have as large a salary settled upon me as most have out of Boston."

But it was time for him to go.

CHAPTER 21

Willoughby Gap

TOMMY SAT ON his father's front porch in the quiet of a late summer afternoon. He had a couple of hours to chat before going on duty. Bill said that yesterday he'd been playing around with his new cordless telephone. He'd decided to place a call to Tommy's mother. "I picked it up and said, 'Jane, where have ya been? I haven't seen ya in two years.' And suddenly the phone rang, and I was startled. 'Jesus Christ,' I said. 'I'm not foolin' around with that stuff anymore. I'm more powerful than I thought.' "

From the porch, Forbes Avenue looked like a bower, in dappled green shade. The conversation turned to Rick. "I won't go to see him, because the only reason would be for curiosity," Tommy said. "He's being punished for something he did, and I don't want to make it any easier for him."

Tommy's voice had the kind of forceful determination that seems to undermine itself. Bill didn't speak for a little while. Then he said, "So I wonder what he's doing now, up there at the county jail."

The in vitro procedure had failed once more. Jean didn't want to try again, not soon anyway, and Tommy, too, was ready to give up. All those hormones couldn't be good for her, he reasoned. "I don't want to be childless *and* wifeless." He took Jean out to dinner in Northampton that night. She had her hair pulled back in a ponytail. He gazed at her, then lifted up a glass and said, "The only thing certain, you and me."

Jean lowered her eyes.

She was readier than ever for a new life, Tommy knew, and he wasn't sure he didn't feel the same now. On a day in August he and Jean drove to Boston. She went shopping. He took the FBI's written test. When he sat down and opened the booklet, the same old panicky feeling washed over him, but this time he told himself it didn't really matter if he did badly. Life would be much simpler if he didn't do too well. Questions on paper weren't a true test of a cop. He didn't have to sit here wishing he was smarter than he was. He'd do his best and leave.

Afterward, in downtown Boston, Tommy found a bar, went in, and tossed down two pints of Guinness Stout, one right after the other. Then he went to his rendezvous with Jean. She asked him how he'd done. Her voice sounded expectant.

"I think I did better drinking the Guinness," Tommy said.

The letter came two weeks later: he had passed.

The news didn't seem real. A few weeks after that, in mid-September, he went for a formal interview to New York City, which seemed more unreal still. The cabbie said, as he let him off at the Federal Building, "The FBI's in there. That where you going?"

"Could be," Tommy said. He thought, "This guy could be a plant." He got out. The cabbie called to him. Tommy had forgotten his change.

He'd arrived an hour early. He'd never seen Manhattan before. The density of everything, the crowds rushing by, the car horns, the immense buildings—they'd have come as a shock to the system of anyone from a small place, never mind someone who made it his job to notice everything. Tommy wanted just to stand there and take it all in, but he didn't dare. He thought he might get mugged. After all, this was New York.

He began to feel conspicuous, standing in the middle of a busy sidewalk. "I look like Hillbilly Bob." So he went to a fast-food restaurant. He got inside and looked around, and he realized he was the only white-skinned person in the place. "This is kind of cool. The complete opposite from Northampton." He knew no one. No one knew him. "I'd love to work in a place like New York City," he thought. "It would be something else to learn. I wouldn't know all the players. Great! I *never* would. Even better."

On an evening in early October, out on his rounds, Tommy stopped his cruiser beside Pulaski Park, and in the dim glow from the streetlights, he read the letter again. It began

> I am pleased to offer you a conditional appointment as a Special Agent of the Federal Bureau of Investigation (FBI), United States Department of Justice.

He still had to pass the lie-detector test and the physical. Finally there would be the background investigation. If they got that far, he figured, the feds wouldn't find much to worry them, unless they didn't like a colorless past. "It's disgusting. I'm wearing the same freaking belt I had in seventh grade, as a Police Explorer." He looked down at his belt. "And, I might add, it's on the last hole."

He had weighed 220 pounds when he began his diet, a little before Rick's trial. He had to get to 204 to meet the FBI's standards. He now weighed 194. His uniform pants would hardly stay aloft. His stomach looked flat even with his protective vest strapped around it. His uniform collars defined a vanished girth and he looked a little silly in them, like a boy in his father's shirt trying to wear a necktie. He was growing fitter and fitter. At the FBI Academy—if he got there—he'd have to pass a rigorous series of physical tests. He clocked a five-mile run through Northampton. At the end of each mile he got out with a can of spray paint, looked around to make sure the coast was clear, and, a graffiti vandal for the first time in his life, made a little mark on the road.

He hadn't told anyone in the department, and no one suspected anything. The other cops thought he was on a health kick. No one asked why he had to take a day off now and then. They seemed to think that he and Jean were going to the hospital in Boston; he hadn't told anyone that they'd given up on that. One day he said to one of the captains, "Oh, I hate snow shoveling. I'm gonna put my papers in and move down south."

"What are you gonna do? Become a raconteur?" said the captain. "O'Connor, you're never gonna leave this place."

"Early retirement," said Tommy. "Because of the snow."

"Secret squirrel," people in the department would say when a cop behaved like this. He'd told only a few close friends who weren't on the force, so he wouldn't be publicly humiliated if in the end he got turned down or changed his mind. In the meantime, he could dream of leaving and see what it felt like.

His jogging route took him through the green residential parts of town, along the circumference of the world of his youth. "It doesn't seem to be my town as much anymore," he thought as he ran. "A lot of the people seem different. Most of the kids I knew well are gone. A lot of things are going on that I never thought were going on back then, which I *like* as a cop, but I'm not as sure of its safety as I was. It seems like a lot of other places to me now. So why not try some of those other places?"

He ran a little faster every day, and as he ran he thought of all the reasons that he wouldn't pass the next hurdle the FBI placed before him. It seemed to him that something unexpected was bound to end this fantasy, maybe something unknown, or invented. He wondered if they'd talk to Rick, and what Rick would tell them. He wondered if he'd flunk the physical because of his old shoulder injury, another souvenir of high school football. Or he'd fail the lie-detector test. What had he done that he didn't remember or know about? If he went in believing there was something of that sort, he might appear to answer every question with a lie.

Before work one day in October, Tommy drove north out of town and climbed the lookout tower at the top of Mount Sugarloaf. From the railing, to the south, the valley of the Connecticut stretched away across a mostly level plain. The river looked very blue that afternoon. He watched it running on, between cultivated fields, toward steeples in the distance. "Yeah, it's a beautiful place. But there gotta be other beautiful places," Tommy said. He'd be a fool not to take this opportunity, a fool to wait around to become Northampton's detective sergeant. "And what an adventure. This hometown-boy stuff. There's more to life than that." Everything happened for a reason. Maybe this was why he and Jean couldn't have children: so that they'd be free to go. This would be a way of making something good out of something bad. Jean wasn't sure yet what work she'd do, but she was very happy. You could see it in her face. "And what an adventure. A life of travel. All my life I wanted to do nothing but police work. And this is the FBI! The number one police agency in the country. But that'd be pretty cool. Go into a place. Who are you? *FBI.* Talk about pride in your organization. I'm very proud of the Northampton PD, but this is a thousand times larger. The toys are unbelievable, and if you do a good job, you're doing something really important."

A friend had told him he'd never find another place as nice as Northampton. He'd pondered that. He thought he had an answer now. "Even if you live in Oz, if you live in Oz all your life, you'd want to leave once in a while." From the tower, Northampton lay just out of sight. He thought he could get used to views like that.

The Three County Fair had come and gone. He'd worked security during fair week for a decade. This year seagulls seemed to outnumber people. There wasn't any policing to do. He borrowed a golf cart and raced around the grounds. "One thing I'll miss, screwing around like this. But I bet I can still do it. Have some fun." The fair used to be different, full of runaway teenagers and prostitutes. There used to be brawls at the beer hall. The dog-food-company trucks gathered down by the stables again. But in a lot of the afternoon races, only five horses started. In one race, three turned up lame. The fair was dying, he thought. The festival of restaurants downtown, the Taste of Northampton, had all but replaced it. Northampton had become a town that preferred sushi to cotton candy. He liked the new festival, but this was another way in which Northampton wasn't like his hometown anymore.

He drove back and forth through Hampshire Heights as usual on Cabbage Night. "Ooooh, look at those kids over there. They're going to the store to buy more eggs. It must be something to egg O'Connor's cruiser. This is the shit I'll miss. Listen to me. I probably won't be missing this until thirty years from now."

In Northampton the cycles of crime and punishment were as easy to observe as the cycles of the weather. "It's like sharks' teeth," Tommy said. "One criminal goes to jail and another comes out." But it seemed as though an unusual number of people he'd arrested, people he often dealt with, were going off to jail this fall. Last winter, a judge had thrown out a small marijuana case of his, on Fourth Amendment grounds. Now that case came around again, in a sense. The boy in question had committed an armed robbery and now was headed for the county jail, Camp Hamp. "I don't think that judge did you any favors," Tommy said to him the night of his most recent arrest. "He didn't!" the boy cried. "I thought I could get away with anything!" Which was probably what he thought Tommy wanted to hear. Weeping in his cell at the lockup, he'd begged Tommy to let him become an informant. There were half a dozen others now bound for Camp Hamp, among them the young man "God" whom he'd caught selling LSD in Pulaski Park last year. As Tommy saw it, the kids who loitered in the park were acting as if the place were their living room and bathroom. He'd done his best to make them uncomfortable there. A new graffito, created in chalk on the concrete pavement in front of the benches, commemorated both this attempt and God's sentencing, the image of a tombstone, inside which was written:

> HERE LIES RIP
> THOMAS O'CONNOR
> MAY HE REST IN
> HELL

Tommy took a snapshot. He could hang it in his shrine, or take it with him when he left, if leaving was what Fate wanted. Tommy drove away from the park and his chalk tombstone. "It's going to be a quiet year," he said, thinking of all the people now heading to jail. "I might as well leave. I've cleaned up this town. I've tamed this shrew."

Back at the station, in the Detective Bureau, a letter addressed to Tommy was pinned to the wall over Rusty Luce's desk. Scrawled in large letters in the margins were the words "Help!" and "Please!" It came from the county jail in Ludlow.

She got hurt, Chasing me out—the Window, I got 2 Wittness. All 3 of us. Were out side when she jumped. Please help me out. D.A. want 2 year's and I didn't, do it. Boss, I'm verry Graetfull if you Can help me! Can you Please, Call D.A.? Ockey, I'm sorry for being a pain in the butt. You known I meant Well. I promise, this is the last time, your going to hear—me and Carmen Court problems. Sorry to do all this— "Crying" I'd should had, leastsend to you a long time ago. I'd Learn my lesson, the hard way. I'm getting a new Wife. I have to give up, on Carmen. We Just Can't make it together. Love is blind, and so was I.

There was no point in answering. With Frankie, it had been the same old thing over and over again: Carmen and crack; crack and Carmen. Peter said he felt bad for Frankie. Tommy said, "I've gone and seen him many times in jail. I'm not doing it anymore. There'll be other Frankies." He got a strange feeling, though, when he walked back into his office at the station, and there sitting on his desk was the stack of other letters from Frankie in jail. He used to say, when Frankie had disappeared for a time, that in the midst of life's uncertainties there was always one sure thing: Frankie would show up again. It had always been true. Some months from now, Frankie would shamble up to the side door and say to the cop who opened it, "Hey, tell Oakie I'm here. Tell him it's eighty-eight." And Tommy wouldn't be there. He could hear Frankie's sneaky voice. "Let's get this guy, Oakie. He's gettin' too big for his bridges." He could see Frankie slithering off his chair with laughter. Frankie richly deserved to go to jail. But he'd miss him. He put the letters away in his desk drawer.

Rick had become yesterday's news. He had made the front page of the *Gazette*: OFFICER PLEADS GUILTY TO ASSAULT ON CHILD. The next day he'd dropped back to the second section of the paper, and, of course, it hadn't been long before Rick's name had fallen out of public view, like Rick himself.

The Hampshire County Jail stands on a promontory commanding lordly views of Mount Tom and the Holyoke Range. It seems an odd place for those fortresslike buildings surrounded by fences topped with razor wire. Tommy had often gone inside—to interview prisoners; often to visit Frankie in the sally port, out of sight of other inmates. The jail used to be just another landmark on his drive home after work around midnight. He liked that drive, the landscape darkening with trees, the night air sweet in the spring, winy in fall, sharp with whiffs of wood smoke in winter. After tours of duty that took him into squalid places, the drive home seemed like a bath. He could feel his body relaxing, a welcome relief from welcome tension. But ever since last August, whenever his headlights had brushed across the sign for the jail up ahead, he had thought about Rick, up that hill, inside that fence, behind those beige, blank walls.

He'd heard some news about Rick inside. A local jailhouse boss of a Latino gang had supposedly threatened him, but apparently nothing had come of it. He heard Rick had been placed for a while in a room with another convicted sex offender. "Some short little guy who did his own daughter," Tommy was told. Most recently, Rick had been put in a cell with God, and apparently he and Rick weren't getting along very well.

None of this seemed real. As he drove by the jail, Tommy told himself that Rick was a convicted felon now, that departmental regulations prohibited Northampton cops from socializing with convicted felons, that the FBI probably had even stricter rules. He'd gotten a letter from Rick. He'd stopped at these lines and read them again:

> I guess you'll never know until you have kids of your own. I hope for your and Jean's sake that happens soon. There is nothing better in this world, no truer love.

What was Rick saying? Why would he want to bring that up? To taunt him? Was that the sort of thing Rick would talk about if he visited him? Tommy kept himself angry for weeks.

One night as he passed by the jail, he realized that he might be gone before Rick got out. He might never see him again. Ever again. The thought struck him as odd, a chord in a strange key. When you parted ways with old friends, you didn't usually know it was for the last time. They left town, and you simply lost touch. He didn't feel angry at Rick anymore. But the prospect of visiting him in jail was all painful. He didn't want to see him reduced to that state. Rick belonged to another part of his life, and he wanted to leave him there, as he used to be.

Bill O'Connor wasn't one to say a thing outright, but when Tommy had told him about the FBI, he'd said, "That's great, Tom. It'll give me another place to visit." His father had said nothing would make him prouder, except maybe Tom's becoming pope. "And there's Jean, so I guess you're disqualified." Bill made his laugh. It sounded genuine, and it came as a great relief to Tommy. He'd fretted for days about telling his father.

Bill went walking every day in Look Park. One thing Bill liked was that he always ran into a lot of other old-timers there, getting their exercise, too. "Old folks," Bill called them. Usually, when he started on his walk, another of the old folks would tell him some gossip, invariably false. Didn't he think there was something funny about Mayor Ford? As he walked on, past the tennis courts and duck ponds, Bill knew that the story was moving on ahead of him, so that by the time he got back to his car another of the old folks was bound to sidle up and say, "Can you believe it, Bill? Our mayor's a lesbian. And I got that from the source." The other morning Tommy had gone along on the walk, and they kept running into old folks, who would say hello to both of them. One said to Bill, "You got your bodyguard with you." Afterward, Bill said, "It makes you feel good." But Bill didn't take a melancholy tone with Tommy. Around Tommy the old man seemed positively cheerful at the thought of his son's going away.

Tommy kept up his daily runs around Northampton, five miles, faster and faster. Every day he'd finish at his father's house. They'd have lunch together, and in the evening, while on duty, Tommy would stop again for his forty. He kept asking his father if it really would be all right for him to leave, if by some miracle he did get into the FBI. Maybe he asked too often.

One night, Bill wiped his mouth with his napkin and said,

"Yes, when I started high school, I had to choose. I had to take the classical course or the commercial course. I came home to my mother and told her.

" 'What are the Paddens doin'?' she said.

" 'They're takin' the commercial course.'

" 'You're takin' the classical,' she said. 'You're goin' to college.' "

Bill sighed. Those were the years of the Great Depression. There was barely enough money for the family to live on, in their apartment down in Holyoke. Never mind sending Bill to college. "So in 1934 I graduated from high school. Well, the CCCs were hirin' and down we went to the city hall, me and Jimmy Burke. They said, 'You have to be eighteen.'

"I said, 'I'm seventeen.'

"The clerk says to another fella in the office, 'Jubinville, you can fix that right now, can't you?'

"In a matter of seconds I became eighteen. I'm actually a lot younger than I look. Like Abraham in the Old Testament. I wound up at Fort Devens. They were pushin' us through the line to get uniforms. I said to the sergeant, 'I want to call my mother.' And they started laughing. I was supposed to be home for supper. It was the first time in my life I was more than five minutes from home, except for the trolley ride to Springfield. I was about to cry. They were laughin'.

"So, they let me call her. She says, 'Oh, my God, Billy, you're down at Fort Devens.'

"She seemed upset. And *I* was upset. Then I said, 'Thirty-five dollars a month, Mom, and twenty-five of it goes home.'

" 'Oh!' she says. 'That's not bad.'

" 'I'm really feeling like crying,' I said.

" 'That's good, Billy,' she says. 'Good-bye.' "

Bill went on, "From the playground one minute to Fort Devens. And then they put us on a rattly old train to Lyndonville, Vermont. I remember this captain with shiny boots up to his knees. 'Tomorrow morning, they'll wake you up at six.' But it was beautiful scenery. We passed through Willoughby Gap, and I said to Jimmy Burke, 'This isn't too bad.' After gettin' out of Catholic school, after twelve years, you were free. Choppin' trees. There were real wildcats up there. And I'd call up my mother and say, 'My term is up now.' She'd say, 'There's nothing here for you, Bill. And God we can use that twenty-five dollars.' "

Bill laughed. Then Tommy did, too.

"I stood fifteen months up in that place," said Bill.

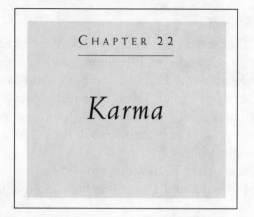

CHAPTER 22

Karma

THE OLD TOWN seemed to look down kindly on the rituals invented for it, like a god who likes flattery: Smith's Mountain Day and the ringing of the bell in the tower of College Hall, which for years beyond memory had declared one day every fall too pretty for classes. High school football on Friday nights, the cheers for Hamp High rising up from the fields below Elm Street. And the party clothes the inhabitants put on the old place to announce the coming holidays—the Christmas tree in the river, the lights all over town. Eighty-three children were born in December, nine months from last year's final big snowstorm—only an average number, in spite of predictions. Now the snows came again, but in moderate amounts, just enough to turn the town white. There is something somber and exciting about the sight of fresh snow around old buildings made of brick and stone. It summons up sensations that feel like pathways between the old and new, time past and time reborn. A few days before Christmas, traffic offenders trooped into District Court to answer for their crimes at the last preholiday session, Judge W. Michael Ryan presiding. The proceedings that day had a seasonal flavor.

A young university student stood at the defendant's lectern.

The youth had been caught speeding over in Amherst. He said he didn't think he was going that fast.

For a moment the black-robed, gray-bearded judge looked stern. Then he said, "It's obviously a case of Amherst working their police too hard." A trace of a smile crossed his face. He wiped it away, stroking his beard. "I find you not responsible."

The young man at the lectern beamed. "Thank you, sir."

Then up came a young woman. Judge Ryan studied the documents on her case. Then he declared, "The proper citation here would have been speeding. I find you not responsible."

She grinned. Leaving the courtroom, she did a little skip.

Then another young man. "The Westhampton police did not respond. I find you not responsible," said Judge Ryan.

That defendant punched the air with a fist. "Yes!"

The next charge was more serious. The man at the defendant's lectern looked disheveled, as if he had slept in his clothes. He'd been caught driving without a license a year ago, and had failed to show up in court. Last night he'd been picked up by the police on a default warrant, and had spent the night in jail.

Judge Ryan scratched his head. "Why didn't you come back to answer this?"

"I can't really answer that," said the defendant. "But I would like to resolve all this."

"What image of a resolution do you have in mind?" asked Judge Ryan.

The young man shrugged.

Judge Ryan leaned forward, his elbows on the bench. "Well, let me ask you this. What were you hopin' to get away with?"

The old part of the Hampshire County Courthouse faces Main Street, the Romanesque part with the lawn out front and the bust of Calvin Coolidge and the wrought-iron fence with little spears on top. Nowadays almost all of the business was conducted to the rear, in the tall, modern, warehouse-like annex, largely hidden from Main Street. In the outer lobby of the annex, beside the metal detector, there was a blackboard with this label at the top: WEAPONS INTERCEPTED. The court officers had begun keeping track in the fall of 1989, after being asked repeatedly why they bothered to search people in a crime-free place like Northampton. The running tally on the blackboard read: "14,634 knives, 1,606 mace, 346 pistols, 14 switch blades, 13 double edged knives, 4 stun guns, 1 set nunchucks, 1 ninja star, 1 set of metallic knuckles, ammo, razors, 2 mock bombs." This was the kind of raw statistical data that confirms people's worst thoughts about the general state of society. You looked at numbers like those and wondered about the educational system. How could so many people think they'd get away with carrying stuff like that through a metal detector? But this was, after all, the courthouse. Most of its clientele wouldn't have been coming here at all if they had done better in school.

Frankie didn't come in the front entry, not this time. He was led in handcuffs from the back door of the Hampden county jail van, through a brief taste of winter air, and into the courthouse through a side door, the door to the holding cells, where he was deposited to wait for his turn in court. Carmen's latest allegations had gotten him six months in Ludlow. He'd had no choice but to accept a plea, because the D.A. in Springfield had threatened to send him away to state prison for two years if he insisted on a trial. And because Frankie had pled guilty to those charges, the old motor vehicle ones had been reinstated, the ones that Rusty Luce had gotten suspended for him months ago. Frankie had to face them in court today. Then he'd go back to jail, probably with some time tacked on to his six-month sentence.

Frankie was neatly dressed today. His pants were clean and safely aloft. He'd put on some weight; he always did, in jail. Life wasn't terrible in Ludlow. He had a cousin serving time there who was a big shot in one of the Latino gangs, so no one messed with Frankie. But you couldn't smoke cigarettes in Ludlow as you could at Camp Hamp, and that made the time go by more slowly. And he hated jail as much as ever. He'd never get used to the feeling of being buried alive. He'd been counting the days to his release, and now the prosecutors up here in Northampton wanted to tack on more days, for those stupid old motor vehicle charges. He'd helped these prosecutors out. He'd bagged that crack dealer Tyrone for them, and now they were going to punish him for something that never would have happened in the first place, if the cops had treated him as decently as he'd treated them and had helped him get his license back.

Frankie languished in the holding cell, thinking angry thoughts. He didn't want any more time tacked on to his sentence. It was long enough already. He needed a strategy, but he couldn't think of one.

Frankie sat all morning in the courtroom lockup. He sat there half the afternoon. By the time he was led into Courtroom 2, most of the cases were over. Only a couple of spectators remained in the gallery. In one corner, a lawyer stood talking softly into a defendant's ear. Frankie sat in handcuffs, on the bench reserved for defendants already in custody. He looked around the all-but-empty room, looking for Rusty, looking for Peter, looking for Oakie. All his old friends had abandoned him, except for the public defender. She was a very nice young woman. Kind of pretty, too, he thought. She had represented him before.

The gray-haired, gray-bearded judge above him on the bench didn't look familiar. Frankie had stood in front of him once before, around Thanksgiving many years ago, but Frankie had seen too many judges. They all looked the same to him now. As the judge heard another case, Frankie turned a sorrowful-looking, attentive face toward him. You never knew. The judge might notice and see how sorry Frankie was. Finally, the clerk called Frankie's surname, mispronouncing it as usual. His was the last case of the day. He stood at the lectern in the well of the courtroom, beside his young, pretty lawyer. She wore nice perfume. The clerk intoned the old motor vehicle charges. The judge asked, "How do you want to plead?"

"Not guilty," said Frankie. He added, "Uh, sir."

Then his lawyer took over. "I was Mr. Sandoval's attorney on another matter, Your Honor. But he defaulted. I'm glad to represent him again."

Frankie spoke up quickly. "When I defaulted, I was also incarcerated, Your Honor."

"How much time are you doing now?" asked Judge Ryan.

"Six months," said Frankie.

"Do you want to resolve this today?"

"Yes, Your Honor."

The judge called a recess so that Frankie could confer with his lawyer, and then disappeared through a side door. Frankie and his lawyer sat down on the prisoners' bench.

"You're breaking your mother's heart," said the public defender. Moms had called her recently.

"I wasn't really doin' anything," said Frankie. "My wife promised she'd behave. I got her an apartment. I had two jobs. My therapist told me it was an addictive relationship."

The lawyer bowed her head, probably to hide her smile. Then she started reading through Frankie's printed record. She shook her head. Frankie looked over her shoulder. "You think that's a lot. I met this guy, he's got a hundred and seventy-two charges."

Frankie wondered if she could talk the prosecutor into helping him get a driver's license. "Because I heard of something called a Cinderella license, where you can't drive after dark."

She looked over at him, at the wide, copper-colored face. She smiled. "You'd look good as a pumpkin."

Then she got down to business. The prosecutor wanted Frankie to get ten days "on and after" for these old, reinstated motor vehicle charges, ten days added to his six-month sentence. It was just as Frankie had feared. But his lawyer was hopeful, she said, because of the judge sitting here today. Frankie should plead guilty and throw himself on this judge's mercy. "I think he might make those ten days concurrent," the public defender explained.

"I hope so," said Frankie. He scowled, thinking of the prosecutors and the cops. "I helped them out, and they dropped this. Now look what they want."

"What are you going to do when you get out?" asked the lawyer.

"Go to work," said Frankie. "I got a job in Springfield, with Hearth 'n Home Construction. It's like home repairs."

The lawyer made a note on her yellow pad.

Maybe, after all, there is such a thing as karma. If so, Frankie's had never been anything but mixed, bad one moment, good the next.

Judge Ryan sat in his chambers, a well-appointed private room, full of law books. He read over Frankie's record. He didn't recognize the name; he'd seen so many names. In here earlier today, the probation officer on duty had described the pending cases, and near the end of the listing he'd told the judge, "And we've got a shitbum from Ludlow on some motor vehicle charges." But now, reading Frankie's rap sheet, Judge Ryan murmured to himself, "I've seen worse records."

As a rule, Judge Ryan didn't like adding time to the sentence of a defendant already in jail. Moreover, he never felt happier up on the bench than when he had a chance to construct an artful sentence. Like the one he'd given a locally famous anti-war demonstrator, a Quaker woman, during the Gulf War. She was found guilty of trespassing at an air force base and said she would refuse to do community service. So, she told him in effect, he'd have to set her free or else send her to jail. But he outfoxed her. He sentenced her to give classes on nonviolence at the high school. "I'll do it," she'd said fiercely. "But not because you told me to."

This case wasn't nearly as challenging, but it left some room for invention. Ten extra days of jail time wouldn't do this Mr. Sandoval any good, and to give him ten days that ran concurrently with his other sentence wouldn't accomplish anything either. So Judge Ryan would give him another suspended sentence. It was possible that Mr. Sandoval would go straight and never sin again. That was always possible, in Judge Ryan's philosophy. It wasn't likely, though, he thought, pondering the rap sheet. And if he gave Mr. Sandoval a plain old suspended sentence on these charges, and Mr. Sandoval committed another sort of crime, then these charges would once again be reinstated, and then the same thing that was happening today would happen all over again, wasting the court's time. There was only one logical solution. He'd give Mr. Sandoval a suspended sentence, and add the proviso that these charges could not be brought forward again unless Mr. Sandoval committed identical offenses. Because it was a lenient sentence, Judge Ryan would deliver it in a stern voice, full of opprobrium.

He walked back into the courtroom. He had his mind all but made up. But first he'd hear the lawyers' arguments.

The court officer said, "All rise." Frankie and the public defender returned to the lectern. And Judge Ryan led Frankie through the standard colloquy, Frankie answering all the questions in his sweet, soft voice. He was forty-two. He'd made it as far as tenth grade in school. He wasn't under the influence of drugs or alcohol, just now.

"And how do you plead?"

"Guilty, Your Honor."

The prosecutor made his pitch for severity. "He has a very long record, Your Honor. He's in jail on other matters. The Commonwealth feels he shouldn't be let off on a concurrent sentence as he would normally. That's why we're asking for ten days on and after."

It wasn't a strong argument, and it was delivered a little wearily. It was an end-of-the-day argument. Judge Ryan didn't feel swayed. Even if he had, he would have been swayed back by the public defender. He liked to reward public defenders when they did a good job. They were crucial to the system, and they weren't paid well or often thanked for their work. And this public defender's argument, he thought, verged on eloquence.

She started out in a routine way, attesting to the side of Frankie's character that, as Frankie would have said, meant well. And finally, as is proper at the ends of arguments on behalf of human beings, she spoke of new beginnings. "He has a job waiting for him when he's released, Your Honor." She glanced at her yellow pad. "With Hearth 'n Home Construction."

It was news that seemed calculated to strike fear in the hearts of homeowners. A smile flickered around Judge Ryan's eyes.

"He plans to get his license back," the public defender continued. "He is eligible for parole soon, and I sincerely think that it is Mr. Sandoval's wish to put all of this behind him." She paused, and then, looking up at Judge Ryan, declared, "Because frankly, Your Honor, he's too old for this nonsense."

CHAPTER 23

Free at Last

FEELING SURE THAT he must have guilty secrets, but unable to root them out, feeling a little as he had as a boy at confession, but with no intention of making something up this time, the way he used to for the priest, Tommy sat down and let the polygraph operator hook him up to the machine. He confessed everything. The time he appropriated a ream of paper from the Detective Bureau to do some work at home. The time when, as a teenager, he tried to smoke a joint with an old friend—and, of course, they should know about that old friend. Even the times he told Jean he'd taken out the trash when he actually hadn't yet.

The test went on for hours. Afterward, the operator laughed. He said Tommy was one of the few completely honest husbands he could remember examining. So Tommy figured he'd probably passed.

Tommy had a young friend named Luis Ramos, who lived in the Hampton Gardens apartment complex. They went way back. Tommy remembered Luis as a child and young teenager. In years past, when there was trouble at the Gardens, Tommy would drive up to the scene and usually find Luis on the sidelines. "What's goin' on?" Tommy would ask, and Luis would invariably say, "I don't know. I just got here." At first this was annoying. But eventually Tommy realized that Luis acted out of a sense of honor. Tommy found it hard not to like a young teenager who wouldn't do everything his friends did but wouldn't rat them out either.

Luis had complicated the view through cruiser windows. "It's all in who you hang out with." That was one of Father O'Connor's favorite sayings. But, at one time or another, Tommy had arrested half the friends of Luis's youth, and he'd never had a reason to arrest Luis. When Tommy was a young cop, he used to say he wasn't interested in why people did things, just in what they'd done. He wondered about Luis, though. Luis was an orphan essentially, abandoned by his parents and raised in Northampton by grandparents who spoke no English. He and the former gangster Felix, an old friend of Luis's, had similar backgrounds. The other night Tommy had asked him what the difference was. Luis had shrugged. "My grandparents gave me everything I needed. Maybe his parents didn't."

On a night in November, when the only things that remained between Tommy and the FBI were the physical and the background check, he drove into Hampton Gardens, looking for Luis. He found him standing outside his apartment. Luis was a tall young man, with his head shaved like Tommy's—but in his case for fashion.

Tommy parked and Luis got into the cruiser. He had been a star on the Hamp High basketball team. He was twenty-one now. He had a part-time job, which Tommy had gotten for him, and was taking courses in law enforcement at Holyoke Community College. Luis said one of his teachers had gone to the FBI Academy. "Ever think of doing it, O'Connor?"

"You never know. Keep all the doors open."

"Why don't you just do it?"

"Because you're here, Luis. I couldn't leave *you*." Tommy smiled. Then in a serious voice, he asked, "What do you think the kids around here would say if I did?"

"They'd be happy you were gone, actually. Relief."

Tommy smiled again, then changed the subject. Recently, Luis had said he didn't want to be a cop. He wanted to be a probation officer. Tommy thought he was wavering, though. "The Border Patrol is hiring. Take every exam for every force you can. It's a good idea to start young. The state police, they don't look at *anything* but what you do on their test, which is wrong, but you being a minority, you get extra points. You'd do fine."

"I'd rather work in the daytime," said Luis.

"Well, I'll tell you what, son, you'll get used to nights. You need nothing. You've got life by the balls. Twenty-one years old. Of course, I'm twelve years older than you."

"God, I hope I don't have a head like yours in twelve years. Hey, O'Connor, I have to get my girlfriend a fake I.D. You know anybody who's doing them?"

"Yeah, I do. But they're all in jail."

"So. You want to go back to detective?"

"Yeah, I do."

"Not dressed?"

"Not in this uniform."

"If you're a detective, do you go to other towns?"

"Sometimes."

"Do you go undercover?"

"Not often."

"I'd like to go undercover," said Luis. He changed the subject. "It's scary. I'm getting older. I wish I could just stay this age."

"No, you don't."

"Pretty soon I'll be going to doctors, getting bald like you."

"It's all in how you look at it, Luis. If you get stuck in a rut, it's bad, but not if you move on and enjoy yourself. Hey, any rumors around that I have the virus, because I lost weight?"

Luis hadn't heard any. He wondered if he could ride along with Tommy for a shift. Tommy said he should come to the station the following night.

When Luis arrived, a drunk was being led in handcuffs

down the hall toward the Booking Room. The drunk was saying, in a garbly voice, "You're locking me up illegally."

"You're locking him up illegally?" Luis asked.

"Yeah, we do that all the time," said Tommy. He had some paperwork, but it could wait. He took Luis right out to the cruiser. "By the way, Luis. I know you're not hanging with any of the troublemakers, but just don't tell them things, like the fact that there were only three cruisers out tonight. Like Felix."

"Felix wouldn't be smart enough to ask me a question like that."

Tommy had hoped for a busy night, but the city was quiet, settling down into winter again. He spent most of the evening showing Luis the city that a cop saw—the murderer paroled here long ago, out for a stroll; the dirt-floored cellars behind the tenement on Graves Avenue, where people had obviously been camping; the scruffy woods near the railroad tracks, Northampton's main alternative homeless shelter. He stopped to show Luis the snapshot he kept in his logbook, a photo of himself in his wig and fake mustache.

"Christ, I'd love to do that," said Luis.

"You're helping people. Sometimes they'll change. But you're not gonna stop the drugs from coming in."

He showed Luis the bars where drug dealing was common, and Luis said, "There's a lot of goddamn coke in this town. I just hear it from people. I've heard of lots of kids trying powder. Kids who surprise me."

Tommy didn't ask for the names.

"Let's go down to the Meadows, Luis." The dirt roads were still open. Across the cornfields, the trucks on the Interstate looked afloat, like lighted ships. It was a strange and lovely landscape, redolent of old cases. Tommy remembered, from many years ago, driving down here an hour or so before dawn. He drove into a wooded section. Uphill, about two hundred yards away, lay the South Street neighborhood and the mansion to which Calvin Coolidge had retired and the house where the mayor was sleeping. In the dark gray light, Tommy saw a parked car. He got out. Then he saw a figure walking up the dirt road toward him. He lit the figure with his flashlight. It was a man, and he was naked, except for a plastic garbage bag, wrapped around him like a loincloth or a diaper.

"If there's a body down here, I want you to take me to it."

The man began to weep. It turned out he was a respectable citizen from a nearby town. And no murderer. He had a dildo as large as Tommy's PR-24 in his anus, beneath the trash bag. He came down here to masturbate, he said, still weeping. He begged Tommy not to tell his wife.

"Tell your wife?" thought Tommy. "Jesus Christ! I'd rather do a death notification." He'd let him go, with advice as usual: "Go home, and next time use someone else's meadows. And get yourself some help. Because that thing'll kill ya."

He decided not to tell that story to Luis. Time enough for this wholesome boy to find out about such things.

It was almost eleven, almost the end of the shift, when, out on Mount Tom Road, they came upon a police cruiser parked behind a Northampton taxi. Tommy lifted a thumb to the cop, who lifted a thumb in reply, to say no help was needed.

Tommy drove on, then turned around and headed back toward downtown, but as he was passing the cruiser and taxi again, his eyes went to his mirror. "Who are those jamokes?"

He pulled over. "Luis, you better stay in the cruiser."

Luis watched from a distance: the two male passengers climbing out of the taxi, talking to O'Connor with animated hands. Luis couldn't hear what O'Connor said to them, just O'Connor's voice uttering cryptic remarks and questions over the radio. Then Peter, the drug detective, arrived, a hulking figure. Luis knew him. In a moment there was a scuffle. Then handcuffings. Then another cruiser arrived. The two men from the taxi were loaded up. They drove off, and Tommy got back into the driver's seat. "Oh, God, am I good!"

"What happened?" asked Luis.

The young cop had stopped the taxi for speeding, Tommy explained. The cop had been writing up a ticket, and hadn't thought to question the passengers. "One of them's wanted in New York, for shooting a guy in the stomach. The other has warrants for heroin distribution."

"How'd you know?"

"It just didn't make sense, two guys in a taxi coming back from Holyoke. Why are two grown men taking a taxi back from Holyoke at ten o'clock at night?" Tommy started driving toward the station. He looked over at Luis. "Okay, this is your lesson for the night. You always look further." Tommy went on, "I asked the guy with the topknot, 'What's your name?' 'Uh, Dunbar Martin.' I said, 'No. You're Shorty Ortiz.' I just made that up. He said, 'No, you're wrong.' I said, 'Dunbar, I have dealt with you. It's gonna come back to me. Talk to me.' Then he wouldn't talk. I kept staring at him. Then it came to me. I reached over and touched his hair, the little topknot? 'Googie!' "

"Was that Googie?" said Luis. "He used to drive a Nova."

"Yeah, he comes from your neighborhood. We got one cuff on and he started fighting. After we were done with him, I went to work on the other guy. 'And what's your name?' 'Uh, Alex Alexander.' 'Ever arrested, Alex Alexander?' 'No.' 'And you hang around with this fucking clown? No one who hangs around with him is an angel.' But Peter identified him. His real name is Angel. I told him, 'I stand corrected. You *are* an angel.' "

"Do you get credit for this?" Luis asked.

"The credit is I know I did a good job."

Peter was standing by the side door of the station. He walked over and slapped a high five with Tommy. "Hey," said Peter. "You can't hide from us."

Luis stood there, smiling. Tommy turned to him. "See, Luis, we don't spend all our time in the Gardens." Tommy put on his wild-looking grin, his parody of mania. "It was fucking masterful, *masterful* police work." Then he got serious. "That officer was young, Luis. And alone."

"So how long did it take you to become sergeant?" asked Luis. They stood at the side door.

"Five years to get into the Detective Bureau, ten years to make sergeant, twelve years to make detective sergeant, actually eleven, but they've screwed around with me for a year. Well, there you go, Luis. What do you think? It's a fun job, isn't it?"

"Yeah!"

"What I want is to get you out of college and out on the street."

"Yeah," said Luis. "Me, too."

On an afternoon in early December, Tommy walked into the Detective Bureau in plainclothes: boots, khaki pants, and a flannel shirt, his pistol and his badge attached to his civilian belt. The lieutenant of detectives rooted around in a corner of his office and found a rusty sword, an old piece of evidence. He tapped Tommy with the flat of the blade on either shoulder. "I hereby knight you Detective Sergeant."

Tommy gazed at his name on the bureau roster. "It feels good to be back," he said. But this long-awaited moment had come too late. He thought, "It's nice. Everyone thinks this is a promotion, and if I go out, I want to go out on top."

The doctor thought the old football injury to Tommy's shoulder had healed well enough for federal service. The doctor didn't seem like a person to joke around with, but Tommy couldn't help himself. He was nervous about the rectal exam.

"Well, I'm all yours, Doc."

"Good. Could you turn around, please?"

The doctor discarded his rubber glove. "You're all set."

"Can I get your first name?" Tommy asked.

The doctor looked at him.

"Well, you've been more intimate with me than any man ever has. I just think we should be on a first-name basis."

"Don't worry about it, Mr. O'Connor. Go get a drink."

"Well, I kinda feel like I should ask you to come along."

Then the doctor laughed, which was encouraging, in several ways. All that remained was the background investigation. Soon an agent would arrive and start asking questions around the station, which would give away his secret. He'd have to do that job himself, and soon.

Tommy lay in bed, awake in the dark. "Now I really *may* be leaving," he thought. He made himself say it over and over in his mind. "Now I really *may* be leaving."

The chief was in his office working at his computer, with the stereo on. "I only have a couple of minutes," he said. He had a meeting to go to.

"I don't know how to put this, Chief."

Tommy talked for a while. When he said, "Then they gave me a test and I passed it," the chief leaned over and snapped off his stereo. "Well, that got his attention," Tommy thought.

Tommy said he wanted to thank the chief for all the opportunities he'd given him over the years, which was what had made this possible.

The chief slapped himself on the forehead, as if to say he regretted making that mistake.

"I've been here in this station since ninth grade, realistically," Tommy said. "It's not easy to pick up and leave, but on the other hand, I've never been anywhere."

The chief said, "I think it's great." But the FBI had frustrations, too. He should sit down and talk with some agents.

"I have," said Tommy.

"Hey, I'm happy for you," said the chief. "Gotta say I'm sad for me."

Tommy walked into the Ready Room. A crowd of uniformed cops sat there, the patrol shifts of both Days and Evenings. They'd been told to wait for an announcement.

Tommy told the whole story. "And if I pass the background investigation, with a little help from my friends . . ."

"Don't worry, Tom," said Preston Horton. He was one of the gay officers. "Our secret's safe with me."

Most of the cops laughed. Tommy smiled. "But they do a lot of neat things," he went on. "Mafia, organized crime, robbery squads. It's all pretty much a big hit to me. I've been here since ninth grade. So. That's the deal."

He was done. The Ready Room was very still for a moment. The broken bench on the far wall creaked under its load of officers. It was a cheerless-looking room, like a shipping room in a factory, full of ghosts for some of the people now in it, those who had been around long enough for it to have acquired subjective adornments. Some of the officers looked as if they were staring into their futures and didn't like what they saw.

Horton's loud voice broke the silence. "Congratulations!"

Then one of the young men from Tommy's shift clapped. Then they all started clapping, a swelling sound, Tommy standing before them wetting his lips and blushing, a blush on a blush.

The Ready Room cleared out. Several of the older officers from Evenings—Carlos, Micker, Scotty—sat at one of the folding tables, each looking in a different direction, none speaking, all their faces glum. Dorothy, one of the detectives, was weeping.

Out in the hallway Peter, who had just arrived, said, "What's Dorothy crying about?"

"Because Tommy's leaving."

"Hey, Tommy, come over here so I can cry over you."

Tommy was in the Report Room, saying to one of the secretaries, "I've been here since ninth grade. I would come in twice a week as an Explorer Scout. Do a shift at the desk . . ."

The third week of January, Tommy got word that his background was clean. Both the *Gazette* and the *Union-News* told Northampton the news, in long articles and big headlines— local boy, local cop, makes the big time. He went to District

Court, probably for the last time, for a hearing on an old case of his. As he walked down the corridor, the voices of probation and court officers, of prosecutors and some defense lawyers, kept coming at him: "Gonna miss ya." "Hey, congratulations." Even some defendants walked up to say good-bye: "So you never comin' back, O'Connah?"

The hearing was a plea. The defendant said he'd been a soldier in Vietnam, a certifiable combat hero. Tommy had caught him bringing a dozen bags of heroin back from Holyoke last summer.

"So did Vietnam get you hooked up with drugs?" Tommy asked him, while they waited for the judge.

"Nah. I was doin' drugs before. Stealin' cars, too. I can't blame Vietnam for nothin'. I got seventy thousand for post-traumatic stress disorder. I said I didn't have it. They told me I was in denial. What the hell? I knew I couldn't keep the money. I knew I'd just shoot it up. So I bought a house for my daughter."

Tommy shook his head. "Hey, you know what? You're the last case I'll be doing as a Northampton cop."

He said good-bye to city hall. Jean came along. They sat down with Mayor Ford, a slightly odd good-bye because of the stiffness underneath. Recently, jokingly, Mayor Ford had said to Bill O'Connor that it might be just as well for her that Tommy was leaving, because if he stayed, political ambitions might blossom.

"Is it really true? Is it official?" Mayor Ford said, smiling. "Congratulations, you son of a bitch."

"We're extremely excited, but scared as hell."

"Well, you really deserve it, not only with what you've done, but with having the vision to apply. And your dad's proud."

"Yeah. It's either this or pope."

Mary laughed heartily.

"And Jean kind of took care of that," said Tommy. He went on, "The only reason I got the job was because of what I did here, and because of the chief. He let me do the drug stuff, instead of saying he didn't want to know about any drugs here."

"Which is something we want to continue," said the mayor.

Tommy said, "You know, I've never been anywhere. I was born and raised here. I don't know where I'm gonna buy lunch or get my car fixed."

"You'll have to find an old dumb radio station like WHMP," she said. "A station that carries obituaries and Engelbert Humperdinck."

They stood up. Mayor Ford had begun to open her arms, but Tommy made a slight sideways movement, and she stuck out her hand instead.

There had been one moment that seemed more than just polite, a reflective moment for each of them. Mandatory retirement came at fifty-seven for FBI agents, Tommy had said.

"You're gonna retire back here," Mary replied. "I probably won't be in this office then."

"Hey, if the chief's position is open," Tommy had said. "Fifty-six isn't that old. Is it MacArthur who said, 'I shall return'?"

He couldn't walk more than a few steps downtown without someone coming up and wishing him well, and his beeper kept going off and the phone went on ringing, at work and at home. All of his informants called, even a few of the people he'd arrested. One caller said, in a shaky female voice, "This is someone who is very, very proud of you."

"Mrs. B!" His history teacher, who used to have him sit beside her desk, to try to curb his chattering.

Puttering around the station, Tommy found an engraving tool. He got a ladder and engraved in the cement-block wall above the side door, "83 1997." He stood back. It was hard to see. There was a better place, on the wall beside the rack where officers hung the keys to the cruisers. In small letters in the concrete block, he engraved, "83—1997 FBI." Maybe officers going on duty, getting their keys, would stop there and think of him, and years from now maybe some rookie would wonder at the meaning of the inscription, and ask, "Who was Eighty-three?"

He spent the rest of that evening cleaning out his desk. The next afternoon, his last day on duty, he retired from plain-clothes. He went down to the locker room and put on his uni-form, and all his medals. Tommy was under instructions not to make any arrests if he could help it, because he wouldn't be around to testify about them. So he drove his usual patrol routes, looking for people to say good-bye to.

Fresh snow lay on the roadside. The air was cold and there weren't many people out. He drove slowly through the Heights. "I wish it was summertime and I was leaving. I'd con-vene a gathering. All right, everybody get over here. You're free." He pulled up beside a small group of boys. "Well, gentle-men, whuss goin' on?"

"FBI, yo," said one. He read the paper, apparently. He came up to the window and shook hands.

"Good luck to ya. Stay out of trouble."

At a little after five, he met Jean and his father at the Look Restaurant. He hoisted his chocolate milk. "To the last forty at the Look."

And it was back to the station again. A few nights ago, a couple of officers had spent a few hours checking parking lots for teenagers drinking in their cars. They had rounded up about a dozen. For tonight the lieutenant had planned a larger operation. Now he began to brief the troops. "Everybody bring extra cuffs."

Tommy took a pair of handcuffs off his belt. "I'll be locking up Gotti with these."

"What we're doing here is sending a message," the lieu-tenant said. "So hit the streets and good luck."

They had borrowed a paddy wagon from the county jail to transport the arrestees to the station. Tommy rode along, a younger cop at the wheel. By a little before eleven, the van had made half a dozen trips and boys and girls lined the hallway inside the police station. The kids were being booked, then bailed out, one after another. A court clerk had arrived to manage the transactions. Tommy looked at his wristwatch. It was almost eleven. He'd almost forgotten. He took his portable radio off his belt, and broadcast into the night air of Northampton, "Eighty-three to all members of the three-to-eleven shift. Thank you very much for a very pleasurable two years. And I hope we can do it again someday. In a different capacity, of course. I'm *not coming back*."

He returned to the hallway. Several of the girls caught drinking were crying. Tommy surveyed the arrested youths. Most wore party clothes. "Just relax," he told them. "It's not the crime of the century."

Another vanload arrived. Tommy went out into the frigid night. He helped five young women and a young man out of the van. All were handcuffed. The boy looked scared. Tommy led him in. "Hey, look at it this way. How many guys at UMass can say, 'I spent last night with five girls in handcuffs.' " There were a dozen standing in the hall. A few of the girls still wept. "Ladies and gentlemen, we're doing this because we don't want people drinking in our parking lots," said Tommy. "You'll be out in half an hour and it won't go on your records."

But one girl went on sobbing into her hands. He walked over to her. "Where do you go to school?"

"Wu-Wu-Westfield State."

"Westfield State? So did I! You probably learned a lesson, huh?"

"I learned a really good lesson!"

He addressed the assembled youths again. "You seem like nice kids. You wouldn't be reacting like this if you weren't."

He stared at them, but they still seemed much too scared. So he started asking them where they went to school, then introduced them to each other. "Westfield State meet Holyoke Community College."

This seemed to work. In a moment one of the girls, her cheeks still streaked with tears, was giving advice to one of the boys. "If you want to pick up a girl," she told him, "you shouldn't be wearing those shoes with those pants."

It was past midnight now. Time to go home. He went into his office and began unclipping items from his belt. He laid them one by one on his desk—ammo pouches, portable radio, baton, flashlight, pouch for rubber gloves, handcuffs, pepper spray, pistol. He took off his clip-on tie and put it on top of the pile, then his round hat. He was aiming for a bigger hat, a bigger badge, and far, far better toys, but the boy had yearned to carry those things now lying on the desk, and the young man had acquired them, and now he was letting them go. He could hardly bear to look at them, sitting in a heap, abandoned.

He opened all the drawers in his desk. All were empty, except that a box of staples lay in one. He pocketed the staples. "I already took the polygraph." Suddenly, he snapped his fingers. "Frankie!"

Frankie had to be out of Ludlow by now, but no one had heard from him. Tommy went back to the Radio Room and ran a Bureau of Probation check. It amounted to a farewell. He was "BOPping" Frankie good-bye. When the printer finished, Tommy picked up the long sheet of paper. There were no new charges on it. "He's disappeared," said Tommy. He looked puzzled for a moment. Then he lifted an index finger. "But! I BOPped him under 'Frankie Sandoval.' No telling who he is now."

Tommy went back to the patrol sergeant's office, the tiny chamber off Records, opened up his filing cabinet, and got out Frankie's file. He opened the folder and picked out the Samson Rodriguez license and studied the photograph. "He's someone whose funeral I'd go to." Then Tommy put the license back, closed the folder, and put it on Peter's desk. He turned out the lights and locked the door to the Detective Bureau. Then he went outside.

The van was departing again, to pick up more underage drinkers. Tommy stood by the side door, watching it go. "Well, that's it. I'm defunct. Ain't got a badge. No gun. Who the fuck am I?"

It was snowing lightly, like moths in the lights over Center Street. He looked all around him. He felt sick to his stomach. "Well. It's just good-bye. Just walk out, I guess."

Tommy said he was glad there wouldn't be a big farewell party. He really didn't seem to know Northampton wouldn't let him go so easily. Jean told him they were going out for supper. As they drove up to the Elks Club, Tommy said, "What the hell is going on in town tonight? Oh, you *bastards.*"

The Elks basement, a huge, low-ceilinged, smoky bingo parlor, was entirely filled. The emcee, Brian Rust, a police lieutenant, declared, "Ladies and gentlemen, Tom O'Connor." Hundreds of people, a fair cross-section of respectable Northampton, stood and cheered—most of the city cops, most of the D.A.'s office and the D.A. herself, all of Tommy's state police detective friends, much of his family, virtually all the probation and court officers, nurses from the ER, dozens of ordinary citizens, some scanner buffs among them, city councillors, childhood friends.

Naturally, there were speeches, from the mayor and the chief. And Judge Ryan bravely took the microphone. It wasn't the judge's kind of crowd: too many police officers. He and Tommy exchanged a few quips, Ryan saying that Tommy had an uncanny knack for catching criminals, Tommy calling from the head table, "And then *you* let them go!" The room erupted.

Ryan smiled, waiting for the laughter to die down. Then he went on, "When I encounter Tom in the court, it's not a trial. It's a motion to suppress. He made a stop. He ended up with half the drugs in New England. He has a radar sense. Unfortunately, the Constitution doesn't recognize this radar sense." That quieted the crowd. Then the judge said Tommy had a reputation for being funny. "But compared to his father he's only a half-wit." Which brought down the house. Ryan finished up with the night's benediction. "It wouldn't be right if I didn't send you off with an Irish blessing. I think I may have stolen it from your dad. Blessings on your friends and blessings on your enemies. Turn their hearts. If the Lord won't turn their hearts, we'll ask the Lord to turn their ankles, so you'll know them by their limp."

And Bill O'Connor got up, and received a standing ovation. "I'm delighted to be here tonight. I'm delighted to be anywhere. But, really, how many fathers live long enough to attend their sons' retirement parties? After listening around the table the past few evenings, I said, 'Tom, you deserve everything you get at Quantico. You earned it.' And his wife—they're a great couple—they're goin' on to a new adventure. I hope I hear from them now and then."

Finally, Tommy took the mike. "When you get on the job, they start telling you about, 'Oh, you remember when this guy, remember when that guy,' and the new guy wonders who the hell they're talkin' about? I really hope that someday somebody's gonna say, 'Remember that O'Connor guy?' " His face drained of color. He held the microphone away from him. "All right. It's not a wake. But, Christ! It's not a bad wake if it was one! I just wanta . . . Thanks a lot."

In January, near the end of his nights of duty, Tommy had gone to the house of a suicide, along with other detectives. They went to make sure it wasn't a murder, but there wasn't much question of that. A note lay on the coffee table beside the corpse: "See you later. Please forgive me." The undertaker's assistant was unceremonious as he stuffed the corpse into the black body bag. Tommy carried the feet.

"Harry? If I'm gone from this area and something happens to my dad? Be gentle."

"It's different with people I know," said the undertaker.

"Somebody knew *him*," Tommy said, as they carried the corpse out the door.

He had two weeks in Northampton as a civilian. He was driving his own car toward his father's house for supper when he saw a man, a familiar face, on Main Street. There was a warrant out for him. Tommy reached for a microphone that wasn't there. Many times he drove past people he felt he should question. Finally, he got over this. He was driving up King Street toward the gym. Up ahead he saw the aftermath of an accident, two cars by the side of the street, the drivers outside arguing. He slowed down, then accelerated. "Call the police!" Tommy cried.

"I don't feel responsible for taking care of everybody anymore. It's like I'm a *resident*," he said.

There was a background to this place. He wondered where it had been all these years. Forever, it seemed, he'd scanned the human landscape, picking out from it certain faces and certain kinds of movements, often ignoring the rest. He'd come to suspect mayhem, arguments, squalor, inside every apartment and house in town. The place looked different to him now. "It's kind of weird. It doesn't seem as full of criminals anymore."

Late in January, a couple of weeks before he planned to leave, Tommy heard that Rick had gotten out of jail. A few days later, it snowed. He drove to Northampton to clear his father's driveway. Tommy got the snowblower out of the garage. He was walking along behind the roaring machine, heading down the driveway toward Forbes Avenue, when he saw a red Saab turn off Elm Street, coming his way. He couldn't make out if Rick was at the wheel. Tommy turned and started snowblowing back up the driveway. If Rick wanted to see him, Rick would come over. He made as if he didn't notice the car. He watched it from the corners of his eyes.

The car slowed. Tommy thought, "I should wave." He was

about to raise a hand. Then he thought, "If he waves, I will." The car turned in at Rick's family's house. He was going home. Tommy got a glimpse of him at the wheel, just a brief snapshot of his face inside the car. Then it vanished behind the houses.

Rick must have seen him, and Rick hadn't waved. The moment was gone, probably for good. Tommy carried it around with him as he finished clearing the driveway. It was better this way, he told himself. "Two ships in the night," he thought, as he stamped the snow off his boots at the kitchen door.

JEAN WAS GOING to drive down south with Tommy, then return to Northampton while he was in training. They'd spend a few days in Washington and Richmond on the way to Quantico. They were packed. They'd left their dog, Murphy, with a friend. All was ready, but then Tommy was seized by anxiety that they'd get lost on the way to Washington and wouldn't be able to find the hotel where he and Jean planned to stop for the night. Bill belonged to Triple A. He went to the office to ask them to make a detailed map of the route, a TripTik. But the officious clerk said they couldn't make one up that fast. Bill said, "Oh, that's too bad, because this is for the FBI," and the clerk said he'd make the TripTik right away. "I laughed," said Bill, retelling the story the next morning. "See? I'm usin' it already."

A map of the United States was spread on the kitchen table in the house on Forbes Avenue. Bill and Jean's mother and Tommy and Jean stood over it, discussing which duty stations Tom should apply for after the academy.

Bill said, "Los Angeles."

Tommy looked at him, wetting his lips. Bill was looking down at the map and couldn't have noticed.

Tommy held two small boxes, gift-wrapped and beribboned. Now he handed one to Bill and one to Jean's mother. "Here's a gift for the two a ya."

"Oh, jeez, can we open it now?" said Bill. He started opening the box.

"There's an explanation that goes along with it," said Tommy.

"I'm trying so hard not to break down," said Bill.

Tommy stared at him again.

"They're dog tags!" said Bill. "I could get *my* dog tags."

Jean laughed. Tommy said, "I don't expect you to wear these."

"We'll just keep 'em," said Bill.

"It's the St. Michael's medal, it's the protector of the police," said Tommy.

"Oh," said Jean's mother.

"I haven't worn anything around my neck since I stopped wearing my scapular medal," said Bill.

"Engraved with the date my academy starts."

"Very good," said Jean's mother.

"The date your academy starts," said Bill.

"Protestants don't believe in saints?" said Tommy to Jean's mother.

"I wouldn't say that."

"Well, there's one that'll keep me safe."

"So now, you're lucky you're going today," said Bill.

"You are," said Jean's mother. "Tomorrow's supposed to be a bad day. It is. That's what it said last night."

They all looked down at the map on the table again.

"All right," said Tommy. "Well, we won't extend this any longer." He held out his hand toward his father. They shook.

"No," said Bill. "Okay, well, good luck. And you got a new challenge, and you'll do good. Keep your head up no matter how hard they tackle you."

Tommy kept staring at him. "I'll be back in about six weeks." He meant for a visit. The course was four months long.

"What you're thinkin' is, you're saying, 'I hope he's here in six weeks,' " said Bill, and he winked at Jean's mother.

She laughed. Jean laughed nervously.

Tommy was still staring at his father, and the color was gone from his face.

"Let's look at the brighter side," said Bill. It was as if he were ascending an imaginary podium. "The whole thing is going his way. I wish I was going down there. At thirty-three. I wouldn't even turn back. Bet your life. I'd say good-bye to my father and mother and then I wouldn't even think about it."

Tommy said, in a very soft voice, "Am I doing the right thing?"

But Bill's hearing had weakened, the last few years. He couldn't have heard. He was saying, "I'd take an allotment out, send them a memento every month . . ." Then he paused. Tommy had turned and hurried out of the room.

"So," said Bill.

Everyone was silent, eyes looking for somewhere to go. From the kitchen you could hear water running in the bathroom. Bill looked down at the road map again, and said to Jean's mother, "Well, let's see. I'll be chartin' it here. I figure they'll be in New York by two. See, that keeps me goin'." He chuckled. "Then they're headed for Washington. Philadelphia'll be another two hours or so. If they're driving like Jack. They'll be in Philadelphia, see, and then go around there and then first thing you know he'll be in Arlington. With all the good people that live there and work in Washington. Huh?"

"Yes, well, they live outside," said Jean's mother.

"Yeah, in Arlington. It's a nice spot. The hotel, I understand, is in a good spot." He turned to Jean. "Shall we start wearing our medals now?" Bill held up his. "The new look. I'll put this on a chain."

Tommy still hadn't reappeared. In a little while, Bill went looking for him. He found him standing in the adjacent room, in front of the staircase. "Okay," Bill said. Tommy bowed his head and extended his hand to shake again, and Bill extended his, and Tommy began to sob, noiselessly. Bill's mouth gaped open, as if to exhale one of his laughs. His shoulders shook. They stood there, mouths open, hands still clasped. "You guys go out!" Tommy yelled toward the kitchen.

He had his dark glasses on when he got into the driver's seat beside Jean. He rolled down the window and called to Bill and Jean's mother, who were standing on the stoop, "Pray for a warm spot."

It was a cold sunny morning, the sunlight blinding against the snow. He backed out, beeped his horn, paused, beeped again, cleared his throat, made a choking cough, and then drove slowly down Forbes Avenue toward Elm. Jean looked pensively out the windshield.

"Got the TripTik. But we can still get lost," said Tommy. He coughed. "Better off to be miserable in the sun, I guess, huh?" He wasn't really speaking to her and she didn't answer.

"Well, will your mother wear her medal?"

Jean laughed.

"I heard my father. 'Shall we start wearing our medals now?'"

"I bet he'll be wearing it."

"He'll be fine," said Tommy.

"He's sending you off to a good place. Not to a war."

Tommy put on a stentorian voice. "It's a war out there anyway, Jean. A war against crime."

He stopped at the police station, to drop off a few more pieces of equipment. "There's one that never said boo to me," he murmured, spotting one of the veteran cops of the day shift heading for a cruiser. On his way out of the station, he paused in the Ready Room to look at the inscription he'd engraved in the wall by the key rack: "83—1997 FBI." Someone had painted it over. It must have been someone on the day shift. He made a sour face, then left the station whistling.

He stopped again at the intersection of King and Main, waiting for the light to change. Up ahead lay Pleasant Street, the southern route out of town, a piece of the Holyoke Range in the distance. He sat at the wheel, looking straight ahead. "Well, I could have joined a rock-and-roll band when I was eighteen and left. Done a lot of drugs. I guess the FBI's better than that. What else could I have done?"

"Could have gotten divorced," said Jean.

"Could have gotten divorced? Nope."

"Could have lived with somebody before you got married."

"Yup, could've."

The light changed. They passed Alan Scheinman's building. "He was out here in shorts yesterday on the street corner talking to somebody. In the snow," said Jean.

Tommy drove down Pleasant Street in silence, until he passed the bowling alley at the edge of downtown. Then his newly lean jaw stiffened. "It doesn't bother me *one iota* leaving this place," he declared, as he glanced in his rearview mirror at the modest skyline of Northampton, shrinking behind him. "It tears me apart leavin' the old guy, but it's come down to the point where I owe this town *nothing*." Just as he was saying this, as he drove through the gap in the dike where Pleasant Street becomes Mount Tom Road, a car turned left in front of him. It was heading for the dirt back road into the Meadows, now covered in snow and nearly impassable. Tommy's head snapped around to follow that car. His face had the familiar, on-duty look of sudden attentiveness, like the face of a cat that has heard something you can't.

"What are you *doin'*, goin' down there?" Tommy said, peering after the car.

Then he caught himself. His face changed, to a look of great craftiness, a comic-book detective's visage. He said, "Throw on his diaper. Crank his meat in the Meadows."

The entrance to the Interstate loomed up ahead. The back

road to the Meadows lay behind. In his normal voice, Tommy asked, "What *is* he going down there for? It obviously isn't a shortcut anymore."

"There was a big white sheet in the backseat," said Jean.

"Goin' to dump a body," he said. "Well. Peter'll figure it out."

He turned onto the Interstate, heading south. He looked at the speedometer. "Better not get caught speeding now." For now he had nothing to prove he belonged to the society of cops. He lifted his voice. "I don't got no stinking badges in this car! All I have is my *mouth*. Or as Ryan says, my half-wit."

The landscape, the watery southern part of Northampton, began to pour by. The river's oxbow, covered in ice, flashed by on the right. Up ahead loomed the twin hills, Mounts Tom and Holyoke, colored like pinto ponies, brown and freckled white with snow on this frozen, crystalline day.

The sign that marked the city limits flickered by. "Get out the TripTik, bud!" Tommy exclaimed to Jean. "There it is! The Easthampton line! The birds are flying!"

"I have directions for the hotel," said Jean in her normal, soft voice.

"Doo doo de doo doo," Tommy sang. He shouted, "Free at last!" He had never seemed younger, or more mixed up. His tear-reddened eyes were still hidden behind sunglasses, his voice still had the crackle left over from weeping, and he was shouting, "Free at last! Free at last! Thank God almighty I'm . . ." He lost his voice to the kind of laughter that lies in one of nature's boundary conditions, like the one between rain and snow. "Free at last!"

The car entered the water gap between Northampton's mountains, the visual limits of his former jurisdiction, the barrier against what Frankie had called "the malice power," the vanishing background for a life still to come. Tommy lowered his voice, and as if to himself, he said, "Now I got a whole bunch of places to go. Better have a TripTik, though." The car was silent for a moment. Jean reached out and put a hand on his knee.

"At least Murphy didn't throw up," she said. "The way he usually does when he sees suitcases."

To the left the great river gleamed. Behind, there were only the mounts—no steeples, no town anymore. Tommy glanced over at Jean. "Wow, that was tough," he said.

CHAPTER 24

The Judge

IN JUDGE W. Michael Ryan's bedroom, the clock radio comes alive, a glissando ripples up to three long chords, and a voice appears at the judge's ear, saying, "Goo-od morning. It's sixty-six degrees. Russ Murley calls for. Hazy sun. I'm. Ron Hall. A Northampton man is resting at home comfortably . . ." Judge Ryan remembers a four-foot-high wooden radio with doilies on top, downstairs in the living room of this very house. He remembers other voices that came from that audible piece of furniture, including the voice of his own father, the mayor then, who was celebrating the birth of the radio station.

A commercial comes on. "Quality and variety from Serio's Market. Your neighborhood grocery store for more than forty years. Remember the name, Serio's Market." The judge always shops there, when he does the shopping.

His wife, a schoolteacher, arises. He lies in bed awhile, listening to the radio, one of many tethers to this place. Four generations of his family have lived here. What changes each saw and didn't live to see. He wonders sometimes if it is only lack of adventurousness that has kept him here, moving on in his life by moving backward, back where he started, to the same town as his father, the same house, the same job. But even when he went away as a young man to Ireland, it was only in the hope of becoming a writer who would tell tales of Northampton. He never wanted to go far away after that. Now more than ever, when he gets a few miles from the Connecticut River, he feels, as he puts it, discombobulated.

The judge listens on. "Cowls Building Supply. Come see what we saw." The judge thinks of his son, not long out of college. He hopes that the young man will settle down here, and he wants to tell him to get out of town quick, before his life and this place become completely entangled.

On the radio Dennis Lee's voice has replaced Ron Hall's. It's a relatively new voice, only eighteen years on the local airwaves. "That's our Pet Patrol for ya this morning, WHMP, the *Fourteen Hundred* team. This is your station! For *info*rmation and *con*versation. Comin' up, we're gonna talk to Rose from the Oxbow Water Skiing Club."

With half an ear, the judge waits for his second alarm.

"Here's your morning polka for ya. On the Fourteen Hundred team!"

So it's 6:40. Time to get up. On the night before April Fool's Day, the judge would lay out a needle and a full spool of thread on his bureau. In the morning he'd put the spool in his pocket and poke the end of the thread through his suit jacket. He'd let it dangle there until it was spotted by one of the women who work in the courthouse or a female friend encountered downtown. Since no woman alive can resist a loose thread, except for his sisters, who are wise to him, someone would always take hold of it and pull. And pull. And he'd cry out, "My jacket's unraveling!" Most days provide opportunities for mischief. The judge arises to the polka. The music expresses some of what he knows about life in this town, but it is much too cheerful and innocent to express all. This is one reason the judge likes morning polkas.

Henry James spent some time in Northampton, when it was much smaller and much more sedate. In a letter, James wrote of the town, "Life flows on as evenly as ever up here. Letters and scraps of news are very welcome. Sometimes it waxes so stupid that I swear a mighty oath that I will pack off the next day." But in his first novel, partly set in Northampton, James let his protagonist feel the town's beguiling side, on a night walk down what must have been Elm Street.

> As he looked up and down the long vista, and saw the clear white houses glancing here and there in the broken moonshine, he could almost have believed that the happiest lot for any man was to make the most of life in some such tranquil spot as that. Here were kindness, comfort, safety, the warning voice of duty, the perfect hush of temptation. And as Rowland looked along the arch of silvered shadow and out into the lucid air of the American night, which seemed so doubly vast, somehow, and strange and nocturnal, he felt like declaring that here was beauty too—beauty sufficient for an artist not to starve upon it.

Judge Ryan's family home is situated on Dryad's Green, an archway of giant hardwoods adjacent to Smith College, and everything looks much the same as in his youth, except for the trees, which are bigger. The judge still gets his gas at the same service station he went to the day he first got a license, and the walk to work—up Kensington Street to Elm, then down Bedford Terrace to State Street—is the same that he took to St. Michael's parochial school. That building now serves as an apartment house for the elderly, but what used to be there grows more vivid to him each time he passes. He can see the St. Vincent de Paul box that used to sit in front of the school, like a big Dumpster. When they'd been drinking, he and his buddies would call their parents and say they were staying with friends. Then they'd climb into the box and make nests for the night among the soft, donated clothes.

In the judge's recollection, the older Janacek children make this walk with him and his siblings. Mike used to get in fights

on the playground when his classmates teased the sweet
Janacek girl who had cerebral palsy. Those fights led to others,
when, after he'd defended her, classmates accused Mike of
being her boyfriend. He put his head in his hands over lunch
the day last August when he heard the youngest Janacek was
being sent to jail. He imagines that had something to
do with Tommy O'Connor's departure. "Tommy O'Connor
couldn't leave Northampton! He couldn't leave, could he?"
Judge Ryan had wondered aloud when he'd first heard that
news. He used to think that the young O'Connor was a dangerous kind of cop, not violent or dishonest, just too powerful.
But even though they'd never agreed about much and had
often butted heads in his courtroom, he thinks young Tommy's
departure is a loss to the town, another little hole in the native
ground. To the judge the landscape is full of such spots, left by
the dead and departed. They fill in, but they never look quite
the same. In cops, as in most things, he prefers the local and
native, people who know the town well, and, being known by
it, are held accountable for what they do here. Newcomers have
brought many improvements, he thinks, but newcomers tend
to mistake what they see in the foreground for the place itself,
as if they can't imagine Northampton without themselves in it.
His town needs its natives, he thinks, to keep it continuous.

He knows very well that the place owns him, but gradually
it has allowed him to feel that it's his. He found it hard to make
his own way when Northampton seemed to belong to his
father. But a long family history has also felt like protection, so
that he's had his answer ready when nasty rumors have finally
come back to him—that, for instance, he once fixed a case for a
friend, though in fact, when he heard that rumor, he only
wished that he had—or when people criticized actions he took
as district attorney, or when cops have groused about rulings
he's made as a judge. At times like that, the judge thinks, "Screw
you. My people have been here for over a century. I know
what's best for this town." And when people erupt over big

local issues, or a local person's travails make it into the papers and the mouths of gossips shine on the street corners, then, at those times above all, he can see the long view. Experience counts. It has taught him, for example, that bleeding-heart liberals usually make the most bloodthirsty prosecutors. And he knows that the town always rescues itself from the past. He has seen lots of storms come and go here. No trouble was ever so dire that it hadn't finally become unimportant. So he can believe that redemption is always possible, both for defendants and him, and also for towns.

A couple of blocks past the judge's old school, around the corner from the Elks Club, the courthouse annex slides into view. He looks forward to going inside. Sessions of District Court always contain something unexpected, something amusing. They keep him very busy, but don't usually upset him. For the schoolchildren who periodically visit his courtroom, Judge Ryan draws this distinction: "People who come here to District Court are accused of doing something naughty. People who go upstairs to Superior Court are accused of doing something evil." He has no wish to ascend to the higher court. He feels that he spent enough time in the presence of evil when he served as the district attorney.

Today he will hear short trials. Perhaps the lawyer most given to interminable arguments will come before him. She'd be a good victim for his dangling thread next April Fool's Day. Tonight he'll have dinner with Bertha, a favorite judge friend. He'll go in now and give that garrulous lawyer a good listening to. He'll feel the length of the law that can connect a local shoplifting case with Puritans on the frontier and the Magna Carta before them, when the clerk's voice declares, "Mr. Foreman and members of the jury, hearken to this complaint. The defendant has put himself upon the country, which country you are." As long as he's here—and it should be for a while; District Court judges are rarely impeached, as he likes to say—there will be mercy and geniality in one courtroom at least, to balance the inevitable harshness of law.

On next St. Patrick's Day, God willing, Judge Ryan will again wear his green robe to court, and Bill O'Connor will again preside at the annual breakfast, in the ballroom at the hotel by the Interstate. Bill will begin by reciting the same poem as always, his voice rising toward the end, his own variation,

> Oh, Ireland, how grand ya look,
> Like a bride in a rich adornin',
> And with all the pent-up love in my heart
> I bid ya the top o' the mornin'.

Then Bill will laugh, and laugh at his own jokes, with the laugh that is his best joke of all, and make a few gentle digs at the mayor.

In the Smith Quad the American Legion band will play "Pomp and Circumstance"; the bagpipers will march in, the seniors in a long train behind them; and Laura, inspired, her head full of Eliot, will stride forward, grinning, onto the stage. Extending her hand toward President Simmons, Laura will wobble on her high heels for an instant, almost tripping, just as in the dream she's had all senior year.

Alan will be sighted on Main Street carrying a Rottweiler puppy named Otto, which he bought for Suzanne and adopted himself when she changed her mind. Walking along, the puppy noisily chewing on a slice of pizza, he'll remark, "I wish I had a photograph of this." He'd send it to the behavioral psychologist at McLean with a note that said, "Cured!"—which would be true enough, for most practical purposes.

The mayor will have delivered her speech on the State of the City, before the council and a small live audience, and whoever still watches those polite meetings on cable TV. A great announcement. The city's budget is balanced at last! Problems remain: the fire station, the high school, homelessness. Mayor Ford's voice cracks when she speaks to the town about the Northampton children who are inadequately cared for and

414 / Tracy Kidder

guided, and about the still-rising drug use among them. But, all in all, the state of Northampton is good. She has made some decisions that were both difficult and harsh and has enraged a few more factions in town. But because the ultimate job security is having a job that nobody else really wants, there will be stability in city hall for at least two more years: the mayor, it seems, will run unopposed again next November.

Or almost unopposed. Out in the hallway after the speech, two of the audience confer. One is a young anarchist who often gives lectures during city council public comment time, lectures about corporate greed in America and homelessness in Northampton. His clothes are covered with hardware. A strap connects the legs of his blue jeans, maybe to symbolize his and the nation's imprisonment. The other is a man in late middle age, with a gray ponytail, perennially homeless, who often runs for mayor and usually gets votes in two figures. He thinks he'll improve his chances if he can sign up the anarchist as his speechwriter. "I think I can beat her this time," he says.

"I don't know," replies the anarchist. "It sounds like she's on our side."

Eight years ago, a black university student named Michael Trotman drove into town, fresh from New Jersey, where he'd learned, "You don't use your brakes until you use your horn." He drove down Main Street, saw a pedestrian about to enter a crosswalk, speeded up so as to claim the right of way, as one did back where he came from, and then started yelling, leaning hard on his brakes and his horn. He stopped a few feet from the startled pedestrian. Not an auspicious beginning, and in the years since, Michael had found a lot here to annoy him. He grew up in a New Jersey project. Listening to the large fusses Northampton people tend to make out of small issues, he had sometimes wanted to get on a soapbox downtown, and say, "You're not in college anymore. Get over it." Most of the town's women seemed deliberately dowdy to him. "The female toll takers on the New Jersey Turnpike have more sense of glamour." Often when he passed other black people downtown, ones he didn't know, he smiled at them and they smiled back, little smiles that seemed to say, "Isn't this place weird?" and, "What are *you* doing here?" And yet he had begun to feel something like a booster's pride. This past winter he'd attended a lecture by two famous black intellectuals, delivered at Smith. He'd listened with mounting anger. "White man bad. Black man good." That, he thought, was the lecturers' central message. He felt offended, not personally, but on behalf of his fellow townsfolk. "How dare you talk that way *here,*" he'd wanted to say. "These are some of the nicest white people you'll ever meet."

Every year for the past eight, Michael had decided to leave. He'd taken scouting trips to New York City, Phoenix, Los Angeles. Near the end of every one, he began missing Northampton. He couldn't fully account for the pull it had on him. He had a short answer for friends who asked: "No one's called me a nigger in eight years."

There was, one had to admit, a certain harmony in Northampton. No committee had sat down and arranged the watches of the town, and yet they functioned as if by grand design, so that one's doing this allowed the other's doing that, even if the one didn't know or didn't like the other, even if neither the one nor the other was civic-minded. Here a little contentiousness was good for more than entertainment. The local cops were clearly better cops for feeling that some suspicious eyes observed them, the reformers better reformers for having their homes burglarized occasionally. Northampton wasn't drenched in fellow feeling, and it didn't have to be. The people couldn't always see what they shared, but all their pieces of the town added up to one.

For all its smallness, Northampton had great absorptive powers. The parts mattered less than their combination—geography and history and architecture, workable proportions of human frailty and virtue. If civilization implies more than TVs and dishwashers, more than artistic achievement and wise rules, it implies just this, a place with a life that shelters individual lives, a place that allows people to become better than they might otherwise be—better, in a sense, than they are. The town contained evil, but didn't abide evil. It managed to keep it contained. Of course, dumb luck had helped out the old town, not the least of it the mysterious hold it had on residents' affections. Many people had no better reason for living here than the place itself. For them it wasn't just anywhere, but the place they chose because they felt it had chosen them.

From the steps of city hall late at night, downtown looks like a pop-up card, the spire of the First Church rising up beneath a paper moon. One of the clock faces still tells the wrong time. Gradually, Main Street empties. In stillness, the streetlights burn on, the shadows lie undisturbed, and the façades grow taller, tall as the dark. All of downtown acquires a venerable air. Even the toy castle, city hall, which in daylight seems to say that government here isn't much of a burden—even it acquires dignity.

As downtown empties, it begins filling up. The genius of the place assembles, not an immortal but an enduring presence, made of everything local: both these streets and these buildings and also the dirt and wooden ones that preceded them, the young trees by the sidewalks and the towering elms all gone now. It's a convocation. It consists of the long-vanished canal that used to carry vessels up to State Street and the bridge that now spans its route, under which a while ago boys and girls were smoking dope. It's the tired young man who walks up with a knapsack to the door of the Grove Street Inn—if there's room, he'll get a bed and a decent meal, no questions asked; and the three sisters in hoopskirts so wide that they filled all of Lyman's Lane one eighteenth-century Sunday morning. The local businessman who recently became a shoplifter because he saw his ex-wife in a checkout line and couldn't bear to have her see him buying condoms; and the young Irish woman whose century-old diary fell out of a ceiling a few years ago while a house was being renovated—she had filled page after page with her ardent desire to have her black lover buy her "a suit." All the generations who have passed through town, all the generations to come. The people who have suffered here and the people who have prospered. The residents who traffic in gossip and the residents who add to the town's charity. The natives who have stayed and the natives who have left. The ones who have departed in disgrace and the ones who dream themselves back here when they dream of home.

ACKNOWLEDGMENTS
AND BIBLIOGRAPHY

I am grateful, above all, to the people who appear in this book, for letting me into their lives, for putting up with me, for teaching me.

I want to thank my editor, Kate Medina, for her belief in this project at its inception and for her encouragement and cogent advice throughout. Richard Todd helped immeasurably once again, as did Georges Borchardt, John Graiff, and Jamie Kilbreth. I received generous help from Stuart Dybek, Jonathan Harr, Mark Kramer, and Sam Toperoff. Fran, Diane Harr, and Barnaby and Susan Porter all listened patiently. Jim Moran housed me. Jocelyn Selim performed a series of difficult and challenging tasks of historical research. I am grateful to the estimable copy editor Jolanta Benal and managing editor Amy Edelman.

I must make the usual but entirely accurate disclaimer that none of the people whom I wish to thank bears any responsibility for what I have written.

I am indebted to Corinne Philippides, Tom Hedderich, Mike Vito, and John Musante, all of the mayor's office. Kerry Buckley and Elise Feeley helped to guide me into local history, as did Stanley Elkins, Dan Horowitz, Allison Lockwood, James Parsons, and Neal Salisbury. My thanks to all of the following: Lisa Baskin for letting me spend a very pleasant election day in her company; the management and staff of WHMP for their hospitality, especially Rick Heideman, Ron Hall, Dennis Lee, Mark Vandermeer, and Ted Baker; Tom Arny for a discussion of local weather; John McCarthy for information about the local accent; Polly Baumer for information about New Age beliefs in the area; Sam Brindis for a discussion of local public works; Andrea Cousins and Carolyn Hicks for a discussion about the state of local practices in psychology and psychiatry;

Peter Nelson for a survey of the local music scene; Chris Brennan for allowing me to spend a day at Northampton High with Benjamin Baumeister, and the teachers whose classrooms I visited; Marge Bruchac for several conversations about the local Indians and about Jonathan Edwards in Stockbridge; various editors and reporters for the *Gazette*, including Jim Danko, Jim Foudy, Laurie Loisel, and Suzanne Wilson; Dave Reid of the *Union-News;* Frank Godek for a tour of the Hampshire County Jail and for his great courtesy when I interviewed prisoners there; Wayne Feiden and Nancy Denig for tours of downtown; Sam Goldman for a long conversation about downtown's renaissance, and Brink Thorne and Mazie Cox for a long talk on the same subject; former mayors Sean Dunphy and David Musante for interviews they granted; and George Quinn for allowing me to accompany him during his election campaign. I want to say a special thanks to Mary Humphries, who gave me many valuable insights into the Ada Comstock program; to the nurses and doctors at the emergency room of the Cooley Dickinson Hospital; to the ministers Gene Honan, Peter Ives, David McDowell, James Munroe, and Victoria Safford; and to the staff at the Ada Comstock office. And many thanks to Richard Abuza, Michael Bardsley, David Borbeau, Paul Britt, Marcia Burick, Jim Cahillane, Vin Callo, Marisol Cruz, Judith Fine, Hal Gibber, Pat Goggins, Claire Higgins, Jon Hite, Cindy Langley, Ralph Levy, Ed Maltby, Barry Moser, Steven Murphy, Bill Newman, Nora Owens, John Richards, Peter Rose, Kim Rosen, Charles Ryan, Gary Schaeffer, Ruth Simmons, Lauren Simonds, Michael Sissman, Barry Smith, Melinda Sofer, Jim Stevens, Carol Stewart, Sam Topal, Diane Walsh, and Jill Walton.

I received great courtesies from many people in the local courts and law-enforcement organizations—among others, Mike Andrews, David Angier, Gary Burt, Jim Conley, John Cummings, Ed Etheredge, Tom Foley, Steve Gawron, Harry Jeckanowski, Gen Keller, Bill Kokosinski, Jane Mulqueen,

Kevin Murphy, Aurelio Roldan, David Ross, Betsy Schiebel, Tim Sicard, Dan Soto, Tom Soutier, and Roger Trudeau. I want to thank *all* the local court officers and *all* the members of the Northampton Police Department, including Mike Allard, Martha Blair, Dan Block, Chris Bruneau, Dave Callahan, John Cartledge, Mitch Cichy, Art Clewley, Eddie Cooper, John Cotton, Luanne Duso, Sue Farrell, Ken Hartwright, Pablo Jimenez, Jack Kandrotas, Jim Kandrotas, Craig Kirouac, Joe Koncas, Don Labato, Steve Laizer, Billy Lynch, Michelle Lussier, Chet Maslowski, Digger Morawski, Bob Moriarty, Dave Netto, Ken Nichols, Bob Powers, Pablo Rodriguez, Brian Rust, Al St. Onge, Scott Savino, Steve Superba, Joe Ustaitis, Dave Vitkus, Mike Wall, Joe Yukl. And special thanks for putting up with me are due Bobby Dunn, Peter Fappiano, Dorothy Gagne, Pat Garvey, Ray Goulet, Preston Horton, Carlos Lebron, John McCarthy, Ann McMahon, Bobby Nicol, Ken Patenaude, Ken Watson. I owe great debts to Rusty Luce and even greater ones to Chief Russ Sienkiewicz, who let me hang around.

Doubtless, I have forgotten to name some people who helped me. To them, my thanks and apologies.

The following is a listing of some of the materials I used in my research, arranged more or less by subject. (What is now called the *Daily Hampshire Gazette* was first published on September 9, 1786. It was called *The Hampshire Gazette* until it merged on November 1, 1858, with *The Northampton Courier* and was called *The Hampshire Gazette and Northampton Courier* until 1890, when it became the *Daily Hampshire Gazette.* For the sake of simplicity, I refer to it throughout these notes as the *Gazette.*)

NORTHAMPTON

Bain, George W., and Howard A. Meyerhoff. *The Flow of Time in the Connecticut Valley: Geological Imprints.* Springfield, Mass., and Amherst, Mass.: Connecticut Valley

Historical Museum and Pratt Museum, Amherst College, 1963.

City of Northampton, Annual Budget Adopted by City Council, Fiscal Year—1995, 1996.

Clark, Christopher. *The Roots of Rural Capitalism: Western Massachusetts, 1780–1860.* Ithaca, N.Y.: Cornell University Press, 1990.

History of the Connecticut Valley in Massachusetts with Illustrations and Biographical Sketches of Some of Its Prominent Men and Pioneers, 2 vols. Philadelphia: Louis H. Everts, 1879.

Holland, Josiah Gilbert. *History of Western Massachusetts,* 2 vols. Springfield, Mass.: Samuel Bowles and Company, 1855.

Horowitz, Helen Lefkowitz, and Kathy Peiss, eds. *Love Across the Color Line: The Letters of Alice Hanley to Channing Lewis.* Amherst, Mass.: University of Massachusetts Press, 1996.

Johnson, Clifton. *Historic Hampshire in the Connecticut Valley: Happenings in a Charming Old New England County from the Time of the Dinosaur Down to About 1900.* Springfield, Mass.: Milton Bradley Company, 1932.

Kurath, Hans, with the collaboration of Marcus L. Hansen, Bernard Bloch, and Julia Bloch. *Handbook of the Linguistic Geography of New England.* Providence: Brown University Press, 1939.

MacDonald, William L. *Northampton, Massachusetts, Architecture and Buildings.* Northampton, Mass.: published by the author, 1981.

Manning, Alice H. "Meadow City Milestones: A Collection of Historical Sketches." Printed by the *Daily Hampshire Gazette,* Northampton, February 1987.

Moore, J. Michael. *The Life and Death of Northampton State Hospital: The Experience of Work in an Institution for the Mentally Ill.* Northampton, Mass.: Historic Northampton, 1994.

Nobles, Gregory H. *Divisions Throughout the Whole: Politics and Society in Hampshire County, Massachusetts, 1740–1775.* New York: Cambridge University Press, 1983.

O'Connell, James C., ed. *The Pioneer Valley Reader.* Stockbridge, Mass.: Berkshire House Publishers, 1995.

Robinson, William F. *Abandoned New England: Its Hidden Ruins and Where to Find Them.* Boston: New England Graphic Society and Little, Brown, 1976.

Smith, Joseph H., ed. *Colonial Justice in Western Massachusetts, 1639–1702: The Pynchon Court Record.* Cambridge, Mass.: Harvard University Press, 1961.

Szatmary, David P. *Shays' Rebellion: The Making of an Agrarian Insurrection.* Amherst, Mass.: University of Massachusetts Press, 1980.

Tercentenary Editorial Committee. *The Hampshire History: Celebrating 300 Years of Hampshire County, Massachusetts.* Northampton, Mass.: Hampshire County Commissioners, 1964.

The Tercentenary History Committee. *The Northampton Book: Chapters from 300 Years in the Life of a New England Town, 1654–1954.* Brattleboro, Vt.: Alan S. Browne, 1954.

Trumbull, James Russell. *History of Northampton Massachusetts from Its Settlement in 1654,* 2 vols. Northampton, Mass.: Press of Gazette Printing Co., 1898, 1902.

CENSUS DATA

1990 Decennial Census of Population. U.S. Bureau of the Census, Washington, D.C.

Street List. City of Northampton, November 1996.

SYLVESTER JUDD

Hall, Arethusa, ed. *Memorabilia from the Journals of Sylvester Judd of Northampton, Massachusetts.* Northampton, Mass.: privately published, 1882.

Judd, Sylvester. "The Judd Manuscript," 5 vols. Kept at Forbes Library, Northampton; filmed 1958. (A very useful abridged version with commentary is Gregory H. Nobles and Herbert L. Zarov, eds., *Selected Papers from the Judd Manuscript.* Northampton, Mass.: Forbes Library, 1976.)

———. Notebooks, 8 vols., 1833–1860, kept at Forbes Library, Northampton.

NEWTON ARVIN

Many newspaper articles describe the case. I am indebted to Frank Ellis of Smith College for putting me onto a very fine undergraduate honors thesis, which contains the best rendering of the affair that I have found: Sklar, Stacey M., "The Newton Arvin Case," unpublished honors thesis, Amherst College, April 7, 1989.

TOWNS AND CITIES

Fishman, Robert. *Urban Utopias in the Twentieth Century.* New York: Basic Books, 1977.

Francaviglia, Richard V. *Main Street Revisited.* Iowa City: University of Iowa Press, 1996.

Howard, Ebenezer. *Garden Cities of Tomorrow.* Edited by F. J. Osborn. Cambridge, Mass.: MIT Press, 1965.

Jacobs, Jane. *The Death and Life of Great American Cities.* New York: Vintage Books, 1992.

Mumford, Lewis. *The City in History: Its Origins, Its Transformations, and Its Prospects.* New York: Harcourt, Brace, and World, 1961.

———. *The Culture of Cities.* New York: Harcourt, Brace, and Company, 1938.

Plato. *The Laws.* Translated by A. E. Taylor. London: Everyman's Library, 1966.

Vallentin, Antonina. *Leonardo da Vinci: The Tragic Pursuit of*

Perfection. Translated by E. W. Dickes. New York: Viking Press, 1938.

DRUG USE IN NORTHAMPTON'S SCHOOLS

Report on the Northampton Public Schools. Michigan Alcohol and Other Drugs School Survey, conducted through the Kercher Center for Social Research, Western Michigan University, Kalamazoo, Michigan, 1992.

Summary Report on the Hampshire County Youth and Substance Abuse Survey. Prepared by the staff of the Hampshire Alcohol/Drug Abuse Prevention Partnership of the Tri-County Partnership to Prevent Alcohol/Drug Abuse and the Project Evaluators of the Donahue Institute. Fall 1995.

Michigan Alcohol and Other Drugs 1995 School Survey Report for Northampton Schools. The Donahue Institute, University of Massachusetts, January 1996.

LACK OF OSTENTATION AS A TRADITION

Drake, Samuel G. *Annals of Witchcraft in New England and Elsewhere in the United States.* Boston: W. Elliot Woodward, 1869.

Dwight, Timothy. *Travels in New-England and New-York.* London: printed for William Baynes & Son, 1823. Vol. 1, letters XXXIII and XXXIV.

Gere, Henry Sherwood. *Reminiscences of Old Northampton: Sketches of the Town as It Appeared from 1840 to 1850.* Published by the *Daily Hampshire Gazette*, 1902.

Miller, Perry, and Thomas H. Johnson, eds. *The Puritans.* New York: American Book Company, 1938.

Stebbins, Daniel (1766–1856). Notebooks of Daniel Stebbins, 2 vols. Kept at Forbes Library, Northampton.

"Witchcraft Slander." *Gazette*, June 3, 1904.

PHILANTHROPY AND CARE OF THE POOR

Clark, Christopher. *The Communitarian Moment: The Radical Challenge of the Northampton Association.* Ithaca, N.Y.: Cornell University Press, 1995.

Ebbeling, Donald C. *Courtroom Crucible: The Smith Charities.* Northampton, Mass.: Trustees of the Smith Charities, 1976.

Forbes, Charles Edward. Last Will and Testament. Kept at Forbes Library.

Judd, Sylvester. "The Judd Manuscript" and *Personal Diaries;* and Nobles and Zarov, *Selected Papers.* Complete citations for these works appear above, in the section headed "Sylvester Judd."

Lockwood, Alison McCrillis. *No Ordinary Man: Judge Forbes and His Library.* Northampton, Mass.: privately published, 1994.

Trumbull, James Russell. *History of Northampton.* A complete citation appears on p. 437.

Winthrop, John. "A Modell of Christian Charity." In Perry Miller and Thomas H. Johnson, eds., *The Puritans.* New York: American Book Company, 1938.

I also used the following articles; all of which appeared in the *Gazette.* "The Poorhouse Problem," May 21, 1891; "The Poor Farm," May 23, 1891; "The City Poor House and Farm. Wretched Old Buildings Rotten and Dilapidated," May 27, 1891; "The City Council Grapples with the Sewer, Poor House, and Upper Route Questions," May 28, 1891; "The City Poor, How They Fare Under the City Guardianship," October 18, 1898; and "Almshouse Here Is Now the 'Infirmary,'" May 5, 1927.

THE FOUNDING OF SMITH COLLEGE

I am greatly indebted to Jacque Bradley, a former Ada Comstock scholar and undergraduate history major, for both materials and commentary on the founding of Smith College.

I used the following materials:

Bradley, Jacque. "Sophia's Choice: An Annotated Bibliography of Books Owned and/or Read by Sophia Smith." Smith College, July 1996.

Greene, John M. Journals and scrapbooks, 1857–1917. John M. Greene Papers, held at the Smith College Archives.

————. Line-a-day diaries, 1882–1919 (broken). John M. Greene Papers, Smith College Archives.

————. "Sketch of the Life and Character of Miss Sophia Smith, Founder of Smith College." *Gazette*, August 3, 1875. (This is just one of many flattering portraits that Greene drew of Sophia after her death. In general, the portraits grow increasingly flattering as the years go on.)

Greenwood, William. Letter to John M. Greene about Sophia Smith, July 27, 1875. The Sophia Smith Collection, Smith College.

Hanscomb, Elizabeth Deering, and Helen French Greene. *Sophia Smith and the Beginnings of Smith College.* Northampton, Mass.: Smith College, 1926.

Horowitz, Helen Lefkowitz. "To Preserve Her Woman-liness." *Alma Mater: Design and Experience in the Woman's Colleges from Their Nineteenth-Century Beginnings to the 1930s,* 2nd ed. Amherst, Mass.: University of Massachusetts Press, 1993.

Miller, Mary Esther. "Sophia Smith's Will." *Gazette,* November 13, 1877 (description of Smith).

Quesnell, Quentin. "Whatever Happened to Sophia Smith?" *Smith Alumnae Quarterly,* vol. 86, no. 2, spring 1995.

Seelye, L. Clark. *The Early History of Smith College.* Cambridge, Mass.: Riverside Press, 1923. (This book contains a copy of Sophia's will, which can also be found in a number of other places.)

Smith, Charles. Letter to Greene about Sophia, July 29, 1875. The Sophia Smith Collection, Smith College.

Smith, Sophia. Personal journal, 1861–70. Smith College Archives.

Smith College Board of Trustees. "Smith College Mission and Objectives Statement," May 2, 1987, and January 29, 1997.

Tyler, William S. Letter to Greene about Sophia, August 28, 1875. The Sophia Smith Collection, Smith College.

I also used the following articles and letters to the editor: Untitled article, *Gazette,* July 5, 1870 (squabble over Smith's will); "Local Intelligence," *Northampton Courier,* August 30, 1870 (squabble over Smith's will); "Reasons for Voting against the Proposition to Raise by Taxation $75,000 to Aid Smith College," *Gazette,* March 11, 1873; "Smith College and Who Accumulated a Majority of Its Funds," *Northampton Courier,* March 27, 1888 (stories of Austin); *Gazette,* letters appearing on March 11, 18, and 25, 1873; and "Celebrating Sophia: Rally Day '96," *The Sophian* (Smith College), February 22, 1996.

THE STORY OF HALLIGAN AND DALEY

James M. Camposeo, "Anti-Catholic Prejudice in Early New England: The Daley-Halligan Murder Trial," *Historical Journal of Western Massachusetts,* vol. 6, no. 2 (spring 1978).

Gallen, P. H. "Father Cheverus in Northampton." In *How Popes Are Chosen and Other Essays.* Boston: The Stratford Company, 1927.

Garvey, Richard C. "The Hanging of Daley and Halligan," in Tercentenary History Committee, *The Northampton Book.* For a full citation see p. 437.

History of the Connecticut Valley in Massachusetts (see p. 436), vol. 1, p. 214, contains the following passage: "As an interesting fact connected with this it may be added that years afterward, on his death-bed, the real murderer of the mail-carrier acknowledged his guilt and vindicated—too late—the innocence of the lads who were executed for the crime." Various commentators have settled on this assertion as if it were fact.

But it remains unsubstantiated, in spite of the efforts of many.

Huen-Dubourg, J. *The Life of Cardinal Cheverus.* Translated from the French by E. Stewart. Boston: James Munroe & Company, 1839.

Melville, Annabelle M. *Jean Lefebvre de Cheverus, 1786–1836.* Milwaukee: Bruce Publishing Company, 1958.

A Member of the Bar. *Report of the Trial of Dominic Daley and James Halligan for the Murder of Marcus Lyon Before The Supreme Judicial Court.* Northampton, Mass.: S. & E. Butler Booksellers, 1806.

Peck, Chauncey E. "The Marcus Lyon Murder," in *The History of Wilbraham, Massachusetts,* published by the Town of Wilbraham, 1914.

Shepherd, Mary Pomeroy. Journals, 1803–1809. Held at Historic Northampton.

Sullivan, Robert. "The Murder Trial of Halligan and Daley—Northampton, Massachusetts, 1806." *Massachusetts Law Quarterly,* September 1964, pp. 211–24. The most careful and thorough of the secondary accounts of the judicial proceedings and of the popular hysteria the murder created.

Trumbull, James Russell. "Execution of Dailey [*sic*] and Halligan," in *History of Northampton* (see p. 437), vol. 2, pp. 589–92.

"A Brief Account, etc. of the Execution of Dominic Daley and James Hallagan [*sic*] for the Murder of Marcus Lyon." This document carries no date or publisher. It is held at Forbes Library.

I also consulted the following stories from the *Gazette* (some untitled): a short account of the trial, according to which the jury retired at ten P.M. and returned with their verdict "in a few moments," April 30, 1806; a small notice of the hanging "Thursday last," which sets the size of the crowd at 15,000, June 11, 1806; "The Hanging of Halligan and Daley, for the Murder of Marcus Lyon at Wilbraham," September 6, 1806; "More Reminiscences of Olden Times,"

July 6, 1869; "Old Times," July 20, 1869; "Murder of Marcus Lyon, An Account of It by a Man Who Saw the Murderers Hung in 1806," March 3, 1899; "On Gallows Hill and Pancake Plain," April 30, 1906; "150th Anniversary of Death on Gallows of Innocent Pair Points Up Changes, Progress" (quotes in full a statement by Luke Ryan on the case), April 24, 1956; Alice Manning, "That Great Boulder at the Hospital Grounds—Why Is It There?" December 8, 1972; "Gubernatorial Pardon Being Sought in 19th Century Murder Case Here," June 10, 1982; "50 Attend Ceremony for Irish Pair," June 14, 1982; "Murder Pardons Doubtful," December 21, 1982; "1805 Murder, Mass Held for Irish Who Were Executed," June 7, 1984. I also used *The Hampshire Federalist,* January 7, 1806.

SYLVESTER GRAHAM

Nissenbaum, Stephen. *Sex, Diet, and Debility in Jacksonian America: Sylvester Graham and Health Reform.* Chicago: The Dorsey Press, 1988.

OBSESSIVE-COMPULSIVE DISORDER

I am indebted to Randy Frost of Smith College for providing me with research materials and for several long explanations of the current state of knowledge about the illness and its therapies.

Freud, Sigmund. "Notes Upon a Case of Obsessional Neurosis ('Rat Man') and Process Notes for the Case History." In *The Freud Reader.* Peter Gay, ed. New York: Norton, 1989.

Frost, Randy, and Tamara Hartl. "A Cognitive-Behavioral Model of Compulsive Hoarding." *Behavioral Research Therapy,* vol. 34, no. 4 (1996), pp. 341–50.

Jenike, Michael A., Lee Baer, and William E. Minichiello, eds. *Obsessive-Compulsive Disorders: Theory and Management,* 2nd ed. Chicago: Year Book Medical Publications, 1990.

Pitman, Roger K. "Obsessive Compulsive Disorder in Western History." In *Current Insights in Obsessive Compulsive Disorder*. E. Hollander, J. Zohar, D. Marazzati, and B. Olivier, eds. New York: John Wiley & Sons, 1994.

Steketee, Gail, and Randy Frost. "Obsessive Compulsive Disorder." In *Comprehensive Clinical Psychology*. Vol. 6: *Adults: Clinical Formulation and Treatment*. A. S. Bellack and M. Hersen, eds. Oxford, England: Pergamon Press, 1998.

SOJOURNER TRUTH

Clark, Christopher. *The Communitarian Moment*. For a full citation see p. 440.

Davis, Hope Hale. "The Northampton Association of Education and Industry." In *The Northampton Book*. For a full citation see p. 437.

Painter, Nell Irvin. *Sojourner Truth: A Life, a Symbol*. New York: Norton, 1996.

Washington, Margaret, ed. *The Narrative of Sojourner Truth*. New York: Vintage Books, 1993.

JONATHAN EDWARDS

Aaron, Daniel. "Jonathan Edwards." In *The Northampton Book*. For a full citation see p. 437.

Conforti, Joseph A. *Jonathan Edwards, Religious Tradition, and American Culture*. Chapel Hill: University of North Carolina Press, 1995.

Edwards, Jonathan. "A Farewell Sermon." In *Selected Sermons of Jonathan Edwards*. H. Norman Gardiner, ed. New York: Macmillan, 1904.

"Jonathan Edwards." *Gazette*, January 28, 1873 (a selection from an article originally printed in *Harper's Weekly*).

Miller, Perry. *Errand into the Wilderness*. Cambridge, Mass.: The Belknap Press of Harvard University Press, 1964.

————. *Jonathan Edwards.* Amherst, Mass.: University of Massachusetts Press, 1981.

Smith, John E., Harry S. Stout, and Kenneth P. Minkema, eds. *A Jonathan Edwards Reader.* New Haven: Yale University Press, 1995.

Tracy, Patricia J. *Jonathan Edwards, Pastor: Religion and Society in Eighteenth-Century Northampton.* New York: Hill & Wang, 1980.

Trumbull, James Russell. *History of Northampton.* For a full citation see p. 437.

Winslow, Ola. *Jonathan Edwards, 1703–1758: A Biography.* New York: Macmillan, 1940.

HENRY JAMES IN NORTHAMPTON

Edel, Leon, ed. *Letters of Henry James.* Cambridge, Mass.: The Belknap Press of Harvard University Press, 1974.

James, Henry. *Roderick Hudson.* New York: Charles Scribner's Sons, 1935.

HOME TOWN

TRACY KIDDER

A Readers Club Guide

ABOUT THIS GUIDE

The suggested questions are intended to help your
reading group find new and interesting angles and
topics for discussion for Tracy Kidder's *Home Town*.
We hope that these ideas will enrich your conversation
and increase your enjoyment of the book.

Many fine books from Washington Square Press
feature Readers Club Guides. For a complete listing,
or to read the Guides on-line, visit

http://www.simonsays.com/reading/guides

A Conversation with Tracy Kidder

Q: What compelled you to write this particular book? Why Northampton instead of any other town?

A: I had visited Northampton regularly for nearly 20 years, and I had seen it change a great deal, particularly in its old downtown. On the surface, it seemed to be a town that was functioning well. I wondered why. I also wondered if its appearance wasn't in some ways deceptive. When I first took a ride around the town with a local cop—Tommy O'Connor—I realized that my impressions of the place weren't exactly wrong but were certainly incomplete, and that realization made the town all the more interesting to me. I also chose Northampton because it seemed to be full of surprising, colorful characters, and because, living nearby, I wouldn't have to travel far to study it. I've often written about people close to home, here in New England. I'm very fond of the region, and I figure that if writing about matters close to home was good enough for writers like William Faulkner and Flannery O'Connor, it's certainly good enough for me.

Q: In what sort of community did you grow up? How has it changed or remained the same since your childhood?

A: I grew up on Long Island, in New York. I was a child in the era just before the great suburban migration. Long Island back then was a place of woods and farms and rich marine estuaries. I grew up, in other words, in a place that no longer exists. I wandered around a fair amount as a young man, looking for a replacement place, and found it in New England.

Q: One of your book's chief preoccupations is with the notion of "home," and the various ways this word resonates with different Northamptonites. What is your own definition of home?

A: A home is one thing, a town another. They can turn out to be identical, but they aren't necessarily, which is why I separated the two words in the title of this book. For me, I guess home is a complicated stew of geography and architecture and feeling, usually attractive, sometimes not.

Q: With its detailed characterizations, dramatic narrative arc, and rich insights into human nature, *Home Town* reads much like an intricately structured work of fiction—particularly like the classics of Sinclair Lewis and Sherwood Anderson. Were you especially influenced by these or any other novelists as you worked on this book?

A: I first read Sherwood Anderson's *Winesburg, Ohio* many years ago. It lingered in my mind over the years, as did Edgar Lee Masters' *Spoon River Anthology*. When I was thinking about writing this book, I thought about those two. It seemed like an interesting project—to try to do something like what they'd done, but in nonfiction. I think that notion comforted me; precedents are often comforting. I did try to pay small homage to *Winesburg* in this book, with one of the chapter titles and in a line that appears near the end of the next-to-last chapter. But I wasn't greatly influenced, at least not consciously, by literary precedents while I wrote.

Q: Over the years, you've garnered one of the most devoted followings of readers around. And this is made all the more remarkable by the fact that you never repeat yourself: each of your books has mined a completely different cultural arena. What has steered you toward writing about such disparate subjects?

A: One of the wonderful things about my job is that it allows me to look into parts of the world that interest me. I like changing subjects every three or four years. I can't imagine a better profession. I can get paid for satisfying my curiosity, and I can change the subject of my work every few years without changing jobs.

Q: Your work is regularly celebrated for its elegance and lyricism—qualities generally associated more with poets and novelists than journalists and nonfiction writers. Tell us about your background and training in writing. Will we ever read a Tracy Kidder novel?

A: I started writing in earnest in college, mainly under the tutelage of the poet and great translator Robert Fitzgerald. I wrote fiction—short stories—then. After serving in Vietnam, I came home and wrote a novel about experiences I didn't have in Vietnam. It was never published, thank God. Then I went to The Writer's Workshop at the University of Iowa, intending to write fiction. I'm not quite sure how I came to write nonfiction. Memory grows furtive, as A.J. Liebling once wrote. I really don't think that fiction and narrative nonfiction are very different. They both rely on techniques of storytelling that never have belonged exclusively to fiction. For me, the crucial difference is that when I write nonfiction, I don't make things up. I have written some fiction in the last

25 years. All of it was published. But the sum total is three short stories. I like to imagine that I will write a novel some day, but wanting to write a novel is a far less useful desire than having a novel one wants to write.

Q: How did you meet Tommy O'Connor? How much time did you spend with him while you researched and wrote the book?

A: One day—back in 1994, I think—I was at the gym in Northampton, the one that the local cops use, and a very gregarious, rather loud-voiced young man with a shaved head started talking to me. After awhile, he said, "You don't remember me, do you?" I said I didn't, and he said, "I stopped you for speeding five years ago." Then I did remember. This was the face of the once curly-haired young cop who had given me a ticket and then had said, with great sincerity "Have a nice day." I also remembered that he'd stopped my wife for speeding the same day he'd stopped me, and he hadn't given her a ticket. (As I later learned, this cop—Tommy O'Connor—didn't usually give women speeding tickets, because he hated to see women cry. If a women did start crying, though, he'd figure, "Well, she's already upset, so I might as well write her up.") Anyway, we talked some more, and then he said, in words like these, "Why don't you come out in the cruiser with me some night. I'll show you a Northampton you never thought existed." I accepted the invitation. I ended up riding around with him almost every evening he was on duty for roughly a year and a half.

Q: Tommy's story is the glue which holds *Home Town* together. Through him, we are introduced to every one of the book's other characters. How did you decide to structure the book this way? Why not choose, for instance, Judge Ryan—another prominent native son—to be the central figure?

A: A nonfiction writer like me has to go where the light is good. Tommy let me into his life. I don't think Judge Ryan could have done that to the same degree. But I wouldn't have followed Tommy for so long if he hadn't been interesting in himself and if he hadn't offered me an interesting perspective on the town. Indeed, I can't think of anyone who could have offered me as interesting a perspective. I can't think of anyone who knew the place better, or who loved it more. And, finally, his story was a very good one, for me—a story that was in itself powerful and poignant, and also illuminating in relation to the place.

Q: What sorts of reactions and responses have you received from the people featured in *Home Town*?

A: None of the people I wrote about have yelled at me, at least not yet. Of all the reactions, I think Alan Scheinman's has been the most interesting. A number of people have come up to him and in effect apologized, saying they hadn't known the depth of his trouble. He has told me that since he was already notorious in town, it could only improve matters for some of the actual facts about him to be known as well.

Q: Are there any elements of present-day Northampton which you would have liked to have explored and illuminated more thoroughly if given the opportunity?

A: The process of writing a book is inevitably selective. I did not write this book as a sociologist would have. Many lesbians live in Northampton, and there is no lesbian depicted in my book. It's not as though I pretend that there are no lesbians in town, but I didn't think of this as a paint-by-the-numbers project. In the course of doing my research, I met hundreds of people, including some lesbians, most of them interesting. But there's always less room in a book than I think there will be at the start of a project, and I ended up writing about the people who seemed particularly interesting to me, and who were willing to let me into their lives. If one of those had been a lesbian, I might have written about one. But it didn't happen. I see my job, in part, as freeing people from their groups, rather than making them emblems or symbols. If I had written about a lesbian, lesbianism might well have been the least important thing in the portrait. Tommy O'Connor is a cop, but he doesn't stand for cops. He stands for Tommy O'Connor.

Q: What do you imagine will come of small-town America in the new century?

A: I don't believe in predictions. In my experience, people who predict the future are nearly always wrong. I hope that small towns survive in America, and I hope that neighborhoods survive in big cities. They provide forms of sustenance for life that other kinds of human association just can't provide.

Reading Group Questions and Topics for Discussion

1. Tracy Kidder's Foreword to *Home Town* functions much like the opening shot of a movie, affording a panoramic view of the entire town of Northampton. "From the summit, the cornfields are a dream of perfect order, and the town seems entirely coherent, self-contained, a place where a person might live a whole life and consider it complete, a tiny civilization all its own." What does Kidder achieve by starting the book this way? Describe the tone and style of the Foreword, and compare them with the tone and style employed throughout the rest of the book.

2. In what ways is this initially idyllic, sweeping vision informed, supported, and challenged by the rest of the book, when Kidder zooms in for a series of lingering, tightly focused close-ups?

3. How would you describe *Home Town* to a friend? What themes does it explore? What sorts of emotions does it inspire in you? What books can you compare it to?

4. Although *Home Town* is not a novel, in what ways does the book resemble a work of fiction? Does the story unfold in the arc of a traditional novel?

5. At one point in his detailed rendering of the people, places, and history of Northampton, Kidder refers to the seemingly effortless "genius of the place." What does he mean?

6. Describe Kidder's narrative technique. Why do you suppose he avoids explicitly inserting himself into the proceedings of the book? Why does he never use the authorial "I"?

7. Although Kidder himself is not an actual character in *Home Town*, in what ways, if any, is his presence felt throughout the narrative?

8. Discuss what sort of book *Home Town* would be if we were introduced to Northampton not through a semi-omniscient narrator but through the eyes of a first-person narrator who is physically involved in the book's action. Would this serve to bring us closer to the action, or move us farther away? Explain.

9. To the central figures in *Home Town*, history is very much a living and breathing presence. Who and what are the "living ghosts" to which Kidder refers throughout *Home Town*? How do they affect the denizens of Northampton?

10. Compare and contrast the lives of Tommy O'Connor and Judge Mike Ryan, the two "townies." What role does the past play in Tommy's life? In Judge Ryan's? What impact does history and the presence of memory seem to have upon the choices these men make regarding their respective futures?

11. Why do you suppose Judge Ryan has the compulsion to tell his son to leave Northampton "before it's too late"? Too late for what? Does Ryan regret the decision to stay in Northampton his entire life? Explain.

12. Tommy is torn between his desire to commit his life to the only place he's ever known—an insulated and intensely local place—and a contrary, equally strong urge to move on the large world. How does this tension resolve itself in *Home Town*?

13. In what ways might Tommy's dilemma be viewed as a universal experience which, to some degree, all of us must face at some point? Compare Tommy's choice to the difficult choices which have shaped the course of your own life.

14. What aspects of Northampton are you especially curious about? Is there anything about Northampton you would've liked to have read more about?

15. Discuss the history of Smith College. To what degree does present-day Smith uphold the ideals upon which the school was founded? Explain. What does Kidder mean when he writes that Sophia Smith "couldn't have imagined Smith. She couldn't have imagined Laura?"

16. Chart the course of Laura Baumeister's life in Northampton, from her rocky first year to her eventual blossoming into a passionate scholar. What does the town represent to her initially? And later? Compare Laura's evolving relationship with the town to that of Alan Scheinman.

17. Where did you grow up? Compare your childhood experience to that of Tommy O'Connor. How has the community where you spent your childhood changed over the years?

18. At the end of the chapter entitled "A Moral Place," Kidder reflects upon all that remains unseen in American communities. "A great deal lay hidden and half-hidden in this small, peaceful town. Well before you understood all of it, you would feel you understood too much." What is going on here? And what does the author mean when he writes about Northampton, "to apprehend it all at once—who could stand it? No wonder so much remains invisible in towns." What might Kidder be suggesting here about the value of privacy in democratic civilization?

19. The same chapter, "A Moral Place," occupies an important position in the book's structure. How does it function to make the disparate stories in subsequent chapters feel connected? Do you think that the chapter's title is ironic? What relationship might exist between this chapter and a later one called "Tearless, Eager, and Longing Eyes?" What point do you think Kidder is trying to make about the histories of places in both of these chapters?

20. Kidder makes a point of underscoring a grand paradox of American life: we are "a famously peripatetic people" consumed by the traveling instinct, but we are simultaneously obsessed by "the idea of home." What are the various ways in which these warring instincts are reconciled by the characters in *Home Town*?

21. Do you see yourself as someone like Frankie Sandoval, who wanders through life carrying a sense of home with him wherever he goes? Or do you have a fixed, unmoving place you consider home, as Judge Ryan does with Northampton? What is your definition of home?

About the Author

TRACY KIDDER graduated from Harvard, studies at the
University of Iowa, and served as an army officer in Vietnam.
He has won the Pulitzer Prize, the National Book Award,
the Robert F. Kennedy Award, and many other literary prizes.
The author of *House*, *The Soul of a New Machine*,
Old Friends, and *Among Schoolchildren*,
Kidder lives in Massachusetts and Maine.

What book will you choose for your next reading group?

Visit

www.SimonSays.com

to keep up on the latest new releases from Washington Square Press as well as author appearances, news chats, special offers and more.

Our WSP Readers Club Guides will help enrich your reading group discussions by offering more questions, better and more focused discussion topics, and exclusive author interviews.

To help choose your next reading group book and to browse through our vast library of available reading group guides, visit us online at **www.simonsays.com/reading/guides** today.